YANKEE·DOODLE'S LITERARY·SAMPLER

of Prose, Poetry, & Pictures

YANKEE·DOODLE'S LITERARY·SAMPLER of Prose, Poetry, & Pictures

Being an Anthology of Diverse Works
Published for the Edification and/or
Entertainment of Young Readers
in America Before 1900

Selected from the Rare Book Collections of
the *Library of Congress* and Introduced by
Virginia Haviland & Margaret N. Coughlan

THOMAS Y. CROWELL COMPANY · NEW YORK

 Published simultaneously in Canada by Fitzhenry & Whiteside Limited, Toronto.

Designed by MINA BAYLIS GREENSTEIN

Manufactured in the United States of America

Library of Congress Cataloging in Publication Data

Haviland, Virginia, 1911

Yankee Doodle's literary sampler of prose, poetry, and pictures.

Bibliography: p.

1. Children's literature, American—Bibliography. 2. Children's literature, American—History and criticism. I. Coughlan, Margaret N., joint author. II. Title.
Z1232.H38 028.52 74-12217 ISBN0-690-00269-6

ISBN 0-690-00269-6

2 3 4 5 6 7 8 9 10

Contents

II. Works Intended to Entertain. *From the Colonial Period to 1900.*

III. The Magazines.
From the Colonial Period to 1900.

No TAX

The Literature Reveals the Times.
An Introduction.

THE HISTORY OF CHILDREN'S BOOKS in America is of interest not only to those concerned with the works as types of literature; these books also tell us a great deal about many other facets of early American life and thought. They reflect our cultural nationalism with their conscious efforts at ideological indoctrination—in personal morality and the Puritan ethic, in humanitarian reform and political thought. F. J. Harvey Darton wrote that he intended in his *Children's Books in England: Five Centuries of Social Life* to furnish "a minor chapter in the history of English social life." In a different way this anthology will afford glimpses into the climate of American life up to 1900, as well as point out the never-ending literary controversy between those stressing improvement and those seeking to provide entertainment in books for young Americans. We believe with the great book collector A. S. W. Rosenbach that "more than any class of literature they [children's books] reflect the minds of the generation that produced them. Hence no better guide to the history and development of any country can be found than its juvenile literature."

The period covered by this anthology of writings and pictorial examples stops at 1900; it has been left for scholars at some later date to estimate the highlights and significant trends of the twentieth century. The selections represent both literary classics and mass-produced works. Some early schoolbooks, as well as books for leisure reading, have been singled out because of their special salience. The whole collection is intended to reveal and typify various important currents in a widening stream, rather than setting forth only those works of aesthetic excellence. Quaintness of format and popular success have contributed to the establishment of collectors' desiderata.

The examples chosen show that side by side in this country from the earliest times there existed both American production and the reissuing of British works. The latter were sometimes altered to reflect a superimposed American outlook.

In the late eighteenth and early nineteenth centuries there came to be expressed clearer indications of the development of the young nation: a love of country and pride in its new nationhood, together with a certain antipathy to Old World sentiments. Noah Webster urged the stabilizing of a spelling that should be American, while he also wrote American history for children. Lydia Maria Child's magazine *Juvenile Miscellany* (1826–1836), which after 1834 was headed by that other zealous female educator, Sarah Josepha Hale, was welcomed for its emphasis on American themes.

By the middle of the nineteenth century, and particularly after the Civil War, a body of American children's literature had become recognized, and there was a regular flow of books in two directions over the Atlantic, though not without denunciations from both sides on copyright infringements. A case in point was that of Samuel G. Goodrich, who under the name of Peter Parley wrote a series of very successful informational books in the 1820's and 1830's with the intention of eliminating the British background from books for children. He was outraged to find his books pirated (along with those of six known spurious Peter Parleys as well), and he himself portrayed as a Peter Parley who loved the queen and lustily sang "Rule, Britannia." Republished in the United States and also imitated here were many English storybooks loaded with theories on learning and the use of leisure, espoused by the "guardians of the young." Examples of these are to be found in Part I of this volume. Literature that would endure traveled, too, across the Atlantic, also in both directions: *Alice in Wonderland* found ready acceptance in America; *Little Men* was published earlier in London than it was in Boston, because its American author, Louisa May Alcott, was visiting England then.

Thus it can be seen that the reading matter of American children had much in common with that of English-reading children abroad. As the nineteenth century progressed, however, more American books and magazines for children began to deal with specifically American subject matter: the Westward expansion; attitudes toward Indians, blacks, and immigrants; the growth of cities and industrial development; the post-Civil War boom and depression. The Civil War itself gave rise to a whole category of fiction about slavery, the war, and also many books giving a rather romanticized picture of the Old South.

A broadening of education and a rising interest in foreign travel led to the appearance of numerous information-packed travelogue storybooks in the late nineteenth century. In the same period, crusading reformers and temperance societies created a flood of pious and sentimental tracts, published by the American Sunday School Union in Philadelphia and by other tract societies in Boston and New York. Sunday School libraries sprang up, dealing out these moral works, to inform and indoctrinate tender young minds with virtue while at the same time they aimed to improve Sunday School attendance. Certain popular scribblers depicted heroines with a persistent tearful saintliness and piety who took stands in strict conformity with the Sunday School movement, speaking out strongly against frivolous literature, profanity, gambling, tobacco, and drink. In contrast, there appeared at the same time the blood-and-thunder school of writing for boys, with dime novels (to which even Louisa May Alcott contributed). Soon there arose the endless other popular series for boys and for girls—predecessors of the factorylike output of the Stratemeyer empire—which has reached down even into the present day.

If the nineteenth century was a time of voluminous hack writing, it was also a period when along the way, beside an Anglophilian import of enduring English fantasies, came some notable American imaginative works—by Clement C. Moore, Washington Irving, Nathaniel Hawthorne, Laura E. Richards, and Howard Pyle, among others—and classic family and adventure stories by a handful of other indigenous greats.

The Illustrators

Children's book illustration in nineteenth-century England was moving from the influence of the wood engraving of Thomas and John Bewick to the great successes of Randolph Caldecott, Walter Crane, and Kate Greenaway (by way of Cruikshank, Hughes, Doyle, and Tenniel). In the New World, Alexander Anderson was called the American Bewick, for his white-line work "after Bewick." The real beginner of fine wood engraving in America, Anderson first became famous with his pictures for Arnaud Berquin's *Looking Glass for the Mind,* published in 1795. Also of early importance was James Poupard, who gained recognition for his engravings on copper for a *Metamorphosis,* published in 1814 (see page 15). A goodly company of American artists attracted attention from the 1840's onward for their contributions to children's book illustration and magazine work. Outstanding among these was Felix Octavius Carr Darley, the best known of all the early American book illustrators (particularly celebrated for his illustrations in 1848 for Washington Irving's *Sketch Book*); Henry L. Stephens, a popular early comic artist (famous for illustrating nursery rhymes); Winslow Homer, who did the title page for the children's series *The Percy Family* in 1858 and work for the *Riverside* and other magazines; Hammatt Billings, who illustrated the first edition of *Uncle Tom's Cabin* (1852), Hawthorne's *A Wonder Book* (1852), and *Tanglewood Tales* (1853), and some of Sophie May's Little Prudy stories; E. B. Bensell, important in *St. Nicholas* as the illustrator for Frank R. Stockton and Charles E. Carryl; Frank T. Merrill, who did the pictures for the 1880 edition of *Little Women* and the first edition of Mark Twain's *The Prince and the Pauper;* A. B. Frost, with his natural expression of humor forever to be connected with the Uncle Remus stories; Reginald Birch, so fully associated with *St. Nicholas* and the books that came out of it; and Howard Pyle, who also did work for *St. Nicholas,* as well as for *Harper's Young People,* and whose influence was widespread and lasting.

As many as three hundred lavishly illustrated "quartos" or gift annuals appeared a year. Among them were Horace E. Scudder's Bodley books, Thomas Knox's Boy Traveller stories, and Hezekiah Butterworth's Zigzag travel books, all guilty of having in them illustrations that had already been used elsewhere. Those in Scudder's books, for instance, had previously appeared in *Riverside Magazine,* of which he was the editor.

The periodicals by presenting the work of the best American artists exerted a strong influence upon American book illustration, especially in the case of books for children. New standards in graphics were set by *Our Young Folks* (1865–1873) and especially by the *Riverside* (1867–1870), which solicited work from the fine artist John La Farge as well as from many of those named above. These two periodicals were soon followed by *St. Nicholas* (1873–1943), which took over illustrators who had appeared in the *Riverside,* and by *Harper's Young People* (1879–1899; its title changed to *Harper's Round Table* in 1895), which considered illustration to be a most important feature. While these magazines were stimulating and revealing the new American literature for children, they were also offering work from England—from such authors and artists as George Macdonald, Rudyard Kipling, Randolph Caldecott, Kate Greenaway, and Arthur Rackham. *St. Nicholas* had an English edition during the years 1872–1917, and *Harper's Young People* was published in England from 1885 to 1891. From Denmark came the hitherto unpublished tales of Hans Christian Andersen.

It was a time of technical advances in engraving and printing and the new age of critical appraisal. When it became possible to do color printing on a popular level, children's book artists naturally were spurred on to new heights of creativity. The end of the nineteenth century and the opening years of the twentieth were rightly called the Golden Age of American illustrating.

The Publishers

Emerging American publishers had necessarily to rely on the English output for their earliest lists of children's books. Benjamin Harris, who came to America from London, is credited with printing here one of the earliest editions of *The New-England Primer,* based on *The Protestant Tutor* he had issued in England, sometime before 1690. The accomplishments of the famous John Newbery and his shop, established in 1744 at The Bible and Crown in London and renamed The Bible and Sun when he moved the next year to St. Paul's Churchyard, were a special stimulus to American printers. John Newbery was both a printer and a bookseller, and he is generally considered to be the "father" of children's books in English. His *Little Pretty Pocket-book,* which first appeared in 1744, was the first book created for children that was deliberately intended for their amusement rather than their improvement. Today the American Library Association's highest award for children's literature is a medal bearing John Newbery's name, given annually to the author whose book has made the greatest contribution to literature for children in the preceding year. Early American printers were quick to capitalize on access to Newbery's works. The Non-Importation Agreement of 1769 was enforced in Boston, where there was a prejudice against anything English, but Hugh Gaines of New York did a thriving business. He made all the Newbery toybooks available, including some he reprinted himself. His 1775 edition of *Goody Two-Shoes* thus preceded the more famous first Worcester edition printed by another well-known early American publisher, Isaiah Thomas, who also built up his list substantially by reprinting the Newbery books and those of his successors. Portions from the Library of Congress copy of the 1787 *Little Goody Two-Shoes* and the first Worcester edition, also of 1787, of Newbery's even earlier *Little Pretty Pocket-book* may be seen in reproduction on pages 80 and 68 of this volume. Isaiah Thomas, who selected so well from Newbery's list, unlike that innovator wrote no books himself but attempted, if crudely, to illustrate. He was the most important imitator and adapter of Newbery's books, and influenced other early printers.

Chapbooks—cheap little paper-covered books—flooded America and were much read in the eighteenth and early nineteenth centuries. Many were imported from England, but others were printed in Boston, Philadelphia, and New York, as well as in smaller places. Most were identical with the English chapbooks from which they were derived, but there were some indigenous ones, usually concerned with Indians and the West. As well as the big city printers—William Charles, Jacob Johnson, and Benjamin Warner of Philadelphia (also Benjamin Franklin Bache, who printed there under the direction of his famous grandfather); Samuel Wood and Mahlon Day of New York, the Babcocks of New Haven and Hartford; Zachariah Fowle, Thomas Fleet, Munroe and Francis, and (before he moved to Worcester) Isaiah Thomas of Boston—there were such printers as Peter Edes of Haverhill, Massachusetts, who in 1794 issued Charles Perrault's fairy tales in an important first American edition.

The nineteenth century saw the growth of New York as the New World's chief publishing center, though Boston was recognized as having the two most distinguished publishers of children's books, and Philadelphia as the prime locale of Sunday School publishing. Their lists, without separate departments and editors for children's books, contained some books considered classics today, as this anthology reveals, and most of them also advertised popular mass-produced series (which are eagerly collected by today's bibliophiles as having been important in their time). Harper and Brothers began publishing in New York in 1827 and in the nineteenth century, as today, had a London branch.

New York also had G. P. Putnam; Charles Scribner's Sons; Dodd, Mead; E. P. Dutton; and Lothrop, Lee and Shepard (after each of the two last named had moved from Boston). In Boston, through various mergers, two famous juvenile houses descended from successful forebears: Little, Brown from Roberts Brothers; and Houghton Mifflin from Ticknor and Fields, incorporating the Riverside Press and the contributions of Horace E. Scudder, who has been called the first children's book editor. But another Boston publishing house, A. K. Loring, notable for the many books of Horatio Alger, Jr., did not survive in spite of that author's runaway success.

The Library of Congress Rare Book Collections

The Library of Congress has amassed a large collection of rare and old children's books. D'Alté Welch in his *A Bibliography of American Children's Books Printed Prior to 1821,* which provides a summary evaluation of institutional collections of rare children's books printed up to that date, cites the Library of Congress holdings as being second only to the holdings of the American Antiquarian Society in Worcester, Massachusetts, an institution that owes its beginning to the printer Isaiah Thomas. Welch cites as examples "a fine copy of the *Children's Bible,* Philadelphia, 1763; *The Child's New Plaything,* Philadelphia, 1763; four editions of *The History of the Holy Jesus; The Mother's Gift,* Philadelphia, 1791; and numerous other outstanding books."

The first copyright law was passed in 1790, but direct receipt of copyrighted books by the Library of Congress did not come until the law of 1870. However, many earlier works deposited elsewhere were transferred to the Library. Thus came first issues of books which have since become valuable collectors' items: such classics as *Little Women* and *The Adventures of Tom Sawyer* and many other widely known titles. Curator Valta Parma decided on a chronological shelf arrangement for most of the books in order to portray graphically the changes in format undergone by children's books over the years. Near these rows are author collections, for the works of such prolific writers as Jacob Abbott, William T. Adams ("Oliver Optic"), Mrs. G. R. Alden ("Pansy"), Horatio Alger, Jr., and Samuel Goodrich. Shelves of *McGuffey Readers* are also housed together here.

Purchases and gifts, as well as copyright deposits, have accounted for valuable acquisitions by the Library. Certain early purchases were made from appropriated funds, such as the Benjamin Franklin Collection in 1882—a library that included early primers and Franklin's own publications, like *The Poor Orphan's Legacy: being a Short Collection of Godly Counsels and Exhortations to a Young Arising Generation. Primarily designed by the author for his own children, but published that others may also reap benefit by them. By a minister of the gospel* (1834). Gifts included that of eighty-six rare juvenile items which came in 1940 from lawyer Frank J. Hogan of Washington, D.C. (The unique 1780 *Cock Robin* [shown on page 115] and one of four known copies of *The Tales of Peter Parley about America* [1827], as well as some valuable *New-England Primers* are in the Hogan Collection.) The Hans Christian Andersen Collection, presented by Jean Hersholt, contains items revealing the important relationship between Andersen and Horace E. Scudder.

The division's chronologically arranged children's books date from the early eighteenth century to the present. A number of current publications, pristine in their book jackets, are added each year for posterity. There are early bound magazines and gift collections, as well as the chronological and special author collections, while specific areas hold the Bible collection, miniature books, and dime novels. Schoolbooks and folios have also yielded works included in this anthology.

The total of some sixteen to seventeen thousand titles of American juvenile literature gathered in the Rare Book Division is considered to have as an aggregate a remarkable richness for research, perhaps even an unrivaled completeness.

The pages that follow provide a rich sampling of the works produced in America for young readers during the eighteenth and nineteenth centuries. All the examples have been culled from the collection of the Library of Congress. Some are familiar, some rare, some famous, some nearly forgotten. Taken together, all provide insight into what literate and well-intended adults felt most worthy of inculcating into young minds, of passing on to the future; they are a sort of "time capsule," a fascinating segment of social history, as well as a survey of a vigorous and varied body of writing for children. Too often American children's literature is considered to be merely an offshoot or imitation of English works. This volume reveals that American books for children, though naturally influenced by England during the colonial years and for a short period thereafter, quickly developed a character and subject matter of their own, with, by the middle of the nineteenth century, a host of excellent and highly original indigenous writers and illustrators. Linked by a common language, influences in children's literature crossed the ocean back and forth between England and America, but American books early declared their independence from their mother country. This anthology, with its various introductions to sections and individual selections, we hope will serve to reveal, through examples, significant early trends in American children's literature.

PLAYING SCHOOL.

I. Works Intended to Instruct or Improve. *From the Colonial Period to 1900.*

Books available to eighteenth-century American children and their English cousins were few indeed, and most of them entirely serious in purpose, reflecting the deep concern of their elders about their relationship to God. Thus, the reading matter for these miniature adults consisted largely of spiritual guides, catechisms, Bibles, testimonial works, and religious schoolbooks, designed to awaken their minds to their inborn sinfulness and depravity and their need to be saved.

Published in England in 1646 and in America in 1656 was the popular religious guide, John Cotton's *Milk for Babes.* Its subtitle reads *Drawn out of the Breast of Both Testaments. Chiefly for the spiritual nourishment of Boston Babes in either England. But may be of like use for any children.* Even more prevalent was James Janeway's *A Token for Children* which appeared in 1671–1672, with the subtitle: *Being an Exact Account of the Conversion, Holy and Exemplary Lives and Joyful Deaths of several Young Children.* This was a much imitated and often reprinted work that did not disappear from the publishing scene until the nineteenth century—a clear testimony to its popularity at least with adults.

The Bible was always available. In 1698 Benjamin Harris, an English printer who had sojourned in Boston for a number of years, brought out in England *The Holy Bible in Verse,* perhaps the first Bible designed for children. There is evidence that John Allen, his first partner in Boston, published the first American edition of this work in 1717. This was followed by other adaptations, often in rhyme. The Library of Congress possesses a copy of the *Holy Bible Abridged,* printed and sold by Samuel Hall of Boston in 1795, and one of Isaiah Thomas's second Worcester edition of 1796, also a 1749 *The History of the Holy Jesus,* printed by J. Bushell and J. Green of Boston. Popular as well were the miniature (or thumb) Bibles and "hieroglyphic" Bibles, in which pictures were used for words throughout the text. (These, too, are represented in the holdings of the Library of Congress.)

Schoolbooks abounded. Earliest came the hornbooks, battledores, primers, and other ABC's intended to provide religious training along with the alphabet. Of these, *The New-England Primer,* with its famous "In Adam's Fall/We sinned all" and other verses of Isaac Watts, exerted an especially wide influence. Next came textbook writers—Noah Webster, Caleb Bingham, and Sarah Josepha Hale—who, along with others governed by a desire to inculcate in the young a sense of patriotism, produced spellers, histories, geographies, and biographies of national heroes. William Holmes McGuffey produced his famous McGuffey's Eclectic Readers to meet a need that was especially felt in the rapidly developing West, where there were few teachers and schools. His *First Reader* was published in 1836, and the others followed.

The desire to impart instruction, always strong in New England, saw a shift in emphasis in the mid-eighteenth century with the spread of John Locke's "instruction through play" and the coming of the Age of Reason and Enlightenment. As in England, a growing interest in natural history resulted in the production of many little books about birds, animals, fishes, and insects. Writers for the young on other subjects, too, proceeded with purposefulness and earnestness thinly disguised to instruct *and* "amuse." By the early years of the nineteenth century, Parson Weems had successfully espoused the writing of biographies, and Samuel G. Goodrich, piously avoiding the horrors of fairy tales, wrote in his Peter Parley books about peoples of the real world—with such phenomenal commercial success that his books were often pirated and translated.

Stories were equally full of purpose. Tracts published to suit the American Sunday School movement multiplied, based on an awareness of corruption and atheism in America seen in part to be an aftermath of the American and French revolutions. Westward expansion, the Industrial Revolution, and consequent waves of immigrants made an impact on social life. To combat illiteracy and sin in the young, concerned American women, like their English counterparts, took up their pens to condemn vice in many forms and to advocate religion and industry. These famous English "guardians of the young," who included the redoubtable Mrs. Trimmer, Hannah More (visited and admired by Samuel Goodrich), and Maria Edgeworth, wielded an enormous influence, and their books were much reprinted in America, while the American tract societies as well as other publishers in the New World brought forth works by such native "guardians" as Lydia Maria Child, Lydia Huntley Sigourney (called "the Sweet Singer of Hartford," a writer of edifying stories and verse for children), and innumerable other unidentified "aunts" and "uncles."

I. Works Intended to Instruct or Improve.

From the Colonial Period to 1900.

A. THE TEACHING OF RELIGION AND MORALS.

A TOKEN FOR CHILDREN, Being An Exact Account of the Conversion, Holy and Exemplary Lives and Joyful Deaths of several Young Children. By James Janeway [1636?–1674], Minister of the Gospel. To which is added, A Token for the Children of New-England, or, Some Examples of Children, in whom the Fear of God was remarkably Budding before they died; in several Parts of New-England. Preserved and Published for the Encouragement of Piety in other Children. With New Additions. Boston: Printed and Sold by Z. Fowle, in Back-Street, near the Mill-Bridge, 1771. 156 pages. 17 cm.

This work was first published in England in one volume of two parts (1671–1672) without the portion shown here, which was written for the American market by the Reverend Cotton Mather. The earliest American printing, cited by d'Alté Welch in his *A Bibliography of American Children's Books Printed Prior to 1821,* is that of 1700 in Boston. An account of youthful piety, in tune with the doctrine of original sin, this is the first of the few narratives that were available to eighteenth-century children in America and undoubtedly the most widely read children's book in the Puritan age. The tone of the whole may be deduced from the title page, reproduced here, and the foreword on the next page.

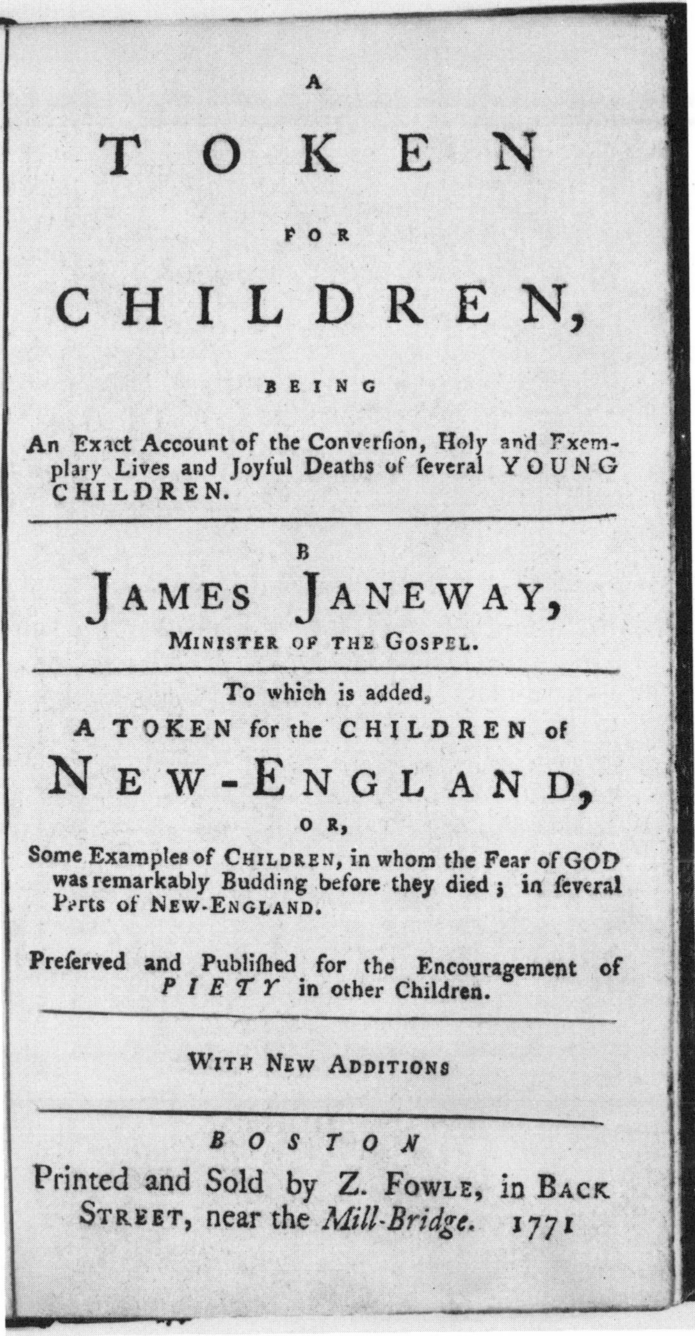

A

TOKEN

FOR

CHILDREN,

BEING

An Exact Account of the Converſion, Holy and Exemplary Lives and Joyful Deaths of ſeveral YOUNG CHILDREN.

B

JAMES JANEWAY,

MINISTER OF THE GOSPEL.

To which is added,

A TOKEN for the CHILDREN of

NEW-ENGLAND,

OR,

Some Examples of CHILDREN, in whom the Fear of GOD was remarkably Budding before they died; in ſeveral Parts of NEW-ENGLAND.

Preſerved and Publiſhed for the Encouragement of *PIETY* in other Children.

WITH NEW ADDITIONS

BOSTON

Printed and Sold by Z. FOWLE, in BACK STREET, near the *Mill-Bridge.* 1771

[107]

A

TOKEN

FOR THE

CHILDREN

OF

NEW-ENGLAND.

IF the Children of New-England *should not with an* Early Piety, *set themselves to* Know *and* Serve *the Lord JESUS CHRIST, the GOD* of their Fathers, *they will be condemned, not only by the* Examples *of* pious Children *in other Parts of the World, the publish'd and printed Accounts whereof have been brought over hither; but there have been* Exemplary Children *in the Midst of New-England itself, that will rise up against them for their Condemnation. It would be a very profitable Thing to our* Children, *and*

[108]

highly acceptable to all the godly Parents *of the* Children, *if, in Imitation of the excellent* JANEWAY's Token for Children, *there were made a true Collection of notable Things, exemplified in the* Lives *and* Deaths *of many among us, whose* Childhood *hath been signalized for what is virtuous and laudable.*

In the Church-History *of* New-England *is to be found the* Lives *of many eminent Persons, among whose Eminencies, not the least was,* Their fearing of the Lord from their Youth, *and their being* loved by the Lord when they were Children.

But among the many other Instances, of a Childhood *and* Youth *delivered from* Vanity *by* serious Religion, *which* New-England *has afforded, these few have particularly been preserved.*

A TOKEN FOR CHILDREN *(continued from page 11)*

THE PRODIGAL DAUGHTER, or A strange and wonderful Relation, Shewing, How a Gentleman of great estate in Bristol, had a proud and disobedient daughter, who, because her parents would not support her in all her extravagance, bargained with the devil to poison them.—How an angel informed them of her design.—How she lay in a trance four days; and when she was put in the grave, she came to life again, and related the wonderful things she saw in the other world.—Hartford: Printed for the Travelling Booksellers, 1799. 12 pages. 18 cm.

(continued on next page)

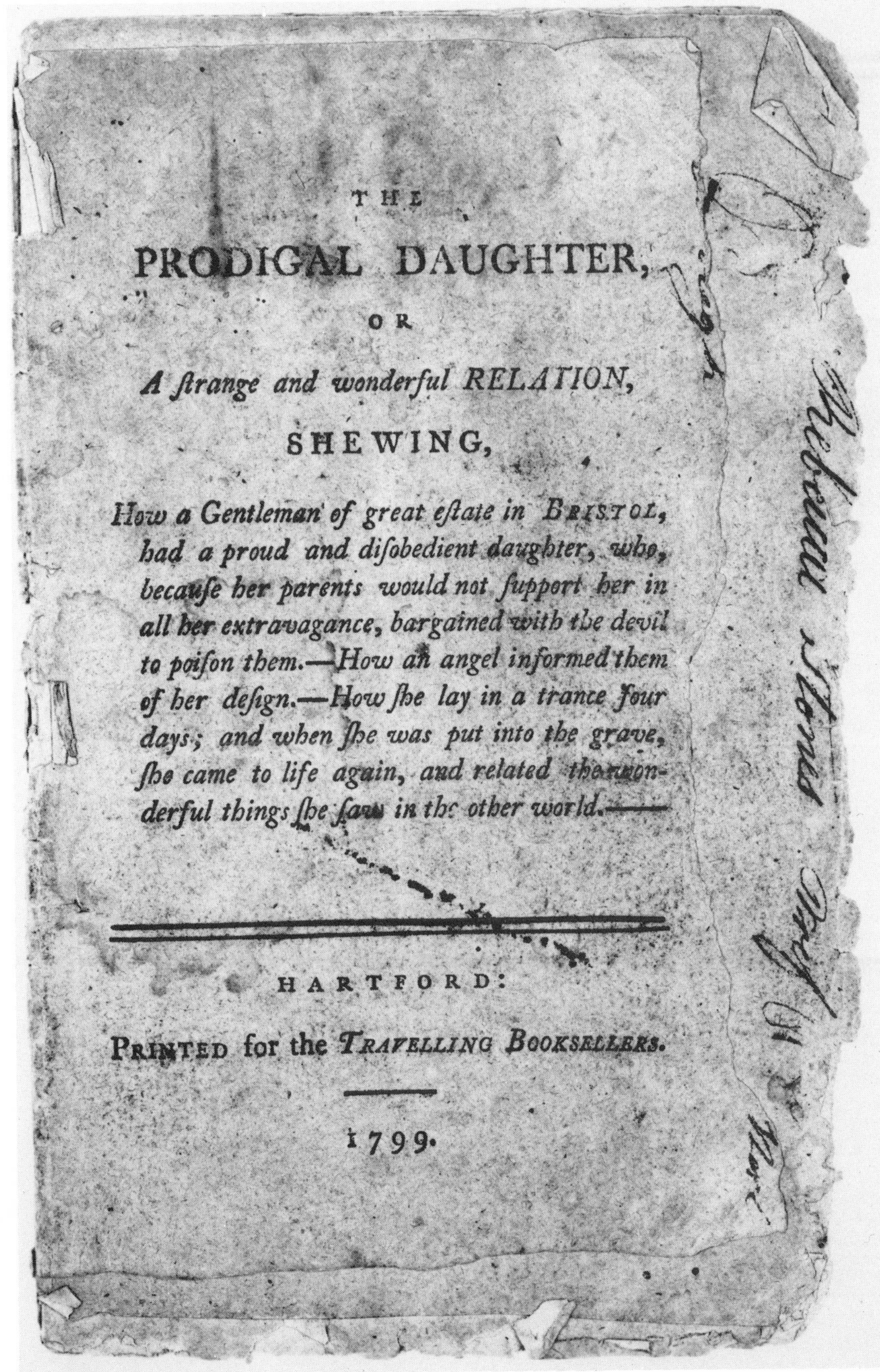

THE

PRODIGAL DAUGHTER,

OR

A ſtrange and wonderful RELATION,

SHEWING,

How a Gentleman of great eſtate in BRISTOL, *had a proud and diſobedient daughter, who, becauſe her parents would not ſupport her in all her extravagance, bargained with the devil to poiſon them.—How an angel informed them of her deſign.—How ſhe lay in a trance four days; and when ſhe was put into the grave, ſhe came to life again, and related the wonderful things ſhe ſaw in the other world.—*

HARTFORD:

PRINTED for the *TRAVELLING* BOOKSELLERS.

1799.

THE PRODIGAL DAUGHTER *(continued from page 13)*

This popular, melodramatic moral tale in rhymed verse, with its somewhat biblical flow of language, represents an early type of chapbook literature that colonial parents considered fit for their children. It is known primarily through its American editions. D'Alté Welch (op. cit.) lists twenty-eight extant editions (dated c. 1737–1741 to 1820), its publishers including Thomas Fleet and Isaiah Thomas. He notes that Irish and English editions differ from the American ones in that the locale of the former is London, rather than Bristol, and that they have a variance in some verses. This Library of Congress edition lacks illustration, as do two others in its holdings, one dated prior to 1811 and the other c. 1819. The last page is shown here.

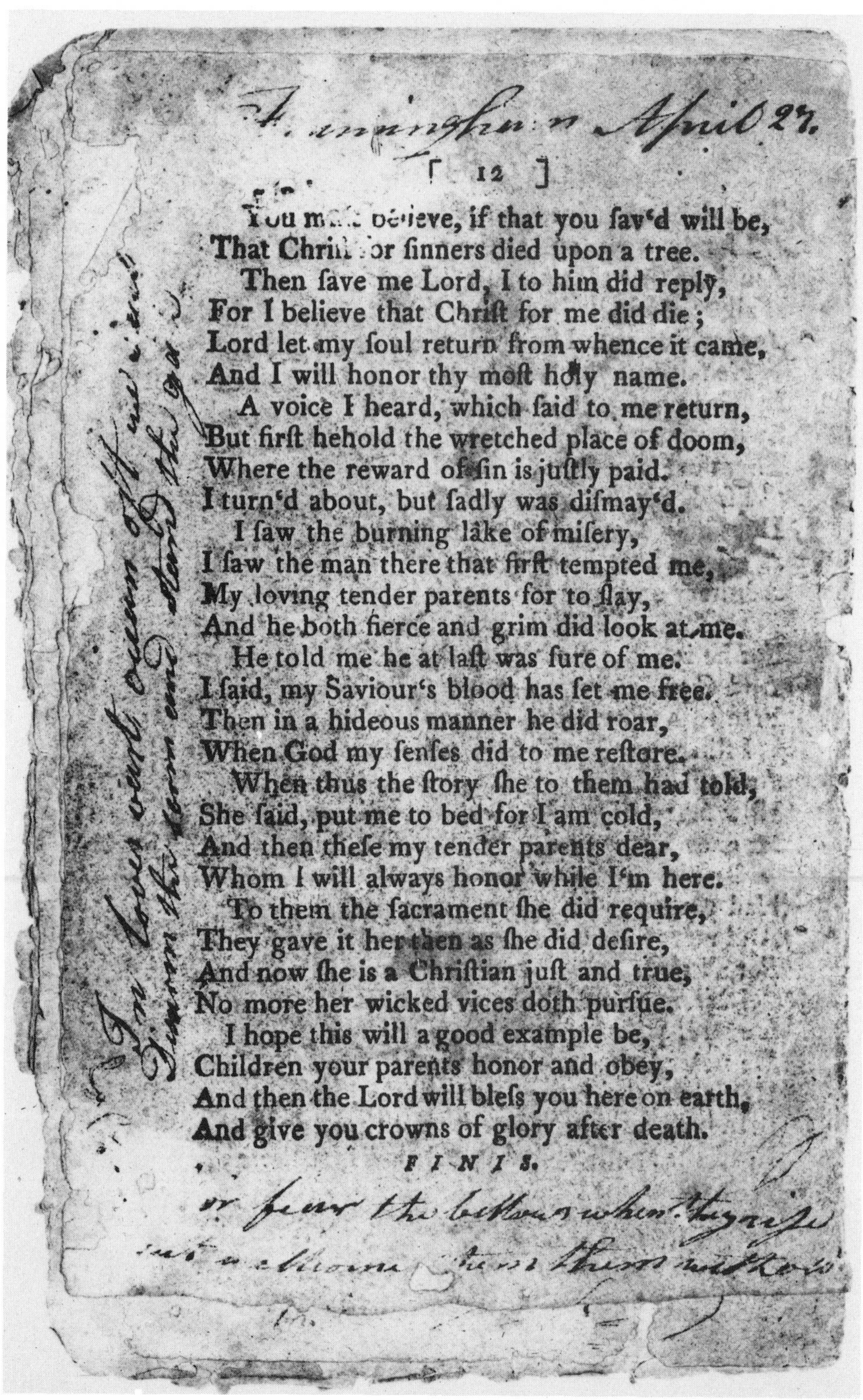

[12]

You muſt believe, if that you ſav'd will be,
That Chriſt for ſinners died upon a tree.
Then ſave me Lord, I to him did reply,
For I believe that Chriſt for me did die;
Lord let my ſoul return from whence it came,
And I will honor thy moſt holy name.
A voice I heard, which ſaid to me return,
But firſt behold the wretched place of doom,
Where the reward of ſin is juſtly paid.
I turn'd about, but ſadly was diſmay'd.
I ſaw the burning lake of miſery,
I ſaw the man there that firſt tempted me,
My loving tender parents for to ſlay,
And he both fierce and grim did look at me.
He told me he at laſt was ſure of me.
I ſaid, my Saviour's blood has ſet me free.
Then in a hideous manner he did roar,
When God my ſenſes did to me reſtore.
When thus the ſtory ſhe to them had told,
She ſaid, put me to bed for I am cold,
And then theſe my tender parents dear,
Whom I will always honor while I'm here.
To them the ſacrament ſhe did require,
They gave it her then as ſhe did deſire,
And now ſhe is a Chriſtian juſt and true,
No more her wicked vices doth purſue.
I hope this will a good example be,
Children your parents honor and obey,
And then the Lord will bleſs you here on earth,
And give you crowns of glory after death.

FINIS.

Title page

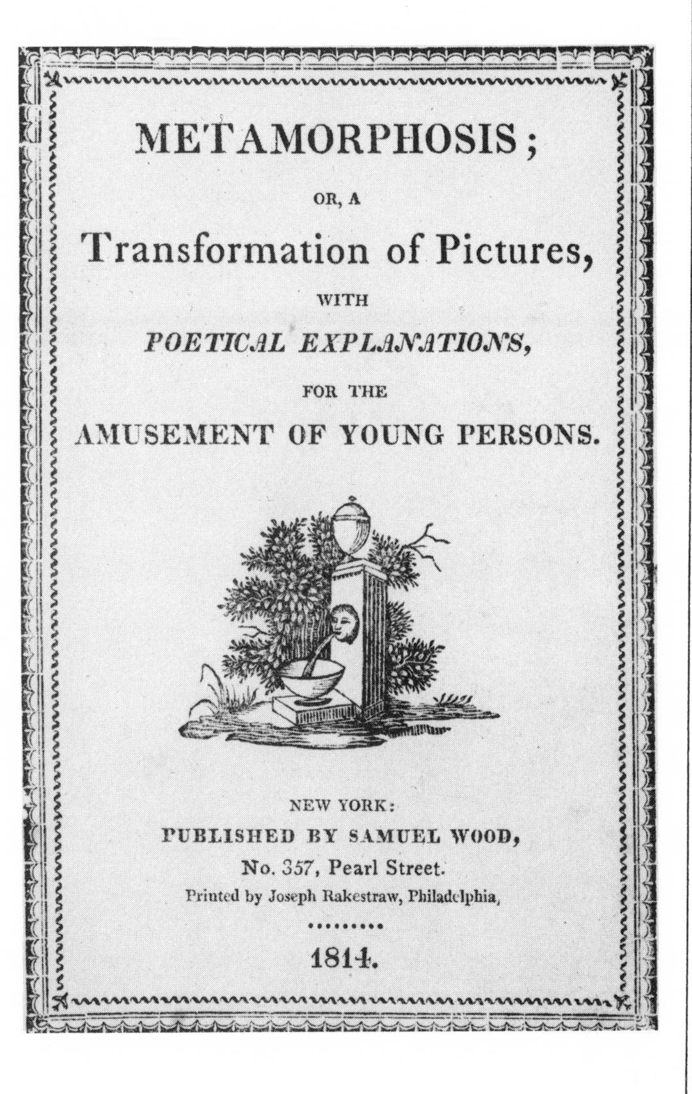
METAMORPHOSIS;
OR, A
Transformation of Pictures,
WITH
POETICAL EXPLANATIONS,
FOR THE
AMUSEMENT OF YOUNG PERSONS.
NEW YORK:
PUBLISHED BY SAMUEL WOOD,
No. 357, Pearl Street.
Printed by Joseph Rakestraw, Philadelphia,
1814.

METAMORPHOSIS; or, a Transformation of Pictures, with Poetical Explanations, for the Amusement of Young Persons. New York: Published by Samuel Wood, No. 357, Pearl Street. Printed by Joseph Rakestraw, Philadelphia. 1814. 8 pages. 15 cm.

One of the "bright inventions" of Robert Sayer, an English printer, this kind of book variously named "harlequinade" or "turn-up" or "metamorphosis" enjoyed about thirty years of popularity in England and then spread across the Atlantic. Over thirty-six American editions of these popular items appeared between the years 1787 and 1820. The earliest Library of Congress edition contains nine lines of explanation, and an illustration of a three-masted schooner sailing under the American flag establishes its nationality, although the text is rewritten from the English edition of 1654.

(continued on next page)

 (continued from page 15)

A page with all flaps folded down.

The same page with top flap unfolded, revealing new verses and part of the underlying picture.

4. A Lion rousing from his den
On purpose for to range,
Is soon turn'd into another shape;
Lift up and see how strange.

6. Behold within the Eagle's claws,
An infant there doth lie!
Which he has taken as a prey
And is prepar'd to fly.

18. The Tree of Life, now in that land,
And knowledge, do well guarded stand,
Lest Adam should the same espy,
And eat thereof and never die,

There Cherubs with a flaming sword,
Are set the Tree of Life to guard:
Now who among our fallen race,
Can hope to see his Maker's face?

Above: The same page with lower flap unfolded.
Right: The metamorphosis completed.

14. In happy Eden see them plac'd,
Who stood or fell for all our race;
In a sweet bower, composed of love,
This happy pair might safely rove.

There was no curse upon that ground,
Nor changing grief there to be found:
There nothing could their joys controul,
Nor mar the pleasures of the soul.

5. A Griffin here you may behold,
As fabled said to be;
Once more do but the leaf downfold,
A stranger sight you'll see.

6. Behold within the Eagle's claws,
An infant there doth lie!
Which he has taken as a prey
And is prepar'd to fly.

18. The Tree of Life, now in that land,
And knowledge, do well guarded stand,
Lest Adam should the same espy,
And eat thereof and never die,

There Cherubs with a flaming sword,
Are set the Tree of Life to guard:
Now who among our fallen race,
Can hope to see his Maker's face?

A NEW

HIEROGLYPHICAL BIBLE

For the amusement & instruction of Children;

BEING

A SELECTION

Of the most useful Lessons,
AND
most interesting Narratives ;

(Scripturally arranged)

From GENESIS to the REVELATIONS.

Embellished with

Familiar Figures, and Striking Emblems.

To the whole is added a sketch of the life of

OUR BLESSED SAVIOUR.

Recommended by the Rev. *Roaland Hul,* M. A.

From an English Edition : Re printed at
JAFFREY N. H.
BY SALMON WILDER:
Sold at his Printing Office. by the gross. doz en or single.—1814.

A NEW HIEROGLYPHICAL BIBLE For the amusement & instruction of Children; Being A Selection of the most useful Lessons and most interesting Narratives; (Scripturally arranged) From Genesis to the Revelations. Embellished with Familiar Figures, and Striking Emblems. To the whole is added a sketch of the life of Our Blessed Saviour. Recommended by the Rev. Rowland Hul, M.A. From an English edition: Reprinted at Jaffrey N. H. By Salmon Wilder: Sold at his Printing Office by the gross, dozen or single, 1814. 56 pages. 15 cm.

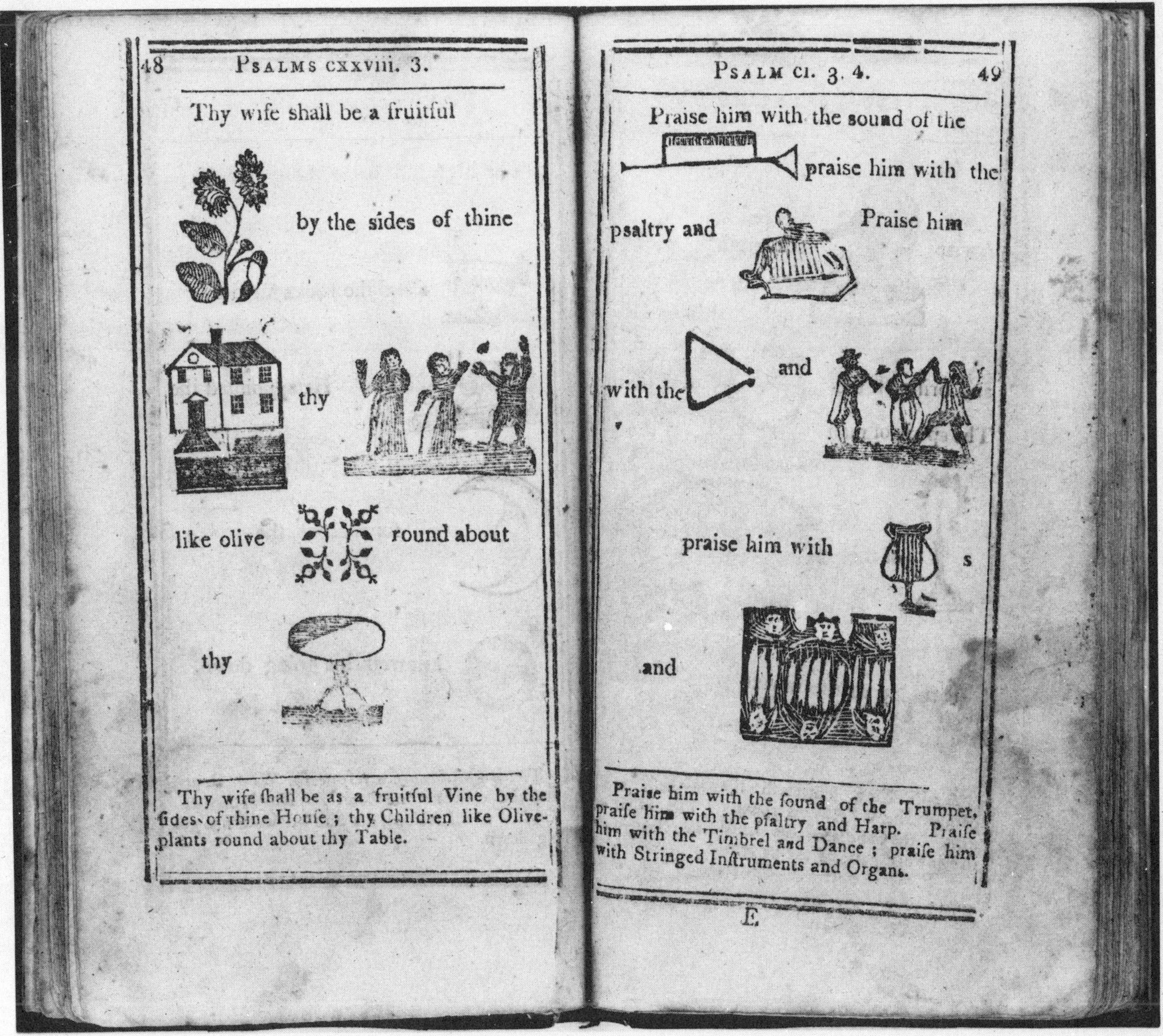

48 PSALMS cxxviii. 3.

Thy wife shall be a fruitful

by the sides of thine

thy

like olive round about

thy

Thy wife ſhall be as a fruitful Vine by the ſides of thine Houſe ; thy Children like Olive-plants round about thy Table.

PSALM cl. 3. 4. 49

Praise him with the sound of the

praise him with the

psaltry and Praise him

with the and

praise him with s

and

Praise him with the ſound of the Trumpet, praiſe him with the pſaltry and Harp. Praiſe him with the Timbrel and Dance ; praiſe him with Stringed Inſtruments and Organs.

E.

Quaint hieroglyphic Bibles, Bibles made attractive to children through the rebus-like substitution of pictures for words, appeared in this country in the eighteenth century. One of the first was issued by Isaiah Thomas in 1788. That shown here, an early Library of Congress copy, was illustrated with woodcuts by American artist Alexander Anderson. (The Library also possesses a 1796 edition printed by "the Booksellers" and two copies of an 1819 edition published by Samuel Wood and Sons.) The title page and a typical double spread are shown here.

I. Works Intended to Instruct or Improve.
From the Colonial Period to 1900.

B. PRIMERS, SPELLERS, AND ABC BOOKS.

THE NEW-ENGLAND PRIMER IMPROVED. For the more easy attaining the true reading of English. To which is added the Assembly of divines, and Mr. Cotton's Catechism. Boston: Printed for, and sold by A. Ellison, in Seven-Star Lane, 1773. 80 pages. 10¼ cm.

Called "the Little Bible of New England," this was the American children's book most widely found in the early colonies and long after (also the first book of American origin to find current use abroad). The earliest edition in the Library of Congress, an imperfect copy, has a manuscript note on its cover: "This is one of the first copies of the New England Primmer [sic]. Printed back of 1700 probably 1695. Traced by those who owned it." It was probably printed by Benjamin Harris, a printer from London, who had issued there in 1679 the *Protestant Tutor,* of which the *Primer* was a copy.

In the Hogan Collection are a rare Providence edition of 1775, which contains the childhood prayer, "Now I Lay Me Down to Sleep," and the only known copy of the Boston edition of 1790.

Editions through many generations varied both in text and illustration. In the many editions at the Library of Congress it can be seen that the frontispiece changed with history: from the picture of "King George the Third, Crown'd Sept. 22d, 1761," to one "ascribed to Paul Revere" of George Washington, in an edition printed and sold in Cambridge "near Charles-River Bridge," 1789. Though there were some changes in the famous rhyming alphabet, the verses were more or less all scriptural, and the opening one "In Adam's fall,/We sinned all" and the concluding "Zaccheus he/Did climb the tree/His Lord to see" remained constant. After the middle of the eighteenth century, Isaac Watts's *Songs for Children* was included. By 1795 the reader was being told that this primer was an "easy and pleasant" guide to reading. An edition of 1796 reads, ". . . much enlarged. And better adapted to the use of children." Shown here are some typical pages of text; the two historic frontispieces are shown on the following page.

A In ADAM's Fall
We ſinned all.

B Heaven to find,
The BIBLE mind.

C Chriſt crucify'd,
For Sinners dy'd.

D The Deluge drown'd
The Earth around.

E ELIJAH hid,
By Ravens fed.

F The Judgment made
FELIX afraid.

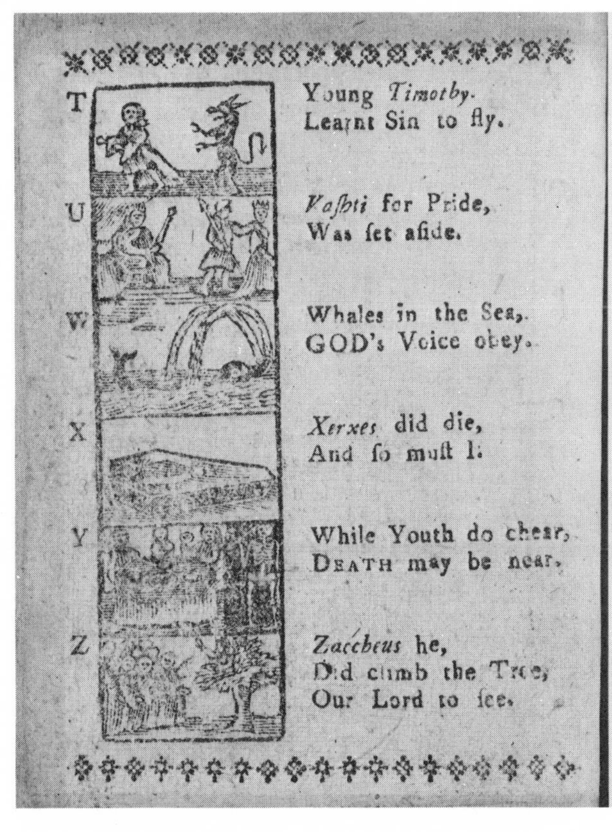

T Young *Timothy*.
Learnt Sin to fly.

U *Vaſhti* for Pride,
Was ſet aſide.

W Whales in the Sea,
GOD's Voice obey.

X *Xerxes* did die,
And ſo muſt I.

Y While Youth do chear,
DEATH may be near.

Z *Zaccheus* he,
Did climb the Tree,
Our Lord to ſee.

Two historic frontispieces from THE NEW-ENGLAND PRIMER

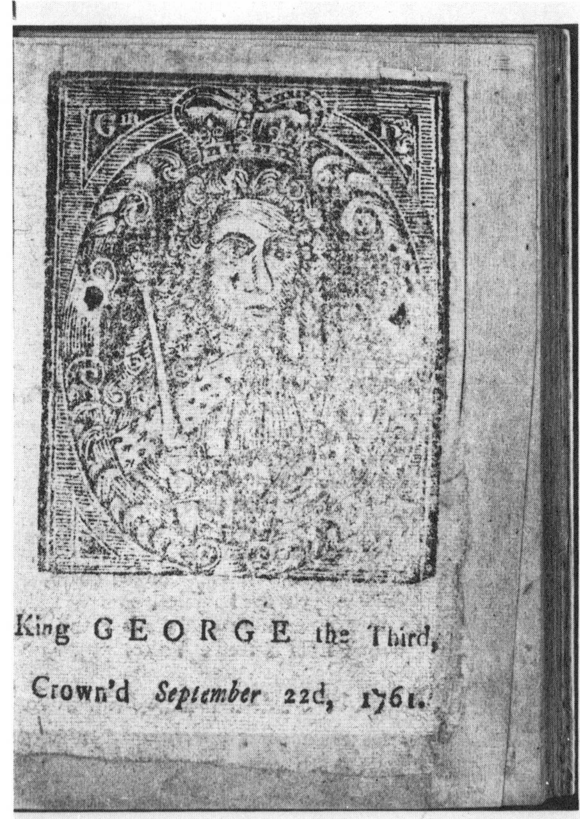

THE AMERICAN SPELLING BOOK: Containing an Easy Standard of Pronunciation. Being the First Part of a Grammatical Institute of the English Language. By Noah Webster, Jun. Esquire [1758–1843]. Author of "Dissertations on the English Language," "Collections of Essays and Fugitive Writings," &c. Thomas and Andrews's Second Edition. With additional Lessons, corrected by the Author. Printed at Boston, by Isaiah Thomas and Ebenezer T. Andrews. At Faust's Statue, No. 45 Newbury Street. Sold, Wholesale and Retail, at their Bookstore; by said Thomas at his Bookstore in Worcester, and by the Booksellers in Town and Country. 1790. 144 pages. 17 cm.

(continued on next page)

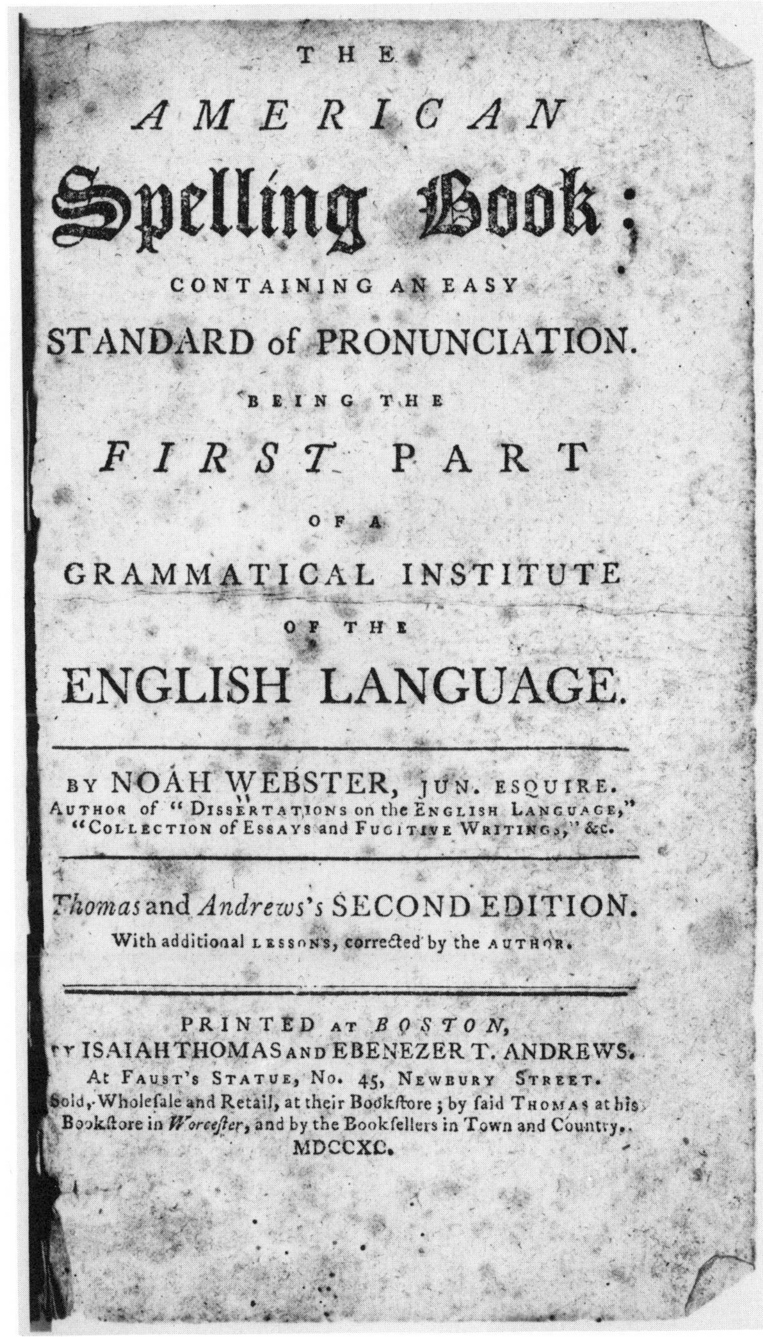

THE

AMERICAN

Spelling Book;

CONTAINING AN EASY

STANDARD of PRONUNCIATION.

BEING THE

FIRST PART

OF A

GRAMMATICAL INSTITUTE

OF THE

ENGLISH LANGUAGE.

BY NOAH WEBSTER, JUN. ESQUIRE.

AUTHOR of "DISSERTATIONS on the ENGLISH LANGUAGE," "COLLECTION of ESSAYS and FUGITIVE WRITINGS," &c.

Thomas and *Andrews's* SECOND EDITION.

With additional LESSONS, corrected by the AUTHOR.

PRINTED AT *BOSTON*,

BY ISAIAH THOMAS AND EBENEZER T. ANDREWS.

At FAUST's STATUE, No. 45, NEWBURY STREET.

Sold, Wholesale and Retail, at their Bookstore; by said THOMAS at his Bookstore in *Worcester*, and by the Booksellers in Town and Country.

MDCCXC.

94 AN EASY STANDARD.

tually promiſed to aſſiſt each other, if they ſhould happen to be aſſaulted. They had not proceeded far, before they perceived a Bear making towards them with great rage. There were no hopes in flight; but one of them, being very active, ſprung up into a tree; upon which the other, throwing himſelf flat on the ground, held his breath, and pretended to be dead; remembering to have heard it aſſerted, that this creature will not prey upon a dead carcaſe. The bear came up, and after ſmelling to him ſome time, left him, and went on. When he was fairly out of ſight and hearing, the hero from the tree calls out—Well, my friend, what ſaid the bear? He ſeemed to whiſper you very cloſely. He did ſo, replied the other, and gave me this good piece of advice; never to aſſociate with a wretch, who in the hour of danger will deſert his friend.

TABLE XXXIII.

Words in which *ch* have the ſound of *k*.

CHRIST, chyle, ſcheme, ache, chaſm, chriſm, tach, chord, loch, ſchool, choir

cho-rus, te-trarch, cha-os, cho-ral, a-poch, o-cher, tro-chee, an-chor, chriſ-ten, chym-iſt, ech-o, chal-ice, ſched-ule, paſ-chal

chol-ic, chol-er, ſchol-ar, mon-arch, or-chal, ſchir-rous, ſtom-ach, pa-tri-arch, eu-cha-riſt, an-ar-chy, chryſ-o-lite

char-ac-ter, cat-e-chiſm, pen-ta-teuch, ſep-ul-cher, tech-nic-al, al-chy-my, an-cho-ret, brach-i-al, lach-ry-mal, mach-i-nate, ſac-char-ine, ſyn-chro-niſm, mich-ael-mas, chor-iſ-ter

OF PRONUNCIATION. 95

chron-i-cle, or-cheſ-tra, och-i-my, chi-me-ra, pa-ro-chi-al, cha-mel-ion, tri-bach-us, arch-an-gel, me-chan-ic, ca-chex-y

cha-lyb-e-ate, a-nach-ro-niſm, ſyn-ec-do-che, pyr-rhich-i-us, am-phib-ra-chus, mel-an-chol-y, chro-nol-o-gy, chi-rog-ra-phy, cho-rog-ra-phy, chro-nom-e-ter

the-om-a-chy, ar-chi-tec-ture, an-ti-bac-chus, cat-e-chet-ic-al, bac-cha-nal-ian, cat-e-chu-men, ich-thy-ol-o-gy

FABLE VII.—*The* TWO DOGS.

HASTY and inconſiderate connections are generally attended with great diſadvantages; and much of every man's good or ill fortune depends upon the choice he makes of his friends.

A goodnatured Spaniel overtook a ſurly Maſtiff, as he was travelling upon the high road. Tray, although an entire ſtranger to Tyger, very civilly accoſted him; and if it would be no interruption, he ſaid, he ſhould be glad to bear him company on his way. Tyger,

THE AMERICAN SPELLING BOOK *(continued from page 23)*

The first edition of this frequently revised text appeared in 1783—the famous "Blue-backed Speller," which is still in print. More than fifty impressions, some of them of 25,000 copies each, appeared before 1800. Noah Webster, a graduate of Yale College, produced the work because as an educator he was unhappy with children's books which revealed an English rather than an American culture—and spelling. He devoted a long life to efforts to promote a distinctively American literature and language through his famous dictionary and many books, including his *History of the United States,* "to which is prefixed a brief historical account of our [English] ancestors, from the dispersion at Babel, to their migration to America, and of the conquest of South America, by the Spaniards, by Noah Webster, LL.D."

Webster's *American Spelling Book* was one of Isaiah Thomas's most heavily published titles and one of the few not originating with Newbery. The title page can be seen on the preceding page; shown here is a typical spread.

EASY AND INSTRUCTIVE LESSONS FOR CHILDREN. Also, The Ladder to learning; or, A selection of fables, consisting of words of only one syllable, being an easy Introduction to the useful Art of Reading. Boston: Printed by Manning & Loring, for Ezekiel Goodale, Bookseller, Hallowell, 1804. 48 pages. 11 cm.

A gaily-flowered cover belies the earnestness of this "easy Introduction to the useful Art of Reading." The heavy tone of the text is relieved by tiny, charming woodcuts for the fables which comprise the second half of the volume.

44 *A Selection of Fables.*

FABLE VIII.

The MAN and his GOOSE.

A POOR fool of a Man once had a Gooſe which laid eggs of gold; and this made the young rogue as proud as a horſe. Come, come, ſaid he, I may now hold up my head with the beſt of them all. Cheer up, my lad, for in a ſhort time you may have a coach to ride in, and make the duſt fly like ſmoke. But why did I ſay in a ſhort time? Bleſs me! what a ſtrange fool I am! It is but to rip up the Gooſe, and then I ſhall be as rich as King George at once. So to work he went, and ript up the Gooſe the ſame day. But he was a great fool for his pains; for when the poor gooſe was dead, he found nought but a few ſeeds, from which, it is true,

A Selection of Fables. 45

more eggs might have been bred, if he had been ſo wiſe as to wait for them; but as there was no life and warmth in the Gooſe, to make them grow, they were of no more worth to him than the eggs of a wren.

MORAL. *All graſp, all loſe.*

FABLE IX.

The Old MAN who called for DEATH.

A POOR Old Man, who was forced to go to the wood to pick up

THE
YOUNG CHILD's
A B C,
OR,
FIRST BOOK.

NEW-YORK:
PUBLISHED BY SAMUEL WOOD,
NO. 362 PEARL-STREET.
1806.

THE YOUNG CHILD'S A B C, OR, FIRST BOOK. New-York: Published by Samuel Wood, No. 362 Pearl-Street. 1806. 16 pages. 10 cm.

The first of Samuel Wood's many nursery books, this is a small chapbook, covered in blue paper, with finely engraved woodcuts illustrating alphabets, syllables, and lists of rhyming words, as in a battledore. The cuts are believed to have been made by Alexander Anderson. The entire text is reproduced here.

A B C D
E F G H
I J K L
M N O P
Q R S T
U V W X
Y Z &

3

a b c d e f g h i j k l m n
o p q r ſ s t u v w x y z

Aa Bb Cc Dd Ee Ff Gg Hh Ii Jj Kk
Ll Mm Nn Oo Pp Qq Rr Ss Tt
Uu Vv Ww Xx Yy Zz

Mm Ii Nn Dd Yy Oo Uu Rr Bb Aa
Kk Ll Cc Ee Gg Tt Vv Ff Hh
Pp Jj Qq Ss Ww Xx Zz

A E I O U Y a e i o u y

b c d f g h j k l m n p q r s t v w
x z

ct ff fi ffi ffl fl ſb ſh ſk ſi ſl ſſ ſſi ſt

ct ff fi ffi ffl fl ſb ſh ſk ſi ſl ſſ ſſi ſt

1 2 3 4 5 6 7 8 9 0

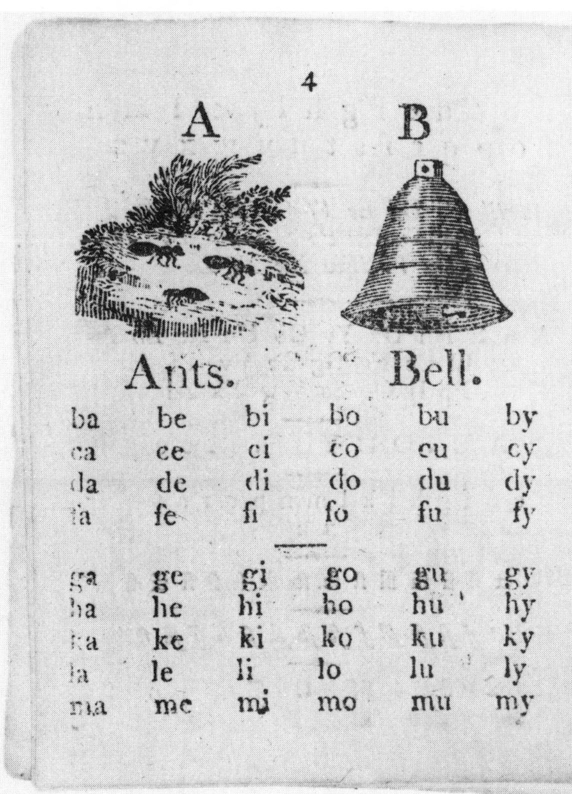

4

A B

Ants. Bell.

ba	be	bi	bo	bu	by
ca	ce	ci	co	cu	cy
da	de	di	do	du	dy
fa	fe	fi	fo	fu	fy
ga	ge	gi	go	gu	gy
ha	he	hi	ho	hu	hy
ka	ke	ki	ko	ku	ky
la	le	li	lo	lu	ly
ma	me	mi	mo	mu	my

5

C D

Cat. Dog.

na	ne	ni	no	nu	ny
pa	pe	pi	po	pu	py
ra	re	ri	ro	ru	ry
sa	se	si	so	su	sy
ta	te	ti	to	tu	ty
va	ve	vi	vo	vu	vy
wa	we	wi	wo	wu	wy
ya	ye	yi	yo	yu	
za	ze	zi	zo	zu	

(continued on next page)

6

E F

Elk. Fox.

ab eb ib ob ub
ac ec ic oc uc
ad ed id od ud
af ef if of uf

ag eg ig og ug
ak ek ik ok uk
al el il ol ul
am em im om um

7

G H

Goose. Horse.

an en in on un
ap ep ip op up
ar er ir or ur
as es is os us

at et it ot ut
av ev iv ov uv
ax ex ix ox ux
az ez iz oz uz

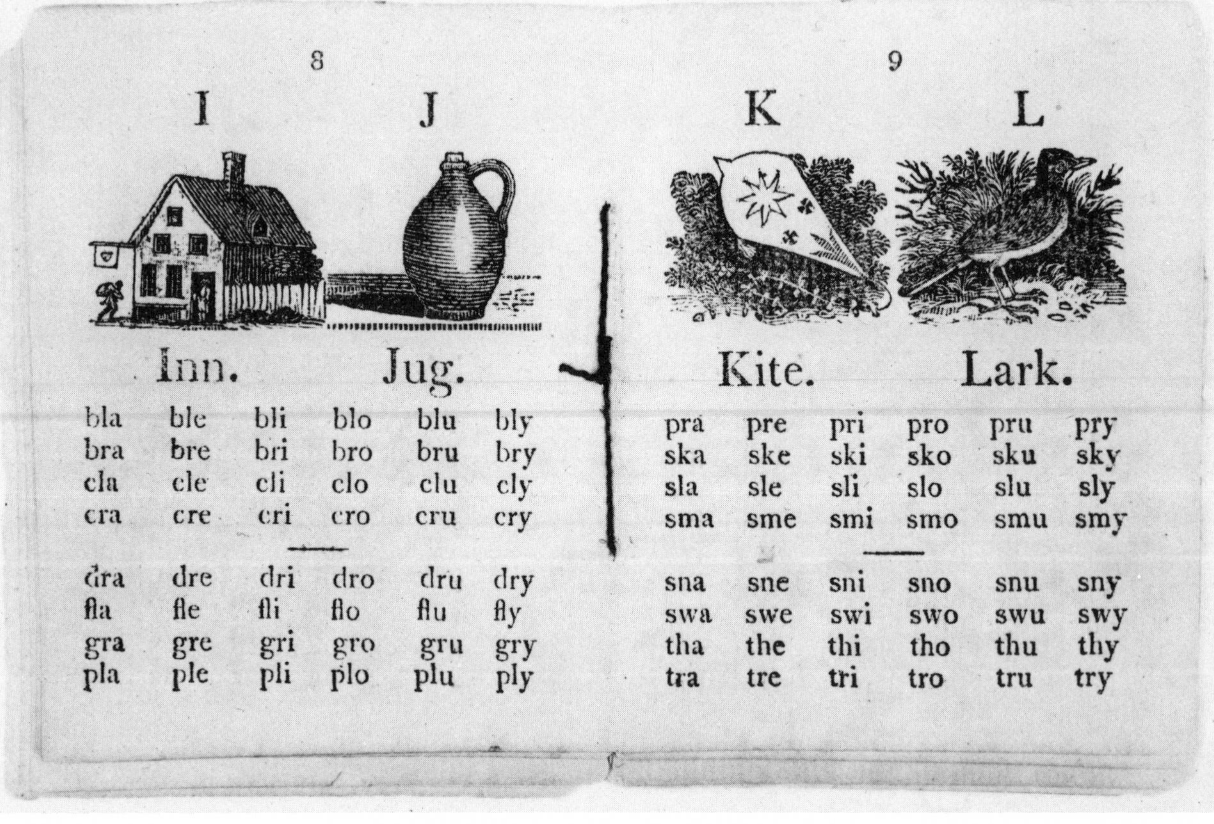

8

I J

Inn. Jug.

bla ble bli blo blu bly
bra bre bri bro bru bry
cla cle cli clo clu cly
cra cre cri cro cru cry

dra dre dri dro dru dry
fla fle fli flo flu fly
gra gre gri gro gru gry
pla ple pli plo plu ply

9

K L

Kite. Lark.

pra pre pri pro pru pry
ska ske ski sko sku sky
sla sle sli slo slu sly
sma sme smi smo smu smy

sna sne sni sno snu sny
swa swe swi swo swu swy
tha the thi tho thu thy
tra tre tri tro tru try

THE YOUNG CHILD'S A B C *(continued from page 27)*

10

M N

Mouse. Nest.

bad	had	lad	mad	sad	bed
fed	led	ned	wed	bid	did
kid	hid	lid	rid	hod	nod
rod	sod	bud	cud	mud	rud

---

bag	cag	hag	lag	nag	rag
bog	cog	fog	hog	jog	log
bat	cat	fat	hat	mat	rat
bin	din	fin	pin	sin	tin

11

O P

Owl. Pump.

beg	can	fan	lap	ran	ten
red	led	six	pig	rip	fig
man	wet	lip	cob	put	for
gun	tar	but	top	pod	fox

---

jar	arm	not	ask	jug	cur
hug	bun	pot	rub	hot	nod
fun	got	box	mop	cut	mug
cup	ink	pen	hot	bit	hip

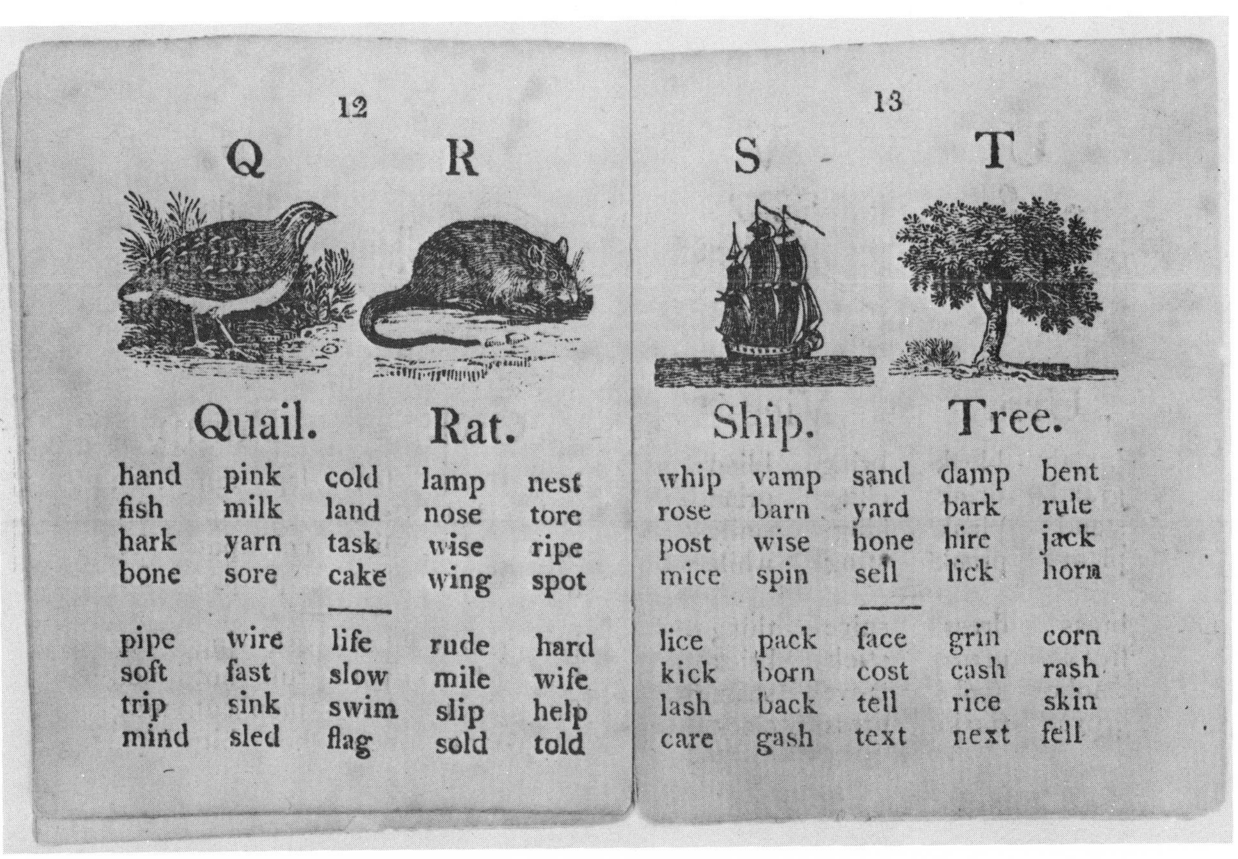

12

Q R

Quail. Rat.

hand	pink	cold	lamp	nest
fish	milk	land	nose	tore
hark	yarn	task	wise	ripe
bone	sore	cake	wing	spot

---

pipe	wire	life	rude	hard
soft	fast	slow	mile	wife
trip	sink	swim	slip	help
mind	sled	flag	sold	told

13

S T

Ship. Tree.

whip	vamp	sand	damp	bent
rose	barn	yard	bark	rule
post	wise	bone	hire	jack
mice	spin	sell	lick	horn

---

lice	pack	face	grin	corn
kick	born	cost	cash	rash
lash	back	tell	rice	skin
care	gash	text	next	fell

(continued on next page)

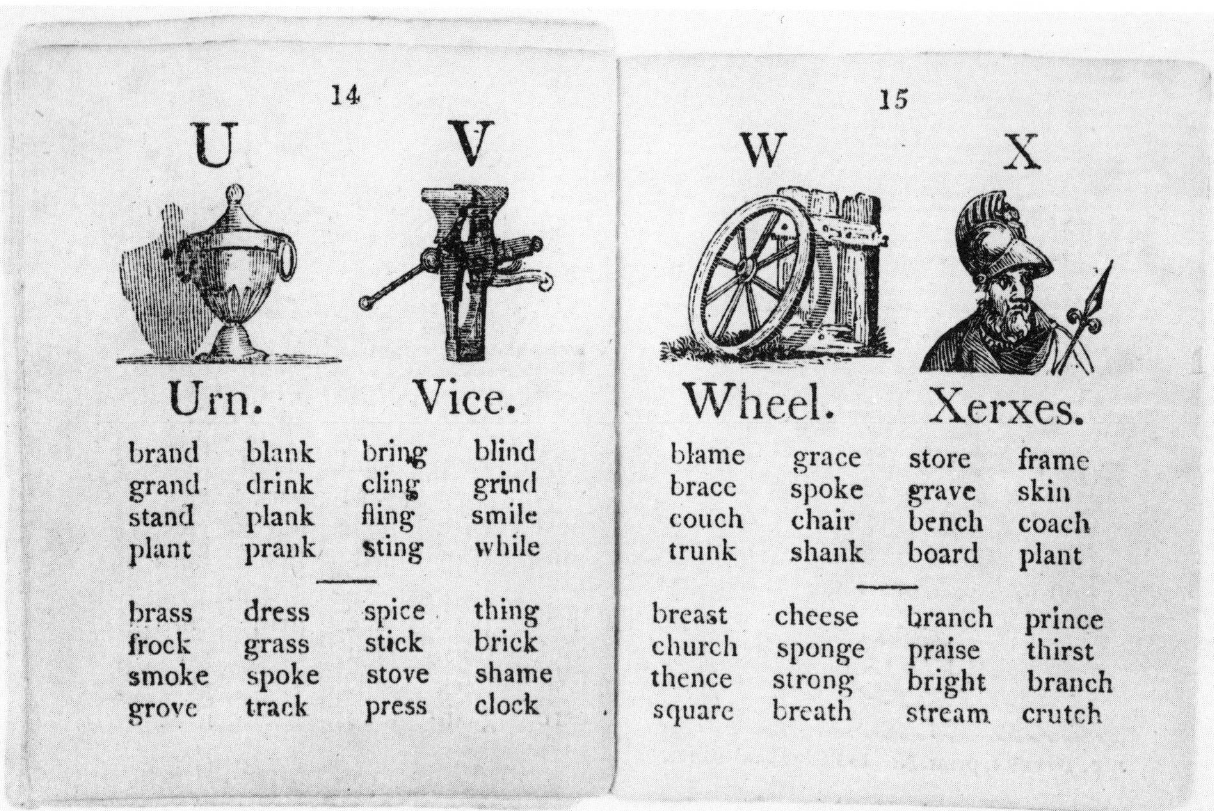

14

U V

Urn. Vice.

brand	blank	bring	blind
grand	drink	cling	grind
stand	plank	fling	smile
plant	prank	sting	while

brass	dress	spice	thing
frock	grass	stick	brick
smoke	spoke	stove	shame
grove	track	press	clock

15

W X

Wheel. Xerxes.

blame	grace	store	frame
brace	spoke	grave	skin
couch	chair	bench	coach
trunk	shank	board	plant

breast	cheese	branch	prince
church	sponge	praise	thirst
thence	strong	bright	branch
square	breath	stream	crutch

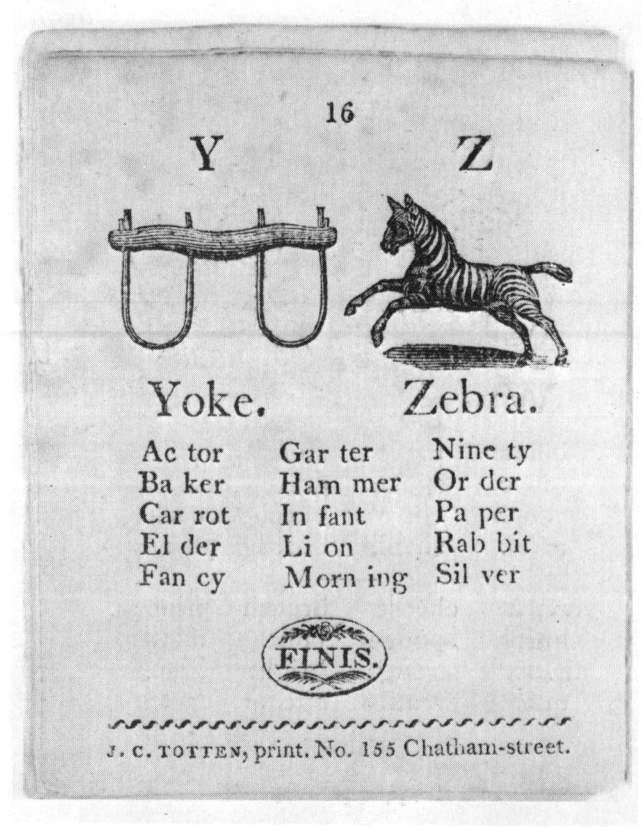

16

Y Z

Yoke. Zebra.

Ac tor	Gar ter	Nine ty
Ba ker	Ham mer	Or der
Car rot	In fant	Pa per
El der	Li on	Rab bit
Fan cy	Morn ing	Sil ver

FINIS.

J. C. TOTTEN, print. No. 155 Chatham-street.

THE ILLUSTRATED PRIMER; or the First Book for Children: Designed for Home or Parental Instruction. Embellished with Numerous Engravings, and Pretty Stories, Which will please the Children amazingly! Oh, what a pretty book! said Charley to Anne. New York: Published by George F. Cooledge & Brother, 323 Pearl Street, Franklin Square. No date. 47 pages. 19½ cm.

(continued on next page)

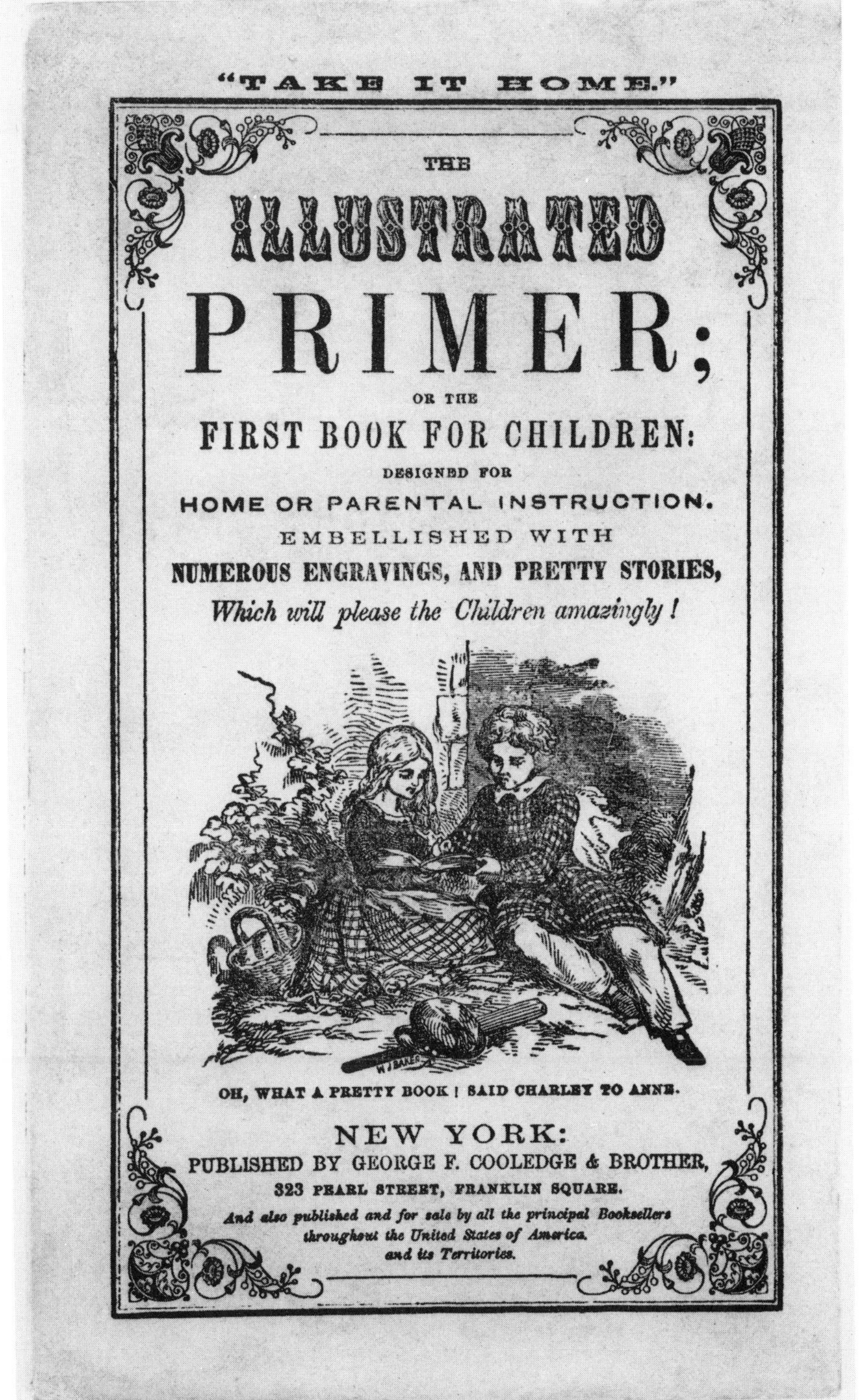

"TAKE IT HOME."

THE

ILLUSTRATED

PRIMER;

OR THE

FIRST BOOK FOR CHILDREN:

DESIGNED FOR

HOME OR PARENTAL INSTRUCTION.

EMBELLISHED WITH

NUMEROUS ENGRAVINGS, AND PRETTY STORIES,

Which will please the Children amazingly!

OH, WHAT A PRETTY BOOK! SAID CHARLEY TO ANNE.

NEW YORK:

PUBLISHED BY GEORGE F. COOLEDGE & BROTHER,

323 PEARL STREET, FRANKLIN SQUARE.

And also published and for sale by all the principal Booksellers throughout the United States of America, and its Territories.

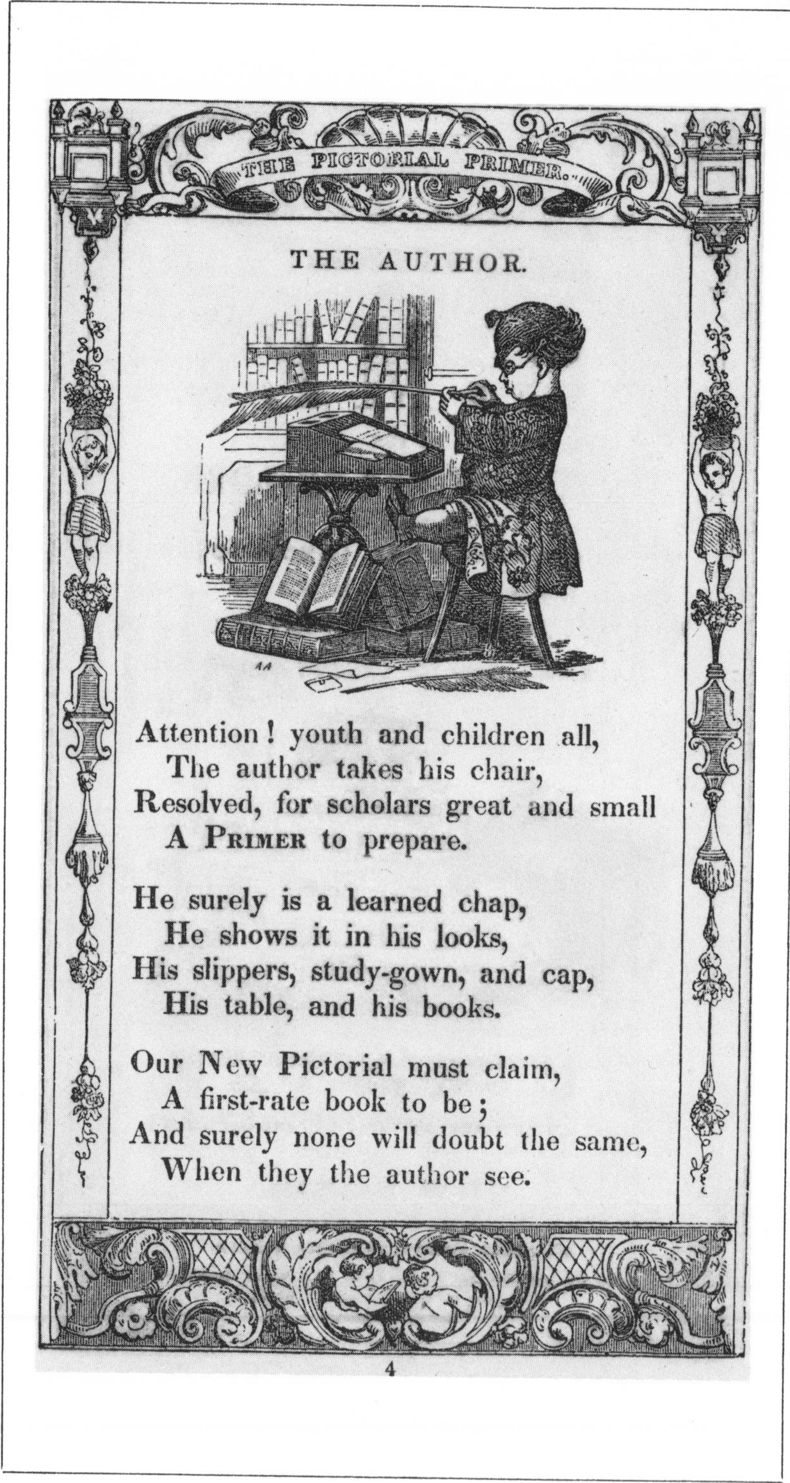

THE PICTORIAL PRIMER.

THE AUTHOR.

Attention! youth and children all,
The author takes his chair,
Resolved, for scholars great and small
A PRIMER to prepare.

He surely is a learned chap,
He shows it in his looks,
His slippers, study-gown, and cap,
His table, and his books.

Our New Pictorial must claim,
A first-rate book to be;
And surely none will doubt the same,
When they the author see.

4

THE ILLUSTRATED PRIMER *(continued from page 31)*

The introductory matter states, "The objects to be aimed at . . . [in this work] are simplicity and attractiveness. It is necessary, not only to catch the eye, and engage the mind of the learner, but to win him, by natural and easy steps, toward the mysteries of language." The title page can be seen on the preceding page; pages 4 and 26 are shown here.

THE PICTORIAL PRIMER.

My First Ride on the Pony.

"Hold on, Charley, never fear,
Pony is kind, and John is near,
Have courage, and you, by-and-by,
Will ride as well as George or I."

"Oh! I'm afraid of Pony Jack,
He trembles so all over his back,
He'll shake me off—I wish I knew,
If riding feels just so to you."

"Yes, always at the first—but then
We try, and try, and try again,
Until, at last, we find the saddle,
As easy as a chair, or cradle."

hold	back	first	last
kind	wish	shake	chair
ride	just	near	then
feel	try	find	fear
cradle	saddle	tremble	again

26

THE UNCLE'S PRESENT, A New Battledoor. Philadelphia: Published by J. Johnson. c. 1810. 5 pages. 18 cm.

The title is taken from the inside of the cover flap. On the cover are the alphabet and numerals, with the words "Read, and Be Wise" above, and with the imprint: "Philadelphia: Sold by Benjamin Warner, 147, Market Street.

Each letter of the alphabet is illustrated with a small picture from the *Cries of London*.

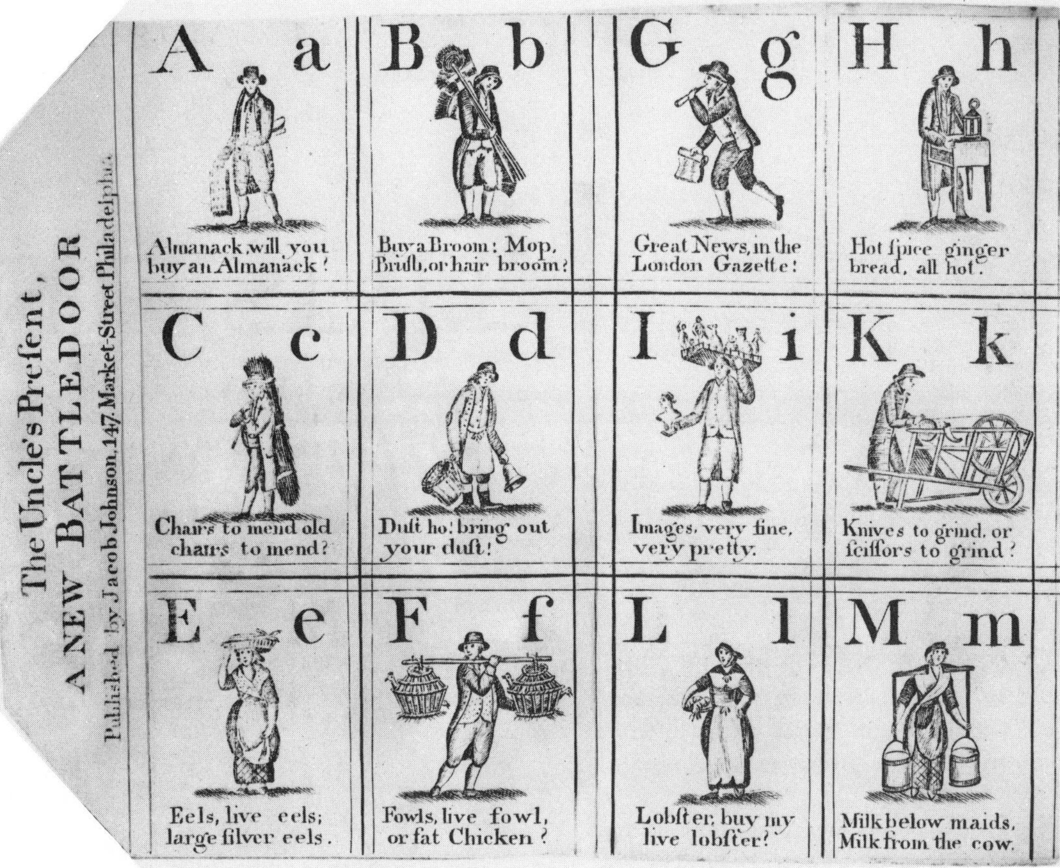
The Uncle's Prefent,
A NEW BATTLEDOOR
Published by Jacob Johnson, 147, Market-Street Philadelphia.
A a
Almanack, will you buy an Almanack?
B b
Buy a Broom: Mop, Brush, or hair broom?
G g
Great News, in the London Gazette!
H h
Hot spice ginger bread, all hot.
C c
Chairs to mend old chairs to mend?
D d
Dust ho! bring out your dust!
I i
Images, very fine, very pretty.
K k
Knives to grind, or sciffors to grind?
E e
Eels, live eels; large silver eels.
F f
Fowls, live fowl, or fat Chicken?
L l
Lobster, buy my live lobster?
M m
Milk below maids, Milk from the cow.

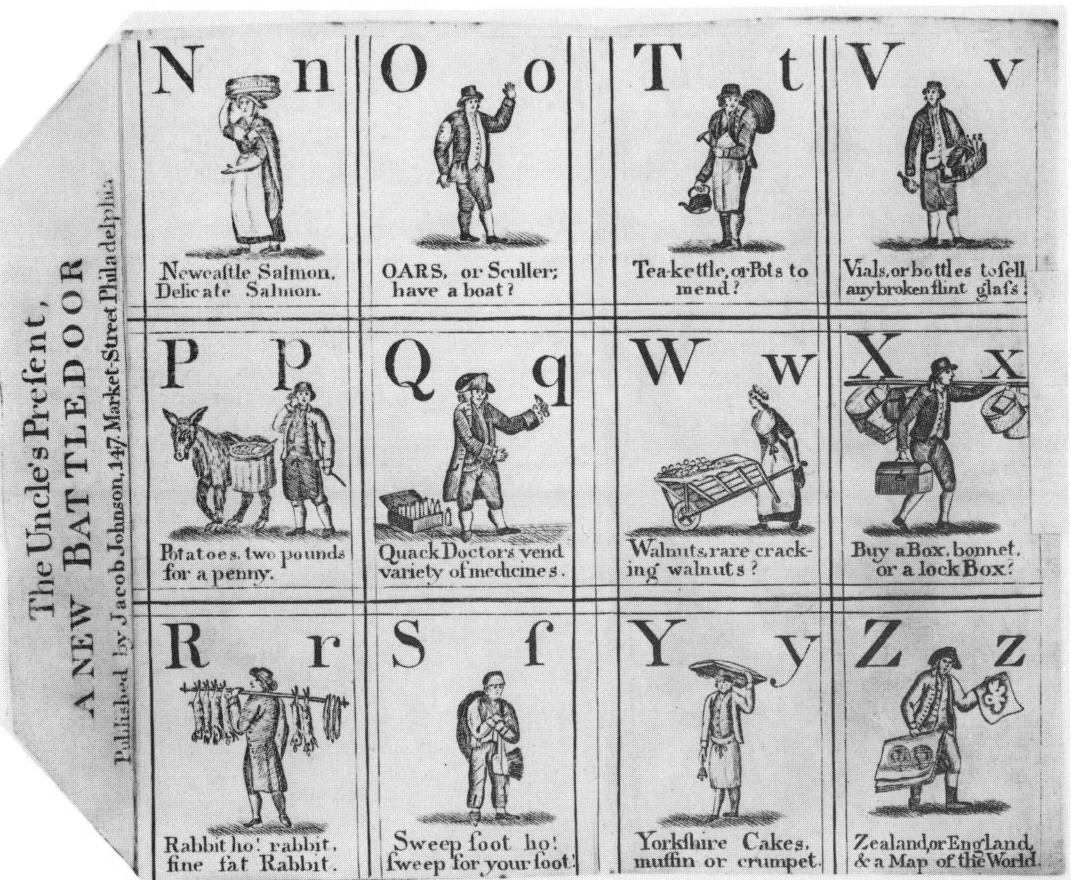
The Uncle's Prefent,
A NEW BATTLEDOOR
Published by Jacob Johnson, 147, Market-Street Philadelphia.
N n
Newcastle Salmon, Delicate Salmon.
O o
OARS, or Sculler; have a boat?
T t
Tea-kettle, or Pots to mend?
V v
Vials, or bottles to sell, any broken flint glafs?
P p
Potatoes, two pounds for a penny.
Q q
Quack Doctors vend variety of medicines.
W w
Walnuts, rare cracking walnuts?
X x
Buy a Box, bonnet, or a lock Box?
R r
Rabbit ho! rabbit, fine fat Rabbit.
S ſ
Sweep foot ho! sweep for your foot!
Y y
Yorkshire Cakes, muffin or crumpet.
Z z
Zealand, or England, & a Map of the World.

A
PICTURE BOOK,
FOR
LITTLE CHILDREN.
PHILADELPHIA:
PUBLISHED BY KIMBER AND CONRAD,
NO. 93, MARKET STREET.
MERRITT, PRINTER.

A PICTURE BOOK, FOR LITTLE CHILDREN. Philadelphia: Published by Kimber and Conrad, No. 93 Market Street. Merritt, Printer. c. 1812. 24 pages. 14 cm.

Two woodcuts to a page illustrate the lessons to be learned by the child. The last two cuts show a finely dressed lady and gentleman, and a peacock. Beneath a picture of the lady and gentleman is the heavily weighted query: "The use of clothes is to cover us, and to keep us warm; what do these people wear theirs for?"

A ship sails on the sea, it can be seen from the rocks when a great way off.

B B

b b

Do not go far from the shore; the boat looks too much like a tub to be a safe one.

It is not genteel to sit back to back—always look at a person when you speak to him.

B B

b b

The bible is the best of all books. Children who can read in the bible, may go to Kimber & Conrad's Store and buy one for themselves.

BEAUTIES OF THE NEW-ENGLAND PRIMER. New York: Published by Samuel Wood & Sons, 261 Pearl Street, c. 1818. 29 pages. 10½ cm.

The publisher describes this as "A selection, with some alterations." It is interesting to compare this with the earlier version shown on page 20. The Library of Congress possesses an earlier edition (1812) of *Beauties of the New-England Primer* (also from Samuel Wood), but with "the first preliminary leaf and the last leaf wanting."

ABCDEFGHIJKLM
NOPQRSTU
VWXYZ.

abcdefghijklmnopq
rstuvwxyz.

ABCDEFGHIJKL
MNOPQRSTU
VWXYZ.

abcdefghijklmnop
qrstuvwxyz.

fi fl ff ffi ffl &—*& fi fl ff ffi ffl*

1 2 3 4 5 6 7 8 9 0

BEAUTIES

OF

THE NEW-ENGLAND

PRIMER.

NEW YORK:

Published by Samuel Wood & Sons,

261 *Pearl-street.*

4

A.

Adam and Eve
Their God did grieve.

B.

Thy life to mend,
This Book attend.

C.

The Cat doth play,
And after, slay.

D.

A Dog will bite
A thief at night.

E.

An Eagle's flight
Is out of sight.

F.

The idle Fool
Is whipt at school,

5

G.

As runs the Glass
Our life doth pass.

H.
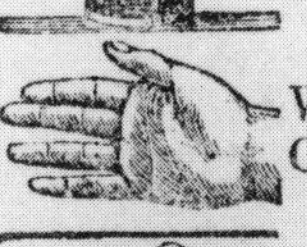
Wrought by the hand
Great works do stand.

J.

Job felt the rod,
Yet bless'd his God.

K.

The paper Kite
Is boys' delight.

L.

The Lion bold
The Lamb doth hold.

M.

The Moon gives light
In time of night.

6

N.

Nightingales sing
In time of Spring.

O.

The Owl at night
Hoots out of sight.

P.

Peter denied
His Lord, and cry'd.

Q.

Queens & kings must
Lie in the dust.

R.

The Rose in bloom
Sheds sweet perfume.

S.

Samuel anoints
Whom God appoints.

7

T.

Time cuts down all,
Both great and small.

U.

Urns hold, we see,
Coffee and tea.

W.

Whales in the sea
God's voice obey.

X.

Xerxes the great
Shar'd common fate.

Y.

Youth should delight
In doing right.

Z.

Zaccheus, he
Did climb the tree
His Lord to see.

I. Works Intended to Instruct or Improve.

From the Colonial Period to 1900.

C. INFORMATIONAL BOOKS.

THE LIFE OF GEORGE WASHINGTON; with Curious Anecdotes, Equally Honourable to Himself and Exemplary to His Young Countrymen. A life how useful to his country led!/How loved! while living!—how revered! now dead!/Lisp! lisp! his name, ye children yet unborn!/And with like deeds your own great names adorn. Seventh Edition—Greatly Improved. By M. L. Weems [Mason Locke Weems (1759–1825)], formerly Rector of Mount-Vernon Parish. Philadelphia: Printed for the Author, 1808. 229 pages. 18 cm.

Desirous of inculcating heroism and love of country in young persons, the writer, known as Parson Weems, was actually an itinerant Southern preacher and purveyor of books and morals. In this well-known book he reveals through anecdotes: "Washington the *dutiful son*—the affectionate brother—the cheerful schoolboy—the diligent surveyor—the neat draftsman—the laborious farmer—the widow's husband—the orphan's father—and poorman's friend . . . Washington the *Hero,* and the Demigod . . . the *sun beam* in council . . . the storm in war." Included in the imaginary reconstruction of Washington's boyhood is the famous cherry-tree episode, reproduced here on pages 42–44.

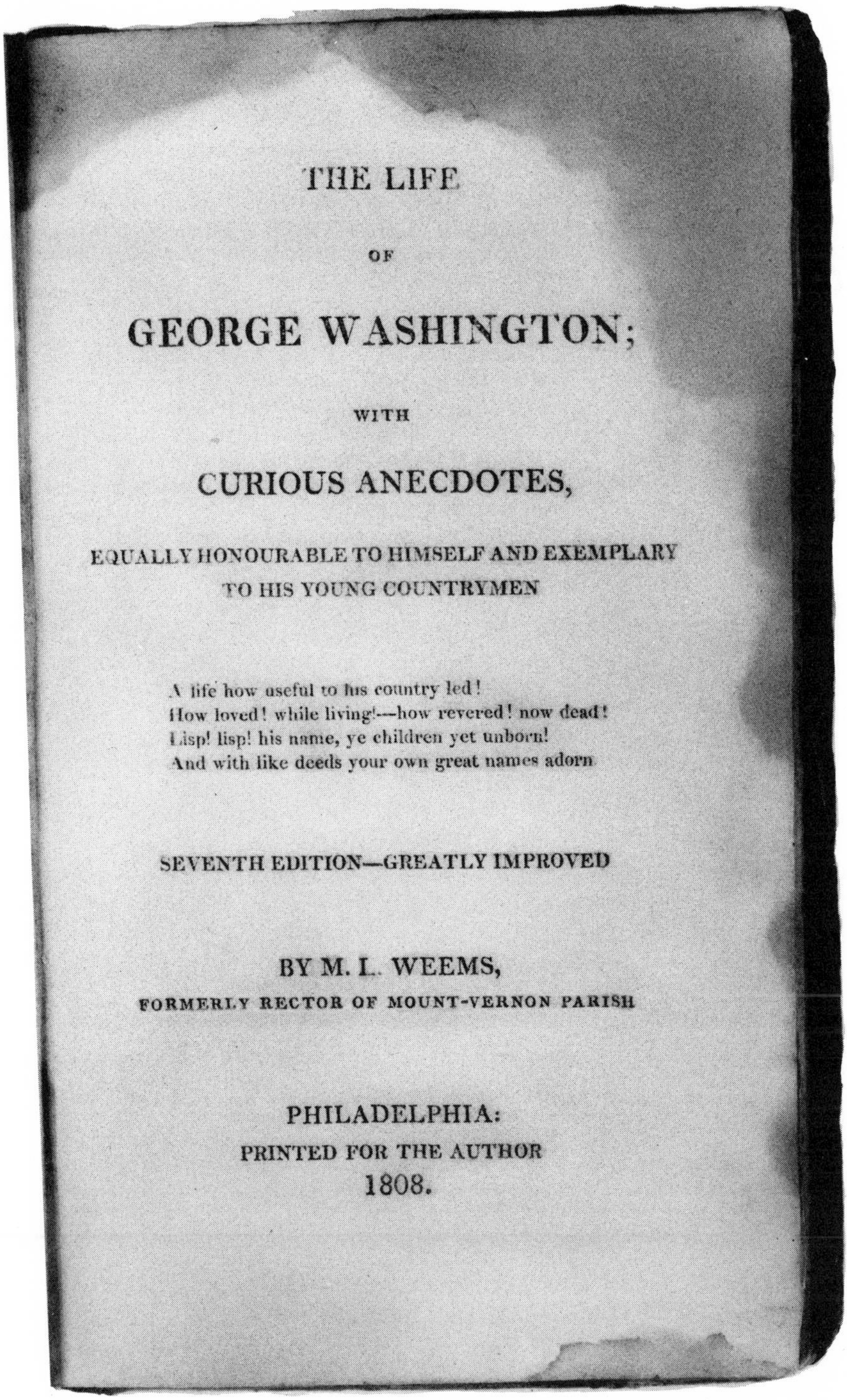

THE LIFE

OF

GEORGE WASHINGTON;

WITH

CURIOUS ANECDOTES,

EQUALLY HONOURABLE TO HIMSELF AND EXEMPLARY
TO HIS YOUNG COUNTRYMEN

A life how useful to his country led!
How loved! while living!—how revered! now dead!
Lisp! lisp! his name, ye children yet unborn!
And with like deeds your own great names adorn

SEVENTH EDITION—GREATLY IMPROVED

BY M. L. WEEMS,
FORMERLY RECTOR OF MOUNT-VERNON PARISH

PHILADELPHIA:
PRINTED FOR THE AUTHOR
1808.

(continued on next page)

Some, when they look up to the oak whose giant arms throw a darkening shade over distant acres, or whose single trunk lays the keel of a man of war, cannot bear to hear of the time when this mighty plant was but an acorn, which a pig could have demolished. But others, who know their value, like to learn the soil and situation which best produces such noble trees. Thus, parents that are *wise* will listen well pleased, while I relate how moved the steps of the youthful Washington, whose single worth far outweighs all the oaks of Bashan and the red spicy cedars of Lebanon Yes, they will listen delighted while I tell of their Washington in the days of his youth, when his little feet were swift towards the nests of birds; or when wearied in the chace of the butterfly, he laid him down on his grassy couch and slept, while ministering spirits, with their roseate wings, fanned his glowing cheeks, and kissed his lips of innocence with that fervent love which makes *the Heaven!*

Never did the wise Ulysses take more pains with his beloved Telemachus, than did Mr. Washington with George, to inspire him with an *early love of truth.* " Truth, George, (said she) is the loveliest quality of youth. I would ride fifty miles, my son, to see the little boy whose heart is so *honest*, and his lips so *pure*, that we may depend on every word he says. O how lovely does such a child appear in the eyes of every body! His parents doat on him; his relations glory in him; they are constantly praising him to their children, whom they beg to imitate him. They are often sending for him to visit them; and receive him, when he comes, with as much joy as if he were a little angel, come to set pretty examples to their children.

" But, Oh! how different, George, is the case with the boy who is so given to lying, that nobody can believe a word he says! He is looked at with aversion wherever he goes, and parents dread to see him come among their children. Oh George! My son! rather than see you come to this pass, dear as you are to my heart, yet gladly would I assist to nail you up in your little coffin, and follow you to your grave. Hard, indeed, would it be to me to give up my son whose little feet are always so ready to run about with me, and whose fondly looking eyes and sweet prattle make so large a part of my happiness: but still I would give him up rather than see him a common liar.

"Pa, (said George very seriously) do I ever tell lies?"

"No George, I *thank God* you do not, my son; and I rejoice in the hope you never will: at least, you shall never, from me have cause to be guilty of so shameful a thing. Many parents, indeed, even compel their children to this vile practice, by barbarously beating them for every little fault; hence, on the next offence the little terrified creature slips out a *lie!* just to escape the rod. But as to yourself, George, you know I have *always* told you, and now tell you again, that, whenever by accident you do any thing wrong, which must often be the case, as you are but a poor little boy yet, without *experience* or *knowledge*, never tell a falsehood to conceal it, but come *bravely* up, my son, like a *little man*, and tell me of it, and instead of beating you, George, I will but the more honour and love you for it, my dear."

This, you'll say, was sowing good seed!—Yes, it was, and the crop, thank God, was, as I believe it ever will be where a man acts the true parent, i. e. the *Guardian Angel*, by his child.

The following anecdote is a *case in point;* it is too valuable to be lost, and too true to be doubted, for it was communicated to me by the same excellent lady to whom I was indebted for the last.

"When George," said she, "was about six years old, he was made the wealthy master of a *hatchet!* of which, like most little boys, he was immoderately

B

(continued on next page)

fond, and was constantly going about chopping every thing that came in his way. One day, in the garden, where he often amused himself hacking his mother's pea-sticks, he unluckly tried the edge of his hatchet on the body of a beautiful young English cherry tree, which he barked so terribly that I don't believe the tree ever got the better of it. The next morning the old gentleman finding out what had befallen his tree, which, by the by, was a great favorite, came into the house, and with much warmth asked for the mischievous author, declaring at the same time that he would not have *taken five guineas* for his tree. No body could tell him any thing about it. Presently George and his hatchet made their appearance. *George*, said his father, *do you know who killed that beautiful little cherry tree yonder in the garden?* This was a *tough question*, and George staggered under it for a moment; but quickly recovered himself; and looking at his father, with the sweet face of youth brightened with the inexpressible charm of all-conquering truth, he bravely cried out, "*I can't tell a lie, Pa, you know I can't tell a lie; I did cut it with my hatchet.*"—*Run to my arms you dearest boy*, cried his father in transports, *run to my arms, glad am I, George, that you ever killed my tree, for you have paid me for it a thousand fold. Such an act of heroism in my son, is more worth than a thousand trees, though blossomed with silver, and their fruits of purest gold.*

It was in this way, by interesting at once both his *heart* and *head*, that Mr. Washington conducted George with great ease and pleasure along the happy paths of virtue. But well knowing that his beloved charge, soon to be a man, would be left exposed to numberless temptations both from himself and from others, his heart throbbed with the tenderest anxiety to make him acquainted with that GREAT BEING, whom to know and love, is to possess the surest defence against vice, and the best of all motives to virtue and happiness.

THE HISTORY OF INSECTS. And God made everything that creepeth upon the earth. Gen. 1.25. New-York: Printed and Sold by Samuel Wood, At the Juvenile Book-store, No. 357 Pearl-street, 1813. 28 pages. 10 cm.

The publisher advertises this small chapbook as one of "a great variety of pretty little books, with neat nuts, calculated to afford to the young mind pleasing and useful information." Title-page spread and several typical pages are shown here.

(continued on next page)

ABCDEFGHIJKL
MNOPQRSTU
VWXYZ.

abcdefghijklmno
pqrstuvwxyz.

ABCDEFGHIJKL
MNOPQRSTU
VWXYZ.

abcdefghijklmnop
qrstuvwxyz.

fi fl ff ffi ffl—*fi fl ff ffi ffl*

THE
HISTORY OF INSECTS.

And God made every thing that creepeth upon the earth. Gen. 1. 25.

NEW-YORK:
PRINTED AND SOLD BY SAMUEL WOOD,
At the Juvenile Book-store,
No. 357, Pearl-street.

1813.

OBSERVE the insect race, ordained to keep
The silent sabbath of a half year's sleep !
Entom'b beneath the filmy web they lie,
And wait the influence of a kinder sky ;
When vernal sunbeams pierce the dark retreat,
The heaving tomb distends with vital heat ;
The full formed brood, impatient of their cell,
Start from their trance, and burst their silken shell,

BARBAULD.

THE HISTORY OF INSECTS.

INSECTS are so called from a separation in the middle of their bodies, seemingly cut into two parts, and joined together by a small ligature, as we see in wasps and common flies.

However small and contemptible this class of beings may appear, at first thought, yet, when, we come to reflect, and carefully investigate, we shall be struck with wonder and astonishment, and shall discover, that the smallest gnat that buzzes in the meadow, is as much a subject of admiration as the largest elephant

4

that ranges the forest, or the hugest whale which ploughs the deep ; and when we consider the least creature that we can imagine, myriads of which are too small to be discovered without the help of glasses, and that each of their bodies is made up of different organs or parts, by which they receive or retain nourishment, &c. with the power of action, how natural the exclamation, O " Lord, how manifold are thy works ! in wisdom hast thou made them all." Under these considerations, that they are the work of the same great, good, and Almighty hand that formed us, and that they are all capable of feeling pleasure and pain, surely every little child, as well as older person, ought carefully to avoid every kind of cru-

5

elty to any kind of creature, great or small.

The supreme court of Judicature at Athens punished a boy for putting out the eyes of a poor bird ; and parents and masters should never overlook an instance of cruelty to any thing that has life, however minute, and seemingly contemptible the object may be.

" I would not enter on my list of friends
(Though grac'd with polish'd manners, and fine sense,
Yet wanting sensibility) the man
Who needlessly sets foot upon a worm."

COWPER.

THE HISTORY OF INSECTS *(continued from page 45)*

6

ELEPHANT-BEETLE.

The elephant-beetle is the largest of this kind hitherto known, and is found in South America, particularly in Guiana, about the rivers Surinam and Oroonoko. It is of a black colour, and the whole body is covered with a shell, full as thick and as strong as that of a small crab. There is one preserved in the musuem that measures more than six inches.

7

GRASSHOPPER.

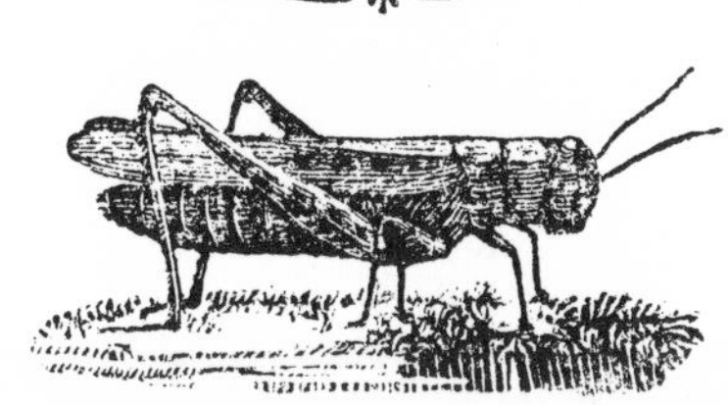

Grsshoppers are too common to need description, as they abound almost wherever there is green grass. One summer only is their period of life; they are hatched in the spring, and die in the fall; previous to which, they deposite their egss in the earth, which the genial warmth of the next season brings to life. They are food for many of the feathered race.

20

these, after a short time, change into large white aureliæ, or chrysales, which are usually called ant's eggs. When a nest of these creatures is disturbed, however great their own danger, the care they take of their offspring is remarkable: each takes in its fore-ceps, a young one, often larger than itself and carries it off.

These little insects form to themselves, with much industry and application, of earth, sticks, leaves, &c. little hillocks, called ant-hills, in the form of a cone: in these, they dwell, breed, and deposite their stores: they are commonly built in woody places: the brushy plains on Long-Island abound with them: they are from one to two feet in height.

21

HONEY-BEE.

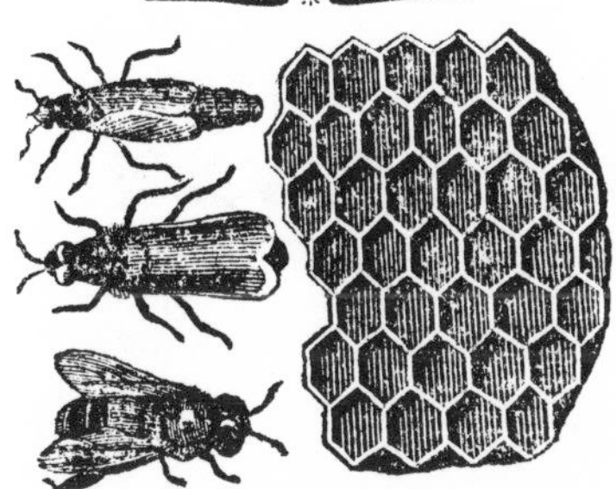

This is an extraordinary, curious, and remarkably industrious little insect, to which mankind are indebted for one of the most palatable and wholesome sweets which nature affords; and which was one of the choice articles with which the promised land was said to abound.

THE TALES OF PETER PARLEY, ABOUT AMERICA [by Samuel Griswold Goodrich (1793–1860)]. With engravings. Boston: S. G. Goodrich, 1827. 144 pages. 14 cm.

In the Library of Congress's Hogan Collection, this is one of four known copies.

Considered to be the first author of American children's books to put as much emphasis on entertainment as on instruction, "Peter Parley" was one of the most prolific writers for children (he produced over a hundred books). Goodrich was eager to offer good informational reading written in a manner children would enjoy, but was unable to see importance in anything unfactual. In these tales his design was to give the child his first ideas of geography and history. Influenced by the English writer Hannah More and her moral tales for the uneducated masses, Goodrich had a strong influence upon the growth of American literature for children. Nearly a million copies of *Peter Parley's Method of Telling about Geography to Children* (1829) were

THE

TALES

OF

PETER PARLEY,

ABOUT

AMERICA.

With Engravings.

S. G. Goodrich....Boston.

....

MDCCCXXVII.

PREFACE.

THE design of this little work is to convey to children, under the guise of amusement, the first ideas of Geography and History. In pursuing this object, the author has connected these grave topics with personal adventures, and exhibited an outline merely, in simple terms, adapted to the taste and knowledge of children.

There is more difficulty, and more importance than is generally supposed, in this humble species of literature. The *difficulty* of it arises from

the want of a language, at the same time copious enough to express a great variety of ideas, and simple enough for the limited comprehension of children; the *importance* of it lies in the powerful aid which it is capable of giving to the cause of infant education.

If the author should be thought to have been tolerably successful in this attempt to contribute something toward promoting juvenile instruction, he proposes to give a series of works of the same kind on Europe, Asia, and Africa.

published in the United States. It was translated into foreign languages and published in several English editions.

Goodrich, one-time American consul in Paris, visited eight countries in Europe. He established his own publishing house in Boston in 1826, and in the next year began his long series of Peter Parleys, which achieved such popularity that many pirated and also spurious books with this name were issued abroad. For his busy enterprise in juvenile publishing, he employed a writing staff; Nathaniel Hawthorne and his sister Elizabeth are known to have been behind *Peter Parley's Universal History on the Basis of Geography (1837)*. The Preface, shown here, sets forth Peter Parley's intentions; the interesting excerpt from the first chapter, which follows on pages 50–56, reveals his attitude toward the American Indians.

Peter Parley. page 5

THE

TALES

OF

PETER PARLEY.

HERE I am. My name is Peter Parley. I am an old man. I am very grey and lame. But I have seen a great many things, and had a great many adventures in my time, and I love to talk about them. I love to tell stories to children, and very often they come to my house, and they get around me, and I tell

them stories of what I have seen, and of what I have heard.

I live in Boston. Boston is a large town, full of houses, with a great many streets, and a great many people or inhabitants in it. When you go there you will see some persons riding about in coaches, and some riding on horseback, some running, and some walking. Here is a picture of Boston.

When I was a little boy, Boston was not half so large as it is now, and that large building which stands very high, as you see in the picture.

Boston. page 6

Indians. page 7.

called the new State House, was not built then. And, do you know that the very place, where Boston stands, was once covered with woods, and that in those woods lived many Indians? Did you ever see an Indian? Here is a picture of some Indians.

The Indians go nearly naked, except in winter. Their skin is not white like ours, but reddish, or the color of copper. When I was a boy, there were a great many that lived at no great distance from Boston. They lived in little huts or

houses called Wigwams. Here is a picture of a Wigwam.

The Indians were very ignorant; they could not read or write; their houses were very small and inconvenient. They had no such fine rooms in them as our houses have, nor had they any chimnies or fireplaces. The Indians had no chairs to sit in, nor tables to eat from. They had no books to read, and had no churches or meeting houses. In winter, they sometimes wore skins of bears and deer, which they shot with bows and arrows, or with guns.

Wigwam, or Indian House. page 8.

(continued on next page)

Indians Shooting a Deer. page 9.

Here is a picture of Indians shooting a Deer.

There are no Indians near Boston now; they are nearly all dead, or gone far west over the mountains. But, as I said before, when I was a boy there were a good many in New England, and they used often to come to Boston to sell the skins of wild beasts, which they had killed.

When I was about twelve years old, an Indian by the name of Wampum, came to my father's house in Boston. He had been a chief or great man among the Indians once,

but he was now poor. He was generally esteemed a good Indian, and he loved my father, because he once saved his life, when he was attacked by some sailors in the streets of Boston. He asked my father to let me go home with him. He told me of the excellent sport they had in shooting squirrels and deer where he lived; so I begged my father to let me go, and he at length consented. Wampum lived near Northampton, at the foot of a mountain called Mount Holyoke, just on the bank of Connecticut River. It is about one

Wampum's House. page 11.

hundred miles from Boston. There are good roads from Boston to Northampton now, and the stage travels it every day. But the roads were bad when I went with Wampum, and there were no stages in America.

So Wampum and I set out on foot. The second day we arrived at Worcester. It was then a very little town, and there were no such fine houses there as now. The fourth day we arrived at Wampum's house, which was a little wigwam at the foot of Mount Holyoke. Here is a picture of it.

In this little house we found Wampum's wife and three children; two boys and a girl. They came out to meet us, and were very glad to see Wampum and me. I was very hungry and tired when I arrived. Wampum's wife roasted some bear's meat, and gave us some bread made of pounded corn, which made our supper. We sat on the floor and took the meat in our fingers, for the Indians had no knives and forks. I then went to bed on some bear skins, and slept very well. Early in the morning, Wampum called me from

my sleep, and told me they were going into the woods a shooting, and that I must go with them. I was soon ready, and set out with Wampum and his two sons.

It was a fine bright morning in October. The sun was shining on the top of Mount Tom and Mount Holyoke. We ascended Holyoke through the woods. At length we climbed a high rock, from which we could see the beautiful valley from below us, in the centre of which was the little town of Northampton, then much smaller than it is now.

(continued on next page)

Do you see those houses? said Wampum to me. When my grandfather was a boy, there was not a house where you now see so many. That valley, which now belongs to white men, then belonged to the red men. Then the red men were rich and happy; now they are poor and wretched. Then that beautiful river, which you see running through the valley, and which is called the Connecticut, was theirs. They owned these fine mountains too, they hunted in these woods, and fished in that river, and were numerous and pow-

erful. Now we are few and weak.

But how has this change happened? said I. Who has taken your lands from you, and made you miserable? I will tell you all about it to-night, said Wampum, when we return from shooting. But hark! I hear a squirrel chattering in the woods; we must go and find him. Whist! said Wampum, and follow me. We all followed accordingly, and soon discovered a fine grey squirrel sitting in the top of a walnut tree, erect on his hind legs, with his tail curled over his back, and a nut in his

fore paws. Wampum beckoned to his youngest son, who drew his bow and discharged his arrow, which whistled over the back of the squirrel, but did not touch him. Wampum's eldest son immediately discharged his arrow, which struck the squirrel in the side, and brought him instantly to the ground.

After this adventure we proceeded cautiously through the woods. We had not gone far, when Wampum beckoned to us all to stop. Look yonder, said he to me, on that high rock above us. I did so, but could

see nothing. Look again, said Wampum. I did, and saw a young deer, or fawn, standing upon the point of a rock, which hung over the valley. He was a beautiful little animal, full of spirit, with large black eyes, slender legs, and of a reddish brown color. Here is a picture of him.

Wampum now selected a choice arrow, placed it on the bow, and sent it whizzing through the air. It struck the fawn directly through the heart. The little animal sprung violently forward over the rock, and fell dead many feet below, where Wam-

pum's sons soon found him. We now returned to Wampum's house, carrying the fawn with us.

In the evening, I reminded Wampum of his promise to tell me how the Indians had been robbed of their lands, and reduced to poverty. He accordingly began as follows.

But a little more than a hundred years ago, there were no white men in this country. There were none but red men or Indians. They owned all the lands, they hunted, and fished, and rambled where they pleased. The woods were then full

of deer and other game, and in the rivers, there were a great many salmon and shad. At length, the white men came in their ships from across the sea. The red men saw them, and told them they were welcome. They came ashore. The red men received them kindly. The white men built houses, and they grew strong, and drove the red men back into the woods. They killed the children of the red men, they shot their wives, they burned their wigwams, and they took away their lands. The white men had guns, the Indians

(continued on next page)

had only bows and arrows. The red men fought and killed many white men, but the white men killed more of the red men. The red men were beaten. They ran away into the woods. They were broken hearted, and they died. They are all dead or gone far over the mountains, except a few, and we are poor and wretched.

The old Indian said no more; he looked sad; his two sons looked sad also; and I almost cried, because Wampum looked so unhappy. I did not understand his story very

well, but when I go back to Boston, thought I, I will ask my grandfather all about it.

THE TALES OF PETER PARLEY ABOUT EUROPE [by Samuel Griswold Goodrich (1793–1860)]. Boston: S. G. Goodrich, 1828. 136 pages. 14 cm.

Also part of the Hogan Collection. Uniform in format with the first in Parley's geographical studies, this successful book was followed by his treatment of Asia, Africa, and so forth. Pages 6 and 7, reproduced here, show an early form of a destructive racial stereotype.

6 PARLEY'S TALES

Here is a picture of the other side of the world; the black place represents Africa; I have made it black because the people are black, and also very ignorant. The white

part represents Europe, and it is white, because the people are white, and because also they are very enlightened. The place which

ABOUT EUROPE. 7

has lines drawn across it in the picture, represents Asia; and that which has lines drawn up and down, is New Holland.

These places which I have thus shown you are land, and all the rest of the surface of the world is water, except islands, which are found in various parts of the ocean.

But I must tell you now about Europe. You have seen the sun rise in the east; well, far in the east over the hills and waters where the sun seems to rise, is Europe. It is a vast country, and there are many nations there. There are also great cities, and splendid palaces, and high mountains, and large rivers, and many other things in Europe, that are interesting.

How many nations do you think there are in Europe? There are no less than fifteen,

Where is Europe?
Is it a great or small place?
What interesting things are there in Europe?
How many nations are there in Europe?

LES CONTES

DE

PIERRE PARLEY

SUR L'AMERIQUE.

AVEC FIGURES.

BOSTON:
CARTER AND HENDEE.
1832.

LES CONTES DE PIERRE PARLEY SUR L'AMERIQUE [by Samuel Griswold Goodrich (1793–1860)]. Avec Figures. Boston: Carter and Hendee, 1832. 144 pages. 14 cm.

The Tales of Peter Parley about America are here "rendered into familiar French, for the use of young persons who are studying the language." The text was translated into French by F. M. J. Surraule.

avec ses sept mille soldats se rendre au Général Washington. Voici l'exposition de la scène.

16. Ce fut là le dernier haut fait militaire. L'Angleterre s'apperçut alors qu'elle ne pouvait pas conquérir l'Amérique. Elle jeta le vieux joug à l'écart, et reconnut son indépendence.

17. Telle fut la guerre connue sous le nom de la révolution Américaine. L'indépendence de notre pays, reposant alors sur une base sûre, n'a cessé de nous faire jouir du bonheur et de la

De quoi l'Angleterre s'apperçut-elle alors? Que fit-elle donc? Qu'est-il arrivé à l'Amérique depuis que son indépendence fut reconnue?

THE YOUTH'S INSTRUCTER IN NATURAL HISTORY; in seven numbers. Each no. containing twenty illustrations. New-York:—E. Bliss. G. L. Austin, printer, 1832. 36 pages each. 14 cm.

The early-nineteenth-century absorption in natural science resulted in the production of many informational chapbooks for the young. This set of six small illustrated volumes devoted to mammals is typical of the genre.

Fig. 90

THE

YOUTH'S INSTRUCTER

IN

NATURAL HISTORY;

IN SIX NUMBERS.

EACH NO. CONTAINING TWENTY ILLUSTRATIONS.

NEW-YORK:—E. BLISS.

1832.

G. L Austin, printer.

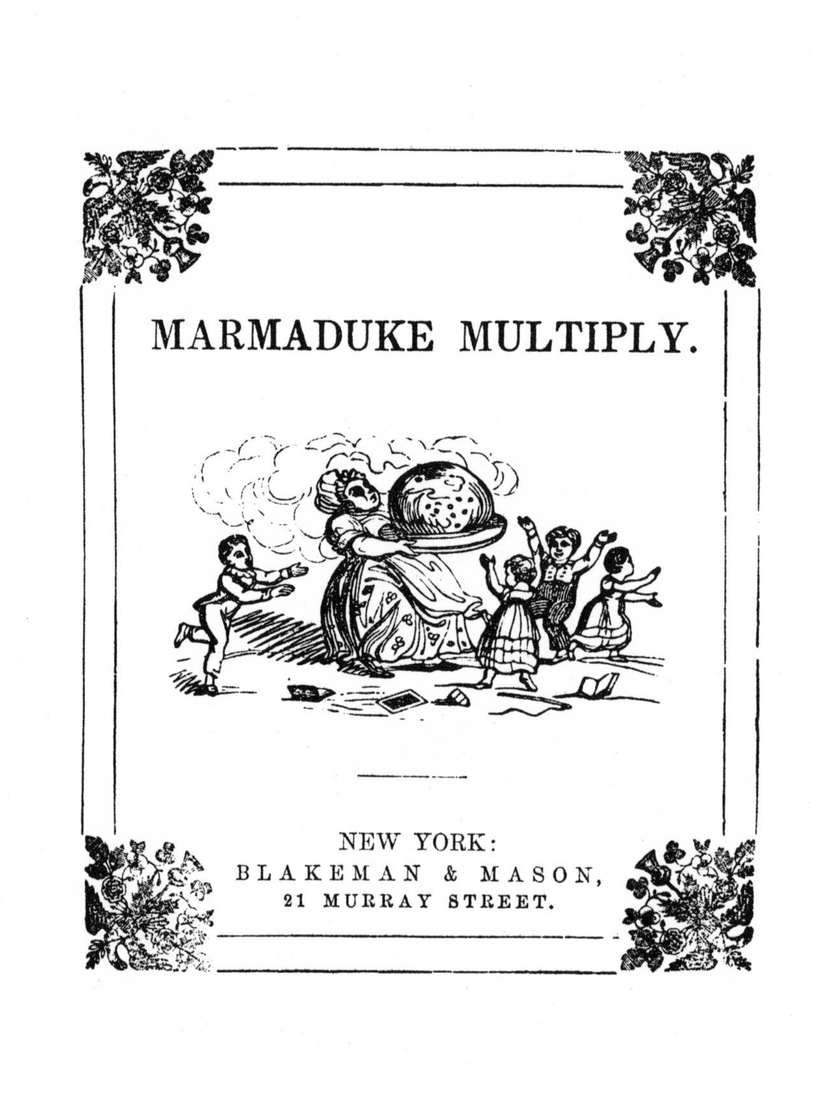

MARMADUKE MULTIPLY. New York: Blakeman & Mason, 21 Murray Street [not before 1851]. 71 pages. 16 cm.

The title page of this Americanized edition omits the familiar amplification of title into "Marmaduke Multiply's Merry Method of Making Minor Mathematicians; or, The Multiplication Table," as it appeared in the John Harris London edition of 1816–1817. A few pages are shown here, from which its humor and charm can be seen.

3

Twice 1 are 2.

This book is something new.

(continued on next page)

34

4 times 11 are 44.

I bought this book at Francis'.

Store.

MARMADUKE MULTIPLY *(continued from page 61)*

(continued on next page)

47

6 times 9 are 54.

My little boat has come ashore.

MARMADUKE MULTIPLY *(continued from page 63)*

71

12 times 12 are 144.

So I bid you good bye, and shut the door.

THE COUNTRIES OF EUROPE, and the Manners and Customs of Its Various Nations. In easy and entertaining verse for children. Edited by Mrs. S. J. Hale [Sarah Josepha (Buell) Hale, (1788–1879)]. With sixteen illustrative embellishments. New York: Published by Edward Dunigan, 151 Fulton-Street [185–?]. 55 pages. 15 cm.

Mrs. Hale is best known for her earlier "Mary's Lamb" (reproduced on page 163). She was widowed early, and with five children

THE

COUNTRIES OF EUROPE,

AND THE

MANNERS AND CUSTOMS

OF IT'S VARIOUS NATIONS.

IN EASY AND ENTERTAINING VERSE, FOR CHILDREN.

Edited by Mrs. S. J. HALE.

WITH SIXTEEN ILLUSTRATIVE EMBELLISHMENTS.

NEW YORK:

PUBLISHED BY EDWARD DUNIGAN,

151 FULTON-STREET.

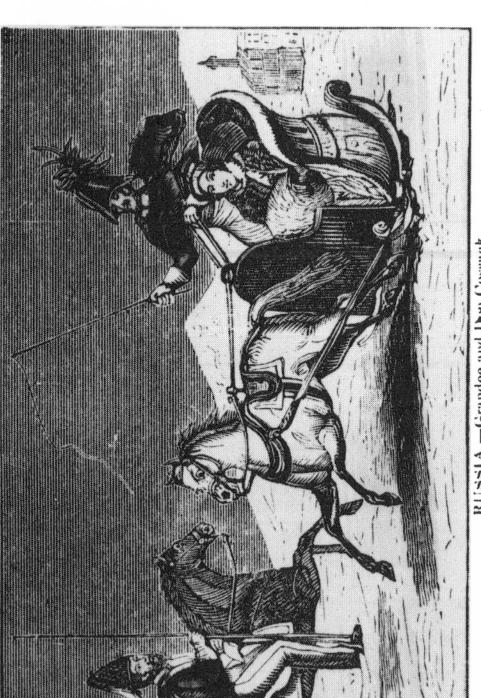

RUSSIA.—Grandee and Don Cossack.

TURKEY.—The Bashaw.

to support, turned seriously to literature. She served for forty years as literary editor of *Godey's Lady's Book* and, discovering the schoolbook field, became one of the leaders in the movement for better juvenile literature.

Here in verse she sets forth colorful facts, illustrated with hand-colored half-page pictures of her subjects: for instance, a woman in a chair being pushed by skaters on a frozen canal in Holland.

THE

COUNTRIES OF EUROPE.

ICELAND.

Now, here's the Map of Europe:
  Here's Iceland farthest north:
Where a volcano, day and night,
  Sends fire and cinders forth.

And though, for more than half the year,
  There's snow and ice around,
Yet streams of water, boiling hot
  Rise steaming from the ground.

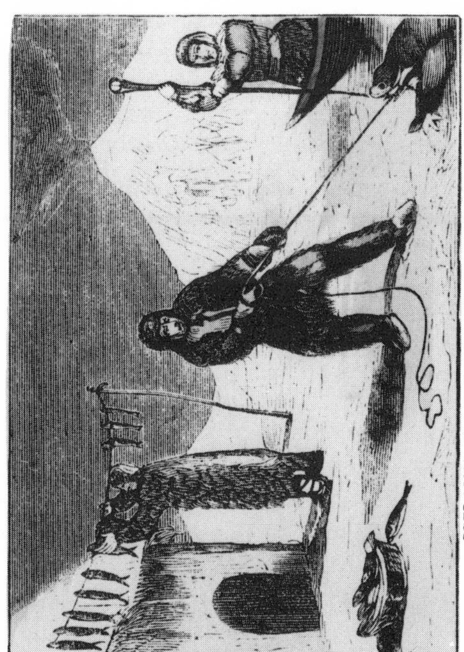

ICELAND.—Seal-catcher, Boiling Springs, and Volcanoes.

I. Works Intended to Instruct or Improve.

From the Colonial Period to 1900.

D. DIDACTIC STORIES AND VERSE.

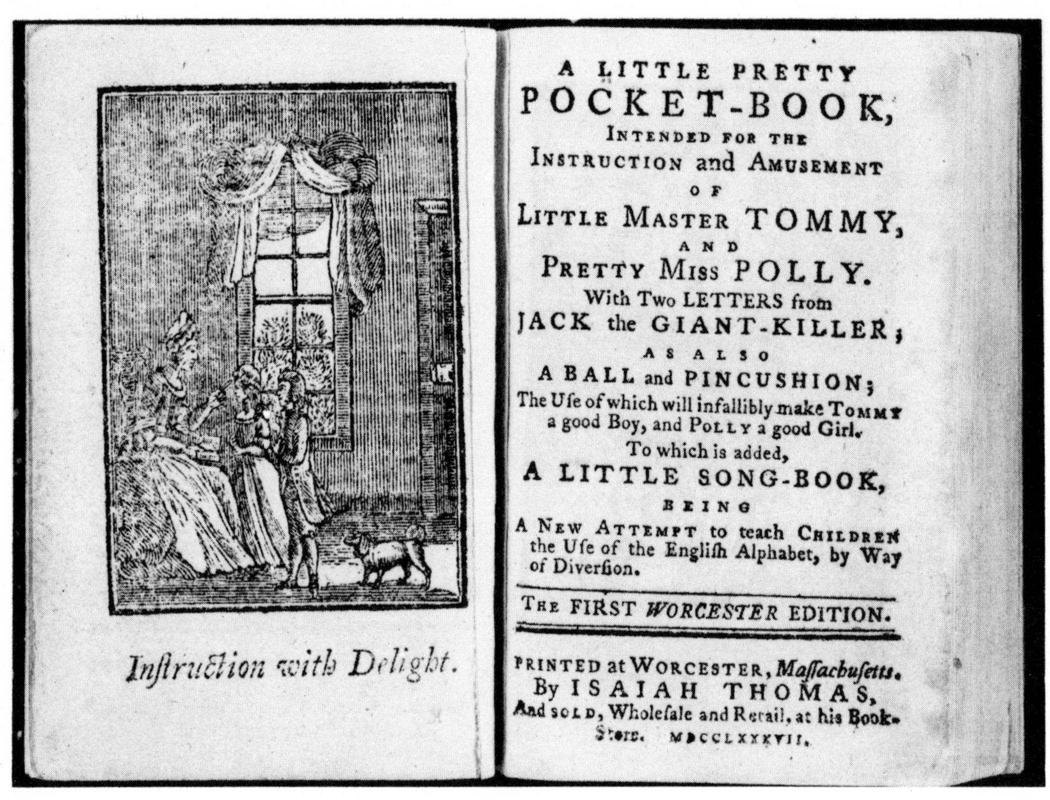
Inſtruction with Delight.

A LITTLE PRETTY
POCKET-BOOK,
INTENDED FOR THE
INSTRUCTION and AMUSEMENT
OF
LITTLE MASTER TOMMY,
AND
PRETTY MISS POLLY.
With Two LETTERS from
JACK the GIANT-KILLER;
AS ALSO
A BALL and PINCUSHION;
The Uſe of which will infallibly make TOMMY
a good Boy, and POLLY a good Girl.
To which is added,
A LITTLE SONG-BOOK,
BEING
A NEW ATTEMPT to teach CHILDREN
the Uſe of the Engliſh Alphabet, by Way
of Diverſion.

THE FIRST *WORCESTER* EDITION.

PRINTED at WORCESTER, *Maſſachuſetts.*
By ISAIAH THOMAS,
And SOLD, Wholeſale and Retail, at his Book-
Store. MDCCLXXXVII.

A LITTLE PRETTY POCKET-BOOK, Intended for the Instruction and Amusement of Little Master Tommy, and Pretty Miss Polly. With Two Letters from Jack the Giant-Killer; as also a Ball and Pincushion; the use of which will infallibly make Tommy a good Boy, and Polly a good Girl. To which is added, A Little Song-Book, Being A New Attempt to Teach Children the Use of the English Alphabet, by Way of Diversion. The First Worcester Edition. Printed at Worcester, Massachusetts. By Isaiah Thomas, And Sold, Wholesale and Retail, at his Book-Store. 1787. 122 pages. 10 cm.

A reprint of the edition which was originally published by John Newbery in London in 1744, with an American addition: "Rules for Behaviour in Children."

This first Newbery publication, although intended deliberately to amuse and for that reason considered the first real piece of children's literature, includes a variety of elements to admonish and instruct: a serious preface addressed to adults, the alphabet, Aesop fables (in verse, with their morals presented in little "letters from Jack the Giant-Killer") and proverbs.

(caption continued on page 70)

24 The *great* A Play.

CHUCK-FARTHING.

AS you value your Pence,
 At the *Hole* take your Aim;
Chuck all safely in,
 And you'll win the Game.

MORAL.

Chuck-Farthing, like Trade,
 Requires great Care;
The more you obſerve,
 The better you'll fare.

The *little* a Play. 25

Flying the KITE

UPHELD in Air, the gaudy Kite,
 High as an Eagle takes her Flight;
But if the Winds their Breath reſtrain,
 She tumbles headlong down again.

RULE *of* LIFE.

Soon as thou ſeeſt the Dawn of Day,
To God thy Adoration pay.

26 The *great* B Play.

Dancing round the MAY-POLE.

WITH Garlands here the May-
 Pole crown'd,
And all the Swains a dancing round,
Compoſe a num'rous jovial Ring,
To welcome in the cheerful Spring.

RULE *of* LIFE.

Leave God to manage, and to grant
That which his Wiſdom ſees thee want.

The *little* b Play. 27

MARBLES.

KNUCKLE down to your *Taw*,
 Aim well, ſhoot away:
Keep out of the *Ring*,
 And you'll ſoon learn to play.

MORAL.

Time rolls like a *Marble*,
 And awes ev'ry State:
Then improve each Moment,
 Before 'tis too late.

(continued on next page)

28 The *great* C Play.

HOOP *and* HIDE.

GO hide out, and hoop,
Whilſt I go to ſleep:
If you I can't find,
My Poſt I muſt keep.

MORAL.

With Carefulneſs watch
Each Moment that flies,
To keep Peace at Home,
And ward off Surprize.

The *little* c Play. 29

THREAD *the* NEEDLE.

HERE Hand in Hand the Boys unite,
And form a very pleaſing Sight;
Then thro' each other's Arms they fly,
As Thread does thro' the Needle's Eye.

RULE *of* LIFE.

Talk not too much; ſit down content,
That your Diſcourſe be pertinent.

30 The *great* D Play.

FISHING.

THE artful Angler baits his Hook,
And throws it gently in the Brook;
Which the Fiſh view with greedy Eyes,
And ſoon are taken by Surprize.

RULE *of* LIFE.

Learn well the Motions of the Mind;
Why you are made, for what deſign'd.

The *little* d Play. 31

BLINDMAN'S BUFF.

BEREFT of all Light,
I ſtumble along;
But, if I catch you,
My Doom is your own.

MORAL.

How blind is that Man,
Who ſcorns the Advice
Of Friends, who intend
To make him more wiſe.

A LITTLE PRETTY POCKET-BOOK *(continued from pages 68–69)*

In tune with the Puritan spirit, Isaiah Thomas added "163 Rules for Behaviour in Children," applicable at the meeting house, home, and school, when in company, abroad, and among other children. On his page of salutation, he addresses "Parents, Guardians, and Nurses, in

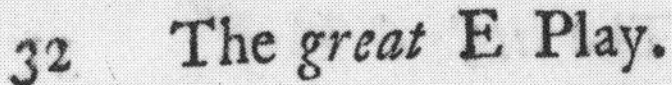
32 The *great* E Play.

SHUTTLE-COCK.

THE *Shuttle-Cock* ſtruck
Does backward rebound;
But, if it be miſs'd,
It falls to the Ground.

MORAL.

Thus chequer'd in Life,
As Fortune does flow;
Her Smiles lift us high,
Her Frowns ſink us low.

The *little* e Play. 33

KING I AM.

AMBITION here fires every
Heart,
And all aſſume the Monarch's Part,
For a few Minutes, though in Play,
Each rules with arbitrary Sway.

RULE *of* LIFE.

Deſcend into thyſelf, to find
The Imperfections of thy Mind.
C

34 The *great* F Play.

PEG-FARTHING.

SOON as the Ring is once compos'd,
The Coin is in the Centre clos'd;
And then the wiſh'd-for Prize to win,
The Top that drives it out muſt ſpin.

RULE *of* LIFE.

Be ſilent if you doubt your Senſe,
And always ſpeak with Diffidence.

The *little* f Play. 35

KNOCK OUT *and* SPAN.

STRIKE out your Man ſtrong;
For the very next one
Will bear off the Prize,
If you come to a *Span*.

MORAL.

This *Span*, my dear Boy,
Shou'd your Monitor be;
'Tis the Length of a Life,
As we oftentimes ſee.

the United States of America" instead of those of "Great-Britain and Ireland." We show here the alphabet, from pages 24 through 67, which omits, as was customary at the time, the letter "J," and also, rather arbitrarily, the letter "V."

(continued on next page)

36 The *great* G Play.

HOP, STEP, *and* JUMP.

HOP ſhort and *Step* ſafe,
To make your *Jump* long;
This Art oft has beat
Th' Efforts of the ſtrong.

MORAL.

This old Maxim take,
T' embelliſh your Book:
Think well ere you talk,
And, ere you leap, look.

The *little* g Play. 37

BOYS *and* GIRLS *come out to Play.*

AFTER a ſultry Summer's Day,
When the Moon ſhines, and
Stars are gay;
The Nymphs and Swains well pleas'd
advance,
And ſpend the Ev'ning in a Dance.

RULE *of* LIFE.

Reflect To-day upon the Laſt,
And freely own thy Errours paſt.

38 The *great* H Play.

I ſent a LETTER *to my* LOVE.

THE Lads and Laſſes here are ſeen,
All gaily tripping o'er the Green;
But one among them, to her Coſt,
The Treaſure of her Heart has loſt.

RULE *of* LIFE.

If proſperous, of Pride beware:
Changes of Fortune frequent are.

The *little* h Play. 39

PITCH *and* HUSSEL.

POISE your Hand fairly,
And pitch plum your Slat;
Then ſhake for all Heads,
And turn down the Hat.

MORAL.

How fickle's this Game!
So Fortune or Fate
Decrees our Repentance,
When oft 'tis too late.

A LITTLE PRETTY POCKET-BOOK *(continued from page 71)*

40 The *great* I Play.

CRICKET.

THIS Leſſon obſerve,
When you play at *Cricket*,
Catch *All* fairly out,
Or bowl down the *Wicket*.

MORAL.

This Maxim regard,
Now you're in your Prime;
Look ere 'tis too late;
By the Forelock take *Time*.

The *little* i Play. 41

STOOL-BALL.

THE *Ball* once ſtruck with Art and Care,
And drove impetuous through the Air
Swift round his Courſe the *Gameſter* flies,
Or his *Stool's* taken by Surprize.

RULE *of* LIFE.

Beſtow your Alms whene'er you ſee
An Object in Neceſſity.

42 The *great* K Play.

SWIMMING.

WHEN the Sun's Beams have warm'd the Air,
Our Youth to ſome cool Brook repair;
In whoſe refreſhing Streams they play,
To the laſt Remnant of the Day.

RULE *of* LIFE.

Think ere you ſpeak; for Words once flown,
Once utter'd, are no more your own.

The *little* k Play. 43

BASE-BALL.

THE *Ball* once ſtruck off,
Away flies the *Boy*
To the next deſtin'd Poſt,
And then Home with Joy.

MORAL.

Thus Seamen, for Lucre
Fly over the Main,
But, with Pleaſure tranſported
Return back again.

(continued on next page)

44 The *great* L Play.

TRAP-BALL.

TOUCH lightly the *Trap*,
And ſtrike low the *Ball*;
Let none catch you out,
And you'll beat them all.

MORAL.

Learn hence, my dear Boy,
To avoid ev'ry Snare,
Contriv'd to involve you
In Sorrow and Care.

The *little* l Play. 45

TIP-CAT.

THE *Gameſter* here his Art diſplays,
And drives the Cat a thouſand Ways,
For ſhould he miſs, when once 'tis toſs'd
He's out—and all his Sport is loſt.

RULE *of* LIFE.

Debates and Quarrels always ſhun;
No one by Peace was e'er undone.

46 The *great* M Play.

FIVES.

WITH what great Force the little Ball
Rebounds, when ſtruck againſt the Wall;
See how intent each Gameſter ſtands;
Mark well his Eyes, his Feet, his Hands!

RULE *of* LIFE.

Know this (which is enough to know)
Virtue is Happineſs below.

The *little* m Play. 47

LEAP-FROG.

THIS ſtoops down his Head,
Whilſt that ſprings up High;
But then you will find,
He'll ſtoop by and by.

MORAL.

Juſt ſo 'tis at Court;
To-day you're in Place;
To-morrow perhaps,
You're quite in Diſgrace.

A LITTLE PRETTY POCKET-BOOK *(continued from page 73)*

48 The *great* N Play.

BIRDS-NESTING.

HERE two naughty Boys,
Hard-hearted in Jeſt,
Deprive a poor Bird
Of her young and her Neſt.

MORAL.

Thus Men, out of Joke,
(Be't ſpoke to their Shame)
Too often make free
With another's good Name.

The *little* n Play. 49

TRAIN-BANDING.

THE *Serjeant Hero* here appears,
Strutting before his *Grenadiers*;
And leads his mighty valiant Men,
Firſt up the Hill, then down again.

RULE *of* LIFE.

Judge not between two Friends, but ſee
If you can bring them to agree.

D

50 The *great* O Play.

All the BIRDS *in the* AIR.

HERE various Boys ſtand round
and ſoon,
Each does ſome favourite Bird aſſume
And if the *Slave* once hits his Name,
He's then made free and crowns the
Game.

RULE *of* LIFE.

Live well, and then die ſoon or late
For ever happy is your State.

The *little* o Play. 51

HOP-HAT.

O'ER this *Hat*, and that,
Boys hop to the laſt;
Which once in their Mouths,
Behind them is caſt.

MORAL.

Thus Men often ſtruggle,
Some Bliſs to obtain;
Which, once in their Pow'r,
They treat with Diſdain.

(continued on next page)

52 The *great* P Play.

SHOOTING.

THO' ſome *Birds*, too heedleſs,
Dread no Danger nigh;
Yet ſtill by the *Fowlers*
They inſtantly die.

MORAL.

From hence we may learn
That, by one thoughtleſs Trip
Strange Accidents happen
'Twixt the Cup and the Lip.

The *little* p Play. 53

HOP-SCOTCH.

FIRST make with Chalk an oblong Square,
With wide Partitions here and there;
Then to the firſt a *Tile* convey;
Hop in—then kick the *Tile* away,

RULE *of* LIFE.

Strive with good Senſe to ſtock your Mind,
And to that Senſe be Virtue join'd.

54 The *great* Q Play.

Who will play at my SQUARES?

THIS well-invented *Game's* de-ſign'd
To ſtrike the *Eye* and form the *Mind*;
And he moſt doubtleſs aims aright,
Who joins *Inſtruction* with *Delight*.

RULE *of* LIFE.

So live with Men, as if God's Eye
Did into every Action pry.

The *little* q Play. 55

RIDING.

IN Queſt of his Game,
The *Sportſman* rides on,
But falls off his Horſe
Before he has done.

MORAL.

Thus Youth without Thought,
Their Amours purſue,
Though an Age of Pain
Does often accrue.

A LITTLE PRETTY POCKET-BOOK *(continued from page 75)*

56 The *great* R.

GREAT A, B, and C,
And tumble down D,
The Cat's a blind buff,
And ſhe cannot ſee.

a, b, c, d.

The *little* r. 57

GREAT E, F, and G,
Come here follow me,
And we will jump over
The Roſemary Tree.

e, f, g.

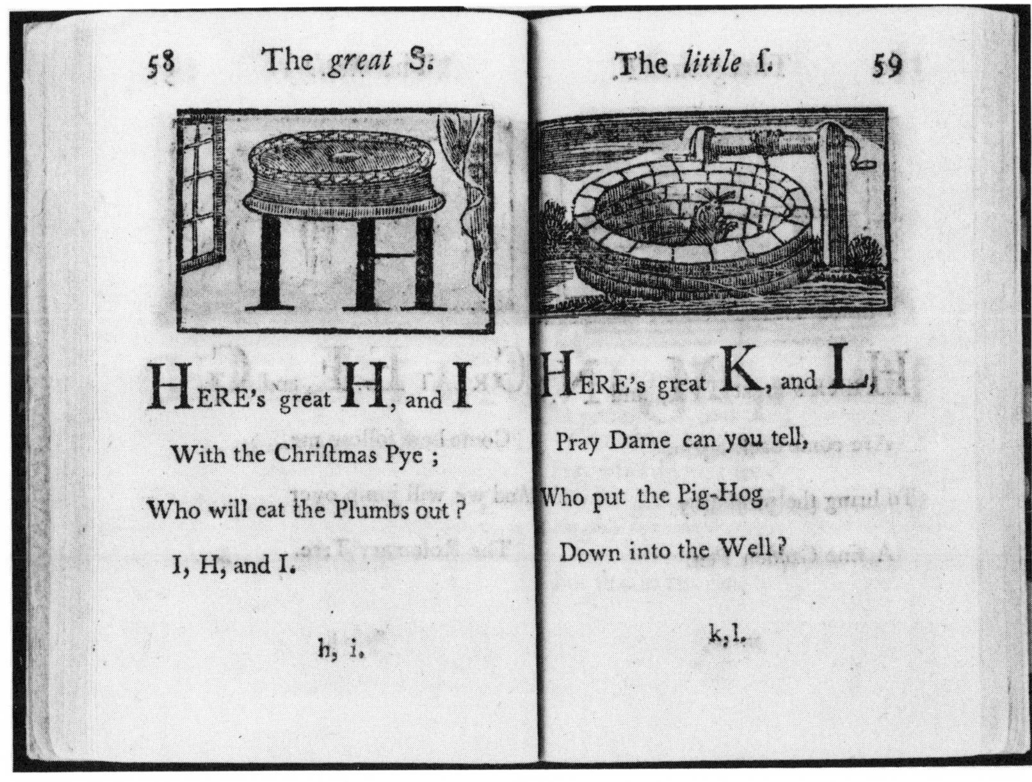
58 The *great* S.

HERE's great H, and I
With the Chriſtmas Pye ;
Who will eat the Plumbs out ?
I, H, and I.

h, i.

The *little* ſ. 59

HERE's great K, and L,
Pray Dame can you tell,
Who put the Pig-Hog
Down into the Well ?

k, l.

(continued on next page)

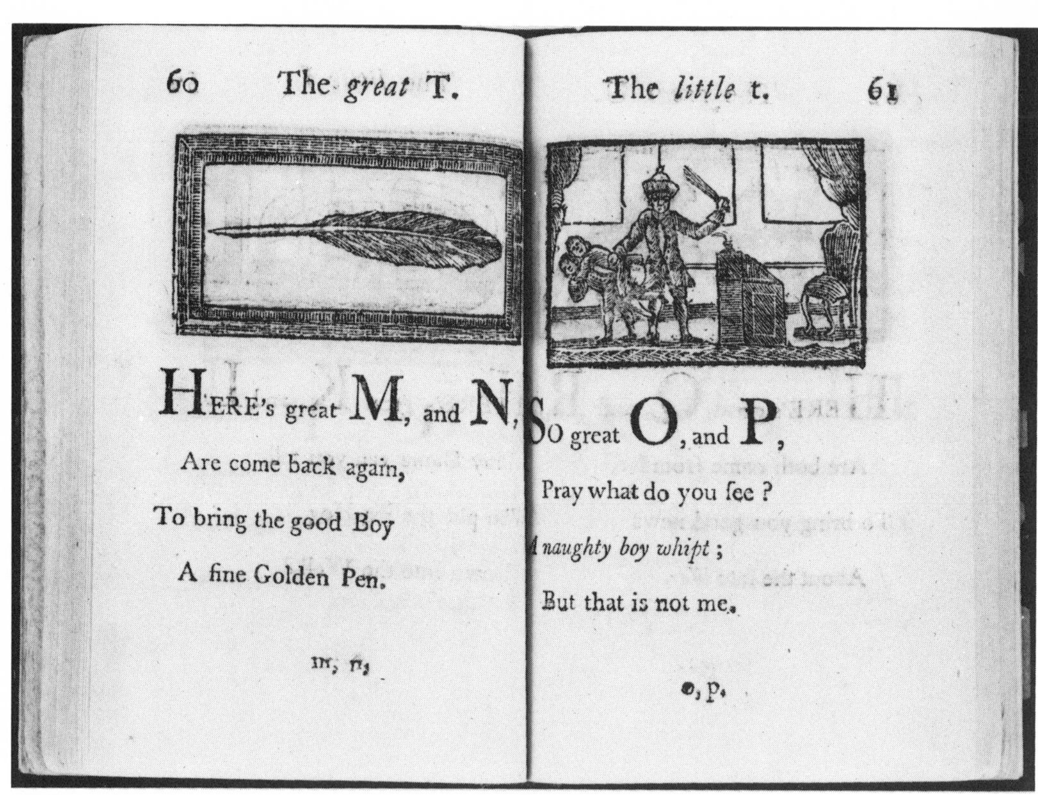
60 The *great* T.

HERE's great M, and N,
Are come back again,
To bring the good Boy
A fine Golden Pen.

m, n,

The *little* t. 61

SO great O, and P,
Pray what do you see ?
A naughty boy whipt ;
But that is not me.

o, p.

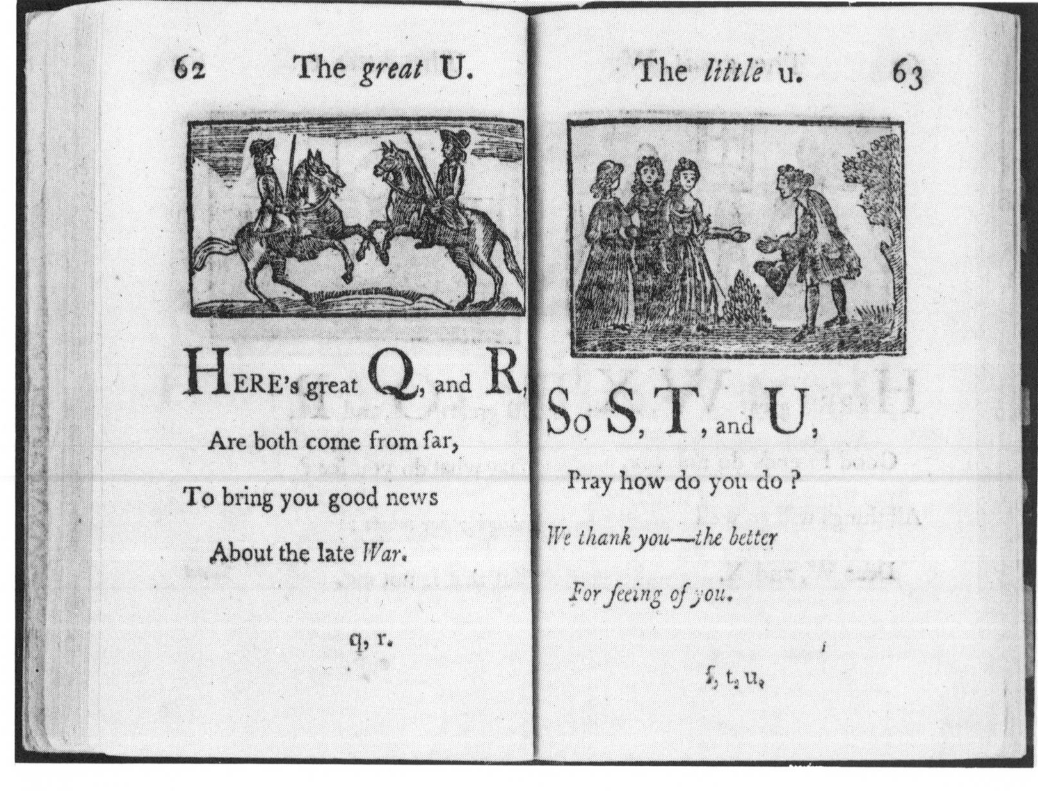
62 The *great* U.

HERE's great Q, and R,
Are both come from far,
To bring you good news
About the late *War*.

q, r.

The *little* u. 63

So S, T, and U,
Pray how do you do ?
We thank you—the better
For seeing of you.

s, t, u,

A LITTLE PRETTY POCKET-BOOK *(continued from page 77)*

64 The *great* W.

HERE'S great W, X,

Good Friends do not vex,

All things will go well

Dear W, and X.

w, x.

The *little* w. 65

THERE'S great Y, and Z,

On a Horſe that is mad :

If you fall down, Farewel

Poor great Y and Z.

y, z.

E

66 The *great* X.

FABLE I.

The WOLF *and the* KID.

AS the Goat went to brouze,
Thus her Charge did begin
Be advis'd, my dear *Kid*,
And let nobody in.
The *Wolf* hearing this
For Admittance did try,
But the *Kid* anſwer'd, No
I'll not truſt you, not I.

The *little* x. 67

To Maſter Tommy, *or Miſs* Polly.

YOU ſee, my Dear, the little Kid, by taking her Parent's Advice, preſerved her own Life; for had ſhe been ſo wicked as to have neglected what the *Goat* (her Mother) ſaid to her, and had opened the Door, the *Wolf* would certainly have torn her to Pieces. Take Care therefore to do always as your Papa and Mamma, or your Maſter and Miſtreſs ſhall direct you, and you will oblige,

Your old Friend,

JACK *the* Giant-Killer.

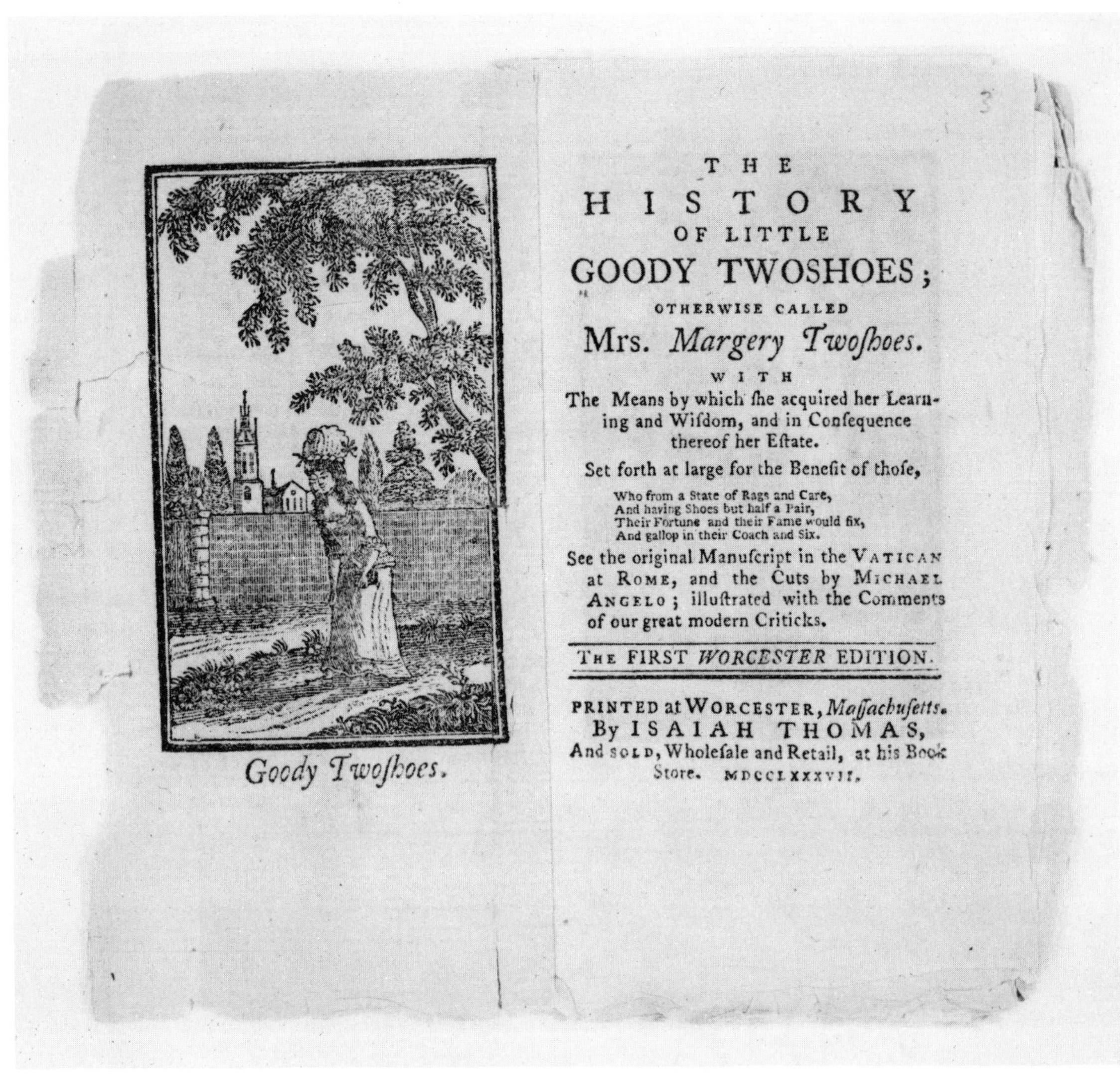

Goody Twoſhoes.

THE
HISTORY
OF LITTLE
GOODY TWOSHOES;
OTHERWISE CALLED
Mrs. *Margery Twoſhoes.*
WITH
The Means by which ſhe acquired her Learning and Wiſdom, and in Conſequence thereof her Eſtate.
Set forth at large for the Benefit of thoſe,

Who from a State of Rags and Care,
And having Shoes but half a Pair,
Their Fortune and their Fame would fix,
And gallop in their Coach and Six.

See the original Manuſcript in the VATICAN at ROME, and the Cuts by MICHAEL ANGELO; illuſtrated with the Comments of our great modern Criticks.

THE FIRST *WORCESTER* EDITION.

PRINTED at WORCESTER, *Maſſachuſetts.*
By ISAIAH THOMAS,
And SOLD, Wholeſale and Retail, at his Book Store. MDCCLXXXVII.

THE HISTORY OF LITTLE GOODY TWOSHOES; otherwise called Mrs. Margery Twoshoes. With The Means by which she acquired her Learning and Wisdom, and in Consequence thereof her Estate. First Worcester edition. Worcester, Massachusetts: Printed by Isaiah Thomas, and sold wholesale and retail, at his book store. 1787. 158 pages. 12½ cm.

Most often attributed to Oliver Goldsmith and originally issued by John Newbery in 1765, this chapbook, published in America in 1775 by Hugh Gaine of New York, and later by Isaiah Thomas of Worcester, is one of the most popular and longest lived of the Newbery publications and is still available today. It describes the harrowing adventures of little Margery after her parents died and her brother went to sea, when she was persecuted by an evil landlord, yet acquired "Learning and Wisdom" and thus rose from rags to riches. (See also pages 84 and 93.)

THE DAISY; or, Cautionary Stories in Verse [by Mrs. Elizabeth Turner (d. 1846)]. Adapted to the ideas of children from four to eight years old. Illustrated with sixteen engravings on copperplate. Philadelphia: Published by Jacob Johnson, No. 147, Market Street. J. Adams, printer. 1808. 36 pages. 14 cm.

First published in London in 1807 by Griffith and Farran, successors to Newbery and Harris. In this edition, many of the illustrations are printed upside down and not opposite the text to which they belong. Despite the poor quality of the printing, the pictures and verses have charm, as can be seen by this example. The Library of Congress possesses another early edition, published in New Haven by Samuel Babcock (Undated. 16 pages. 9 cm.) the gift of Frank J. Hogan, as well as one of 1844 also issued by Babcock.

IV.

Frances and Henry

SISTER Frances is sad,
Because Henry is ill;
And she lets the dear lad
Do whatever he will.

Left her own little chair,
And got up in a minute,
When she heard him declare
That he wish'd to sit in it.

Now, from this we can tell,
He will never more tease her
But, when he is well,
He will study to please her.

A 6

THE ENTERTAINING HISTORY OF GILES GINGERBREAD, a Little Boy who Lived upon Learning. Adorned with Copperplate Engravings. Philadelphia: Published and sold by B. C. Buzby, No. 2, North Third Street, 1810. 22 pages. 13½ cm.

The English original, attributed to John Newbery, appeared in 1764; the first American edition four years later. The edition of 1810, which is shown here, is not cited in d'Alté Welch (see Bibliography). The story is an overt lecture on the merits of industry ("industry intitles [sic] a man to anything") and learning. We show only the title page and a typical spread as the whole is less entertaining than the title would lead one to believe.

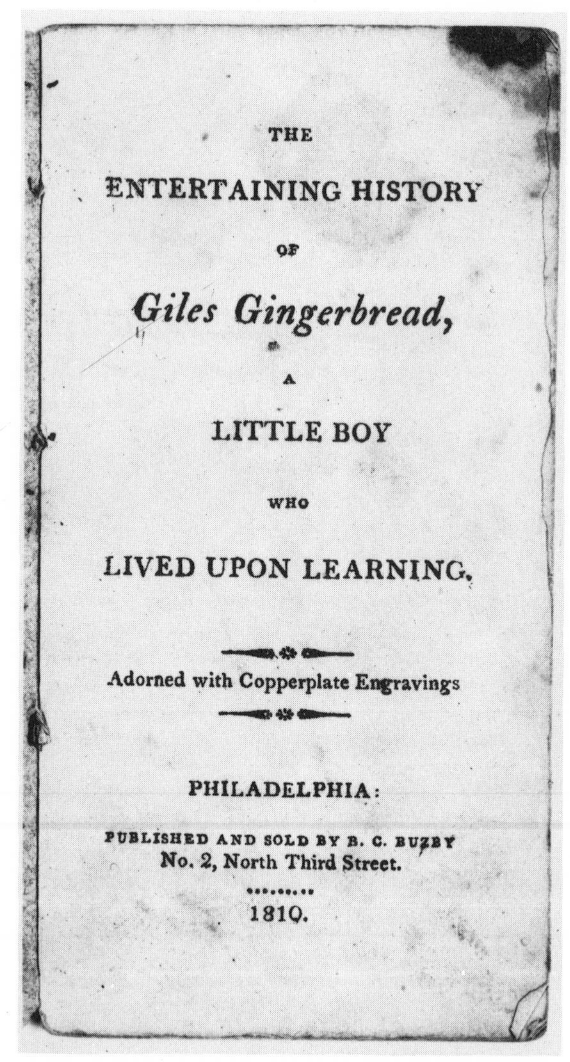

THE

ENTERTAINING HISTORY

OF

Giles Gingerbread,

A

LITTLE BOY

WHO

LIVED UPON LEARNING.

Adorned with Copperplate Engravings

PHILADELPHIA:

PUBLISHED AND SOLD BY B. C. BUZBY

No. 2, North Third Street.

1810.

1
2

should not have done this had I been guilty of the robbery: No, Sir, you have been a father to me, and I have been just and honest to you: but this man has not, (pointing to the thief) for I saw him take goods privately out of the warehouse, and carry them to the pawn-broker's. The master found the mark, saw the boy innocent, and then searched the pawn-broker's, where the goods were found.

Toby knew that it was his duty not only to be honest himself, but if possible to make others so; and you will presently see how God Almighty blessed him for it, and how he was rewarded for his fidelity.

After this, Mr. Goodwill placed great confidence in Toby, and his affairs so prospered, that he became very rich. He then took Toby as a partner with him, and at his death left him the whole trade and a large sum of money, which is still encreasing; and from being a little ragged

THE HISTORY OF TOMMY TWO-SHOES, Own Brother to Mrs. Margery Two-Shoes. Embellished with Cuts. Hartford: Printed by Sheldon & Goodwin. Stereotyped by J. F. & C. Starr [1818?]. 30 pages. 11 cm.

One of "A Variety of Books, Calculated for the instruction and amusement of children," this sequel to *Goody Two-Shoes* repeats part of the earlier work. Here are Tommy's adventures in Africa when, accompanied by a young lion he has tamed, he goes off to find Prester John's kingdom. A passage describes the progress of Tommy and the lion through the jungle: ". . . animals . . . readily ran from the lion, who hunted on one side, to Tommy who hunted on the other so that they were either caught by the lion, or shot by his master and it was pleasant enough, after hunting match, and the meat was dressed, to see how cheek by jowl they sat down to dinner." (See also pages 80 and 93.)

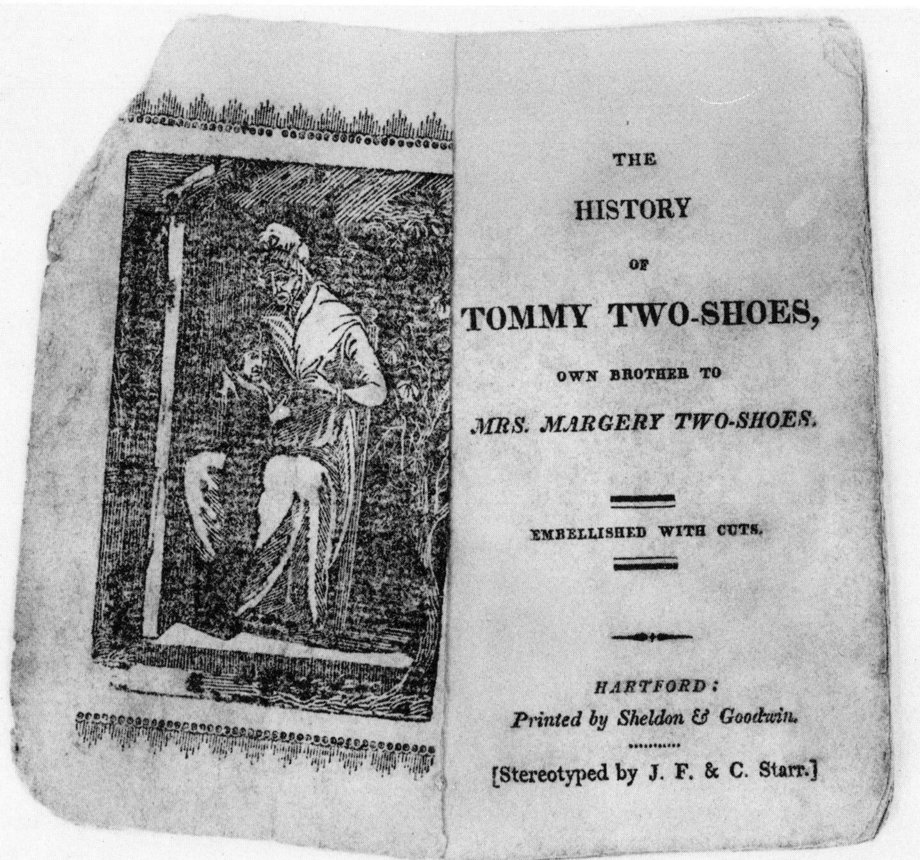

THE HISTORY OF TOMMY TWO-SHOES, OWN BROTHER TO *MRS. MARGERY TWO-SHOES.*

EMBELLISHED WITH CUTS.

HARTFORD:
Printed by Sheldon & Goodwin.

[Stereotyped by J. F. & C. Starr.]

Capital Letters.

A B C D E F G H I J K L M
N O P Q R S T U V W
X Y Z.

Small Letters.

a b c d e f g h i j k l m n o p
q r s t u v w x y z &.

Vowels.

A E I O U Y—a e i o u y.

Points.

, ; : . - ? ! ' ( ) [ ] * † ‡ ‖ § ¶

THE HISTORY OF TOMMY TWO-SHOES

CHAPTER I.

LITTLE Tommy Two-Shoes was born of honest, industrious parents, and although they had the misfortune to be reduced in their circumstances, yet they were very much respected by all who knew them, on account of their fidelity; and it was marked by all the reputable people in the neighbourhood, what care they took in bringing up their children in every christian virtue: however, the

6

Great Disposer and Wise Governour of all things, saw it best to take them early to their reward in heaven, by which means little Tommy, as also his sister Margery, lost the benefit of their parental affection and help; but as the children were careful to remember the instructions given them by their parents, when living, and to act accordingly, that Good Being who had taken the father and mother to himself, took care of the children which were left behind.

7

CHAPTER II.

MR. Smith, a very worthy clergyman, who lived in the parish where little Margery and Tommy were born, and having a relation come to see him, who was a charitable, good man, he sent for these children to him.—The gentleman said he would take Tommy and make him a little sailor, and accordingly had a jacket and trowsers made for him.—When Tommy looked at himself in his new dress, he was mightily pleased with it, and determined to do every thing in his power to merit a continuance of the favours of his new friend.

Mr. Kindheart (for that was the gentleman's name) thought Tommy a little too young to go to sea,

8

and therefore sent him to school; and his attendance to the thing

which he was taught, together with his good behaviour, soon gained him the esteem of his teacher and school-fellows. When he was put to writing, he spared no pains to get complete master of that art; and he succeeded so far, that all the boys in the school were directed to look to him as a

9

pattern. The manner in which he held his pen was admired by all; and his master, who was very expert at drawing, drew the figure of his hand and pen, and hung it up in the school, where it hangs to this day for all the boys to imitate.

(continued on next page)

10

CHAPTER III.

TOMMY having finished his education, Mr. Kindheart told him he intended going to London in a

11

few days, and that he was to go along with him; and as soon as his fortunate ship, the Come-again, could be got ready for sea, he should try his fortune in her.

But I must beg of you to stop a little till I tell you how very affecting the parting was between this little boy and his sister.—Tommy cried, and Margery cried, and

they kissed each other an hundred times; at length Tommy wiped off

12

her tears with the end of his jacket, and bid her cry no more—that he would come to her again when he returned from sea. However as they were so very fond, the gentleman would not suffer them to take leave of each other, but told Tommy he should ride out with him and come back at night. When night came, little Margery grew very uneasy about her brother, and after sitting up as late as Mr. Smith would let her, she went crying to bed, where we must wish her good night.

13

CHAPTER IV.

IT is generally known, that Tommy Two-Shoes went to sea when he was a very little boy, and very poor; and that he returned a very great man, and very rich; but no one knows how he acquired

THE HISTORY OF TOMMY TWO-SHOES *(continued from page 85)*

14

so much wealth but himself and a few friends, who have perused the papers from which I am compiling the history of his life.

After Tommy had been at sea some years, he was unfortunately cast away, on that part of the coast of Africa, inhabited by the Hottentots.—Here he met with a strange book, which the Hottentots did not understand, and which gave him some account of Preston John's country; and being a lad of great curiosity and resolution, he determined to see it; accordingly he set out on the pursuit, attended by a young lion which he had tamed and made so fond of him, that he followed him like a dog, and obeyed all his commands; and indeed it was well for him that he had such a companion, for as his road lay through large woods and for-

15

ests that were full of wild beasts and without inhabitants, he must have been soon starved or torn in pieces, had he not been both fed and protected by this noble animal.

Tommy had provided himself with two guns, a sword, and as much powder and ball as he could carry; with these arms, and such a companion, it was mighty easy for him to get food; for the animals in these wild and extensive forests, having never seen the effects of a gun, readily ran from the lion, who hunted on one side, to Tommy who hunted on the other so that they were either caught by the lion, or shot by his master and it was pleasant enough, after hunting match, and the meat was dressed, to see how cheek by jow' they sat down to dinner.

16

When they came into the land of Utopia, he discovered the statue of a man erected on an open plain, which had this inscription on the pedestal:—*On May-Day in the morning, when the sun rises, I shall have a head of gold.* As it was now the latter end of April, he staid to see the wonderful change, and in the time inquiring of a poor shepherd what was the reason of the statue being erected there, and with that inscription? He was informed, that it was set up many years ago by an Arabian philosopher, who travelled all the world over in search of a real friend; that he lived with, and was extremely fond of a great man who inhabited the next mountain, but that on some occasion they quarrelled, and the philosopher leaving the mountain, retired into the

17

plain, where he erected this statue with his own hands, and soon after died. To this he added, that all people for many leagues round came there every May morning expecting to see the stone head turned to gold.

Tommy got up very early on the first of May to behold this amazing change, and when he came near the statue, he saw a number of people who all ran away from him in the utmost consternation, having never before seen a lion follow a man like a lap-dog. Being thus left alone, he fixed his eyes on the sun, then rising with resplendent majesty, and afterwards turned to the statue, but could see no change in the stone. Surely, says he to himself, there is some mystical meaning in this: This inscription must be an enigma, the

(continued on next page)

18

hidden meaning of which I will endeavour to find, for a philosopher would never expect a stone to be turned to gold. Accordingly, he measured the length of the shadow, which the statue gave on the ground by the sun shining on it and marked that particular part where the head fell; then getting a chopness, (a thing like a spade,) and digging, he discovered a copper chest, full of gold, with this inscription engraven on the lid of it:—

Thy Wit,
O man, whoever thou art,
Hath disclosed the enigma,
And discovered the GOLDEN HEAD
Take it and use it,
But use it with WISDOM;
For know
That GOLD, properly employed,

19

May dispense blessings,
And promote the happiness of mortals;
But when hoarded up,
Or misapplied,
Is but trash, that makes mankind miserable.
Remember
The unprofitable servant,
Who hid his talent in a napkin;
And
The profligate son,
Who squandered away his substance, and fed with the swine.
As thou hast got the GOLDEN HEAD,
Observe the *golden mean*,
Be *good* and be *happy*.

This lesson, coming as it were from the dead, struck him with such awe and reverence for piety and virtue, that before he removed the treasure, he kneeled down

20

and earnestly and fervently prayed that he might make a prudent just, and proper use of it. He

then conveyed the chest away and by his prudence and activity got it safe to *Old England*.

21

As he was now possessed of sufficient wealth, and had it in his power to fix in any part of the kingdom he pleased, he took a straight course for the city of York, knowing it to be a genteel healthful, pleasant, and plentiful situation, where he spent his remaining days in ease and honour; and as he was determined to be as good as he was great, he attended divine service every day at the Minister. He continued this practice for several years, and then died in peace.

THE HISTORY OF TOMMY TWO-SHOES *(continued from page 87)*

MALLEVILLE. A FRANCONIA STORY, by the author of the Rollo Books [Jacob Abbott (1803–1879)]. New York: Harper & Brothers Publishers', 82 Cliff Street, 1850. 219 pages. 17 cm.

This was the first in the famous series of Franconia stories, presenting boys and girls enjoying life in a New England countryside. These are regarded as outstanding among Abbott's many books for children. An educator, he was a disciple of Maria Edgeworth and Thomas Day and, like most didactic writers, was a confirmed enemy of fairy tales and nursery rhymes. He soon became a rival of Samuel Goodrich in his success and in the quantity of his writing, issuing over two hundred titles, of which nearly eight million copies were sold. His work became almost as much known in England as in America.
(continued on next page)

PREFACE.

The development of the moral sentiments in the human heart, in early life,—and every thing in fact which relates to the formation of character,—is determined in a far greater degree by sympathy, and by the influence of example, than by formal precepts and didactic instruction. If a boy hears his father speaking kindly to a robin in the spring,—welcoming its coming and offering it food,—there arises at once in his own mind, a feeling of kindness toward the bird, and toward all the animal creation, which is produced by a sort of sympathetic action, a power somewhat similar to what in physical philosophy is called *induction.* On the other hand, if the father, instead of feeding the bird, goes eagerly for a gun, in order that he may shoot it, the boy will sympathize in that desire, and growing up under such an influence, there will be gradually formed within him, through the mysterious tendency of the youthful heart to vibrate in unison with hearts that are near, a disposition to kill and destroy all helpless beings that come within his power. There is

no need of any formal instruction in either case. Of a thousand children brought up under the former of the above-described influences, nearly every one, when he sees a bird, will wish to go and get crumbs to feed it, while in the latter case, nearly every one will just as certainly look for a stone. Thus the growing up in the right atmosphere, rather than the receiving of the right instruction, is the condition which it is most important to secure, in plans for forming the characters of children.

It is in accordance with this philosophy that these stories, though written mainly with a view to their moral influence on the hearts and dispositions of the readers, contain very little formal exhortation and instruction. They present quiet and peaceful pictures of happy domestic life, portraying generally such conduct, and expressing such sentiments and feelings, as it is desirable to exhibit and express in the presence of children.

The books, however, will be found, perhaps, after all, to be useful mainly in entertaining and amusing the youthful readers who may peruse them, as the writing of them has been the amusement and recreation of the author in the intervals of more serious pursuits.

MALLEVILLE. A FRANCONIA STORY *(continued from page 89)*

ROLLO IN LONDON by Jacob Abbott [1803–1879]. Boston: Reynolds. 1855. 222 pages. 17½ cm.

One of Abbott's innumerable plotless narratives consisting largely of dialogues between the earnest young Rollo and his Uncle George, who served as his mentor for twelve journeys abroad. The travel series was as plainly intended to inform as were the earlier Rollo books. In one of those, "The Little Scholar" learns to talk and in a long list of other books imbibes many facts about the natural world about him, as in *Rollo's Experiments* (1841) and *Learning about Common Things* (Harper's *Picture Books for the Nursery,* Volume 4, 1884). The Library of Congress appears to possess the only surviving copy of *A Picture Book for Rollo* (1835).

(continued on next page)

20 ROLLO IN LONDON.

How the passengers leave the cars on an English railway.

CHAPTER II.

LONDON BRIDGE.

WHEN the train stopped at what is called the London Bridge station, the passengers all stepped out of their respective cars upon the platform. In the English cars the doors are at the sides, and not, as in America, at the ends; so that the passengers get out nearly all at once, and the platform becomes immediately crowded. Beyond the platform, on the other side, there is usually, when a train comes in, a long row of cabs and carriages drawn up, ready to take the passengers from the several cars; so that the traveller has generally nothing to do but to step across the platform from the car that he came in to the cab that is waiting there to receive him. Nor is there, as is usual in America, any difficulty or delay in regard to the baggage; for each man's trunks are placed on the car that he rides in, directly over his head; so that, while he walks across the platform to the cab, the railway porter takes his trunk across and

LONDON BRIDGE. 21

The railway porters. Worth of the English penny.

places it on the top of the cab; and thus he is off from the station in his cab within two min utes sometimes after he arrived at it in the car.

The railway porters, who attend to the business of transferring the passengers thus from the railway carriages to those of the street, are very numerous all along the platform; and they are very civil and attentive to the passengers, especially to those who come in the first-class cars — and more especially still, according to my observation and experience, if the traveller has an agreeable looking lady under his charge. The porters are dressed in a sort of uniform, by which they are readily distinguished from the crowd. They are strictly forbidden to receive any fee or gratuity from the passengers. This prohibition, however, does not prevent their taking very thankfully the shillings or sixpences * that are often offered them, particularly by Americans, who, being strangers in the country, and not understanding the customs very

* Whenever shillings or sixpences are mentioned in this book, English coin is meant. As a general rule, each English denomination is of double the value of the corresponding American one. Thus the English penny is a coin as large as a silver dollar, and it is worth two of the American pennies. The shilling is of the value of a quarter of a dollar; and a sixpence is equal to a New York shilling.

(continued on next page)

22 ROLLO IN LONDON.

The porter and the policeman. An action that spoke louder than words.

well, think that they require a little more attention than others, and so are willing to pay a little extra fee. It is, however, contrary to the rules of the station for the porters to receive any thing ; and, if they take it at all, they try to do it as secretly as possible. I once knew a traveller who offered a porter a shilling openly on the platform ; but the porter, observing a policeman near, turned round with his side to the gentleman, and, holding his hand open behind him, with the back of it against his hip and his fingers moving up and down briskly in a beckoning manner, said, —

" We are not allowed to take it, sir — we are not allowed to take it."

As Mr. George stepped out upon the platform at the London Bridge station his first thought was to find Rollo, who had chosen to come in a second-class car, partly for the purpose of saving the difference in the fare, and partly, as he said, "for the fun of it." Rollo had a regular allowance from his father for his travelling expenses, sufficient to pay his way in the first-class conveyances ; and the understanding was, that whatever he should save from this sum by travelling in the cheaper modes was to be his own for pocket money or to add to his reserved funds.

Caroline M. Hewins, a well-known early librarian in Hartford, Connecticut, believed that Abbott's books should be included in libraries for boys and girls because they contained so much practical wisdom, and as late as 1913 she was still recommending them. The "wisdom" is illustrated in *Rollo in Naples* (1858) wherein Uncle George draws up sensible "Rules for two parties travelling together," many of which might fruitfully be studied by world travelers today, and in the excerpt here on tipping, from *Rollo in London.*

GOODY TWO-SHOES. Illustrated with Ten Pictures. New York: H. W. Hewet, Engraver and Printer, No. 12 Dutch street [c. 1855]. 29 pages. 18 cm.

The story shown here is more appealing to children than the earlier versions because it appears without the original protest against social evils and has less moralizing in general. Although H. W. Hewet's name appears on the title page, this work has been variously attributed to Oliver Goldsmith, Giles Jones, Griffith Jones, and John Newbery. (See also pages 80 and 84.)

(continued on next page)

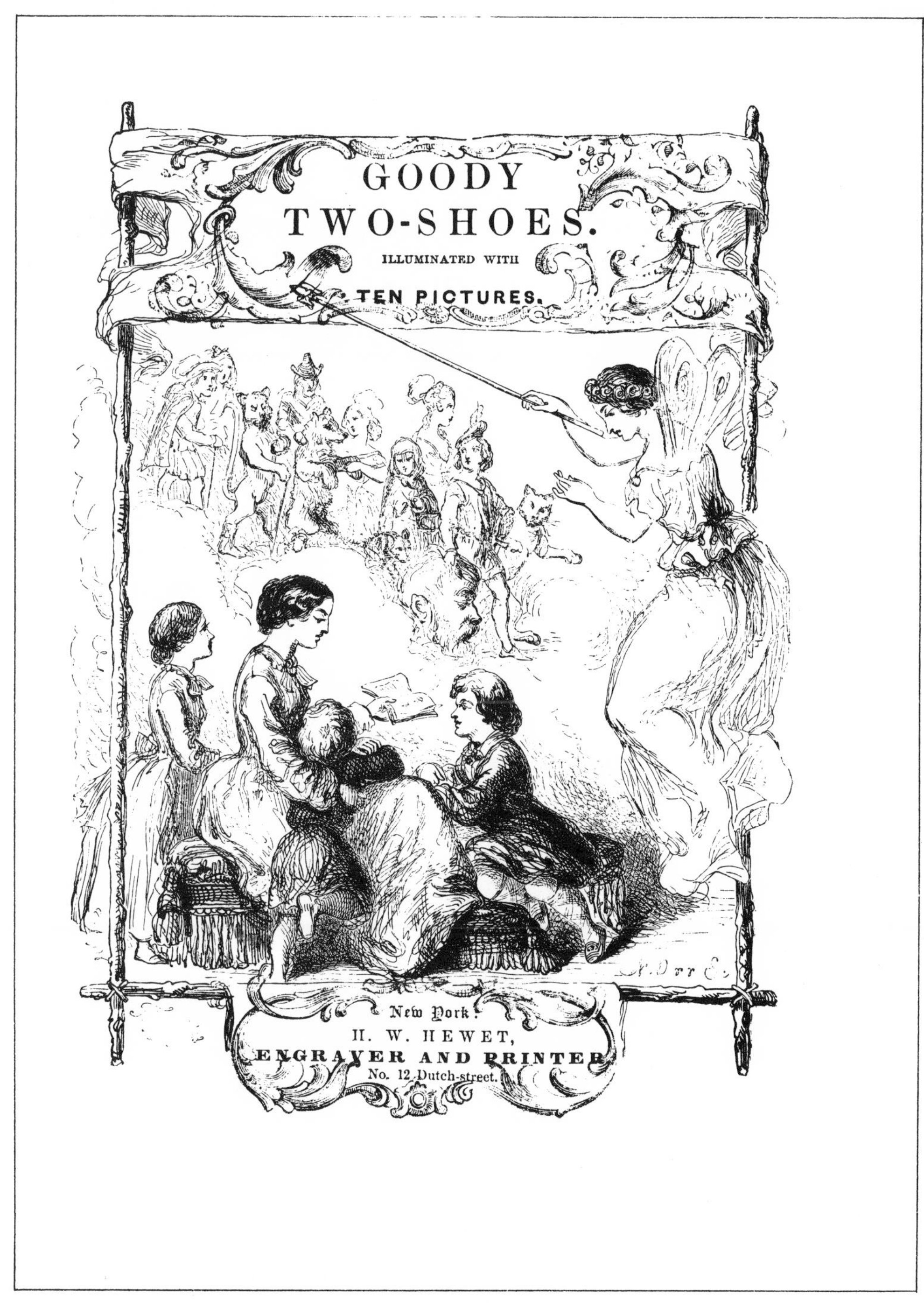

GOODY TWO-SHOES AND HER BROTHER TOMMY AS THEY APPEARED BEFORE THE CLERGYMAN.

GOODY TWO-SHOES.

ALL the world must know that Goody Two-Shoes was not a little girl's real name. No; her father's name was Meanwell, and he was for many years a large farmer in the parish where Margery was born; but by the misfortunes he met with in business, and

A 1

(continued from page 93)

the wickedness of Sir Timothy Gripe, and a farmer named Graspall, he was quite ruined.

Care and discontent shortened the life of little Margery's father. Her poor mother survived the loss of her husband but a few days, and died of a broken heart, leaving Margery and her little brother to the wide world.

It would both have excited your pity and have done your heart good, to have seen how fond these two little ones were of each other. They were both very ragged, and Tommy had two shoes, but Margery had but one. They had nothing to support them but what they picked from the hedges, or got from the poor people, and they slept every night in a barn. Their relations took no notice of them; no, they were rich, and ashamed to own such a poor ragged girl as Margery, and such a dirty curly-pated boy as Tommy.

Mr. Smith was a very worthy clergyman, who

lived in the parish where little Margery and Tommy were born; and having a relation come to see him, who was a charitable, good man, he sent for these children to him. The gentleman ordered little Margery a new pair of shoes, gave Mr. Smith some money to buy her clothes, and said he would take Tommy, and make him a little sailor; and, accordingly, had a jacket and trowsers made for him.

After some days, the gentleman intended to go to London, and take little Tommy with him. The parting between these two little children was very affecting. They both cried, and they kissed each other a hundred times. At last Tommy wiped off her tears with the end of his jacket, and bid her cry no more, for that he would come to her again when he returned from sea.

Nothing could have supported little Margery under the affliction she was in for the loss of her brother, but the pleasure she took in her two shoes.

She ran to Mrs. Smith as soon as they were put on, and stroking down her ragged apron, cried out—"Two Shoes, Ma'am! see, Two Shoes!" And so she behaved to all the people she met, and by that means obtained the name of Little Goody Two-Shoes.

Little Margery saw how good and how wise Mr. Smith was, and concluded that this was owing to his great learning; therefore she wanted, of all things, to learn to read. For this purpose, she used to meet the little boys and girls as they came from school, borrow their books, and sit down and read till they returned. By this means she soon got more learning than any of her playmates, and laid the following plan for instructing those who were more ignorant than herself. She found that only twenty-six letters were required to spell all the words; but as some of these letters are large, and some small, she with her knife cut out of several pieces of wood

ten sets of each. And having got an old spelling-book, she made her companions set up the words they wanted to spell.

The usual manner of spelling, or carrying on the

GOODY TWO-SHOES PARTING WITH HER BROTHER.

game, as they called it, was this: Suppose the word to be spelt was plum-pudding (and who can suppose a better?), the children were placed in a circle, and

(continued on next page)

the first brought the letter *p*, the next *l*, the next *u*, the next *m*, and so on till the whole was spelt; and if any one brought a wrong letter, he was to pay a fine, or play no more. This was their play; and every morning she used to go round to teach the children. I once went her rounds with her, and was highly diverted.

It was about seven o'clock in the morning when we set out on this important business, and the first house we came to was Farmer Wilson's. Here Margery stopped, and ran up to the door—tap, tap, tap! "Who's there?" "Only little Goody Two-Shoes," answered Margery, "come to teach Billy." "Oh, little Goody," says Mrs. Wilson, with pleasure in her face, "I am glad to see you! Billy wants you sadly, for he has learned his lesson." Then out came the little boy. "How do, Doody Two-Shoes?" says he, not able to speak plain. Yet this little boy had learned all his letters; for she threw down the small

alphabet mixed together, and he picked them up, called them by their right names, and put them all in order. She then threw down the alphabet of capital letters, and he picked them all up, and having told their names, placed them rightly.

The next place we came to was Farmer Simpson's. "Bow, wow, wow!" says the dog at the door. "Sirrah!" says his mistress, "why do you bark at little Two-Shoes? Come in, Madge; here's Sally wants you sadly; she has learned all her lesson." "Yes, that's what I have," replied the little one, in the country manner; and immediately taking the letters, she set up these syllables:

ba be bi bo bu	ma me mi mo mu
da de di do du	sa se si so su

and gave them their exact sounds as she composed them; after which she set up many more, and pronounced them likewise.

After this, little Two-Shoes taught Sally to spell

words of one syllable, and she soon set up pear, plum, top, ball, pin, puss, dog, hog, doe, lamb, sheep, ram, cow, bull, cock, hen, and many more.

The next place we came to was Gaffer Cook's cottage. Here a number of poor children were met to learn, and all came round little Margery at once, who, having pulled out her letters, asked the little boy next her what he had for dinner. He answered, "Bread." "Well, then," says she, "set up the first letter." He put up the *B*, to which the next added *r*, and the next *e*, the next *a*, the next *d*, and it stood thus, Bread.

"And what had you, Polly Comb, for your dinner?" "Apple-Pie," answered the little girl. Upon which the next in turn set up a great *A*, the two next a *p* each, and so on till the two words Apple and Pie were united, and stood thus, Apple-Pie. The next had potatoes, the next beef and turnips, which were spelt, with many others, till the game

was finished She then set them another task, and after the lessons were done, we returned home.

As we were returning home, we saw a gentleman, who was very ill, sitting under a shady tree, at the

"TWO SHOES, MA'AM; SEE, TWO SHOES!"

corner of his rookery. Though ill, he began to joke with little Margery, and said, laughingly, "So, Goody Two-Shoes, they tell me you are a cunning little baggage. Pray, can you tell me what I shall do to get well?"

"Yes, sir," says she; "go to bed when your rooks do. You see they are going to rest already. Do you so likewise, and get up with them in the morning. Earn, as they do, every day what you eat, and eat and drink no more than you earn, and you will get health, and keep it. What should induce the rooks to frequent gentlemen's houses, only but to tell them how to lead a prudent life? They never build over cottages or farm-houses, because they see that these people know how to live without their admonition."

The gentleman, laughing, gave Margery sixpence, and told her she was a sensible little girl.

Who does not know Lady Ducklington, or that she was buried in this parish? All the country

round came to see the burying, and it was late before it was over; after which, in the night, or rather very early in the morning, the bells were heard to jingle in the steeple, which frightened the people prodigiously.

They flocked to Will Dobbins, the clerk, and wanted him to go and see what it was; but William would not open the door.

At length Mr. Long, the rector, hearing such an uproar in the village, went to the clerk to know why he did not go into the church and see who was there.

"I go, sir!" says William; "why, I would be frightened out of my wits."

"Give me the key of the church," says Mr. Long.

Then he went to the church, all the people following him.

As soon as he had opened the door, who do you think appeared? Why, little Two-Shoes, who, being

weary, had fallen asleep in one of the pews during the funeral service, and was shut in all night.

She immediately asked Mr. Long's pardon for the trouble she had given him, and said she should not have rung the bells, but that she was very cold, and hearing Farmer Boult's man go whistling by, she was in hopes he would have gone for the key to let her out.

The people were ashamed to ask little Madge any questions before Mr. Long, but as soon as he was gone, they desired she would give them an account of all that she had heard or seen.

"I went to the church," said Goody Two-Shoes, "as most of you did last night, to see the funeral, and being very weary, I sat down in Mr. Jones's pew, and fell fast asleep. At eleven o'clock I awoke. I started up, and soon found that I was shut up in the church. It was dismally dark, and I could see nothing; but while I was standing in the pew some-

thing jumped upon me behind, and laid, as I thought, its hands over my shoulders. Then I walked down the church aisle, when I heard something pit pat, pit

GOODY TWO-SHOES LEARNING TO READ.

pat, pit pat, come after me, and something touched my hand that seemed as cold as a marble monument. I could not think what it was, yet I knew it

(continued on next page)

could not hurt me, and therefore I made myself easy; but being very cold, and the church being paved with stones, which were very damp, I felt my way as well as I could to the pulpit, in doing which something rushed by me, and almost threw me down. At last I found out the pulpit, and having shut the door, I laid down on the mat and cushion to sleep, when something pulled the door, as I thought, for admittance, which prevented my going to sleep. At last it cried, 'Bow, wow, wow!' and I knew it must be Mr. Sanderson's dog, which had followed me from their house to the church; so I opened the door, and called 'Snip! Snip!' and the dog jumped upon me immediately. After this, Snip and I lay down together, and had a comfortable nap, for when I awoke it was almost light. I then walked up and down all the aisles of the church to keep myself warm, and then I went to Lord Ducklington's tomb, and I stood looking at his cold mar-

ble face and his hands clasped together, till, hearing Farmer Boult's man go by, I went to the bells and rung them."

Goody Two-Shoes was so much liked, that most of the differences in the parish were left to her decision; and if a man and his wife quarrelled (which sometimes happened in that part of the kingdom), both parties certainly came to her for advice.

Everybody knows that Martha Wilson was a passionate, scolding jade, and that John, her husband, was a surly, ill-tempered fellow. These were one day brought by the neighbors for Margery to talk to them, when they fairly quarrelled before her, and were going to blows, but she, stepping between them, thus addressed the husband:

"John," says she, "you are a man, and ought to have more sense than to fly in a passion at every word that is said amiss by your wife. And, Martha," says she, "you ought to know your duty bet-

ter than to say any thing to aggravate your husband's resentment. These frequent quarrels arise from the indulgence of your violent passions; for I know you both love one another, notwithstanding what has passed between you. Now, pray tell me, John, and tell me, Martha, when you have had a quarrel overnight, are you not both sorry for it the next day?"

They both declared that they were.

"Why, then," says Goody, "I'll tell you how to prevent this for the future, if you will both take my advice."

They both promised her.

"Then," continued Goody, "you must solemnly agree that, if one speaks an angry word, the other will not answer till he or she has counted twelve, and the other not reply till he or she has told twenty. By this means your passions will be stifled, and reason will have time to take the rule."

In short, as Margery grew in size, so she increased in goodness and wisdom, till she was the favorite of the whole village.

GOODY TWO-SHOES TEACHING THE CHILDREN THEIR LETTERS.

There was in the same parish a Mrs. Williams, who kept a college for instructing little gentlemen and ladies in the science of A, B, C, who was at this time very old and infirm, and wanted to decline this important trust. This being told to Sir William Dove, he sent for Mrs. Williams, and desired she would examine little Two-Shoes, and see whether she was qualified for the office. This was done, and Mrs. Williams made the following report in her favor: namely, that little Margery was the best scholar, and had the best head and the best heart of any one she had examined. All the country had a great opinion of Mrs. Williams, and this character gave them also a great opinion of Mrs. Margery, for so we must now call her.

The room in which Mrs. Margery taught her scholars was very large and spacious; and as she knew that nature intended children should be always in action, she placed her different letters or alphabets all round the school, so that every one was obliged to get up and fetch a letter, or to spell

a word, when it came to their turn, which not only kept them in health, but fixed the letters firmly in their minds.

One day, as Mrs. Margery was going through the next village, she met with some wicked boys, who had taken a young raven, which they were going to pelt with stones. She wanted to get the poor creature out of their cruel hands, and therefore gave them a penny for him, and brought him home. She called him by the name of Ralph; and a fine bird he was.

Now this bird she taught to speak, to spell, and to read; and as he was fond of playing with the large letters, the children used to call them Ralph's Alphabet.

Some days after she had met with the raven, as she was walking in the fields, she saw some naughty boys, who had taken a pigeon, and tied a string to its legs, in order to let it fly and draw it back again

when they pleased, and by this means they tortured the poor bird with the hopes of liberty and repeated disappointment. This pigeon she also bought, and taught him how to spell and read, though not to talk. He was a very pretty fellow, and she called him Tom. And as the raven Ralph was fond of the large letters, Tom the pigeon took care of the small ones.

The neighbors knowing that Mrs. Two-Shoes was very good, as, to be sure, nobody was better, made her a present of a little sky-lark. She thought the lark might be of use to her and her pupils, and tell them when it was time to get up. "For he that is fond of his bed, and lies till noon, lives but half his days, the rest being lost in sleep, which is a kind of death."

Some time after this a poor lamb had lost its dam, and the farmer being about to kill it, she bought it of him, and brought him home with her

to play with the children, and teach them when to go to bed; for it was a rule with the wise men of that age to "rise with the lark, and lie down with the lamb." This lamb she called Will.

GOODY TWO-SHOES AND HER DOG SNIP AT LORD DUCKLINGTON'S TOMB.

No sooner was Tippy, the lark, and Will, the ba-lamb, brought into the school, than that sensible rogue Ralph, the raven, composed the following verse, which every good little boy and girl should get by heart:

> "Early to bed, and early to rise,
> Is the way to be healthy, wealthy, and wise."

Soon after this a present was made to Mrs. Margery of a little dog, whom she called Jumper. The place assigned for Jumper was that of keeping the door; so that he might have been called the porter of a college, for he would let nobody go out nor any one come in, without leave of his mistress.

Billy, the ba-lamb, was a cheerful fellow, and all the children were fond of him; wherefore Mrs. Two-Shoes made it a rule that those who behaved best should have Will home with them at night, to carry their satchel on his back, and bring it in the morning.

Mrs. Margery, as we have frequently observed, was always doing good, and thought she could never sufficiently gratify those who had done any thing to

serve her. Those generous sentiments naturally led her to consult the interest of her neighbors; and as most of their lands were meadow, and they depended much on their hay, which had been for many years greatly damaged by the wet weather, she contrived an instrument to direct them when to mow their grass with safety, and prevent their hay being spoiled. They all came to her for advice, and by that means got in their hay without damage, while most of that in the neighboring village was spoiled. This occasioned a very great noise in the country; and so greatly provoked were the people who resided in the other parishes, that they absolutely accused her of being a witch, and sent old Gaffer Goosecap, a busy fellow in other people's concerns, to find out evidence against her. The wiseacre happened to come to her school, when she was walking about with the raven on one shoulder, the pigeon on the other, the lark on her hand, and the lamb and

the dog by her side, which indeed made a droll figure, and so surprised the man, that he cried out—"A witch! a witch! a witch!"

Upon this, she laughingly answered, "A conjurer! a conjurer!" and so they parted. But it did not end thus, for a warrant was issued out against Mrs. Margery, and she was carried to a meeting of the justices, whither all the neighbors followed her.

At the meeting, one of the justices, who knew little of life and less of the law, behaved very badly, and, though nobody was able to prove any thing against her, asked who she could bring to her character.

"Who can you bring *against* my character, sir?" says she. "There are people enough who would appear in my defence, were it necessary; but I never supposed that any one here could be so weak as to believe there was any such thing as a witch. If I am a witch, this is my charm, and" (laying a baro-

GOODY TWO-SHOES SHOWS HOW SHE TAUGHT THE FARMERS TO KNOW THE STATE OF THE WEATHER, AND CAME TO BE ARRESTED AS A CONJURER.

meter upon the table) "it is with this," says she, "that I have taught my neighbors to know the state of the weather."

All the company laughed; and Sir William Dove, who was on the bench, asked her accusers how they could be such fools as to think there was any such thing as a witch. And then he gave such an account of Mrs. Margery and her virtue, good sense, and prudent behavior, that the gentlemen present returned her public thanks for the great service she had done the country. One gentleman, in particular, Sir Charles Jones, had conceived such a high opinion of her, that he offered her a considerable sum to take the care of his family, and the education of his daughter, which, however, she refused; but this gentleman sending for her afterwards, when he had a dangerous fit of illness, she went, and behaved so prudently in the family, and so tenderly to him and his daughter, that he would not permit her to

leave his house, but soon after made her proposals of marriage. She was truly sensible of the honor he intended her, but would not consent to be made a lady till he had provided for his daughter.

All things being settled, and the day fixed, the neighbors came in crowds to see the wedding But just as the clergyman had opened his book, a gentleman, richly dressed, ran into the church, and cried, "Stop! stop!"

This greatly alarmed the congregation, and particularly the intended bride and bridegroom, whom he first accosted, desiring to speak with them apart. Presently the people were greatly surprised to see Sir Charles stand motionless, and his bride cry and faint away in the stranger's arms; for you must know that this gentleman so richly dressed was little Tommy Meanwell, Mrs. Margery's brother, who was just come from sea, where he had made a large fortune, and hearing, as soon as he landed, of his sister's

intended wedding, had ridden post to see that a proper settlement was made on her, which he thought she was now entitled to, as he himself was able to give her an ample fortune. They soon returned to the communion-table, and were married in tears, but they were tears of joy.

Sir Charles and Lady Jones lived happily for many years. Her ladyship continued to visit the school in which she had passed so many happy days, and always gave the prizes to the best scholars with her own hands. She also gave to the parish several acres of land to be planted yearly with potatoes, for all the poor who would come and fetch them for the use of their families; but if any took them to sell, they were deprived of that privilege ever after.

In short, she was a mother to the poor, a physician to the sick, and a friend to those in distress. Her life was the greatest blessing, and her death the

greatest calamity that ever was felt in the neighborhood.

THE NEIGHBORS WAIT UPON GOODY TWO-SHOES WHEN SHE IS MARRIED TO SIR CHARLES.

THE INDIAN CHIEF AND THE LITTLE WHITE BOY. Philadelphia: Theodore Bliss & Co. [c. 1855]. 96 pages. 12 cm. Contents: The Indian Chief and the Little White Boy.—The Little Flower Girl. —The Drowned Boy.—Story of the Petrel.—A Fox and Her Young Ones.

This interesting book, of which only the title page and frontispiece are shown here, is an amalgam of facts and earnest little stories. The first tale describes the attempt of an upstanding white family to buy land from seven Indian chiefs. The oldest chief demands that the family's little boy go off with him for three days before he will give his answer. The family consents (with great trepidation). The child is returned unharmed and happy at the end of the three days, and the chief declaims: "White strangers, *you* have had *confidence* in an Indian—*I* will have confidence in *you*. I will now sell you my land for you are good people. If all whites had been like you, all the bloody wars between the red and the white men would never have happened. Hereafter, so long as I live, I am your friend."

THE BRANDY DROPS; OR, CHARLIE'S PLEDGE. A Temperance Story, by Aunt Julia. New York: Published by Carlton & Porter, Sunday-School Union, 200 Mulberry-Street. [c. 1858]. 103 pages. 15½ cm.

A typical temperance tract, published in a vast outpouring from the American Sunday School Union and other concerned societies. The tale opens with the witnessing by small boys of a drunken woman, their later eating of brandy drops—on a dare—their repentance, and the forming of a temperance society by many little boys persuaded to join and sign "The Pledge":

United in a joyous band,
We'll sign the pledge with heart and hand;
The ruby wine we'll lay aside,
And be our country's hope and pride.

'T will keep the roses on the cheek,
Preserve the spirit mild and meek;
The eye will beam expression bright,
The mind improve in wisdom's light.

It makes the home of labor sweet,
And happy faces there you'll greet;
It leads the way to honest wealth,
And gives earth's choicest blessing—health.

THE

BRANDY DROPS;

OR,

CHARLIE'S PLEDGE.

A Temperance Story.

BY AUNT JULIA.

New-York:
PUBLISHED BY CARLTON & PORTER,
SUNDAY-SCHOOL UNION, 200 MULBERRY-STREET.

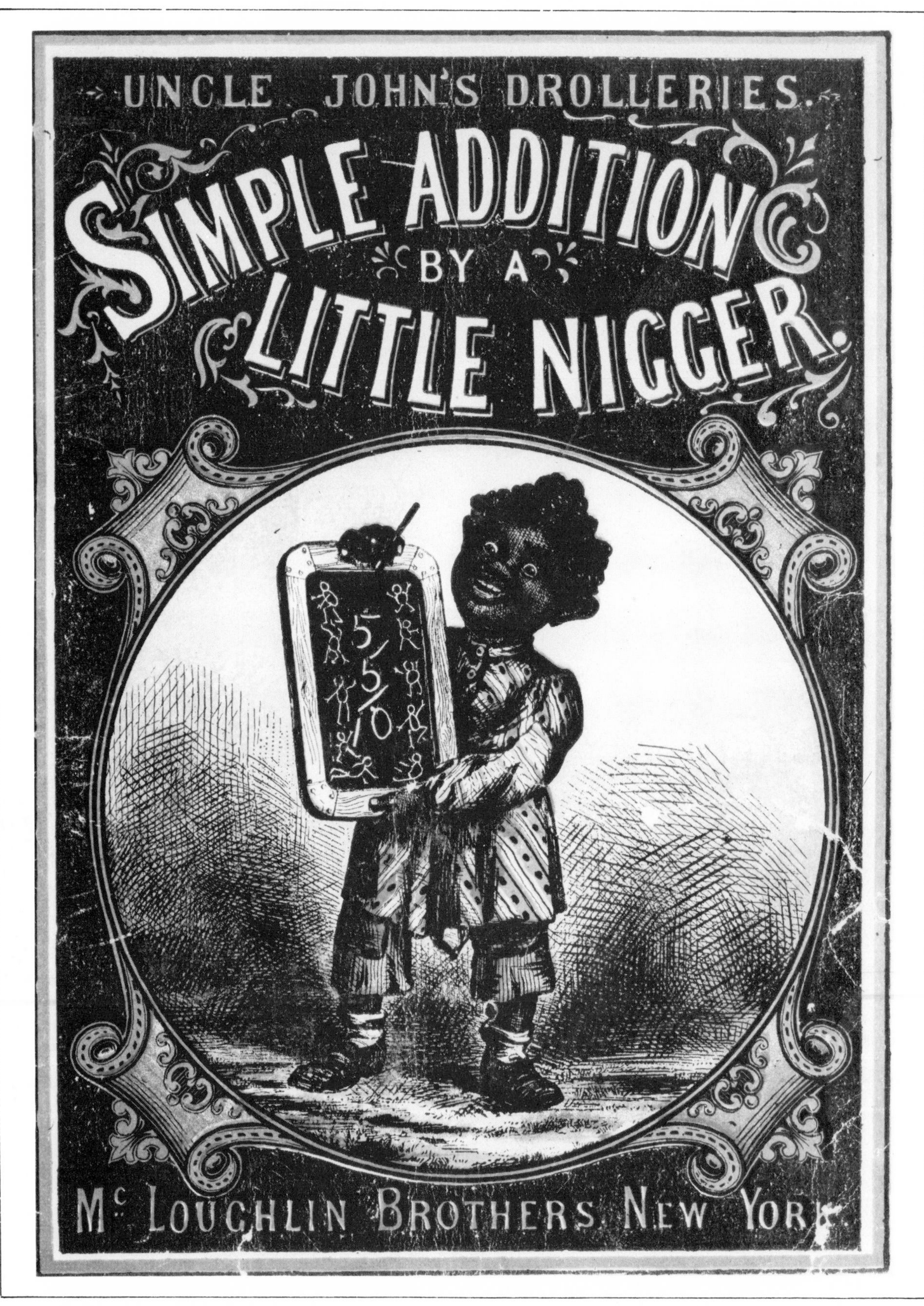

SIMPLE ADDITION BY A LITTLE NIGGER. Uncle John's Drolleries. New York: McLoughlin Bros. [18–?]. Unpaged. 26 cm.

This book, printed in bright, full color, is one of the few early picture books to use black characters throughout. However, the use of the word "nigger" and the exaggerated draw-

ONE little nigger feeling rather blue,
Whistled out another nig, and that made 2.

ing of the features in this work exemplify a stereotype frequently encountered from the mid-nineteenth to the mid-twentieth century. The only dialect employed appears in the doggerel at the end of the counting rhyme:

Dis colored chile am done, dat sum;
"Five and five's ten,"—and now's gwine hum.

(continued on next page)

Two little niggers shook an apple tree,
Down fell another nig, that made 3.

SIMPLE ADDITION BY A LITTLE NIGGER *(continued from page 105)*

Three little niggers wanting one more,
Had'nt any trouble in getting number 4.

(continued on next page)

SIMPLE ADDITION BY A LITTLE NIGGER *(continued from page 107)*

Hired a colored coachman --that made 5.

(continued on next page)

SIMPLE ADDITION BY A LITTLE NIGGER *(continued from page 109)*

Added one apiece, to make their number 10.

(continued on next page)

SIMPLE ADDITION BY A LITTLE NIGGER *(continued from page 111)*

II. Works Intended to Entertain.
From the Colonial Period to 1900.

THE CHANGE IN BOOKMAKING from sober little chapbooks, such as "Jack the Giant-Killer" or "Jack and Jill," with woodcut-illustrated pages measuring not much more than two by three inches, to the sumptuous, gilt-edged annual quartos, which filled bookshops for Christmas giving toward the end of the nineteenth century, reveals much of the changing state of society and of children's literature.

It was in chapbooks, from the early part of the eighteenth century and into the nineteenth, that children of the times found most of their entertainment in reading, for many of these cheap, crudely printed, tiny paperbacks contained popular folktales, rhymes, and riddles. A continuous flow of imports from abroad and reissues in America provided not only the famous English tales and rhymes but also the fairy tales of Perrault and *Aesop's Fables*. In the latter part of the nineteenth century, doggerel verses in the style of the old rhymes, filled the profitable stream of larger, brightly colored, stiff paper-bound picture books (to the delight of today's specialist collectors), most of which were published by McLoughlin. This firm, established in 1828, and which a quarter of a century later became McLoughlin Brothers, claimed to be the "first American publisher to issue children's books illustrated in color." Among the many artists employed by the brothers were such greats as Thomas Nast, Howard Pyle, and Palmer Cox, although their work was largely unsigned—almost all the McLoughlin books had anonymous artwork.

Another kind of original verse, the often sentimental and lifeless imitations of the English Taylor sisters, the poets Jane and Ann, appeared with increasing frequency in tiny books and in the magazines—most of them now forgotten. But not lost were the lines of Clement C. Moore's "A Visit from St. Nicholas," Sarah Josepha Hale's "Mary's Lamb," and Lydia Maria Child's

"The New-England Boy's Song" ("Over the river and through the woods. . . .").

The same disparity in quality characterized the creation of stories. Forerunner in a new succession of dolorous tales was Susan Warner's *The Wide, Wide World* (1850), rightly described by Van Wyck Brooks as "a swamp of lachrymosity." Suitable for the Sunday School library, it consisted of a welter of bathos and religiosity, but it became immensely popular, both in this country and abroad, where it was translated into several languages. It succeeded as the first story to be written for girls in their teens about the American scene and American characters. *Queechy* (1852), the author's second book, had a similar commercial success. (As a sampling of the lachrymose, see on pages 227–246, a famous scene from *Elsie Dinsmore* by Martha Farquharson Finley.) Fortunately girls were to have other styles of stories, of varying degrees of excellence—in series by "Pansy," Mrs. A. D. T. Whitney, Elizabeth Champney, Laura E. Richards, Susan Coolidge (the *Katy* books), and Margaret Sidney (*Five Little Peppers*).

The adventure story for boys literally exploded into publication. Into a marketplace filled with sensational dime novels came more than a hundred vigorous—and moral—"Oliver Optics" by William T. Adams (a Massachusetts schoolteacher who urged Horatio Alger to write). Harry Castlemon (Charles Austin Fosdick), W. O. Stoddard, Elijah Kellogg, Noah Brooks, John Townsend Trowbridge, Charles A. Stephen (especially important to *The Youth's Companion*), and Charles C. Coffin were members of a company of writers who introduced variously realistic pictures of life at sea, on the farm, and on the battlefield, and they were widely read. But leading all these in popularity were Horatio Alger's stories of urchins adrift in New York, where if diligent and thrifty, they were "bound to rise."

If all this seems like an overwhelming mass of ephemera—though admittedly now of interest to the collector—there were also literary highlights in fiction writing, some represented here in "Stories after 1850." Justifiably recognized, in addition to those excerpted, were Mrs. Cecilia Jamison's *Lady Jane* (1891), Mark Twain's masterpieces about Tom, Huck Finn, and the prince and the pauper who changed clothes, and John Bennett's *Master Skylark* (1897).

Fully as significant as these latter for injecting new life into American children's literature was the stream of fantasy and folklore retellings. In the 1850's came Hawthorne's reworking of the Greek myths and original fantasies by Christopher Pearse Cranch sampled here. Charles E. Carryl (probably inspired by Lewis Carroll) produced witty nonsense in *The Admiral's Caravan* and *Davy and the Goblin,* while Laura E. Richards turned out her enduring "hurdy-gurdy" verses with a Lear-like genius for nonsense. From folklore motifs Howard Pyle and Frank R. Stockton created their own tales which are still in print and continue to delight children. Important at the end of the century were classic retellings of heroic legends—not only by Howard Pyle, with his Robin Hood, but also by Sidney Lanier (King Arthur) and James Baldwin (Siegfried and Roland).

II. Works Intended to Entertain.

From the Colonial Period to 1900.

A. TRADITIONAL AND POPULAR TALES; RHYMES, RIDDLES, AND CRIES

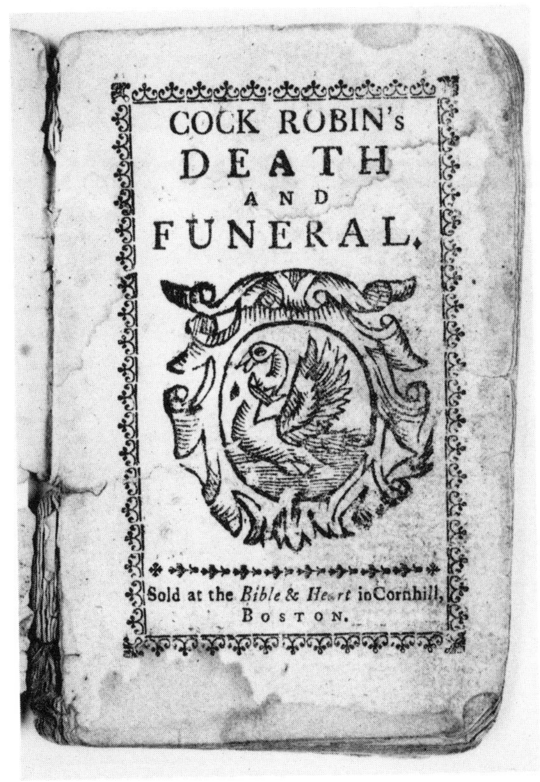
COCK ROBIN's
DEATH
AND
FUNERAL.

Sold at the *Bible* & *Heart* in Cornhill,
BOSTON.

COCK ROBIN'S DEATH AND FUNERAL. Boston: Sold at the Bible & Heart in Cornhill [1780]. 32 pages. 9½ cm.

This very early, tiny toy-book version of one of the most famous traditional nursery rhymes (first recorded about 1744), which came to the Library of Congress as the only known complete copy of this earliest American edition, forms part of the Hogan Collection.

In a notably rich collection of early issues of this rhyme, the Library owns also a copy of a rare edition of 1798 in a larger chapbook format, entitled *The Death and Burial of Cock Robin with the Tragical Death of A, Apple Pie: The Whole Taken from the Original Manuscript, in the Possession of Master Meanwell.*

(continued on next page)

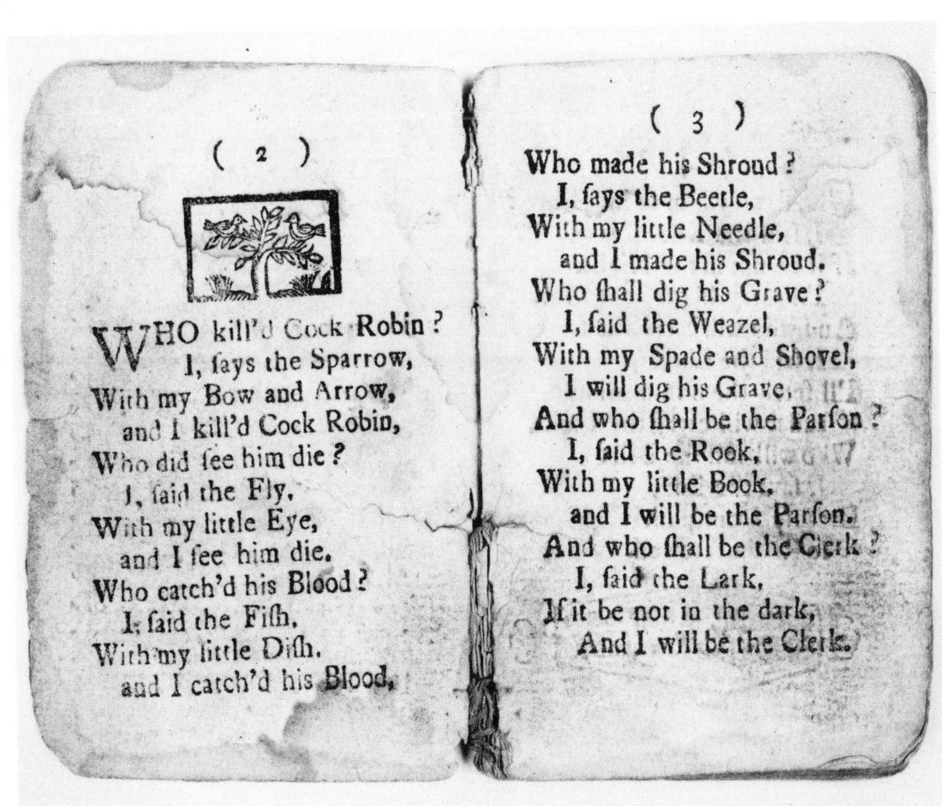
(2)

WHO kill'd Cock Robin?
I, ſays the Sparrow,
With my Bow and Arrow,
and I kill'd Cock Robin,
Who did ſee him die?
I, ſaid the Fly,
With my little Eye,
and I ſee him die.
Who catch'd his Blood?
I, ſaid the Fiſh,
With my little Diſh,
and I catch'd his Blood,

(3)

Who made his Shroud?
I, ſays the Beetle,
With my little Needle,
and I made his Shroud.
Who ſhall dig his Grave?
I, ſaid the Weazel,
With my Spade and Shovel,
I will dig his Grave,
And who ſhall be the Parſon?
I, ſaid the Rook,
With my little Book,
and I will be the Parſon.
And who ſhall be the Clerk?
I, ſaid the Lark,
If it be not in the dark,
And I will be the Clerk.

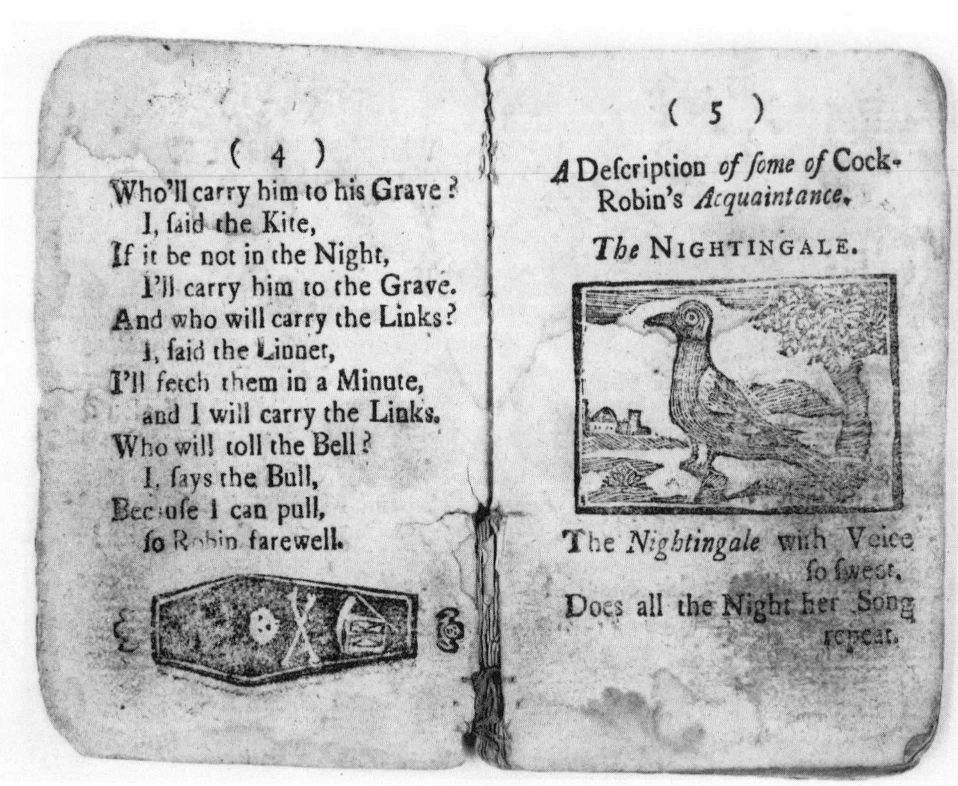

(4)

Who'll carry him to his Grave?
I, ſaid the Kite,
If it be not in the Night,
I'll carry him to the Grave.
And who will carry the Links?
I, ſaid the Linnet,
I'll fetch them in a Minute,
and I will carry the Links.
Who will toll the Bell?
I, ſays the Bull,
Becauſe I can pull,
ſo Robin farewell.

(5)

A Deſcription *of ſome of* Cock-Robin's *Acquaintance*.

The NIGHTINGALE.

The *Nightingale* with Voice ſo ſweet,
Does all the Night her Song repeat.

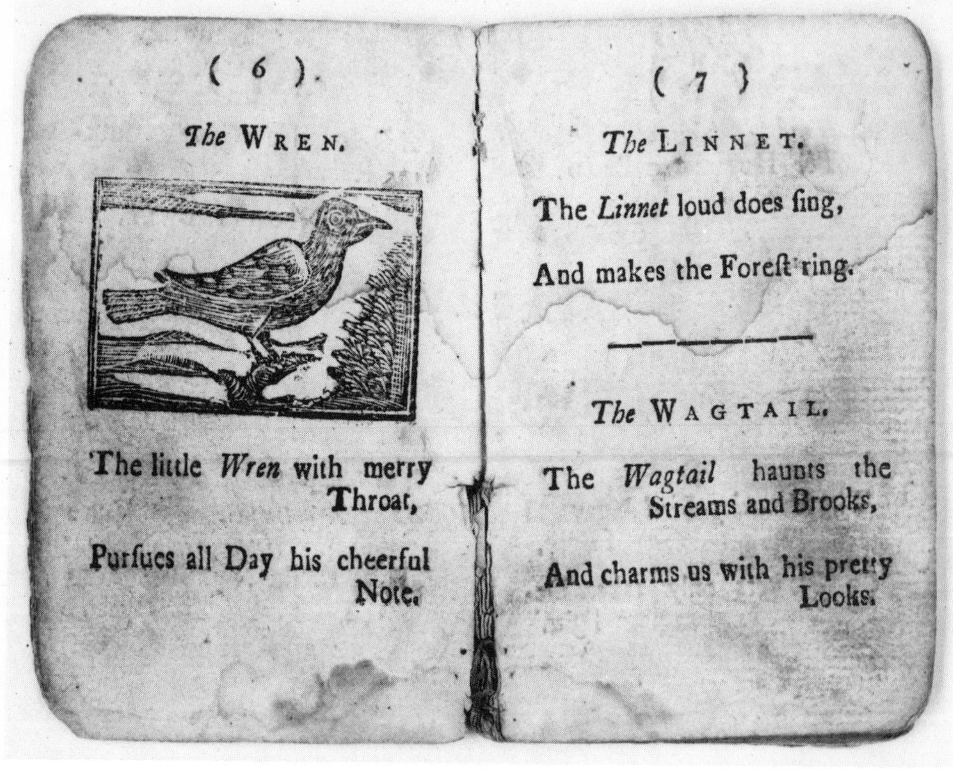

(6)

The WREN.

The little *Wren* with merry Throat,
Purſues all Day his cheerful Note.

(7)

The LINNET.

The *Linnet* loud does ſing,
And makes the Foreſt ring.

The WAGTAIL.

The *Wagtail* haunts the Streams and Brooks,
And charms us with his pretty Looks.

COCK ROBIN'S DEATH AND FUNERAL *(continued from page 115)*

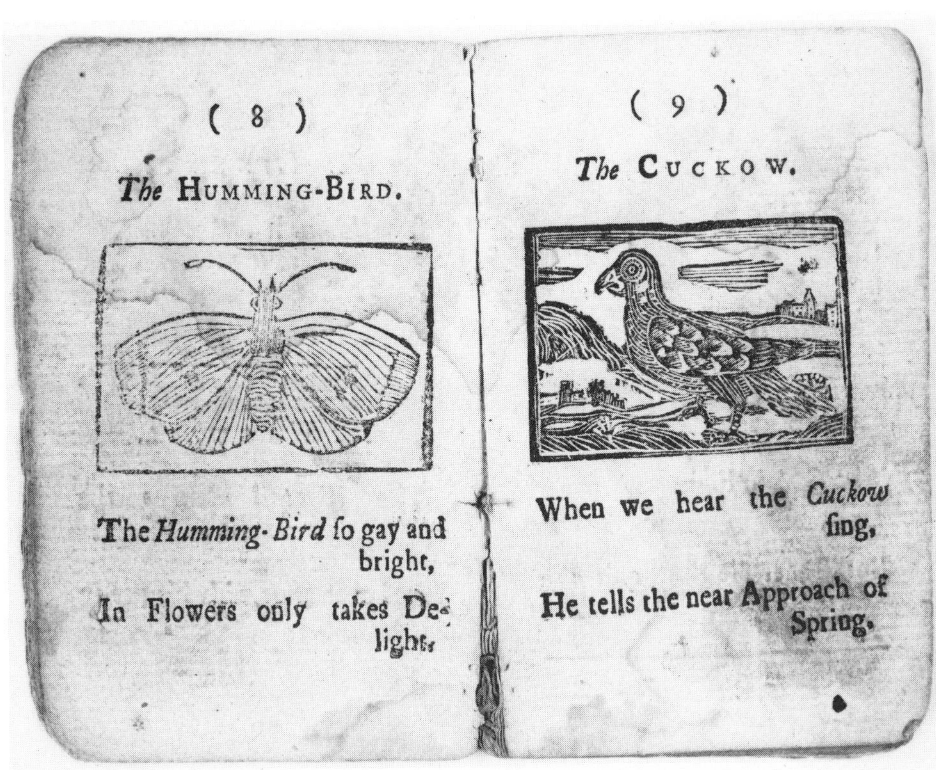

(8)

The HUMMING-BIRD.

The *Humming-Bird* ſo gay and bright,
In Flowers only takes Delight.

(9)

The CUCKOW.

When we hear the *Cuckow* ſing,
He tells the near Approach of Spring.

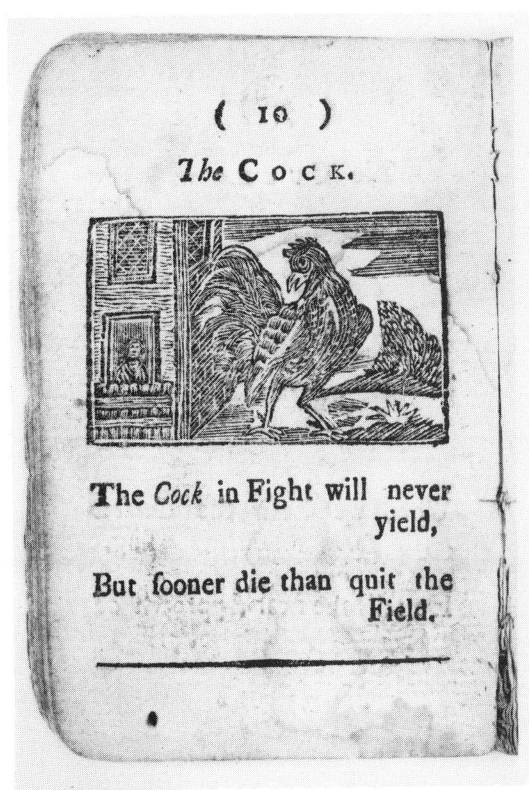

(10)

The COCK.

The *Cock* in Fight will never yield,
But ſooner die than quit the Field.

TALES
OF
PASSED TIMES
By MOTHER GOOSE.

WITH
MORALS.
WRITTEN
In *French* by M. PERRAULT, and
Englished by R. S. GENT.
To which is added a New one, viz.
The DISCREET PRINCESS.

The SEVENTH EDITION, Corrected, and
Adorned with fine Cuts.

NEW-YORK:
Printed for J. RIVINGTON, Bookseller
and Stationer, No. 56, Pearl-Street.
1795.

CONTES
DU
TEMS PASSE
DE MA MERE L'OYE

AVEC DES
MORALES.
Par M. PERRAULT.
Augmentée d'une NOUVELLE, *viz.*
L'ADROITE PRINCESSE.

SEPTIEME EDITION.
avec des jolies Estampes.

NEW-YORK
Imprimé pour J. RIVINGTON
Libraire.
1795.

CONTES DU TEMPS PASSÉ DE MA MÈRE L'OYE. Avec des Morales. Par M. Perrault [Charles Perrault (1628–1703)]. Augmentée d'une Nouvelle, viz L'Adroite Princesse. Septième Edition. avec des jolies Estampes. New-York: Imprimé pour J. Rivington Libraire. 1795. 227 pages. 16½ cm.

This book, which features texts in French and English on opposite pages, was published the year after the first American edition of Perrault (Haverhill, Massachusetts,

1794). The original English title page, missing from this bilingual volume, has been replaced by a copy reproduced from a volume in another collection. A few spreads are shown here, as well as the title page and one of the woodcut illustrations.

A note in a Pierpont Morgan Library exhibition catalog for this edition states that it was "copied from a seventh edition published at The Hague. . . . The woodcuts have been copied by Alexander Anderson from the originals."
(continued on next page)

LE PETIT 7

CHAPERON ROUGE.

CONTE I.

IL étoit une fois une petite fille de village, la plus jolie qu'on eut ſçu voir: ſa mere en étoit folle, & ſa grand-mere plus folle encore. Cette bonne femme lui fit faire un petit Chaperon Rouge, qui lui ſeyoit ſi bien, que par tout on l'appelloit le petit Chaperon Rouge.

Un jour ſa mere ayant fait des galettes, lui dit, va voir comment ſe porte ta grand-mere, car on m'a dit qu'elle étoit malade, porte lui une galete & ce petit pot de beure. Le petit Chaperon Rouge partit auſſi-tot pour aller chez ſa grand-mere, qui demeuroit dans un autre village. En paſſant dans un bois elle rencontra compère le Loup, qui eut bien envie de la manger, mais il n'oſa, à cauſe de quelques Bucherons qui étoient dans la Forêt.

Il lui demanda où elle alloit; la pauvre enfant qui ne ſçavoit pas qu'il eſt dangereux de s'arrêter à écouter un Loup, lui dit, je vais voir ma grand-mere, & lui porter une galette avec un petit pot de beure que ma mere lui envoye. Demeure-t-elle bien loin? lui dit le Loup. Oh oui, dit le petit Chaperon Rouge, c'eſt par de-la

8 *Little Red Riding-Hood.*

the Wolf. *Oh! ay,* anſwered Little Red Riding-Hood, *it is beyond that mill you ſee there, at the firſt houſe in the village. Well,* ſaid the Wolf, *and I'll go and ſee her too: I'll go this way, and you go that, and we ſhall ſee who will be there ſooneſt.*

The Wolf began to run as faſt as he could, taking the neareſt way; and the little girl went by that fartheſt about, diverting herſelf in gathering nuts, running after butterflies, and making noſegays of ſuch little flowers as ſhe met with. The Wolf was not long before he got to the old woman's houſe: he knocked at the door, *tap, tap. Who's there? Your grand-child,* Little Red Riding-Hood (replied the Wolf, counterfeiting her voice) *who has brought you a cuſtard, and a little pot of butter, ſent you by mamma.*

The good grand mother, who was in bed, becauſe ſhe found herſelf ſomewhat ill, cry'd out, *Pull the bobbin, and the latch will go up.* Whe Wolf pull'd the bobbin, and the door opened, and then preſently he fell upon the good woman, and eat her up in a moment; for it was above three days that he had not touched a bit. He then ſhut the door, and went into the grand mother's bed, expecting *Little Red Riding-Hood,* who came ſome time afterwards, and knock'd at the door, *tap, tap, Who's there? Little Red Riding-Hood,* hearing the big voice of the Wolf, was at firſt afraid; but believing her grand-mother had got

CONTES DU TEMPS PASSÉ DE MA MÈRE L'OYE *(continued from page 119)*

got a cold, and was hoarſe: anſwered, *'Tis your grand-child.* Little Red Riding-Hood, *who has brought you a cuſtard, and a little pot of butter, mamma ſends you.* The Wolf cried out to her, ſoftening his voice as much as he could, *Pull the bobbin, and the latch will go up.* Little Red Riding-Hood pulled the bobbin, and the door opened.

The Wolf ſeeing her come in, ſaid to her, hiding himſelf under the bedclothes; *Put the cuſtard, and the little pot of butter upon the ſtool, and come and lye down with me. Little Red Riding-Hood* undreſſed herſelf, and went into bed; where, being greatly amazed to ſee how her grand-mother looked in her night-cloaths, ſaid to her, *Grand-mamma, what great arms you have got? That is the better to hug thee, my dear. Grand-mamma, what great legs you have got! That is to run the better, my child. Grand-mamma, what great ears you have got! That is to hear the better, my child. Grand-mamma what great eyes you have got! It is to ſee the better, my child. Grand-mamma, what great teeth you have got! That is to eat thee up.* And, ſaying theſe words, this wicked Wolf fell upon poor *Little Red Riding-Hood*, and eat her all up.

The MORAL.

From this ſhort ſtory eaſy we diſcern
What conduct all young people ought to learn.
But above all, young, growing miſſes fair,
Whoſe orient roſy blooms begin t'appear:

Who,

fille le petit Chaperon Rouge, qui vous apporte une galette & un petit pot de beure que ma mere vous envoye. Le Loup lui cria, en adouciſſant un peu ſa voix; tire la chevillete, la bobinette cherra. Le petit Chaperon Rouge tira la chevillette, & la porte s'ouvrit.

Le Loup la voyant entrer, lui dit, en ſe cachant dans le lit ſous la couverture; mettez la galette & le petit pot de beure ſur la huche, & viens te coucher avec moi. Le petit Chaperon Rouge ſe deſhabille, & va ſe mettre dans le lit, où elle fut bien étonnée de voir comment ſa grand-mere étoit faite en ſon deſhabille, elle lui dit: ma grand-mere que vous avez de grands bras! C'eſt pour mieux t'embraſſer, ma fille: ma grand-mere que vous avez de grandes jambes! C'eſt pour mieux courir, mon enfant: ma grand-mere que vous avez de grandes oreilles! C'eſt pour mieux écouter, mon enfant: ma grand-mere que vous avez de grands yeux! C'eſt pour mieux voir, mon enfant. Ma grand-mere que vous vez de grandes dents: C'eſt pour te manger. Et en diſant ces mots, ce méchant Loup ſe jetta ur le petit Chaperon Rouge, & la mangea.

MORALITÉ.

n voit ici que des jeunes enfants,
ur tout de jeunes filles,
elles, bien-faites, & gentilles,
nt très-mal d'écouter toutes ſortes de gens,

Et

(continued on next page)

12 *Little Red Ridding-Hood.*

Who, beauties in the fragrant ſpring of age,
With pretty airs young hearts are apt t'engage.
Ill do they liſten to all ſorts of tongues,
Since ſome inchant and lure like Syrens *ſongs.*
No wonder therefore 'tis, if over-power'd,
So many of them has the Wolf *devour'd.*
The Wolf, *I ſay, for* Wolves *too ſure there are*
Of every ſort, and every character.
Some of them mild and gentle-humour'd be,
Of noiſe and gall, and rancour wholly free;
Who tame, familiar, full of complaiſance
Ogle and leer, languiſh, cajole and glance;
With luring tongues, and language wond'rous ſweet,
Follow young ladies as they walk the ſtreet,
Ev'n to their very houſes, nay, beſide,
And, artful, tho' their true deſigns they hide:
Yet ah! theſe ſimpering Wolves *who does not ſee*
Moſt dang'rous of all Wolves *in fact to be?*

Le petit Chaperon Rouge. 13

Et que ce n'eſt pas choſe étrange,
S'il en eſt tant que le Loup mange;
Je dis le Loup, car tous les Loups
Ne ſont pas de la même ſorte;
Il en eſt d'une heumeur accorte,
Sans bruit, ſans fiel & ſans couroux,
Qui privez, complaiſans & doux
Suivent les jeunes Demoiſelles,
Juſques dans les maiſons, juſques dans les ruelles,
Mais helas! qui ne ſait que ces Loups doucereux,
De tous les Loups ſont les plus dangereux.

B Les

CONTES DU TEMPS PASSÉ DE MA MÈRE L'OYE *(continued from page 121)*

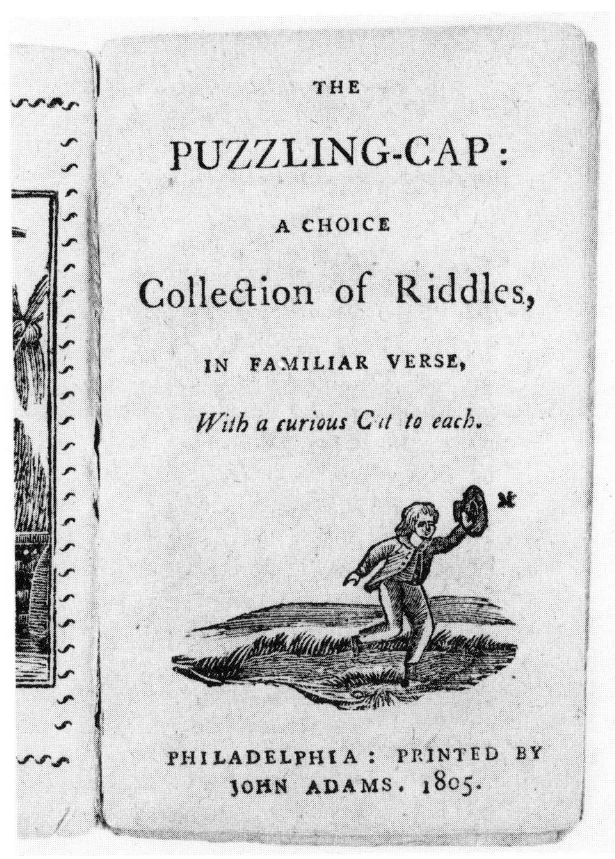

THE

PUZZLING-CAP:

A CHOICE

Collection of Riddles,

IN FAMILIAR VERSE,

With a curious Cut to each.

PHILADELPHIA: PRINTED BY
JOHN ADAMS. 1805.

THE PUZZLING-CAP: A Choice Collection of Riddles, in Familiar Verse With a curious Cut to each. Philadelphia: Printed by John Adams, 1805. 31 pages. 10½ cm.

The last of the fourteen riddles reads as follows:

There was a man bespoke a thing,
Which when the maker home did bring,
This same maker did refuse it;
He who bespoke it did not use it;
And he who had it did not know,
Whether he had it, yea or no.

ANSWER: *a coffin*

(continued on next page)

20 The Puzzling-Cap.

A PAIR OF SPECTACLES

The Puzzling-Cap. 21

RIDDLE IX.

WITHOUT a bridle or a
ſaddle,
Acroſs a ridge I ride and ſtrad-
dle;
And ev'ry one, by help of me,
Tho' almoſt blind, are made to
ſee.
Then tell me every pretty dame,
And witty maſter, what's my
name?

24 The Puzzling-Cap

AN OAK.

The Puzzling-Cap. 25

RIDDLE XI.

AN hundred years I once
did live;
And often wholeſom food did
give;
Yet all that time I ne'er did
roam
So much as half a mile from
home.
My days were ſpent devoid of
ſtrife,
Until at laſt I loſt my life:
And ſince my death, 'tis ſtrange
to hear,
I oft have travell'd far and near.

THE PUZZLING-CAP *(continued from page 123)*

TOM THE PIPER'S SON. Philadelphia: Published and sold wholesale by William Charles, and may be had of all the booksellers, 1808–1810. In two parts. 8 pages. 13 cm.

The Library of Congress possesses both parts, although d'Alté Welch mentions only the ownership of the first. Part One is reproduced here. Part Two consists of a political satire about Tom's being sent to France to make "Master Boney" (Napoleon) dance.
(continued on next page)

TOM THE PIPER

TOM he was a PIPERS SON
He learn'd to play when he was young,
All the tunes that he could play
Was over the hills and far away.

TOM with his pipe made
Such a noise,
He pleased both the girls and Boys
They'd dance and sing while
He did play
Over the hills and far away.

Now TOM after this learned
to play with such skill
That whoever heard him could
never keep still
As soon as he play'd they began
for to dance,
Even PIGS on their hind legs
would after him prance.

As DOLLY was milking her cow
one day,
TOM took out his pipe and began
for to play;
And DOLL and her cow danc'd the
cheshire round,
Till the pail was knock'd down
And the milk on the ground.

The GOAT was a going to shave
off his beard,
But soon he was done when TOMS
music he heard,
He ran out of doors in a kind
of a passion,
And danced this fine dance
Which is now all the fashion.

He met old DAME TROT with
a basket of eggs,
He used his pipe and she used
her legs,
She danced about till her eggs,
were all broke,
Then he left her to fret while
he laugh'd at the joke.

TOM THE PIPER'S SON *(continued from page 125)*

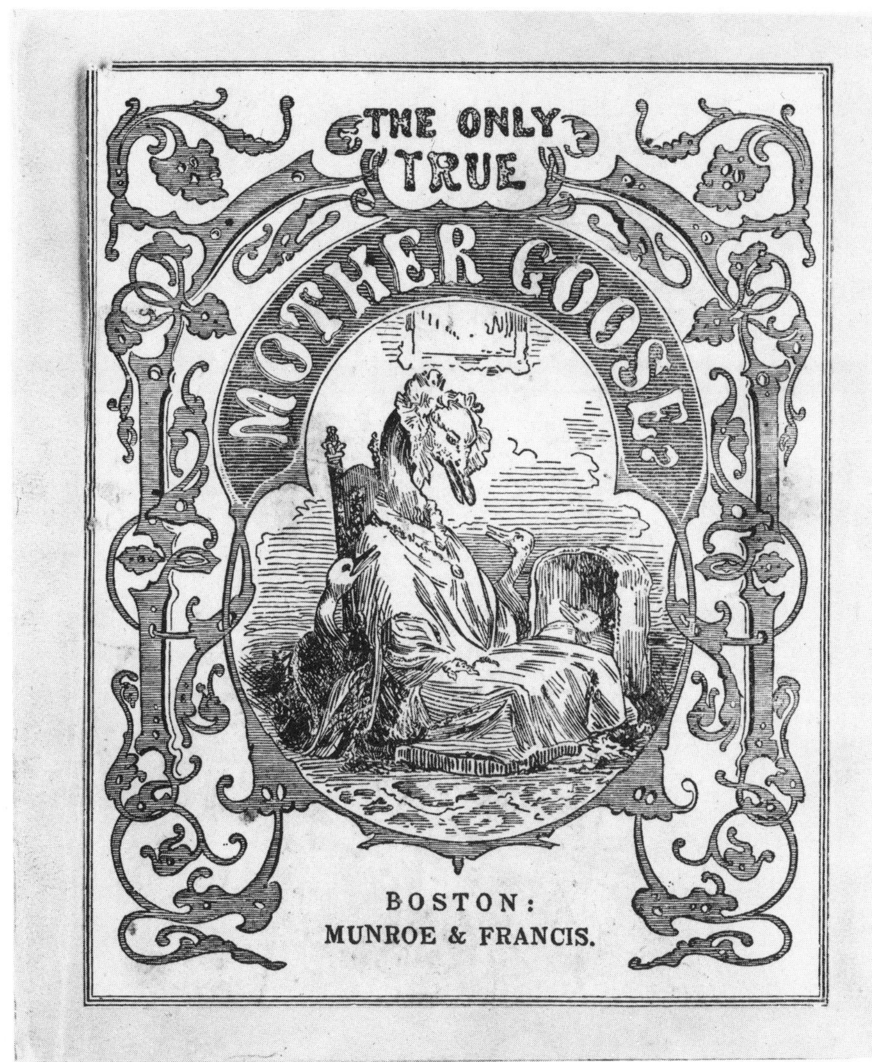

THE ONLY TRUE MOTHER GOOSE MELODIES, without addition or abridgment. Embracing, also, a reliable Life of the Goose Family, never before published. Numerous illustrations. Entered according to Act of Congress, in the year 1833, by Munroe & Francis, in the Clerk's Office of the District Court of Massachusetts. Boston: J. S. Locke & Company [c. 1833]. 95 pages. 14 cm.

An account of the legendary Boston origin for the Mother Goose rhymes is to be found here in the life of printer Thomas Fleet's mother-in-law, Dame Goose (or Mistress Vergoose), whose verses he was credited with publishing in 1719. Since no copy of such work has ever been found, the legend is only that. It is reproduced here, for its interest.
(continued on next page)

THE ONLY TRUE

MOTHER GOOSE

MELODIES,

WITHOUT ADDITION OR ABRIDGEMENT.

EMBRACING, ALSO, A RELIABLE

LIFE OF THE GOOSE FAMILY,

NEVER BEFORE PUBLISHED.

NUMEROUS ILLUSTRATIONS.

Entered according to Act of Congress, in the year 1833, by MUNROE & FRANCIS, in the Clerk's Office of the District Court of Massachusetts.

BOSTON:
J. S. LOCKE & COMPANY,

(continued from page 127)

The first appearance of *Mother Goose's Melodies* is believed to be Isaiah Thomas's *Mother Goose's Melody: Or Sonnets for the Cradle* (1786), of which only an incomplete copy remains. His second edition of 1794 is an almost verbatim reprinting—but with a change of location from London to Boston in the rhyme:

See saw, sacaradown,
Which is the way to Boston Town?
One Foot up the other Foot down,
That is the way to Boston Town.

HEAR WHAT MA'AM GOOSE SAYS!

My dear little Blossoms, there are now in this world, and always will be, a great many grannies besides myself, both in petticoats and pantaloons, some a deal younger to be sure; but all monstrous wise, and of my own family name. These old women, who never had chick nor child of their own, but who always know how to bring up other people's children, will tell you with very long faces, that my enchanting, quieting, soothing volume, my all-sufficient anodyne for cross, peevish, won't-be-comforted little bairns, ought to be laid aside for more learned books, such as *they* could select and publish. Fudge! I tell you that all their batterings can't deface my beauties, nor their wise pratings equal my wiser prattlings; and all imitators of my refreshing songs might as well write a new Billy Shakespeare as another Mother Goose: we two great poets were born together, and we shall go out of the world together.

No, no, my Melodies will never die,
While nurses sing, or babies cry.

HISTORY OF THE GOOSE FAMILY.

[*From the Boston Transcript.*]

COTTON MATHER AND MOTHER GOOSE.

Mr. Editor:—Your correspondent, N. B. S., has so decisively given a *quietus* to the question as to the birth place of Cotton Mather, that there is no danger of its ever being revived again. But there is another question of equal importance to many, to the literary world in particular, which should in like manner be put to rest. *Who was Mother Goose?* and *when* were her melodies first given to the world? These are questions which have been often asked, but have never been satisfactorily answered. The recent publication of a book called "Mother Goose for Old Folks" has again

revived these questions, which serves to show that the subject has not yet lost its interest.

Many persons imagine that Mother Goose is a myth,—that no such person ever existed. This is a mistake. *Mother Goose* was not only a veritable personage, but was born and resided many years in Boston, where many of her descendants may now be found. The last that bore the ancient paternal cognomen died about the year 1807, and was buried in the Old Granary Burying Ground, where probably lie the remains of the whole blood, if we may judge from the numerous grave-stones which mark their resting place. The family originated in England, but at what time they came to this country is unknown,—but probably about the year 1656. This was the "*Wealthy family of Goose,*" which is immortalized by Mr. Bowditch in his book of Suffolk Names, who at the same time has immortalized

himself. They were land holders in Boston so early as 1660. Nearly half the space between West and Winter streets, on Washington street, and extending westerly towards Tremont street, 275 feet, belonged to this family, as did also a large tract of land on Essex, Rowe and Bedford streets, upon which now stand two churches and a large number of dwelling houses. *So much for Mother Goose.* Now for her melodies.

It is well known to antiquarians that more than *two* hundred years ago there was a small book in circulation in London bearing the name of "Rhymes for the Nursery; or Lulla-Byes for Children," which contained *many of the identical pieces* which have been handed down to us and now form part of the "Mother Goose's Melodies" of the present day. It contained also other pieces much more silly, if possible, and some that the *American* types of

(*continued on next page*)

the present day would refuse to give off an impression. The "cuts" or illustration thereof were of the coarsest description,

The first book of the kind known to be printed in this country bears the title of "*Songs for the Nursery; or, Mother Goose's Melodies* for Children." Something probably intended to represent a goose with a very long neck and mouth wide open, covered a large part of the title page, at the bottom of which, Printed by T. Fleet, at his printing house, Pudding lane, 1719. Price, two coppers. Several pages were missing, so that the whole number could not be ascertained.

This T. Fleet, according to Isaiah Thomas, was a man of considerable talent and of great wit and humor. He was born in England, and was brought up in a printing office in the city of Bristol, where he afterwards worked as a journeyman. Although he was considered a

6

man of sense, he was never thought to be overburdened with religious sentiments; he certainly was not in his latter days. Yet he was *more* than suspected of being actively engaged in the riotous proceedings connected with the trial of Dr. Sacheverell, in Queen Ann's time. In London, Bristol, and many other places, the mobs and riots were of a very serious nature. In London several meeting houses were sacked and pulled down, and the materials and contents made into bonfires, and much valuable property destroyed. Several of the rioters were arrested, tried and convicted. The trials of some of them are now before me. How deeply Fleet was implicated in these disturbances was never known, but being of the same mind with Jack Falstaff, that "the better part of valor is discretion," thought it prudent to put the Ocean between himself and danger. He made his way to this country and arrived

7

in Boston, 1712. Being a man of some enterprise, he soon established a printing office in Pudding lane (now Devonshire street), where he printed small books, pamphlets, ballads, and such matter as offered. Being industrious and prudent, he gradually accumulated property. It was not long before he became acquainted with the "wealthy family of Goose," a branch of which he had before known in Bristol, and was shortly married to the eldest daughter.

By therecord of marriages in the City Registrar's office, it appears that in "1715, June 8, was married by Rev. *Cotton Mather*, *Thomas Fleet* to *Elizabeth Goose*." The happy couple took up their residence in the same house with the printing office in Pudding lane. In due time, their family was increased by the birth of a son and heir. Mother Goose, like all good grandmothers, was in ecstacies at the event; her joy was unbounded; she spent her

8

whole time in the nursery, and in wandering about the house, pouring forth, in not the most melodious strains, the songs and ditties which she had learned in her younger days, greatly to the annoyance of the whole neighborhood—to Fleet in particular, who was a man fond of quiet. It was in vain he exhausted his shafts of wit and ridicule, and every expedient he could devise: it was of no use—the old lady was not thus to be put down; so, like others similarly situated, he was obliged to submit. His shrewdness, however, did not forsake him; from this seeming evil he contrived to educe some good; he conceived the the idea of collecting the songs and ditties as they came from his mother, and such as he could gather from other sources, and publishing them for the benefit of the world—not forgetting himself. This he did—and thus "*Mother Goose's Melodies*" were brought forth.

9

 (continued from page 129)

The adoption of this title was in derision of his good mother-in-law, and was perfectly characteristic of the man, as he was never known to spare his nearest friends in his raillery, or when he could excite laughter at their expense.

Cotton Mather and Mother Goose thus stand in juxtaposition ;—and as the former was instrumental in cementing the union, which resulted in placing the latter so conspicuously before the world, it is but just that it should be so,—although the one was a learned man, a most voluminous writer, and published a great many books, some wise and some foolish, it may well be doubted whether any one, or all of them, together, have passed through so many editions,—been read by so many hundreds of thousands, not to say millions,—put so many persons to sleep, or in general done so much good to the world as the simple melodies of the other. REQUIESCAT.

10

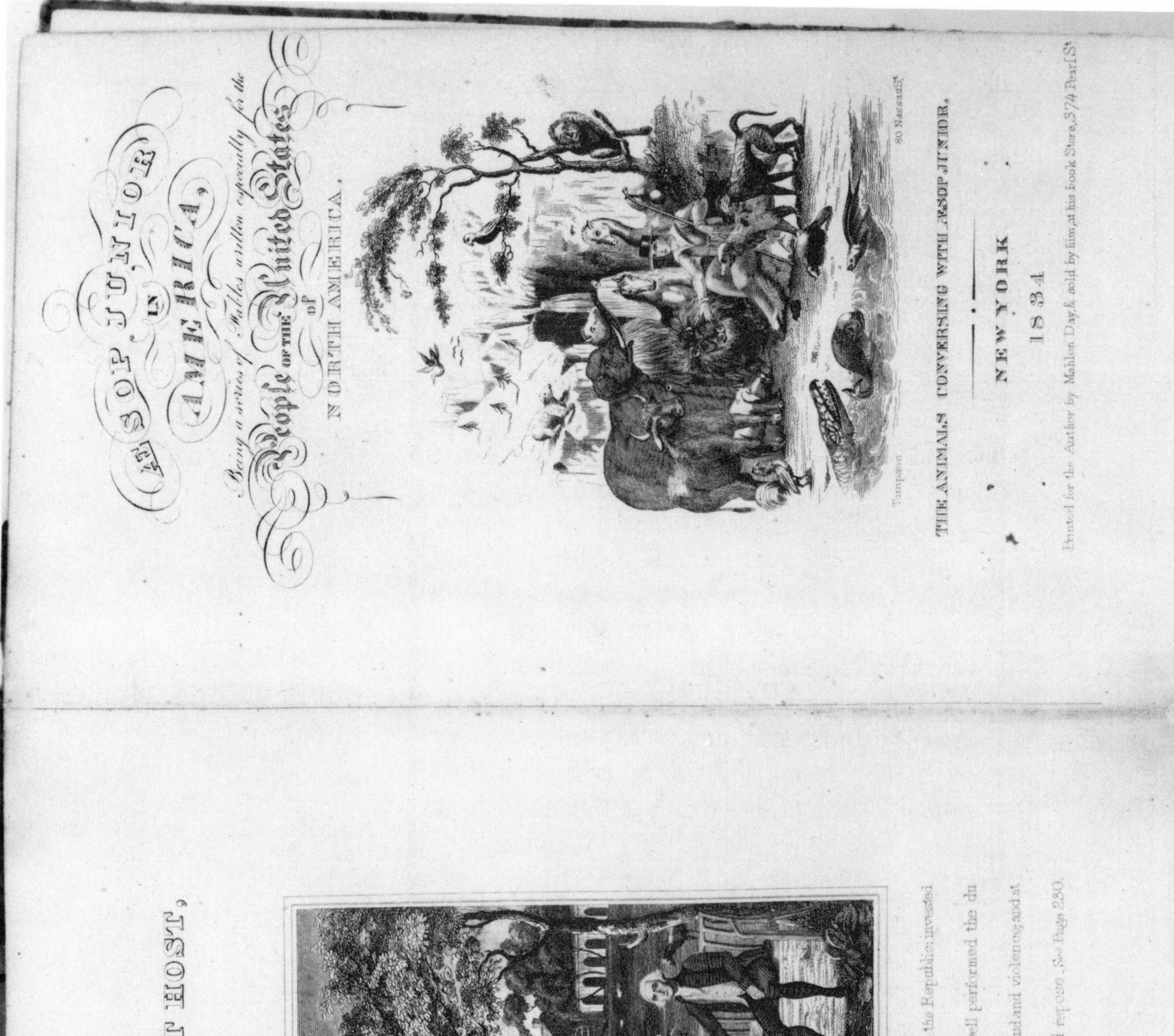
CHIEF of the PATRIOT HOST,
An example to the citizens; an ornament to the Republic; invested
with the highest executive magistracy, he well performed the du
ty of protecting industry and restraining fraud and violence; and at
length he enjoyed, for a short time a dignified repose. See Page 230.
ÆSOP JUNIOR
IN
AMERICA,
Being a series of Fables written especially for the
People of the United States
of
NORTH AMERICA,
Tompson
80 Nassau St
THE ANIMALS CONVERSING WITH ÆSOP JUNIOR,
NEW YORK
1834
Printed for the Author by Mahlon Day, & sold by him at his book Store, 374 Pearl St

84 JACK THE GIANT KILLER.

Each standing on the other's head,
Had scarce o'er topped the monster dread;
The brim of his hat, so consider*able*,
Was half as big round as the king's Round Table;
His massive club was a maple's trunk:—
He might have made great Arthur "funk."
Arthur the First, or Arthur the Second,
As ARTHUR of WELLINGTON may be reckoned
Slockdollagos was rather less,
But he wasn't very short, I guess:—
He was fashionably drest,
In the style of a wizard of the west.

XXIV.

"Clear off, now," was the giant's cry;
"The oldest man in all Kentucky
My father whopp'd—my father, I:—
Absquotilate, and cut your lucky!"
Catawampus looked on every side,
But not a single soul espied;
To the right and left he grimly grinned,
Till the trunks of the very trees were skinned.
"Come out!" he bawled, "or I swear I'll dash
Your brains into an immortal smash!
Don't raise my dander; if you do,
You won't much like me,—*I* tell you.

Jack slays the Yankee Giant, Catawampus.

ON OPPOSITE PAGE:

AESOP JUNIOR IN AMERICA, Being a series of Fables written especially for the People of the United States of North America. The Animals Conversing with Aesop Junior. New York: Mahlon Day, 374 Pearl St., 1834. 234 pages. 19 cm.

Appropriate, often lengthy, morals accompany these fifty-one fables in the vein of Aesop. In an excessively long appendix to the last fable, "The Horse Resolved to Be Free," the anonymous author exhorts his countrymen thus:

Let me add, republicans must find
In manners simple, and in speech sincere,
In meet endeavors to improve their minds,
And cultivate their moral qualities. . . .

JACK THE GIANT KILLER [by Frederic William Naylor Bayley (1808–1853)]. With illustration by Leech. New York, Burgess, Stringer, & Co., 1845. 96 pages. 19 cm.

This is the first of four tales issued in a cloth-bound volume lettered "Comic Nursery Tales." The four elaborated retellings in verse consist of "Jack the Giant Killer" and "Little Red Riding Hood," each illustrated by Leech, and "Blue Beard"—all three told by Bayley; also "Beauty and the Beast" by Albert Smith, "with illustrations, humorous and numerous" by Alfred Crowquill, *pseud.*

The lines beat out a regular rhythm:

I sing the deeds of famous Jack,
The doughty Giant Killer hight;
How he did various monsters 'whack'
And so became a gallant knight.

The giants are named extravagantly: Slockdollagus and Catawampus being two of Jack's oversized but doomed adversaries.

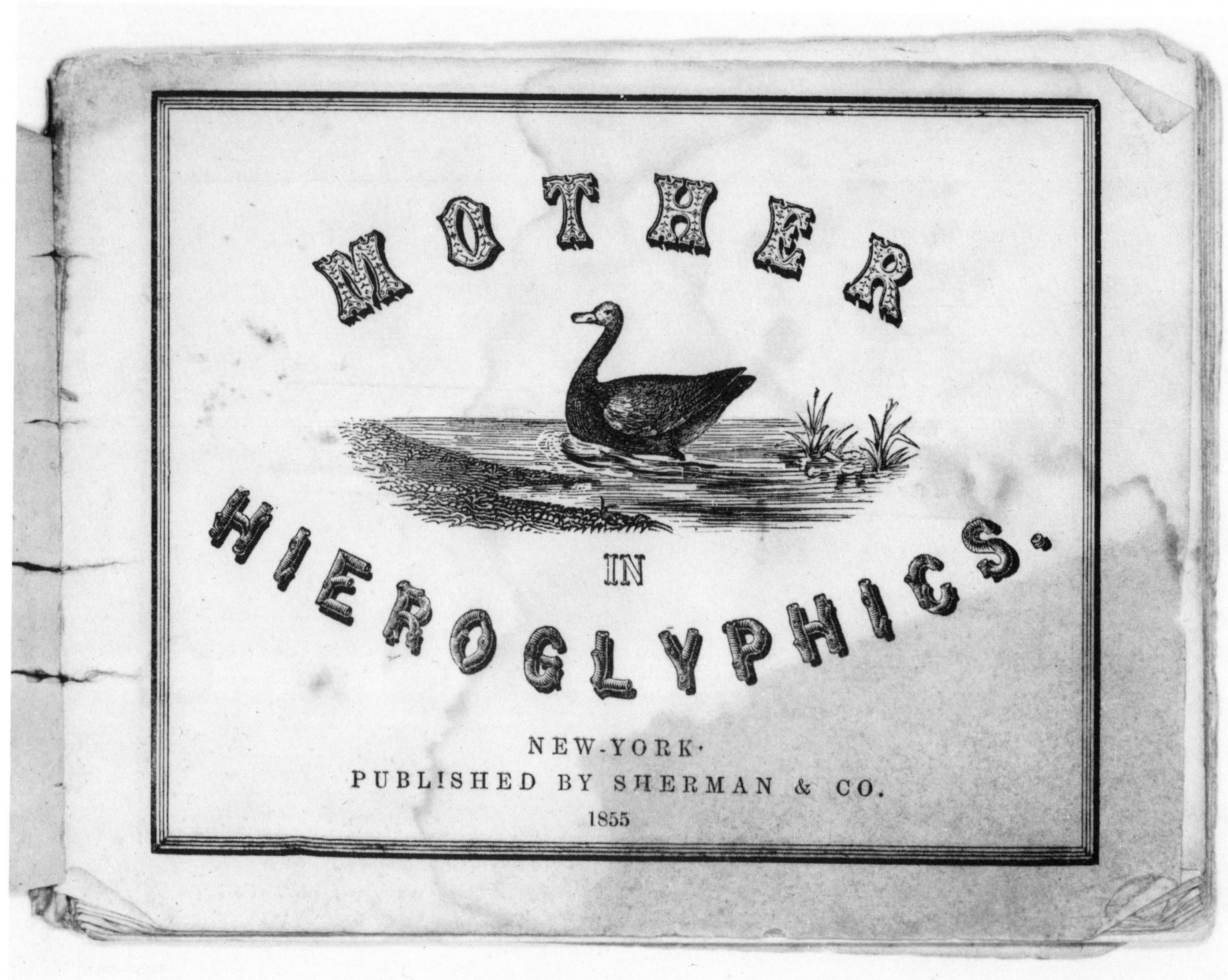

MOTHER [*Goose*] IN HIEROGLYPHICS. New York: Published by Sherman & Co., 1855. 32 pages. 13 cm.

Designed to entertain the young, this rebus is described as "a pretty book, written with pictures, as they wrote in Egypt a long while ago, when folks knew something—about the time when Mother Goose herself was a little gosling."

It is often said that folks now-a-days are a deal wiser than their fathers and grandfathers; but I don't think so; for who has ever written books like Mother Goose, Mother Hubbard, and Mother What's-her-name, that lived a great while ago? and books for children, too, little dears. How many of them owe their lives to the influence of their soothing songs and lullabys! The world would not have been half peopled, had not these old sages once lived and written their invaluable little books for children.

When the doctor sends for physic for a nervous little chick, make a mistake, and go to the bookseller's and buy Mother Goose in Hiero-

(continued on next page)

4 INTRODUCTION.

glyphics; that's what is wanted — a pretty book, written with pictures, as they wrote in Egypt a long while ago, when folks knew something, — about the time when Mother Goose herself was a little gosling.

Yes, buy one of these little books, and when it is torn up, buy another, and another, till the wee ones are old enough to read Robinson Crusoe, and the like. My word for it, there is nothing like books with pictures, to keep children quiet; and this is the best that was ever written, as everybody knows

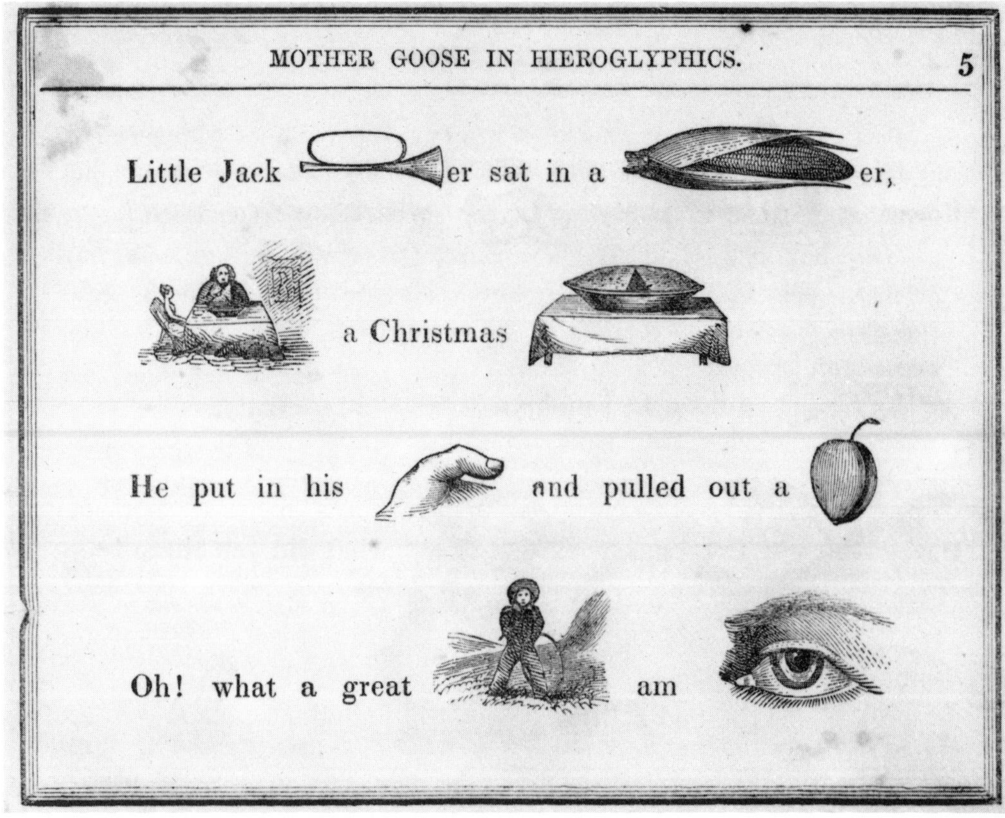

MOTHER GOOSE IN HIEROGLYPHICS. 5

Little Jack er sat in a er,

a Christmas

He put in his and pulled out a

Oh! what a great am

(continued from page 135)

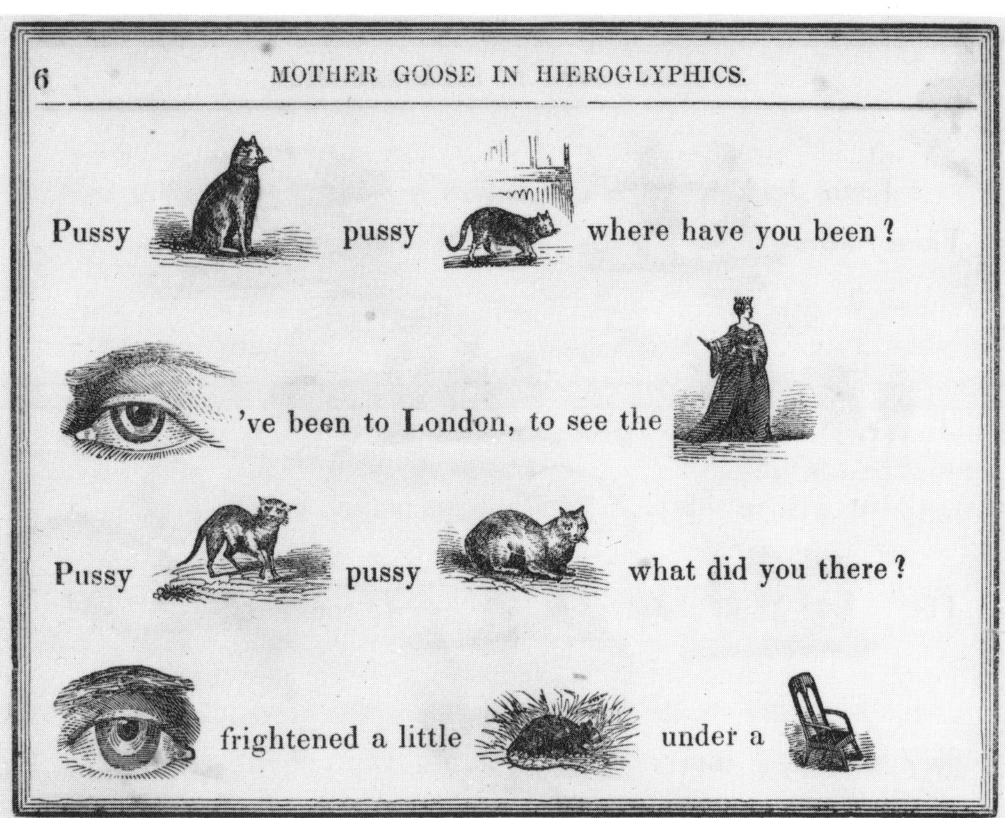

6 MOTHER GOOSE IN HIEROGLYPHICS.

Pussy pussy where have you been?

've been to London, to see the

Pussy pussy what did you there?

frightened a little under a

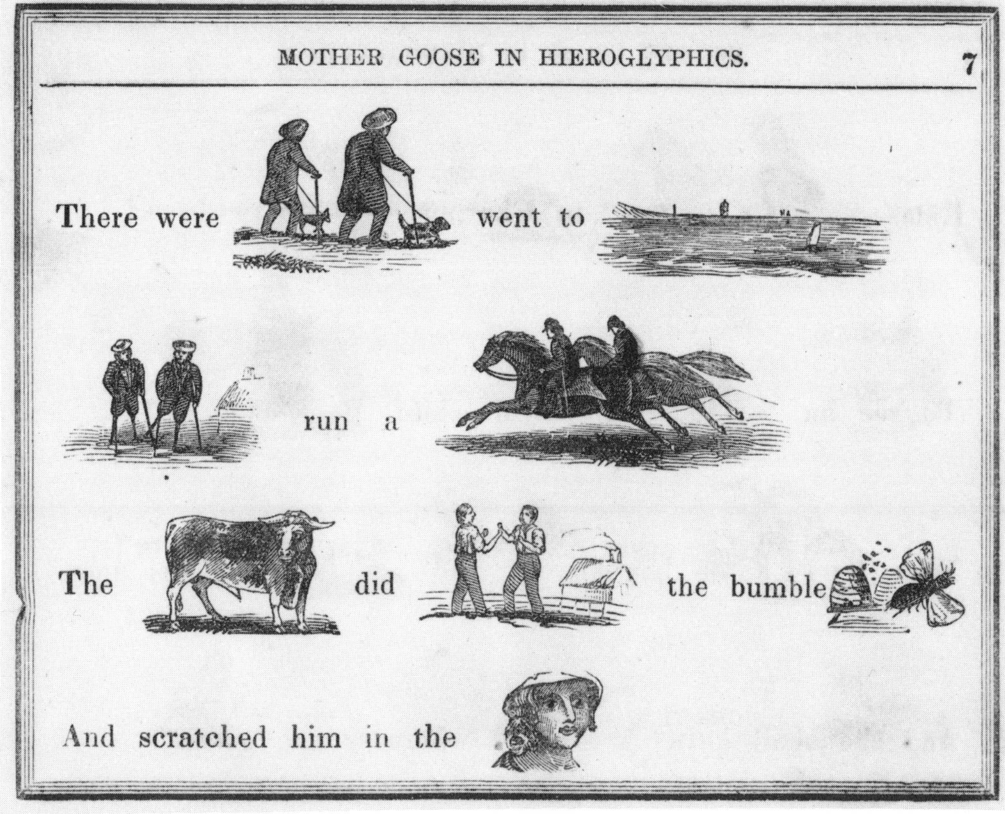

MOTHER GOOSE IN HIEROGLYPHICS. 7

There were went to

run a

The did the bumble

And scratched him in the

(continued on next page)

8 MOTHER GOOSE IN HIEROGLYPHICS.

Ride a to Charing

To see an jump on a white

With on her fingers, and on her toes,

And she shall have wherever she goes.

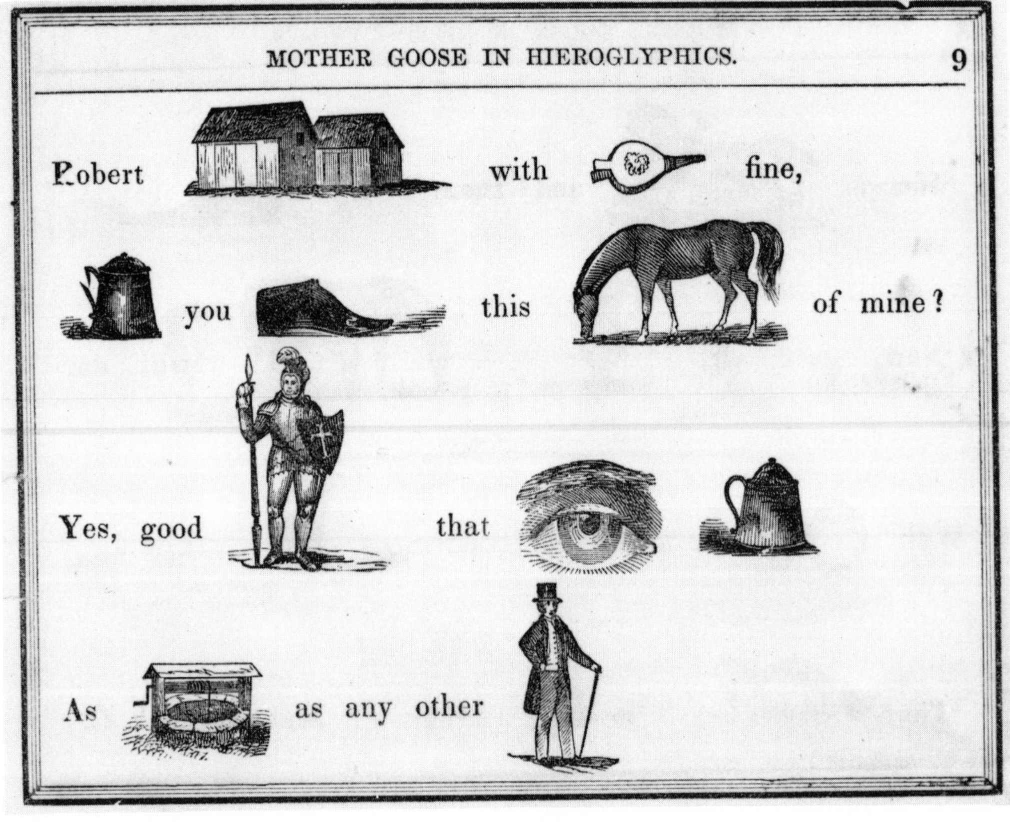

MOTHER GOOSE IN HIEROGLYPHICS. 9

Robert with fine,

you this of mine?

Yes, good that

As as any other

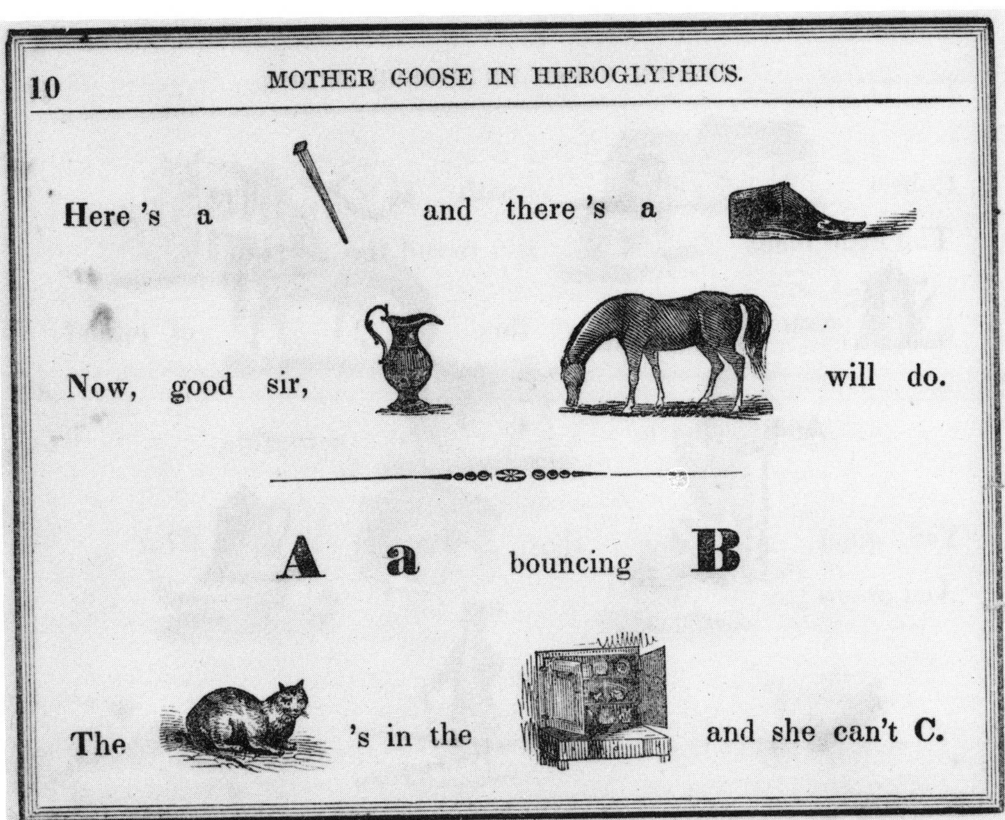
10 MOTHER GOOSE IN HIEROGLYPHICS.

Here 's a and there 's a

Now, good sir, will do.

A a bouncing B

The 's in the and she can't C.

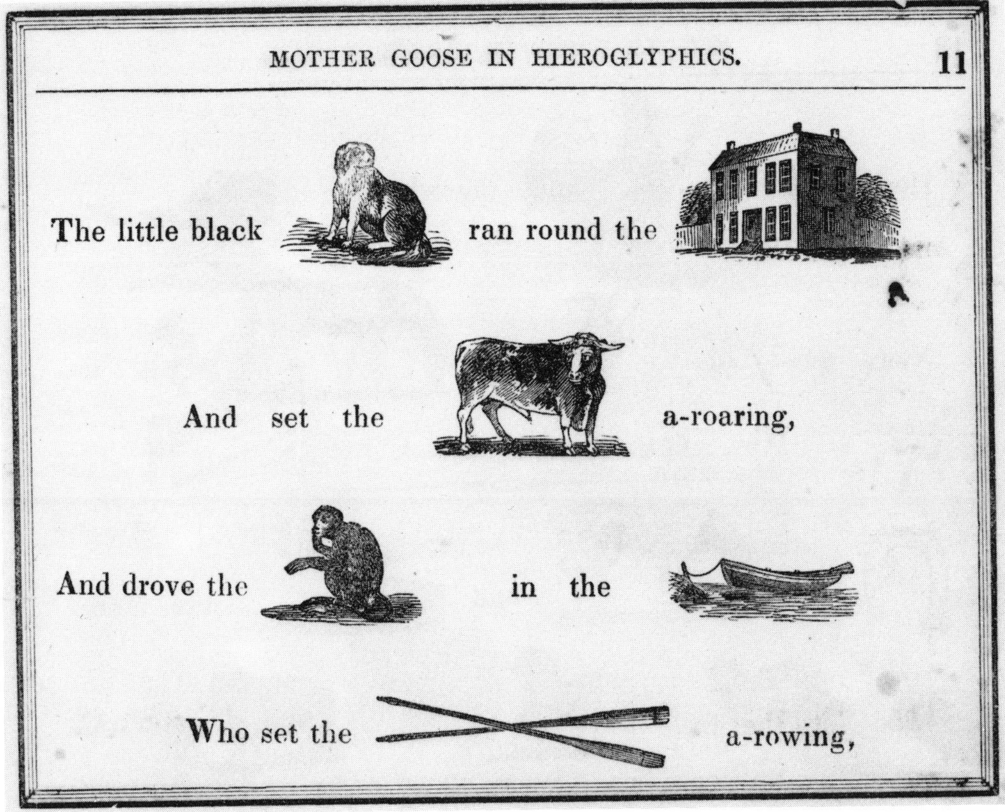
MOTHER GOOSE IN HIEROGLYPHICS. 11

The little black ran round the

And set the a-roaring,

And drove the in the

Who set the a-rowing,

(continued on next page)

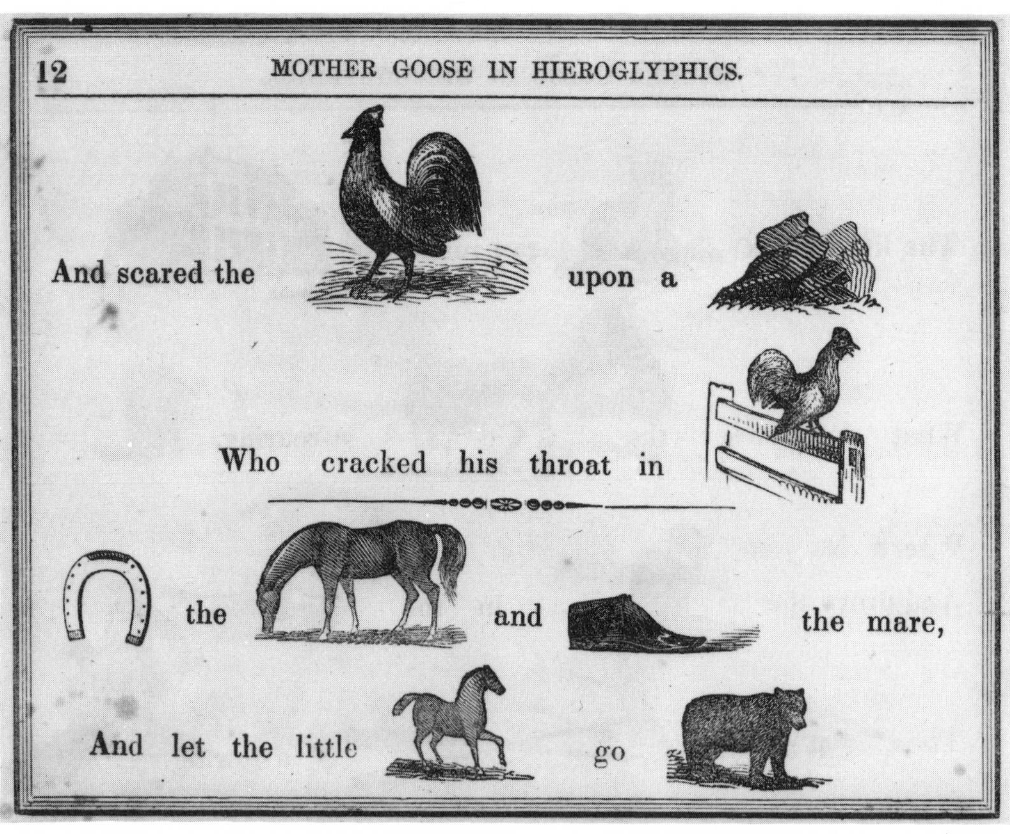
12 MOTHER GOOSE IN HIEROGLYPHICS.

And scared the upon a

Who cracked his throat in

the and the mare,

And let the little go

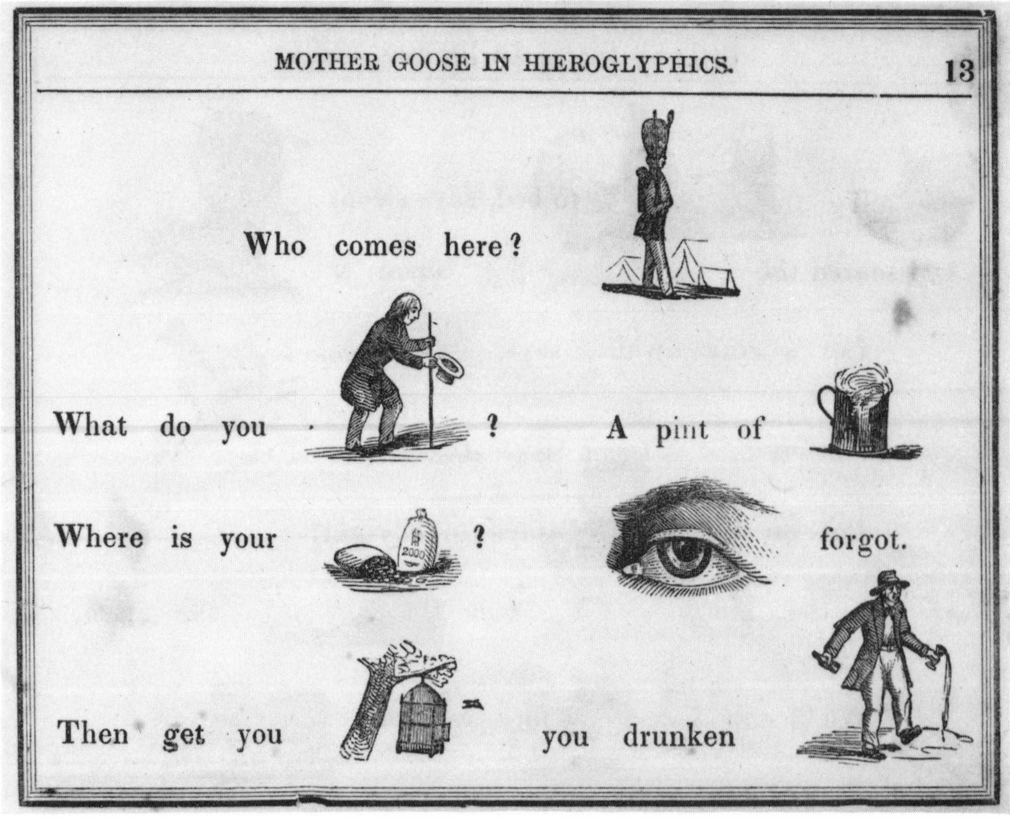
MOTHER GOOSE IN HIEROGLYPHICS. 13

Who comes here?

What do you ? A pint of

Where is your ? forgot.

Then get you you drunken

14 MOTHER GOOSE IN HIEROGLYPHICS.

To [picture] to bed, says sleepy [picture]

Let 's stay awhile, says [picture]

Put on the [picture] says greedy-gut,

We 'll sup [picture] fore we go.

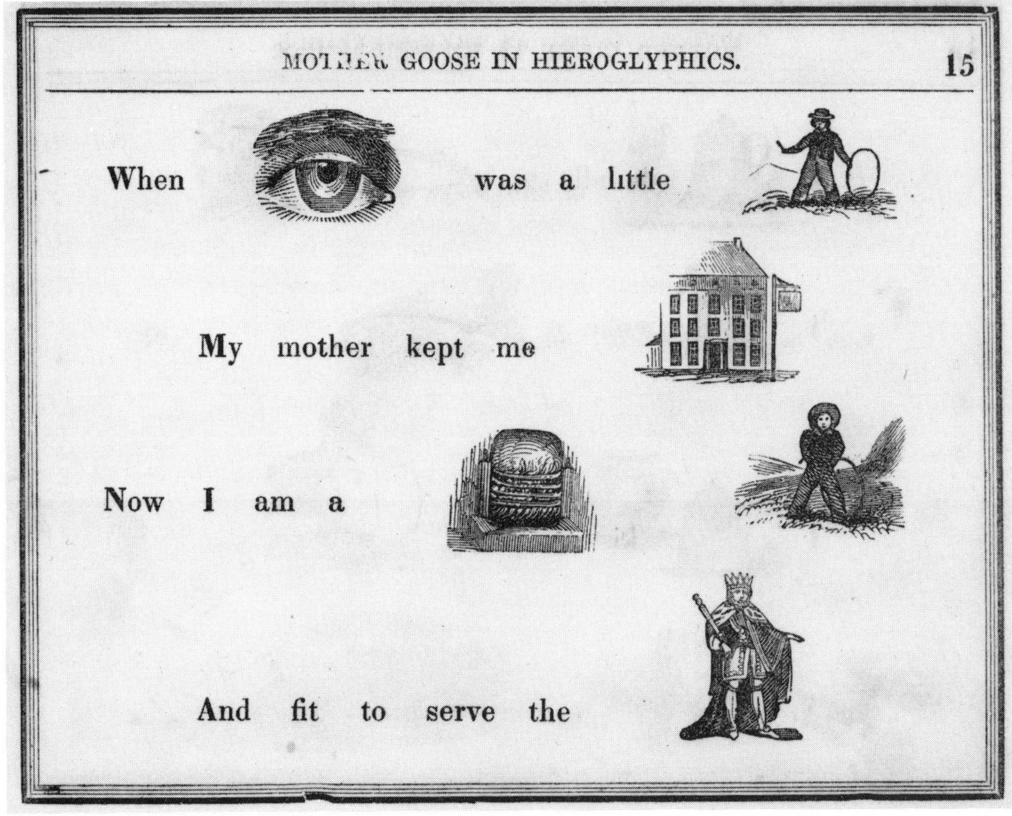
MOTHER GOOSE IN HIEROGLYPHICS. 15

When [picture] was a little [picture]

My mother kept me [picture]

Now I am a [picture] [picture]

And fit to serve the [picture]

(continued on next page)

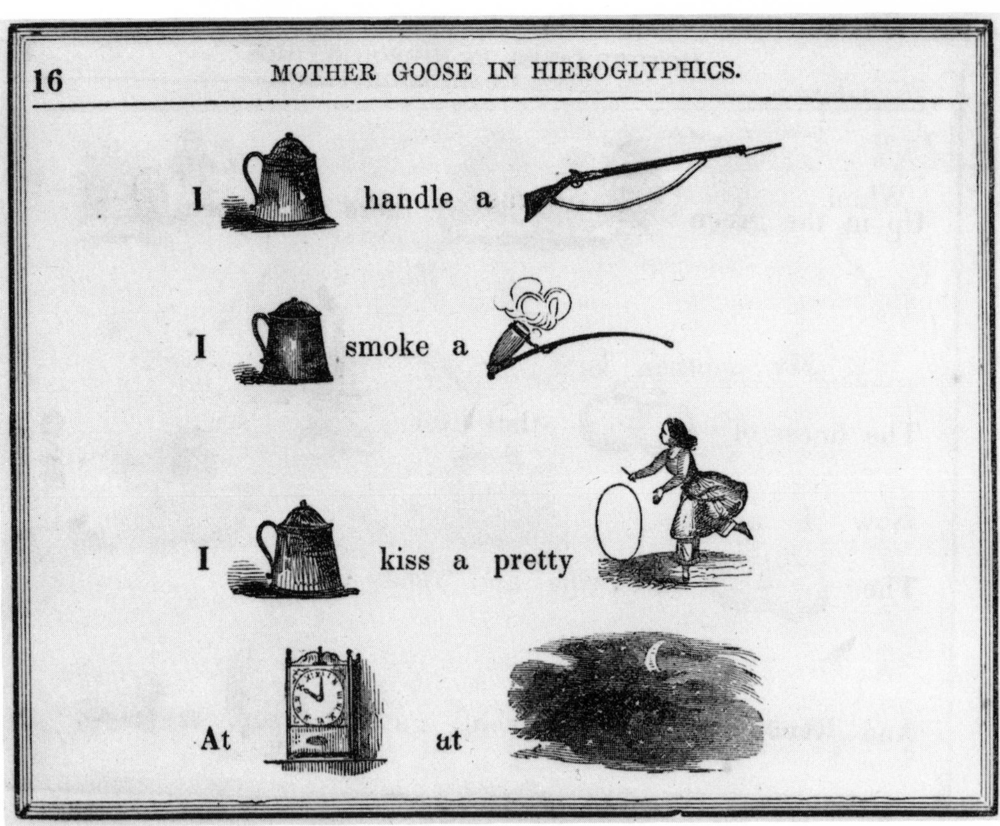

16 MOTHER GOOSE IN HIEROGLYPHICS.

I handle a

I smoke a

I kiss a pretty

At at

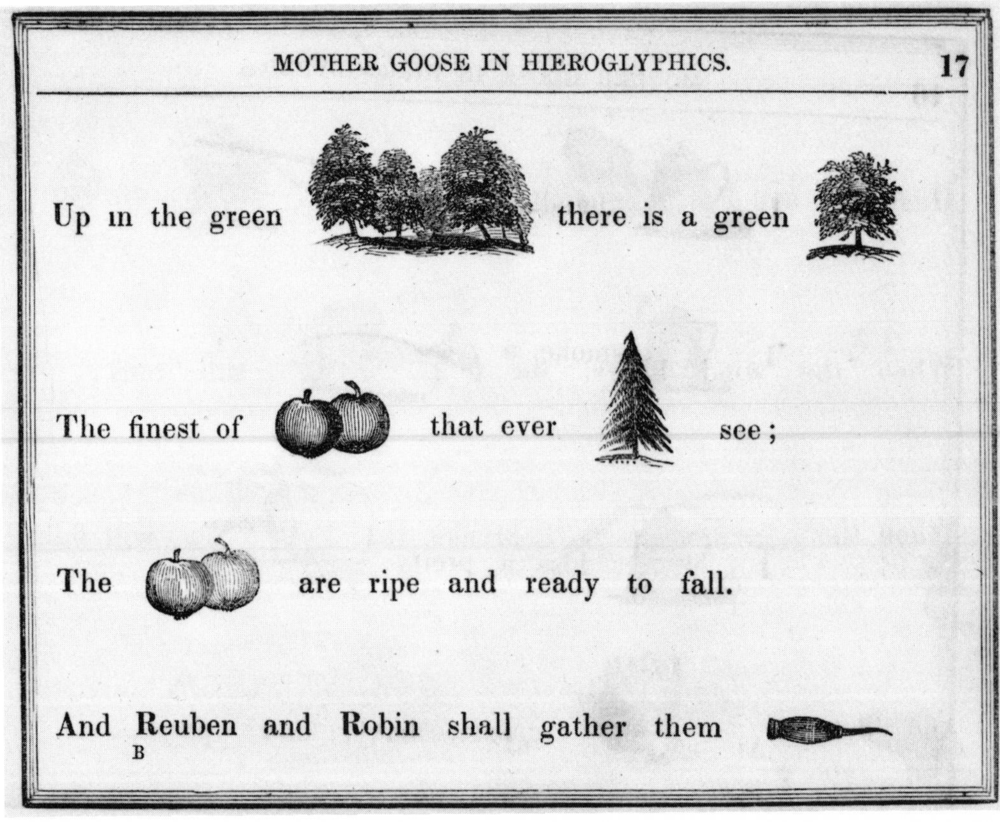

MOTHER GOOSE IN HIEROGLYPHICS. 17

Up in the green there is a green

The finest of that ever see;

The are ripe and ready to fall.

And Reuben and Robin shall gather them

B

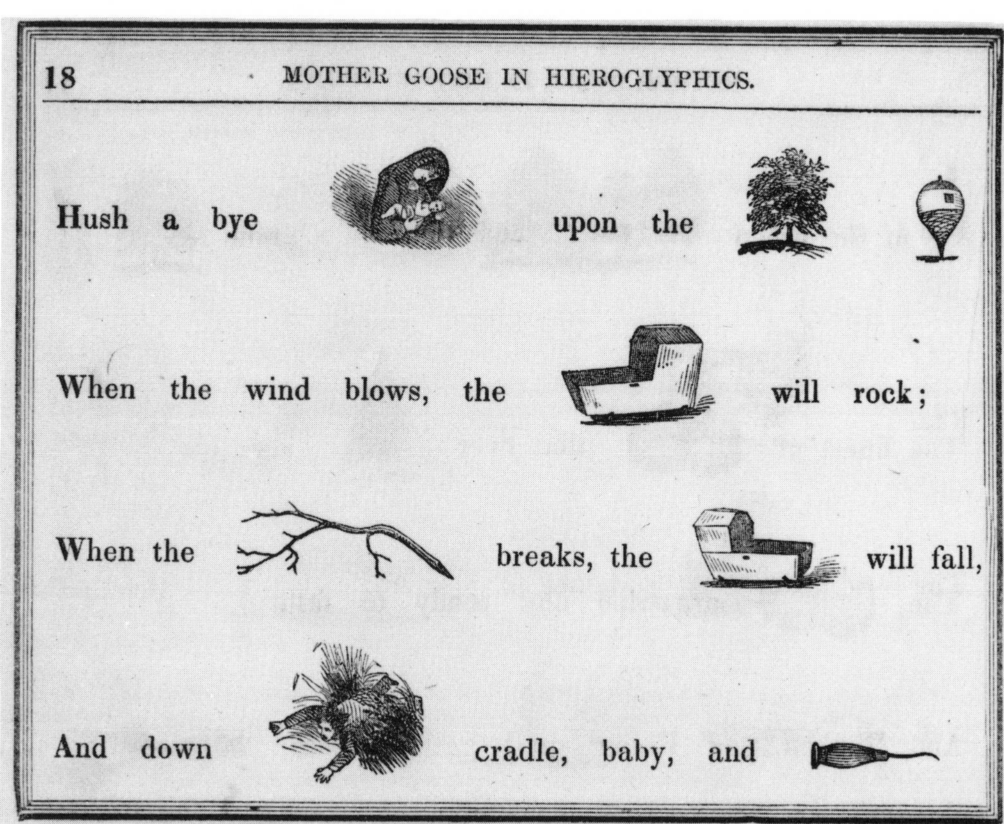

18 MOTHER GOOSE IN HIEROGLYPHICS.

Hush a bye upon the

When the wind blows, the will rock;

When the breaks, the will fall,

And down cradle, baby, and

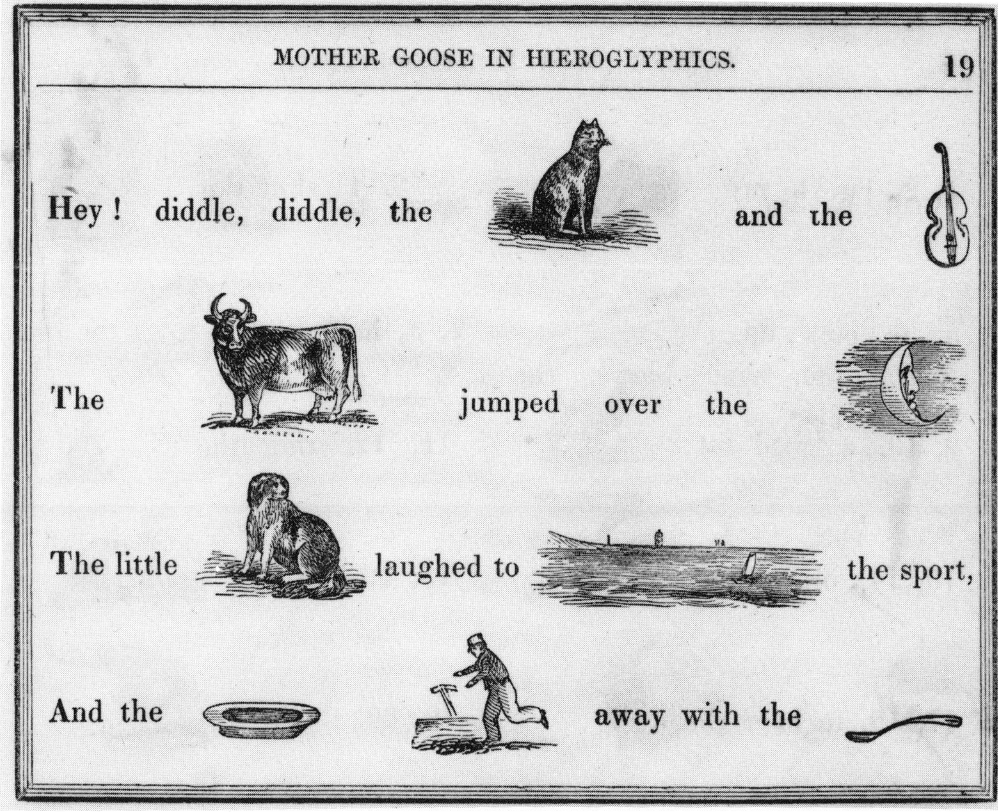

MOTHER GOOSE IN HIEROGLYPHICS. 19

Hey! diddle, diddle, the and the

The jumped over the

The little laughed to the sport,

And the away with the

(continued on next page)

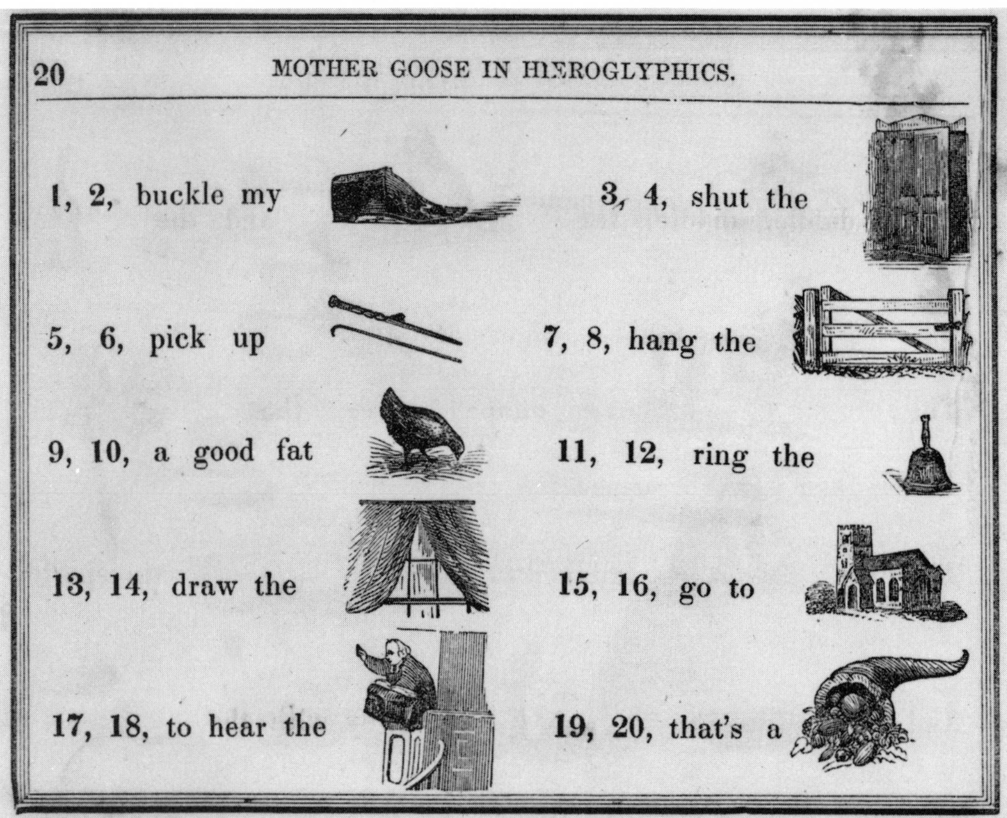

20 MOTHER GOOSE IN HIEROGLYPHICS.

1, 2, buckle my 3, 4, shut the

5, 6, pick up 7, 8, hang the

9, 10, a good fat 11, 12, ring the

13, 14, draw the 15, 16, go to

17, 18, to hear the 19, 20, that's a

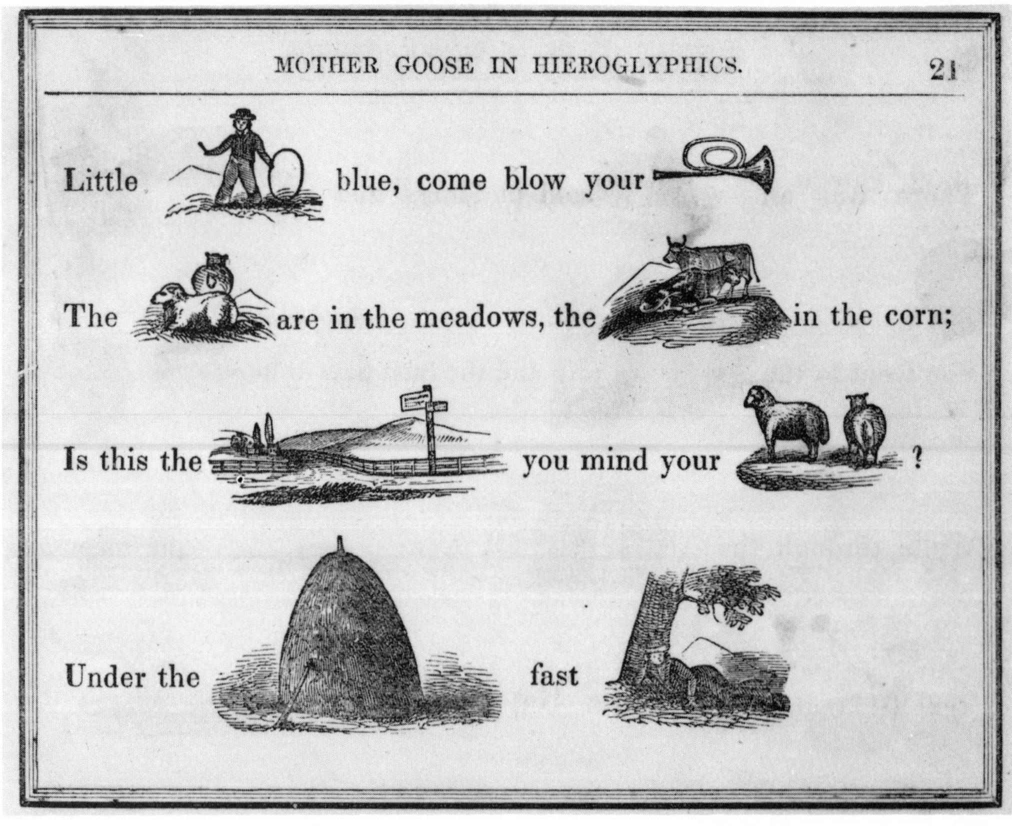

MOTHER GOOSE IN HIEROGLYPHICS. 21

Little blue, come blow your

The are in the meadows, the in the corn;

Is this the you mind your ?

Under the fast

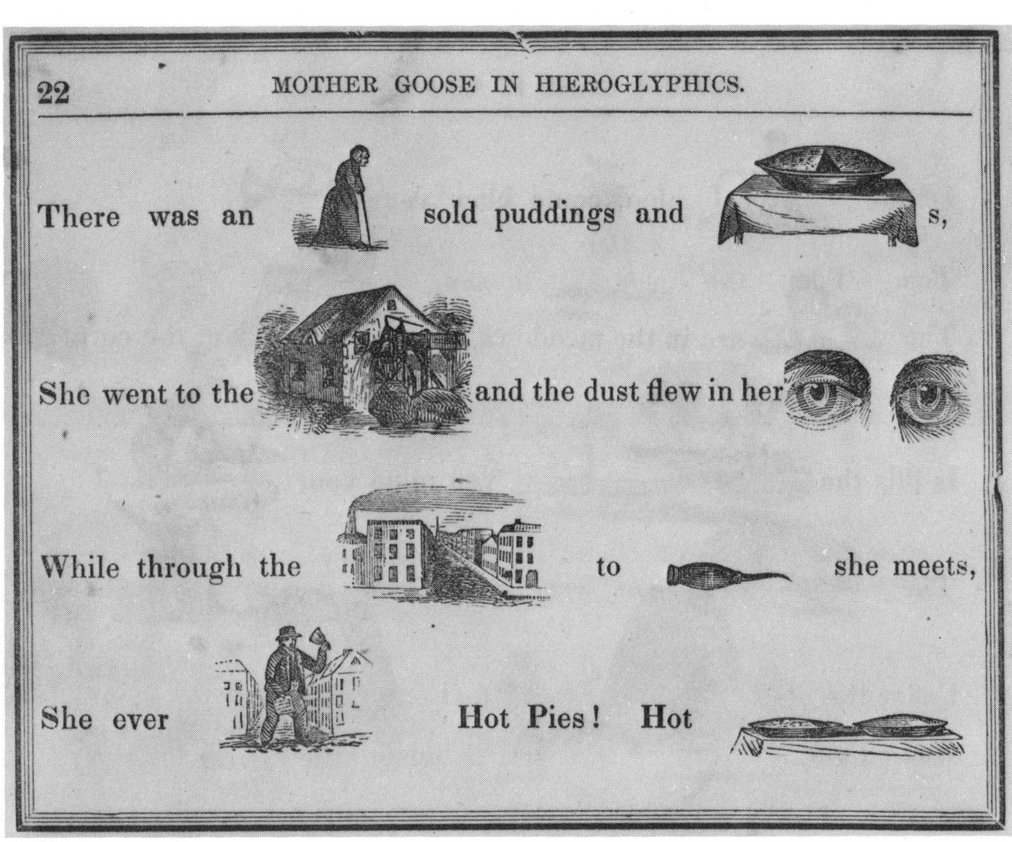
22 MOTHER GOOSE IN HIEROGLYPHICS.

There was an sold puddings and s,

She went to the and the dust flew in her

While through the to she meets,

She ever Hot Pies! Hot

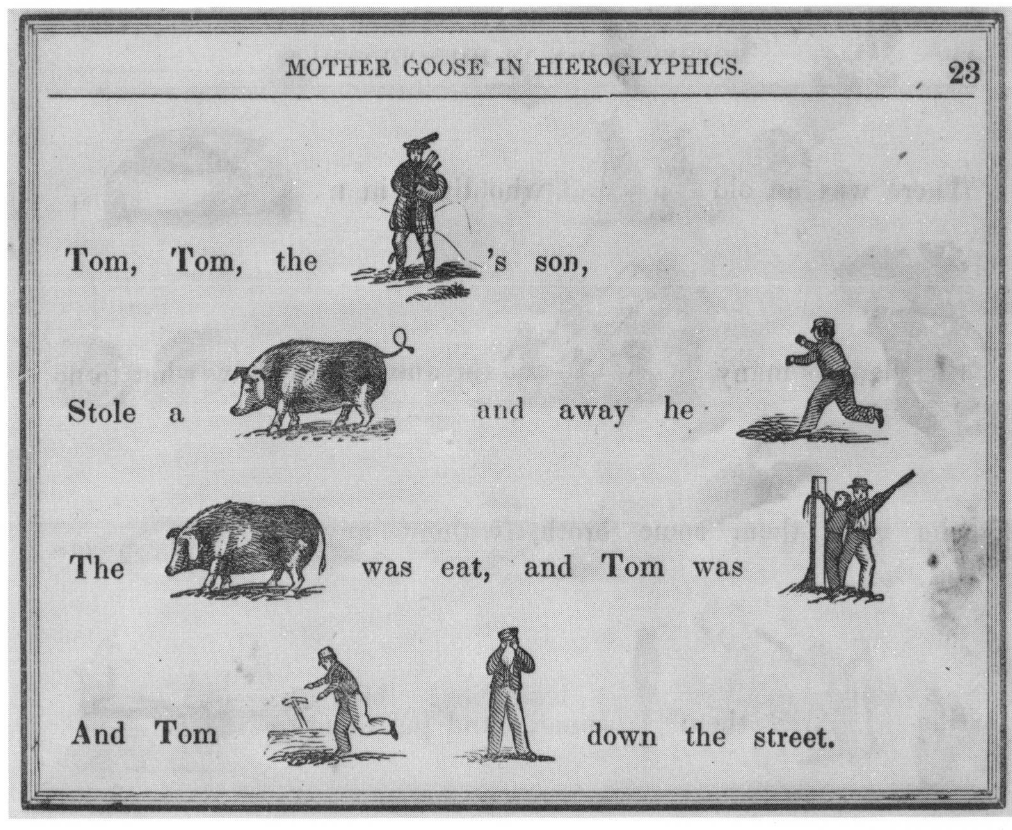
MOTHER GOOSE IN HIEROGLYPHICS. 23

Tom, Tom, the 's son,

Stole a and away he

The was eat, and Tom was

And Tom down the street.

(continued on next page)

24 MOTHER GOOSE IN HIEROGLYPHICS.

There was an old who lived in a

She had so many she did n't know what to do.

She gave them some broth, without any

She them soundly, and put them to

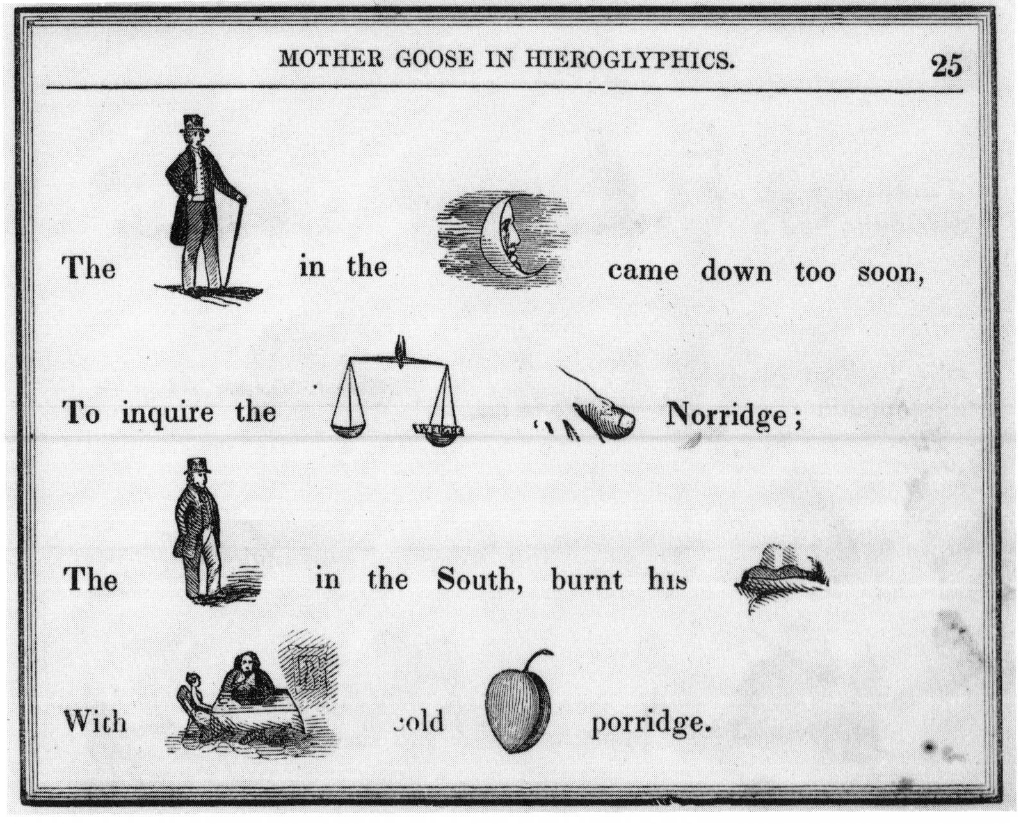
MOTHER GOOSE IN HIEROGLYPHICS. 25

The in the came down too soon,

To inquire the Norridge;

The in the South, burnt his

With cold porridge.

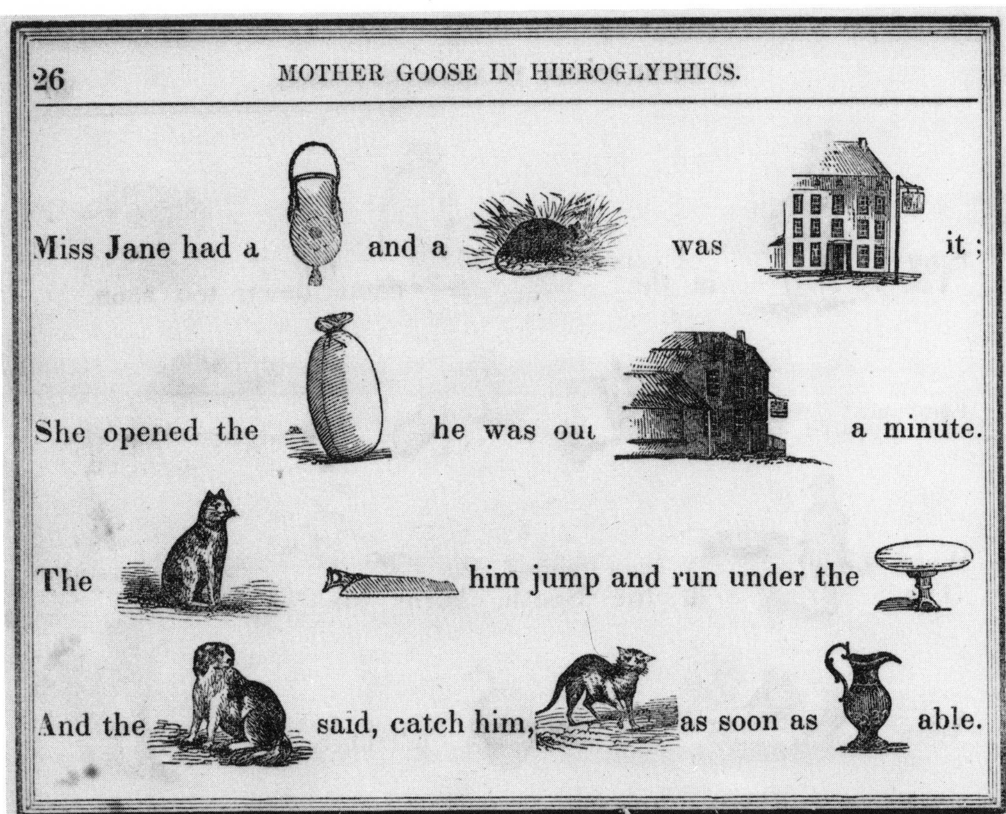

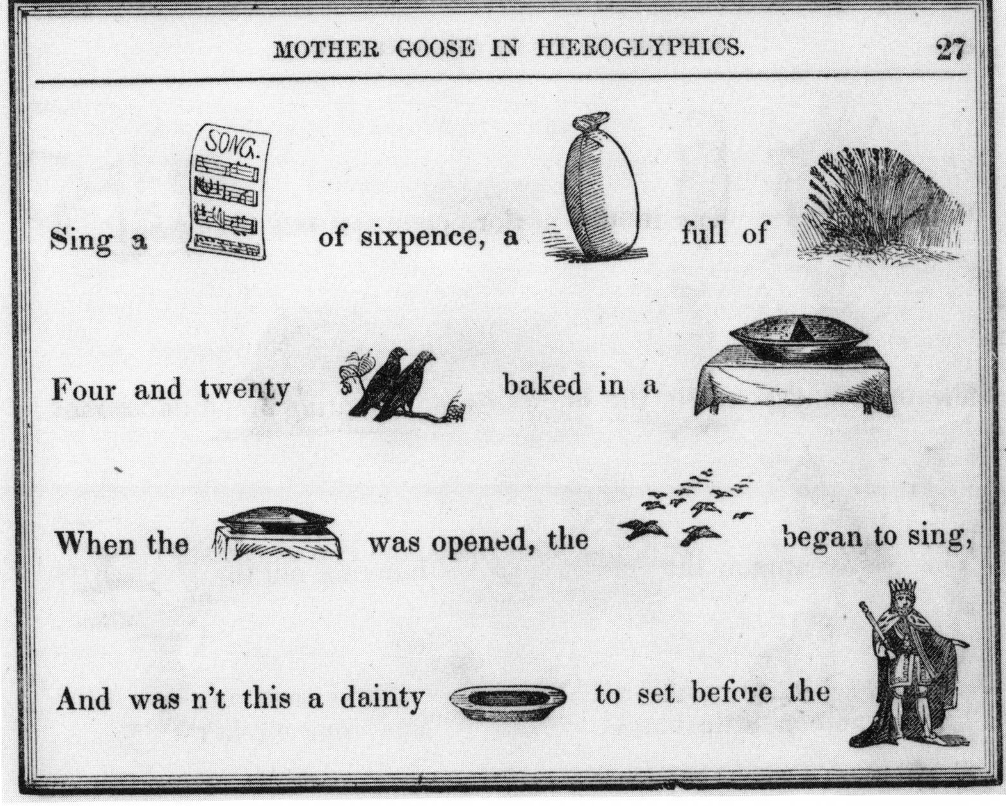

(continued on next page)

28 MOTHER GOOSE IN HIEROGLYPHICS.

The [king] was in the parlor, counting out his [money]

The [queen] was in the [kitchen] eating bread and honey;

The [maid] was in the [garden] hanging out the [clothes]

There came a little black [bird] and nipt off her [nose]

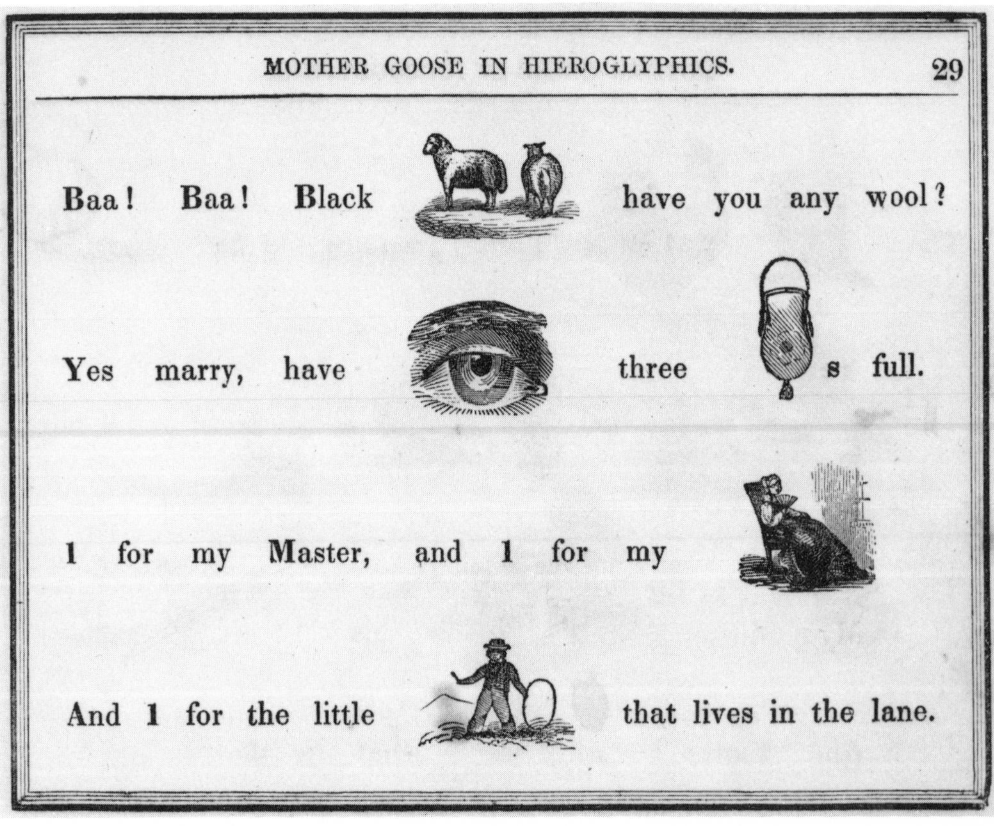

MOTHER GOOSE IN HIEROGLYPHICS. 29

Baa! Baa! Black [sheep] have you any wool?

Yes marry, have [I] three [bag]s full.

1 for my Master, and 1 for my [dame]

And 1 for the little [boy] that lives in the lane.

30 MOTHER GOOSE IN HIEROGLYPHICS.

a doodle doo!

My has lost her

My Master's his

And knows what to do.

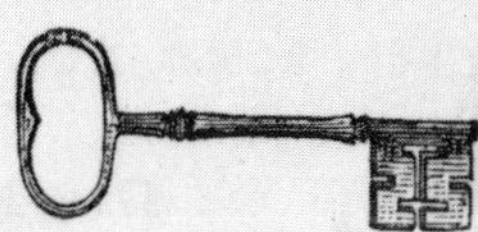

PAGE.

5. Horn, Corn, Eating, Pie, Thumb, Plum, Boy, Eye.
6. Cat, Cat, Eye, Queen, Cat, Cat, Eye, Mouse, Chair.
7. Two Blind Men, Sea, Two Cripples, Race, Bull, Fight, Bee, Face.
8. Jack-horse, Cross, Old Woman, Horse, Rings, Bells, Music.
9. Barns, Bellows, Can, Shoe, Horse, Sir, Eye, Can, Well, Man.
10. Nail, Shoe, Ewer, Horse, Cat, Cupboard.
11. Dog, House, Bull, Monkey, Boat, Oars.
12. Cock, Rock, Crowing, Shoe, Horse, Shoe, Colt, Bear.
13. A Grenadier, Want, Beer, Money, Eye, Gone, Sot.
14. Bed, Head, Slow, Pot, Bee.
15. Eye, Boy, Inn, Grate, Boy, King.

(continued on next page)

32 KEY.

PAGE.	
16.	Can, Musket, Can, Pipe, Can, Girl, Clock, Night.
17.	Orchard, Tree, Apples, Yew, Apples, Awl.
18.	Baby, Tree, Top, Cradle, Bough, Cradle, Tumble, Awl.
19.	Cat, Fiddle, Cow, Moon, Dog, Sea, Dish, Ran, Spoon.
20.	Shoe, Door, Sticks, Gate, Hen, Bell, Curtain, Meeting, Preaching, Plenty.
21.	Boy, Horn, Sheep, Cows, Way, Sheep, Hay-stack, Asleep.
22.	Old Woman, Pies, Mill, Eyes, Street, Awl, Cries, Pies.
23.	Piper, Pig, Run, Pig, Beat, Crying.
24.	Old Woman, Shoe, Children, Bread, Whipped, Awl, Bed.
25.	Man, Moon, Weigh, Toe, Man, Mouth, Eating, Plum.
26.	Bag, Mouse, Inn, Bag, Inn, Cat, Saw, Table, Dog, Puss, Ewer.
27.	Song, Bag, Rye, Blackbirds, Pie, Birds, Dish, King.
28.	King, Money, Queen, Kitchen, Maid, Garden, Clothes, Bird, Nose.
29.	Sheep, Eye, Bag, Dame, Boy, Lane.
30.	Cock, Dame, Shoe, Lost, Fiddlestick, Knot.

ON OPPOSITE PAGE:

THE ADVENTURES OF MISS MINETTE, AND MASTER JOCKO. *To which is added The Marvelous Adventures of Dame Trot and her Wonderful Cat.* New-York: Huestis & Cozans. No. 104 Nassau, corner of Ann St. Stereotyped by Vincent L. Dill [18–?]. 24 pages. 20 cm.

A color-illustrated paperbound book with two stories. The first presents a mischievous monkey whose attempts to dupe a cat cause a series of catastrophes. The second, about a remarkable, playful cat, bears a resemblance to the 1806 text about "Dame Trot and Her Comical Cat." The volume serves as an example of many picture books with nursery humor which were available in America in the latter half of the nineteenth century.

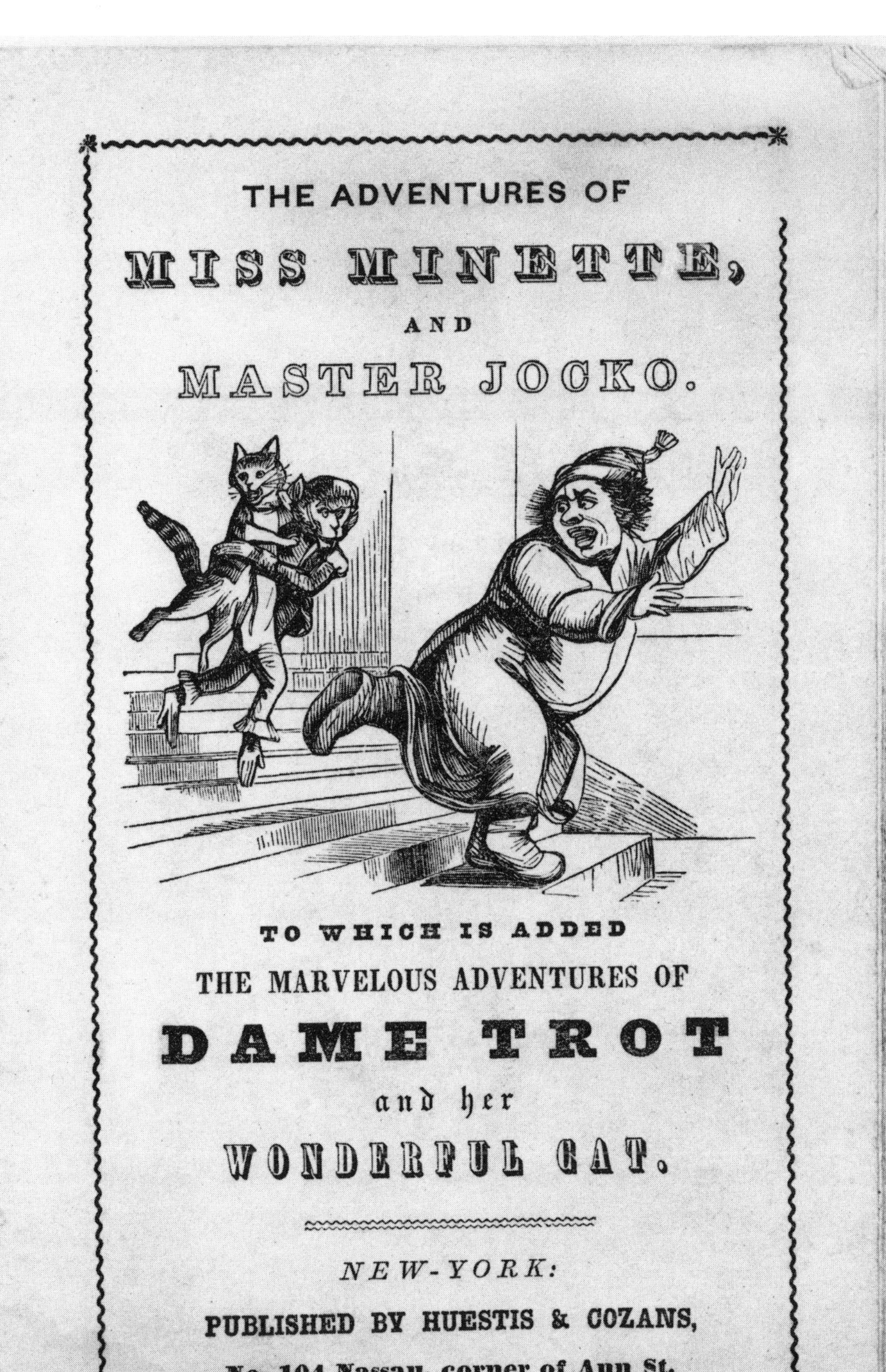

THE ADVENTURES OF

MISS MINETTE,

AND

MASTER JOCKO.

TO WHICH IS ADDED

THE MARVELOUS ADVENTURES OF

DAME TROT

and her

WONDERFUL CAT.

NEW-YORK:

PUBLISHED BY HUESTIS & COZANS,

No. 104 Nassau, corner of Ann St.

STEREOTYPED BY VINCENT L. DILL.

(continued on next page)

THE ADVENTURES OF

DAME TROT AND HER WONDERFUL CAT.

Dame Trot came home one winter's evening quite hungry, and trembling with cold. But her cat had lighted a good fire, and nice roasted a fine fat fowl for the Dame's supper.

Oh how happy the old lady was! the cloth was neatly spread, the juicy fowl smoking on the table ; and this marvellous cat set herself to the duty of carving it up.

When the cloth was removed the Dame exclaimed! what a pity it is not to have something to drink, Miss Puss runs quickly for some wine, and soon returns with a bottle uncorked

But alas! Miss Puss took a glass herself, it soon got in her head; here she is dancing, capering, throwing somersets, and declaring she won't go to bed.

But all things have an end; and see, the fun over, they have all sunk into a sound and peaceful slumber, excepting that the old lady snores rather loud

Early next morning, Miss Puss awakened the Dame! who found breakfast all ready, and Miss Puss ready to do the honours of the table.

(continued on next page)

Breakfast over, Dame Trot went out to visit a neighbour; on her return, she found Miss Puss and her friend Toby engaged in a game of cards.

Another time she came in and found poor Toby with a piteous countenance, seated with his face covered with soap suds, and half of it shaved by the mischievous cat.

Puss having finished her shaving, dressed herself very gaily with a hat and feather on one side, and a rich crimson dress set off with an elegant tippet

She had just finished when Dame Trot came in, who in admiration made her a very low curtesy, which Puss returned with charming grace.

And so they lived very happily together for many years, though truth compels me to add, that Miss Puss, though a very great coquette and an acknowledge beauty, remained and died an old maid. She flirted with our friend Toby for many years, but Toby getting tired one day, went off with a mate, which so affected Miss Puss, that she took to her bed, and never got up again.

WILLIAM RAINE,
Printer and Publisher,
No. 74 BALTIMORE STREET,
BALTIMORE,

Has entered extensively into the publication of

JUVENILE BOOKS.

His facilities for manufacturing Works of this Class, enable him to furnish them at lower prices than any other Establishment in the United States.

NEW COLOURED BOOKS,

New Nursery Book, or, Rhymes for children.
Henry Adair, or, the Youthful Laborer.
Little Tales for Little Folks.
The Months and Seasons, or a Picture of the Year.
First Steps on the Ladder of Learning.
The Picturesque Gift for Children.
The Adventures of Little Red Riding Hood.
The Peahen at Home, or the Swan's Bridal Day.
The Butterfly's Ball, and Grasshopper's Feast.
The Adventures of Little Dame Crump.
Child's First Book.
The Life and Death of Poor Cock Robin.
Child's Own Scrap Book.
My Father.
My Mother.
My Brother.
My Sister.
My Aunt Lucy's Gift.
My Cousin.
Peter Prim's Short Stories for good children.
Mother Goose's Amusing little scraps for children.
The Comical Adventures of the Little Woman.
Dame Wiggins, of Lee, and her Seven cats.
Adventures of Johnny Newcome in the Navy.
The Adventures of Paul Pry, in London.
The History of Wittington and his Cat.
Cinderella, or the Little Glass Slipper.
Adventures of Goody Two Shoes.
The New London Cries.
Adventures of Mother Hubbard.
Puss in Boots.
Dame Trot and her Comical Cat.
Honest Tommy.
Gallery of Birds.
Gallery of Beasts.
Child's Play Book.
The Babes in the Woods.
The House Jack Built.

JUVENILE PRIMER, with 34 col'd Engravings.
PICTURE GALLERY, 144 sheets—all different.

William Raine's Edition.

THE BUTTERFLY'S BALL, AND THE GRASSHOPPER'S FEAST.

EMBELLISHED WITH EIGHT COLORED ENGRAVINGS.

BALTIMORE:
PRINTED & PUBLISHED BY WM. RAINE,
No. 74, BALTIMORE STREET.

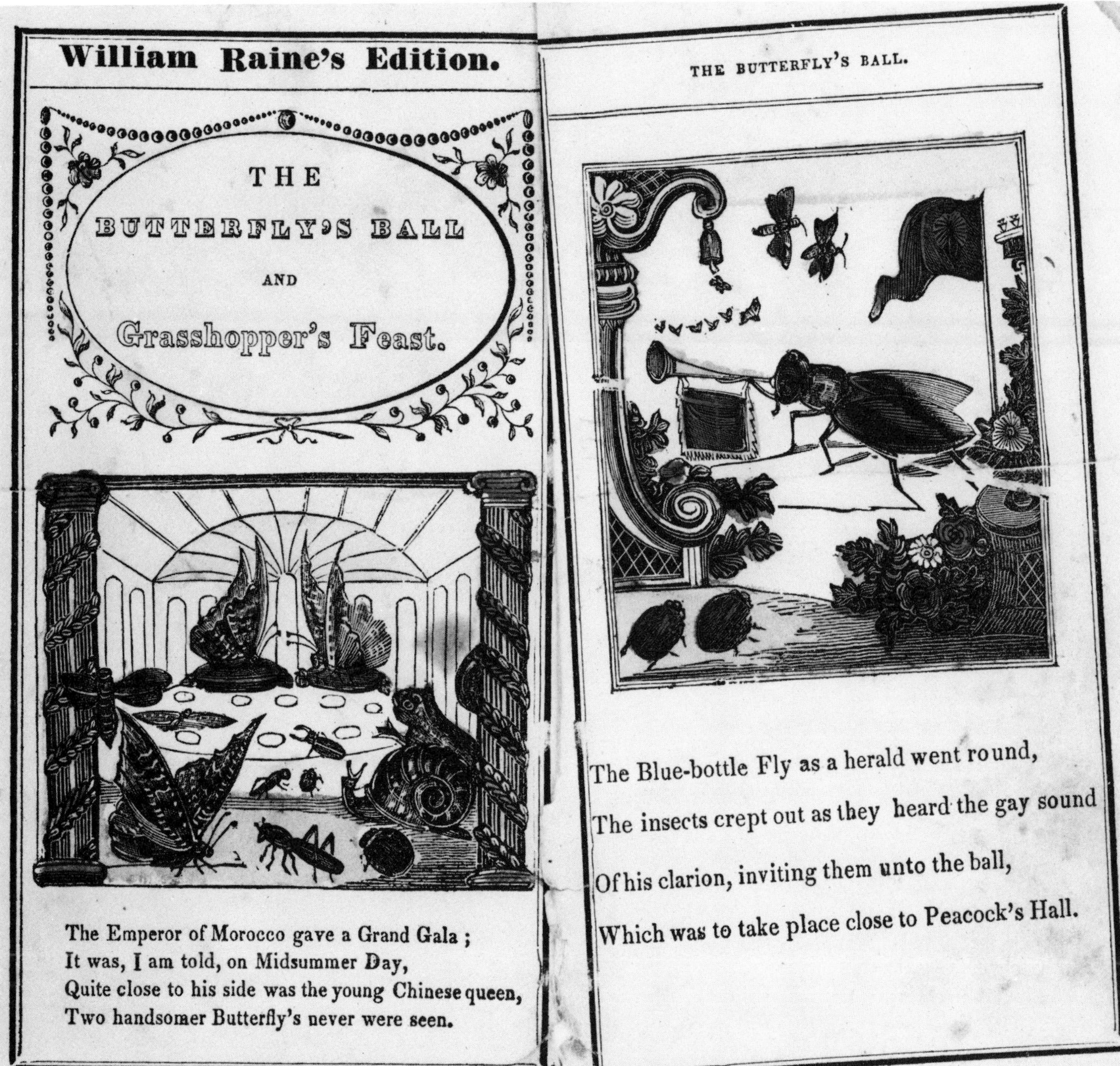

William Raine's Edition.

THE

BUTTERFLY'S BALL

AND

Grasshopper's Feast.

The Emperor of Morocco gave a Grand Gala ;
It was, I am told, on Midsummer Day,
Quite close to his side was the young Chinese queen,
Two handsomer Butterfly's never were seen.

THE BUTTERFLY'S BALL.

The Blue-bottle Fly as a herald went round,
The insects crept out as they heard the gay sound
Of his clarion, inviting them unto the ball,
Which was to take place close to Peacock's Hall.

THE BUTTERFLY'S BALL, AND GRASSHOPPER'S FEAST [after William Roscoe]. Embellished with eight colored engravings. Baltimore: Printed & published by Wm. Raine, No. 74. Baltimore Street [18–?]. 8 pages. 19 cm.

William Roscoe, a member of Parliament and a banker, wrote for his young son the original verses bearing this title. Published by J. Harris of London in 1807, they inspired numerous sequels and imitations in America, of which the work featured here is one. (The Library of Congress owns a copy of the 1807 edition, illustrated by William Mulready in black-and-white cuts. Later, in 1807, Harris published an edition with Mulready's cuts in color.)

(continued on next page)

Such a throng of gay revellers before ne'er was
seen,
Of Moths and Gnats, with Grasshoppers green,
The Bees left their hive, and did quickly repair,
With large bags of honey to add to the fare.

The Cricket came next, a chirping along,
But no one but herself was pleased with the song:
She rode on a Frog, who was a kind fellow,
And she had a small Dock Leaf, for an umbrella.

The Butterfly's subjects came in grand procession,
The scene it was pleasing beyond all expression,
A drawing along, ('tis true I declare,)
Their favorite Prince in a car through the air.

A little Tom Tit was so kind to make tea,
And handed it round to the gay company,
On a small wooden tray, that he placed on his head,
And the Cups and the Saucers of Acorns were made.

(continued on next page)

THE BUTTERFLY'S BALL.

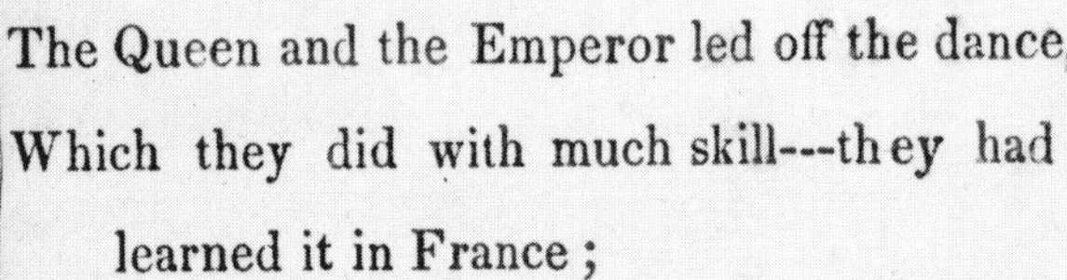

The Queen and the Emperor led off the dance,
Which they did with much skill---they had
learned it in France;
The Frog he stood up, and play'd on the fiddle,
While some little Cockchafers blithe sung
"Diddle diddle."

THE BUTTERFLY'S BALL.

Alas! they unprudently staid till 'twas dark;
They heard the owls hoot and the surly dog bark;
Mr. Frog lost his way, but had the good luck
To make his escape from the gripe of a Duck.
The Butterfly's lay until the next morning,
But rov'd 'mongst the flowers just at the day's
dawning:
Then cards of enquiry to their late guests they
sent,
By a Beetle in boots, who speedily went.

THE LITTLE FROG AND PRETTY MOUSE. Philadelphia: J. B. Keller, 1852. 15 pages. 19 cm.

This is one of many toybooks produced by this publisher. The hand-colored drawings accompanying the doggerel rhymes have great spirit, as the example here indicates.

THE FROG AND MOUSE. 7

Mousey, as bashful as a young
miss,
Retir'd from Froggy's view,
But peeped at him from out
her hole,
As Froggy nearer drew.

Froggy approached and doffed
his hat,
Then, bending on his knee,
Said—Fairest Mouse, pray lis-
ten to
My tale of love for thee.

II. Works Intended to Entertain.
From the Colonial Period to 1900.
B. OTHER VERSE.

THE

SCHOOL SONG BOOK.

ADAPTED TO THE

SCENES OF THE SCHOOL ROOM.

WRITTEN FOR

American Children and Youth.

RY MRS. SARAH J. HALE,
Editor of the Ladies' Magazine, and author of "Flora's Interpreter,"
&c. &c.

BOSTON:
ALLEN & TICKNOR.
1834.

"Mary's Lamb" from THE SCHOOL SONG BOOK. Adapted to the scenes of the school room. Written for American Children and Youth by Mrs. Sarah J. Hale [Sarah Josepha Hale (1788–1789)], Editor of the Ladies' Magazine, and author of "Flora's Interpreter," &c. &c. Boston: Allen & Ticknor, 1834. 98 pages. 15½ cm.

This New England author based her most famous poem "Mary's Lamb" on a true incident from her farm childhood. The verses in *The School Song Book* first appeared in the September–October 1830 issue of *Juvenile Miscellany* (see pages 320–322) and were selected for *McGuffey's Second Reader* (1857). Iona and Peter Opie included it as one of a very few American selections in their *Oxford Book of Children's Verse* (1973).

Vignettes in fine line embellish this little volume.

14

Mary's Lamb.

Mary had a little lamb,
Its fleece was white as snow,
And every where that Mary went
The lamb was sure to go:
It followed her to school one day,
That was against the rule;
It made the children laugh and play
To see a lamb at school.

And so the Teacher turned him out,
But still he lingered near,
And waited patiently about,
Till Mary did appear:
And then he ran to her, and laid
His head upon her arm,
As if he said, "I'm not afraid,
You'll save me from all harm."

15

"What makes the lamb love Mary so?"
The little children cry—
"O Mary loves the lamb, you know,"
The Teacher did reply:
"And you each gentle animal
In confidence may bind,
And make them follow at your call,
If you are always kind."

"The New-England Boy's Song About Thanksgiving Day" from FLOWERS FOR CHILDREN by Mrs. Lydia Maria Child [1802-1880]. Vol. II. For children from four to six years old. New York: C. S. Francis & Co., 252 Broadway. Boston: J. H. Francis, 128 Washington Street, 1844-1845. 178 pages. 15 cm.

"The New-England Boy's Song About Thanksgiving Day," now known as "Over the River and Through the Woods" or "Thanksgiving Day," first appeared on pages 25–28 of this volume, which was the second in a series of three. Of these books, Mrs. Child stated: "About half of each...will consist of new articles written expressly for the occasion;

FLOWERS FOR CHILDREN.

BY

L. MARIA CHILD,

AUTHOR OF THE MOTHER'S BOOK; NEW-YORK LETTERS, ETC.

II.

FOR CHILDREN FROM FOUR TO SIX YEARS OLD.

Of all my things I like it best.
Peep in and take a look!
'T is prettier than all the rest,
My little story book.

NEW-YORK:
C. S. FRANCIS & CO., 252 BROADWAY.
BOSTON:
J. H. FRANCIS, 128 WASHINGTON STREET.
1845.

and the other half will be a selection of what seem to me the best of my own articles, formerly published in the Juvenile Miscellany." The poem was a great success and found its way into many school readers where it can be seen today. Along the way an unknown musician set the words to music, and it is as a song that the poem continues to be enjoyed.

In the same volume Mrs. Child's strong abolitionist feelings are revealed in "The Little White Lamb and the Little Black Lamb." Here Nancy, the black nurse, told the white child, Mary, that "God made the white lambs, and the black lambs. God loves them both, and made them to love each other."

(continued on next page)

THE NEW-ENGLAND BOY'S SONG

ABOUT THANKSGIVING DAY.

Over the river, and through the
wood,
To grandfather's house we go;
The horse knows the way,
To carry the sleigh,
Through the white and drifted snow.

Over the river, and through the wood,
To grandfather's house away!
We would not stop
For doll or top,
For 't is Thanksgiving day.

Over the river, and through the wood,
Oh, how the wind does blow!
It stings the toes,
And bites the nose,
As over the ground we go.

Over the river, and through the wood,
With a clear blue winter sky,
The dogs do bark,
And children hark,
As we go jingling by.

Over the river, and through the wood,
To have a first-rate play—
Hear the bells ring
Ting a ling ding,
Hurra for Thanksgiving day!

Over the river, and through the wood—
No matter for winds that blow;
Or if we get
The sleigh upset,
Into a bank of snow.

Over the river, and through the wood,
To see little John and Ann;
We will kiss them all,
And play snow-ball,
And stay as long as we can.

Over the river, and through the wood,
Trot fast, my dapple grey!
Spring over the ground,
Like a hunting hound,
For 't is Thanksgiving day!

Over the river, and through the wood,
And straight through the barn-yard
gate;
We seem to go
Extremely slow,
It is so hard to wait.

Over the river, and through the wood—
Old Jowler hears our bells;
He shakes his pow,
With a loud bow wow,
And thus the news he tells.

Over the river, and through the wood—
When grandmother sees us come,
She will say, Oh dear,
The children are here,
Bring a pie for every one.

Over the river, and through the wood—
Now grandmother's cap I spy!
Hurra for the fun!
Is the pudding done?
Hurra for the pumpkin pie!

A VISIT FROM SAINT NICHOLAS [by Clement Clarke Moore (1779–1863)]. Illustrated from drawings By F. O. C. Darley. New York: James G. Gregory, Publisher [c. 1862]. Entered according to Act of Congress, in the year 1862 by James G. Gregory, in the Clerk's Office of the District Court of the United States for the Southern District of New York. 8 pages. 26 cm.

Felix Octavius Carr Darley (1822–1888), one of America's best-known early illustrators, admired for the liveliness of his art, produced the three-color pictures for this early edition of the nursery classic, which first appeared anonymously in the *Troy* [*New York*] *Sentinel* on December 23, 1823. Written by Clement Moore for his own family in 1822, it is one of the earliest original stories in American literature for children, owing its longevity to simplicity of style, gaiety, and complete freedom from the didacticism of the period. Another edition of this poem can be seen on pages 247–248.

(continued on next page)

A Visit from Saint Nicholas.

by Clement C. Moore

ILLUSTRATED FROM DRAWINGS

By F. O. C. Darley.

NEW YORK:

JAMES G. GREGORY, PUBLISHER.

(continued from page 169)

A VISIT FROM ST. NICHOLAS.

BY CLEMENT C. MOORE.

'TWAS the night before Christmas, when all through the house
Not a creature was stirring, not even a mouse;
The stockings were hung by the chimney with care,
In hopes that St. Nicholas soon would be there;
The children were nestled all snug in their beds,
While visions of sugar-plums danced in their heads;
And mamma in her kerchief, and I in my cap,
Had just settled our brains for a long winter's nap—

3

(continued on next page)

When out on the lawn there rose such a clatter,
I sprang from my bed to see what was the matter,
Away to the window I flew like a flash,
Tore open the shutters and threw up the sash.
The moon, on the breast of the new-fallen snow,
Gave a lustre of mid-day to objects below;
When, what to my wondering eyes should appear,
But a miniature sleigh, and eight tiny rein-deer,
With a little old driver, so lively and quick,
I knew in a moment it must be St. Nick.
More rapid than eagles his coursers they came,
And he whistled, and shouted, and called them by name:

4

A VISIT FROM SAINT NICHOLAS *(continued from page 171)*

"Now, Dasher! now, Dancer! now, Prancer and Vixen!
On! Comet, on! Cupid, on! Dunder and Blitzen—
To the top of the porch, to the top of the wall!
Now, dash away, dash away, dash away all!"
As dry leaves that before the wild hurricane fly,
When they meet with an obstacle, mount to the sky,
So, up to the house-top the coursers they flew,
With a sleigh full of toys—and St. Nicholas too.
And then in a twinkling I heard on the roof,
The prancing and pawing of each little hoof.
As I drew in my head, and was turning around,
Down the chimney St. Nicholas came with a bound.

(continued on next page)

He was dressed all in fur from his head to his foot,
And his clothes were all tarnished with ashes and soot:
A bundle of toys he had flung on his back,
And he looked like a peddler just opening his pack:
His eyes how they twinkled! his dimples how merry!
His cheeks were like roses, his nose like a cherry;

His droll little mouth was drawn up like a bow,
And the beard on his chin was as white as the snow:
The stump of a pipe he held tight in his teeth,
And the smoke, it encircled his head like a wreath.
He had a broad face, and a little round belly
That shook when he laughed, like a bowl full of jelly.

A VISIT FROM SAINT NICHOLAS *(continued from page 173)*

He was chubby and plump—a right jolly old elf;
And I laughed when I saw him in spite of myself.
A wink of his eye, and a twist of his head,
Soon gave me to know I had nothing to dread.
He spoke not a word, but went straight to his work,
And filled all the stockings; then turned with a jerk,
And laying his finger aside of his nose,
And giving a nod, up the chimney he rose.
He sprang to his sleigh, to his team gave a whistle,
And away they all flew like the down of a thistle;
But I heard him exclaim, ere he drove out of sight,
"MERRY CHRISTMAS TO ALL, AND TO ALL A GOOD NIGHT!"

7

YANKEE DOODLE. Illustrated by F. O. C. Darley. New York: Trent, Filmer & co., 1865. 8 pages. 27 cm.

Assumed by many to have been written by a British doctor serving with General Braddock before the American Revolution, these verses, in spite of their mocking content, were taken over by the Americans. Darley's humorous line drawings are in tune with the character of the Yankee bumpkin of the text. Another edition of this poem, with illustrations by Howard Pyle, can be seen on pages 249–259.

I.

Father and I went down to camp,
  Along with Captain Gooding;
There we see the men and boys
  As thick as hasty-pudding.

CHORUS.

Yankee doodle, keep it up,
  Yankee doodle dandy;
Mind the music and the step,
  And with the girls be handy

(continued on next page)

YANKEE DOODLE.

II.

And there we see a thousand men.
As rich as Squire David ;
And what they wasted every day
I wish it could be saved.
Yankee doodle, etc.

III.

The 'lasses they eat every day
Would keep a house a winter ;
They have as much that I'll be bound
They eat it when they're a mind to.
Yankee doodle, etc.

IV.

And there we see a swamping gun.
Large as a log of maple,
Upon a deuced little cart—
A load for father's cattle.
Yankee doodle, etc.

YANKEE DOODLE.

V.

And every time they shoot it off
  It takes a horn of powder;
It makes a noise like father's gun,
  Only a nation louder.
    Yankee doodle, etc.

VI.

I went as nigh to one myself
  As 'Siah's under-pinning;
And father went as nigh again—
  I thought the deuce was in him.
    Yankee doodle, etc.

(continued on next page)

YANKEE DOODLE.

VII.

Cousin Simon grew so bold,
  I thought he would have cocked it;
It scared me so, I streaked it off,
  And hung by father's pocket.
    Yankee doodle, etc.

VIII.

But Captain Davis had a gun,
  He kind of clapped his hand on't;
He stuck a crooked stabbing iron
  Upon the little end on't.
    Yankee doodle, etc.

IX.

And there I see a pumkin shell
  As big as mother's basin,
And every time they touched it off
  They scampered like the nation.
    Yankee doodle, etc.

YANKEE DOODLE.

X.

I see a little barrel, too,
  The heads were made of leather,
They knocked upon it with little clubs
  And called the folks together.
    Yankee doodle, etc.

(continued on next page)

YANKEE DOODLE.

XI.

And there was Captain Washington,
  And gentlefolks about him ;
They say he's grown so tarnal proud
  He will not ride without 'em.
    Yankee doodle, etc.

XII.

He got him on his meeting clothes,
  Upon a slapping stallion ;
He set the world along in rows,
  In hundreds and in millions.
    Yankee doodle, etc.

XIII.

The flaming ribbons in their hats,
  They looked so tearing fine, ah :
I wanted plaguily to get,
  To give to my Jemima.
    Yankee doodle, etc.

XIV.

I see another snarl of men,
  A digging graves, they told me,
So tarnal long, so tarnal deep,
  They 'tended they should hold me.
    Yankee doodle, etc.

(continued on next page)

YANKEE DOODLE.

XV

It scared me so, I hooked it off,
Nor stopped as I remember;
Nor turned about till I got home,
Locked up in mother's chamber.

CHORUS.

Yankee doodle, keep it up,
Yankee doodle dandy;
Mind the music and the step,
And with the girls be handy.

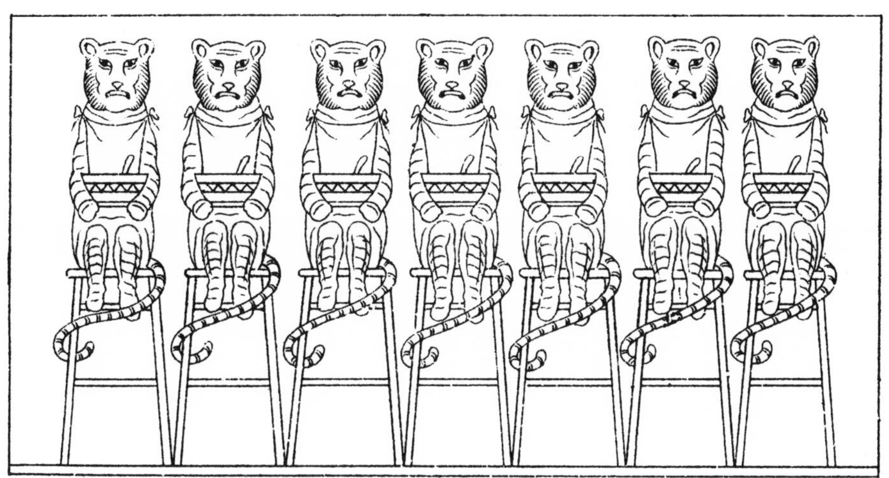

"The Seven Little Tigers and their Aged Cook" from SKETCHES & SCRAPS by Laura E. Richards [1850–1943]. With pictures by Henry Richards. Boston: Estes & Lauriat, 1881. 64 pages. 24 cm.

Endowed with a happy facility with words, and seemingly influenced by Edward Lear, this daughter of Julia Ward Howe (who wrote the "Battle Hymn of the Republic") and Samuel Gridley Howe (noted philanthropist of the Perkins School for the Blind) used her imaginary "hurdy gurdy" to turn out rollicking nonsense verses for her children, sometimes using the back of a placid baby as a writing desk. She also wrote many girls' stories, beginning with *Queen Hildegarde* in 1881. These were greatly loved in their day. However, it is for her blithe verses that she is now known. This book, the only one illustrated by her husband, contains some of the best of these.
(continued on next page)

and their Aged Cook

THE SEVEN LITTLE TIGERS

AND THE AGED COOK.

Seven little Tigers they sat them in a row,
Their seven little dinners for to eat,
And each of the troop had a little plate of soup,
The effect of which was singularly neat.

(continued on next page)

They were feeling rather cross, for they hadn't any
sauce,
To eat with their pudding or their pie.
So they rumpled up their hair in a spasm of despair,
And vowed that the aged cook should die.

THE SEVEN LITTLE TIGERS AND THEIR AGED COOK *(continued from page 187)*

Then they called the aged cook,
and a frying-pan they took
To fry him very nicely for their
supper.
He was ninety-six years old, on
authority I'm told,
And his name was Peter Sparrow-
piper Tupper.

"Mr. Sparrow-piper Tup, we intend
on you to sup!"
Said the eldest little Tiger very sweetly.
But this naughty aged cook, just re-
marking "only look!"
Chopped the little Tiger's head off
very neatly.

Then he said unto the rest, it has always been confessed
That a tiger's better eating than a man.
So I'll fry him for you now, and you all will find, I trow,
That to eat him will be much the better plan.

So they tried it in a trice, and found that it was nice,
And with rapture they embraced one another.
And they said "by hook or crook we must keep this
aged cook,"
So we'll ask him to become our elder brother.
Which they accordingly did.

II. Works Intended to Entertain.

From the Colonial Period to 1900.

C. STORIES AFTER 1850.

A WONDER-BOOK FOR GIRLS AND BOYS. By Nathaniel Hawthorne [1804–1864]. With engravings by Baker from designs by Billings. Boston: Ticknor, Reed, and Fields, 1852. 256 pages. 17 cm.

In spite of the date—1852—on its title page, this book is known to have been published November 8, 1851. Although published first in London, this work by the famous American author was published here in the same year.

Within a framework of storytelling at Tanglewood, in the rolling countryside of the Berkshire Hills of western Massachusetts, the novelist displays his love for Greek mythology, turning the famous tales into versions with elaborated details beloved by children. In attempting to make both this book and its sequel *Tanglewood Tales* (1853) appropriate to the young, he tried out his versions of the stories on his small son and daughter.

In his preface Hawthorne expresses the need for "a great freedom of treatment" and adds that the legends "are marvelously independent of all temporary modes and circumstances. They remain essentially the same, after changes that would affect the identity of almost anything else. He does not, therefore, plead guilty to a sacrilege, in having shaped anew, as his fancy dictated, the forms that have been hallowed by an antiquity of two or three thousand years. . . . by their indestructibility itself, they are legitimate subjects for every age to clothe with its own garniture of manners and sentiment."

Hammatt Billings, the illustrator, contributed to many well-known works. Another edition of this book, with illustrations by Walter Crane, can be seen on pages 260–261.

A

WONDER-BOOK

FOR

GIRLS AND BOYS.

BY

NATHANIEL HAWTHORNE.

WITH ENGRAVINGS BY BAKER FROM DESIGNS BY BILLINGS.

BOSTON:

TICKNOR, REED, AND FIELDS.

MDCCCLII.

PICTURES AND STORIES FROM UNCLE TOM'S CABIN [by Harriet Beecher Stowe (1811–1896)]. Boston: Published by John P. Jewett & Co. [1853]. 38 pages. 22½ cm.

Written in verse and prose, "this little work is designed to adapt Mrs. Stowe's touching narrative [1852] to the understanding of the youngest readers and to foster in their hearts a generous sympathy for the wronged Negro Race of America." The words to the "Little Eva Song" were contributed by John Greenleaf Whittier.

The foreword notes: "The purpose of the Editor of this little Work, has been to adapt it for the juvenile family circle. The verses have accordingly been written by the Authoress for the capacity of the youngest readers, and have been printed in a large bold type. The prose parts of the book, which are well suited for being read aloud in the family circle, are printed in a smaller type, and it is presumed that in these our younger friends will claim the assistance of their older brothers or sisters, or appeal to the ready aid of their mamma."

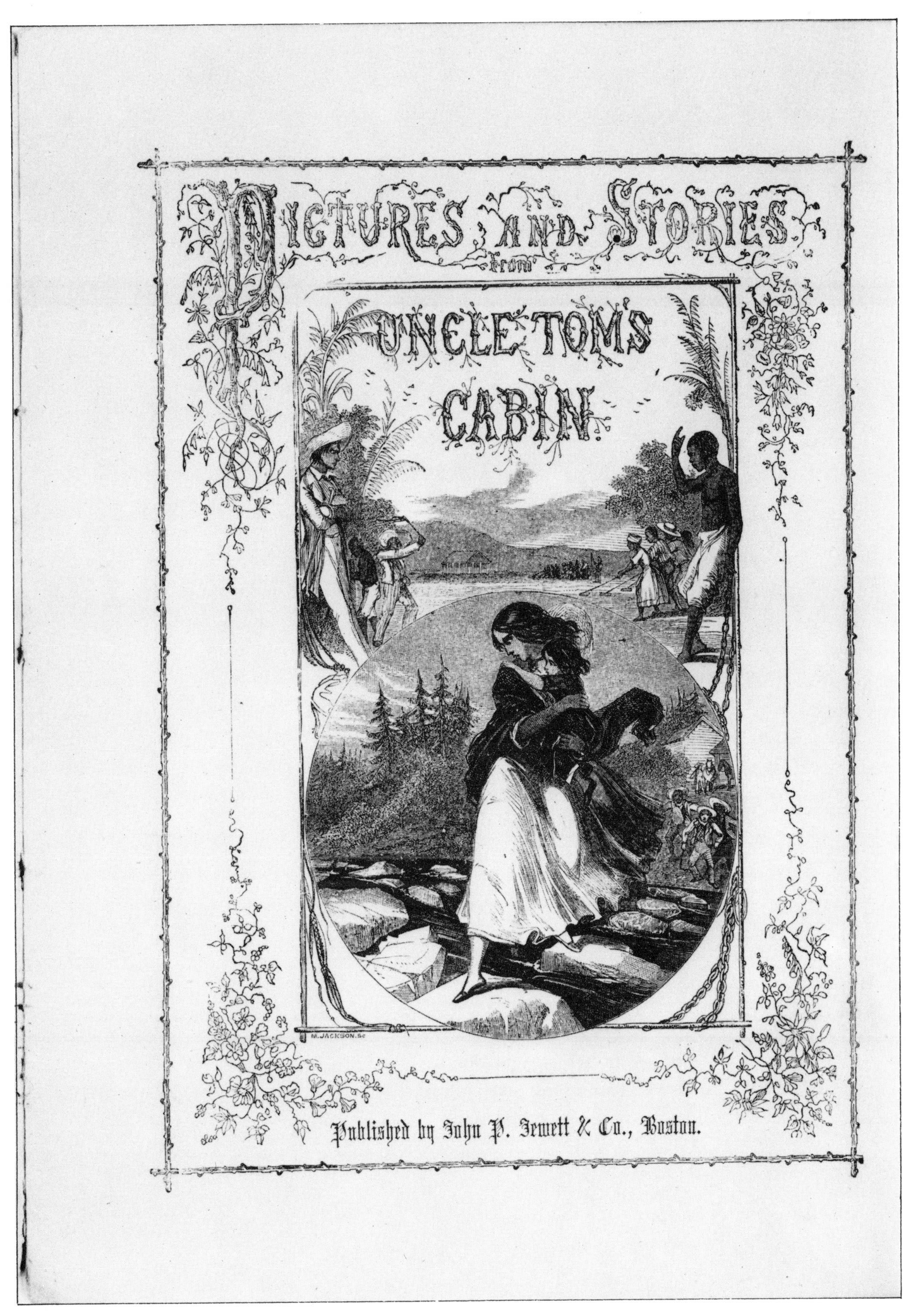

(continued on next page)

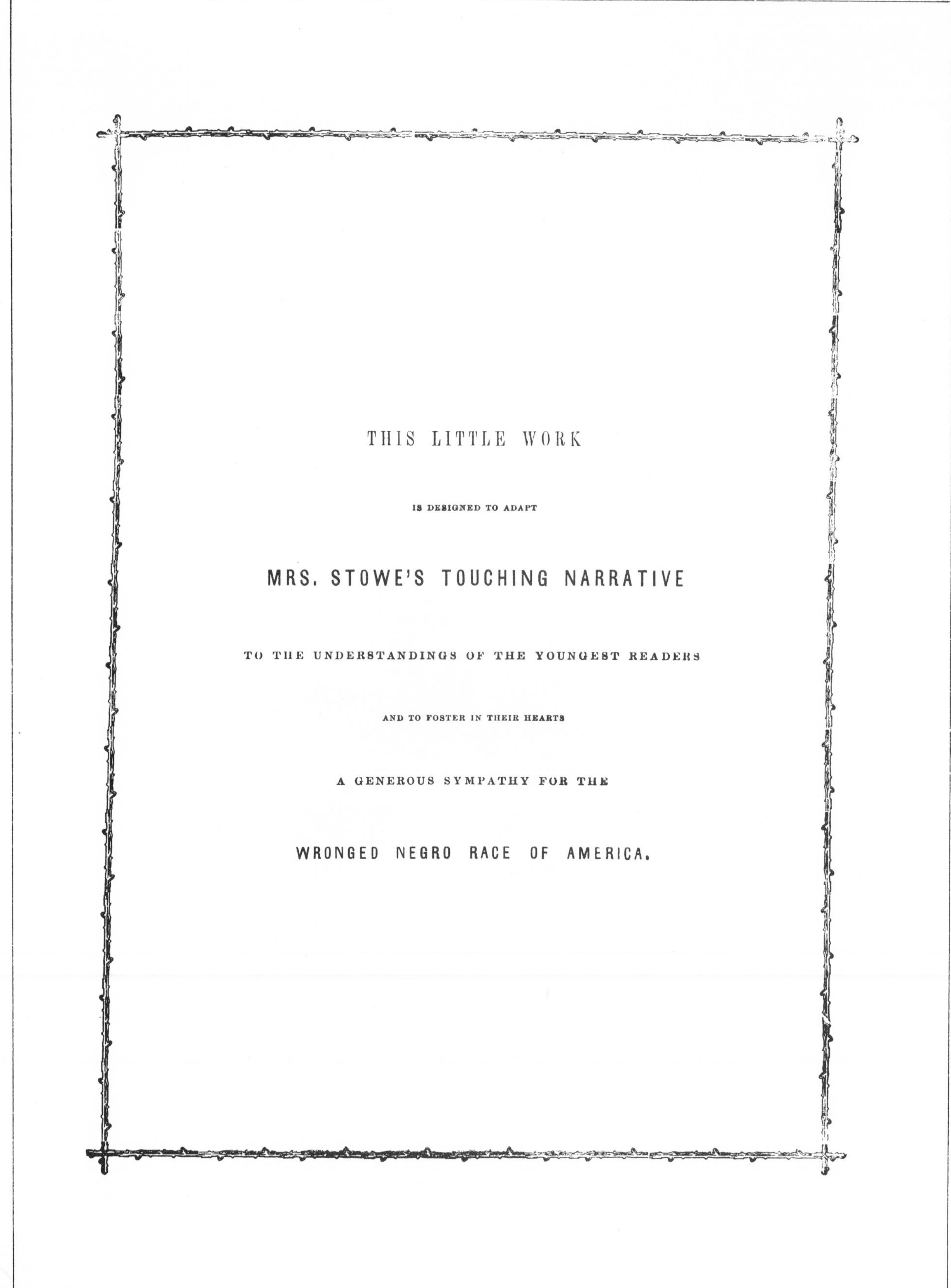

THIS LITTLE WORK

IS DESIGNED TO ADAPT

MRS. STOWE'S TOUCHING NARRATIVE

TO THE UNDERSTANDINGS OF THE YOUNGEST READERS

AND TO FOSTER IN THEIR HEARTS

A GENEROUS SYMPATHY FOR THE

WRONGED NEGRO RACE OF AMERICA.

 (continued from page 193)

TOPSY BRINGING FLOWERS TO EVA.

"Oh mother dear, let Topsy stay,"
Says Eva in her gentle mood,
"She brought such pretty flowers to-day,
Indeed she's trying to be good."

(continued on next page)

LITTLE EVA SONG.

UNCLE TOM'S GUARDIAN ANGEL.

WORDS BY JOHN G. WHITTIER. . . . . . MUSIC BY MANUEL EMILIO.

All is light and peace with Eva;
There the darkness cometh never;
Tears are wiped, and fetters fall,
And the Lord is all in all.
Weep no more for happy Eva;
Wrong and sin no more shall grieve her,
Care, and pain, and weariness,
Lost in love so measureless!

Gentle Eva, loving Eva,
Child confessor, true believer,
Listener at the Master's knee,
" Suffer such to come to me."
O for faith like thine, sweet Eva,
Lighting all the solemn river,
And the blessing of the poor,
Wafting to the heavenly shore.

THE END.

 (continued from page 195)

KOBBOLTOZO: A Sequel to The Last of the Huggermuggers. By Christopher Pearse Cranch [1813–1892]. With illustrations. Boston: Phillips, Sampson and Company, 1857. 95 pages. 22 cm.

The son of a judge in Washington, D. C., Christopher Cranch was a man of many gifts—landscape painter, poet, actor, and caricaturist—who turned his considerable talents to writing and illustrating two fantasies for children as well as his delightful nonsense verse for the *Riverside Magazine*. Illustrations from both *The Last of the Huggermuggers* and *Kobboltozo* and brief extracts from the former are given here to show the lively style of Cranch's writing and his well-drawn pictures.

(continued on next page)

THE MER-KING. See page 67.

THE LAST OF THE HUGGERMUGGERS.

CHAPTER ONE.

HOW LITTLE JACKET WOULD GO TO SEA.

I DARE say there are not many of my young readers who have heard about Jacky Cable, the sailor-boy, and of his wonderful adventures on Huggermugger's Island. Jacky was a smart Yankee lad, and was always remarkable for his dislike of staying at home, and a love of lounging upon the wharves, where the sailors used to tell him stories about sea-life. Jacky was always a little fellow. The country people, who did not much like the sea, or encourage Jacky's fondness for it, used to say, that he took so much salt air and tar smoke into his lungs that it stopped his growth. The boys

1

used to call him Little Jacket. Jacky, however, though small in size, was big in wit, being an uncommonly smart lad, though he did play truant sometimes, and seldom knew well his school-lessons. But some boys learn faster out of school than in school, and this was the case with Little Jacket. Before he was ten years old, he knew every rope in a ship, and could manage a sail-boat or a row-boat with equal ease. In fine, salt water seemed to be his element ; and he was never so happy or so wide awake as when he was lounging with the sailors in the docks. The neighbors thought he was a sort of good-for-nothing, idle boy, and his parents often grieved that he was not fonder of home and of school. But Little Jacket was not a bad boy, and was really learning a good deal in his way, though he did not learn it all out of books.

Well, it went on so, and Little Jacket grew fonder and fonder of the sea, and pined more and more to enlist as a sailor, and go off to the strange countries in one of the splendid big ships. He did not say much about it to his parents, but they saw what his longing was, and after thinking and talking the matter over together, they concluded that it was about as well to let the boy have his way.

(continued on next page)

So when Little Jacket was about fifteen years old, one bright summer's day, he kissed his father and mother, and brothers and sisters, and went off as a sailor in a ship bound to the East Indies.

CHAPTER FOUR.

HOW HUGGERMUGGER CAME ALONG.

Now it happened that Little Jacket was not altogether wrong in his fancies about giants, for there *was* a giant living in this island where the poor sailors were wrecked. His name was Huggermugger, and he and his giantess wife lived at the foot of the great cliffs they had seen in the distance. Huggermugger was something of a farmer, something of a hunter, and something of a fisherman. Now, it being a warm, clear, moonlight night, and Huggermugger being disposed to roam about, thought he would take a walk down to the beach to see if the late storm had washed up any clams* or oysters, or other shell-fish, of which

* The "clam" is an American bivalve shell-fish, so called from hiding itself in the sand. A "clam chowder" is a very savory kind of thick soup, of which the clam is a chief ingredient. I put in this note for the benefit of little English boys and girls, if it should chance that this story should find its way to their country.

(continued on next page)

THE GIANT PICKS UP LITTLE JACKET'S BEDROOM.

he was very fond. Having gathered a good basket full, he was about returning, when his eye fell upon the group of great shells in which Little Jacket and his friends were reposing, all sound asleep.

"Now," thought Huggermugger, "my wife has often asked me to fetch home one of these big shells. She thinks it would look pretty on her mantel-piece, with sunflowers sticking in it. Now I may as well gratify her, though I can't exactly see the use of a shell without a fish in it. Mrs. Huggermugger must see something in these shells that I don't."

So he didn't stop to choose, but picked up the first one that came to his hand, and put it in his basket. It was the very one in which Little Jacket was asleep. The little sailor slept too soundly to know that he was travelling, free of expense, across the country at a railroad speed, in a carriage made of a giant's fish-basket. Huggermugger reached his house, mounted his huge stairs, set down his basket, and placed the big shell on the mantel-piece.

"Wife," says he, "here 's one of those good-for-nothing big shells you have often asked me to bring home."

"Oh, what a beauty," says she, as she stuck a sun-

(continued on next page)

flower in it, and stood gazing at it in mute admiration. But, Huggermugger being hungry, would not allow her to stand idle.

"Come," says he, "let's have some of these beautiful clams cooked for supper — they are worth all your fine shells with nothing in them."

So they sat down, and cooked and ate their supper, and then went to bed.

Little Jacket, all this time, heard nothing of their great rumbling voices, being in as sound a sleep as he ever enjoyed in his life. He awoke early in the morning, and crept out of his shell — but he could hardly believe his eyes, and thought himself still dreaming, when he found himself and his shell on a very high, broad shelf, in a room bigger than any church he ever saw. He fairly shook and trembled in his shoes, when the truth came upon him that he had been trapped by a giant, and was here a prisoner in his castle. He had time enough, however, to become cool and collected, for there was not a sound to be heard, except now and then something resembling a thunder-

(continued on next page)

like snoring, as from some distant room. "Aha," thought Little Jacket to himself, "it is yet very early, and the giant is asleep, and there may be time yet to get myself out of his clutches."

He was a brave little fellow, as well as a true Yankee in his smartness and ingenuity. So he took a careful observation of the room, and its contents. The first thing to be done was to let himself down from the mantel-piece. This was not an easy matter, as it was very high. If he jumped, he would certainly break his legs. He was not long in discovering one of Huggermugger's fishing-lines tied up and lying not far from him. This he unrolled, and having fastened one end of it to a nail which he managed just to reach, he let the other end drop (it was as large as a small rope) and easily let himself down to the floor. He then made for the door, but that was fastened. Jacky, however, was determined to see what could be done, so he pulled out his jackknife, and commenced cutting into the corner of the door at the bottom, where it was a good deal worn, as if it had been gnawed by the rats. He thought that by cutting a little now and then, and hiding himself when the giant should make his appearance, in time he might make an opening large enough for him to squeeze himself through. Now Huggermugger was by this time awake, and heard the noise which Jacky made with his knife.

"Wife," says he, waking her up—she was dreaming about her beautiful shell—"wife, there are those eternal rats again, gnawing, gnawing at that door; we must set the trap for them to-night."

Little Jacket heard the giant's great voice, and was very much astonished that he spoke English. He thought that giants spoke nothing but "chow-chow-whangalorum-hallaballoo with a-ruffle-bull-bagger!" This made him hope that Huggermugger would not eat him. So he grew very hopeful, and determined to persevere. He kept at his work, but as softly as he could. But Huggermugger heard the noise again, or fancied he heard it, and this time came to see if he could not kill the rat that gnawed so steadily and so fearlessly. Little Jacket heard him coming, and rushed to hide himself. The nearest place of retreat was one of the giant's great boots, which lay on the floor, opening like a cave before him. Into this he rushed. He had hardly got into it before Huggermugger entered.

Jacky had a succession of high adventures, on land and on sea, after he succeeded in getting out of the Giant Huggermugger's boot. He, with the other sailors, managed to get to Java and even back to the island of the Huggermuggers where they found the giants to be less dangerous than they'd thought.

THE

SEVEN LITTLE SISTERS

WHO LIVE ON

THE ROUND BALL

THAT

FLOATS IN THE AIR.

With Illustrations.

BOSTON:
TICKNOR AND FIELDS.
M DCCC LXIV.

THE SEVEN LITTLE SISTERS WHO LIVE ON THE ROUND BALL THAT FLOATS IN THE AIR [by Jane Andrews (1833–1887)]. With illustrations. Boston: Ticknor and Fields, 1864. 127 pages. 17½ cm.

An innovation, in an imaginative but truthful and graphic conception, designed to introduce small readers to little girls of other lands.

AGOONACK, THE ESQUIMAUX SISTER,

AND HOW SHE LIVED THROUGH THE LONG DARKNESS.

WHAT is this odd-looking mound of stone? It looks like the great brick oven that used to be in our old kitchen, where, when I was a little girl, I saw the fine large loaves of bread and the pies and puddings pushed carefully in with a long, flat shovel, or drawn out with the same when the heat had browned them nicely.

Is this an oven standing out here alone in the snow?

You will laugh when I tell you that it is not an oven, but a house; and here lives little Agoonack.

Do you see that low opening, close to

1 *

The "seven little sisters" are girls from various countries, and the "round ball that floats in the air" is, of course, the earth. This book, remarkably modern in concept, was followed in 1885 by *Ten Boys Who Lived on the Road From Long Ago Till Now* and stayed in print as late as 1924.

(continued on next page)

the ground? That is the door; but one must creep on hands and knees to enter. There is another smaller hole above the door; it is the window. It has no glass, as ours do, only a thin covering of something which Agoonack's father took from the inside of a seal, and her mother stretched over the window-hole to keep out the cold and to let in a little light.

Here lives our little girl; not as the brown baby does, among the trees and the flowers; but far up in the cold countries, amid snow and ice.

If we look off now, over the ice, we shall see a funny little, clumsy thing, running along as fast as its short, stout legs will permit, trying to keep up with its mother. You would hardly know it to be a little girl; but might rather call it a white bear's cub; it is so oddly dressed in the white, shaggy coat of the bear which its father killed last month. But this is really Agoonack, and you can see her round, fat, greasy little face, if you throw back the white jumper-hood which covers her head. Shall I tell you what clothes she wears?

Not at all like yours, you will say; but, when one lives in the cold countries, one must dress accordingly.

First, she has socks, soft and warm; but not knit of the white yarn with which Mamma knits yours. Her Mamma has sewed them from the skins of birds, with the soft down upon them to keep the small brown feet very warm. Over these come her moccasons of seal-skin.

If you have been on the sea-shore, perhaps you know the seals that are sometimes seen swimming in the sea, holding up their brown heads, which look much like dogs' heads, wet and dripping. If you have n't seen them there, you may have in Boston at the Aquarial Gardens, living among the fishes and snakes and other wonderful inhabitants of that attractive place.

(continued on next page)

The seals love best to live in the seas of the cold countries; and here the Esquimaux (for that is the name by which we call these people of the cold countries) hunt them, eat them for dinner, and make warm clothes of their skins; so, as I told you, Agoonack has seal-skin boots.

Next she wears leggins, or trousers, of white bear-skin, very rough and shaggy; and a little jacket or frock, called a jumper, of the same. This jumper has a hood, made like the little red riding-hoods, which I dare say you have all seen. Pull the hood up over the short, black hair, letting it almost hide the fat, round face, and you have Agoonack dressed.

Is this her best dress, do you think?

Certainly it is her best, because she has no other; and when she goes into the house — But I think I won't tell you that yet, for there is something more to be seen outside.

Agoonack and her mother are coming home to dinner, but there is no sun shining on the snow to make it sparkle. It is dark like night, and the stars shine clear and steady like silver lamps in the sky; and far off, between the great icy peaks, strange lights are dancing, shooting long rosy flames far into the sky, or marching in troops as if each light had a life of its own, and all were marching together along the dark, quiet sky. Now they move slowly and solemnly, with no noise, and in regular, steady file; then they rush all together, flame into golden and rosy streamers, and mount far above the cold, icy mountain-peaks that glitter in their light; and we hear a sharp sound like, Dsah! dsah! and the ice glows with the warm color, and the splendor shines on the little white-hooded girl as she trots beside her mother.

It is far more beautiful than the fireworks on Fourth of July. Sometimes

(continued on next page)

we see a little of it here, and we say there are northern lights, and we sit at the window watching all the evening to see them march and turn and flash; but in the cold countries they are far more brilliant than any we have seen.

It is Agoonack's birthday, and there is a present for her before the door of the house. I will make you a picture of it.

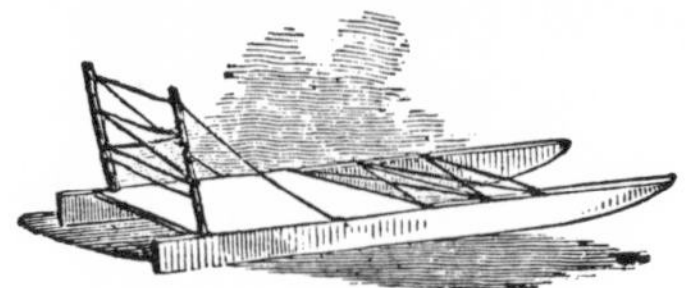

"It is a sled," you exclaim. Yes, a sled; but quite unlike yours. In the far away cold countries no trees grow; so her father had no wood, and he took the bones of the walrus and the whale, and bound them together with strips of seal-skin, and he has built this pretty sled for his little daughter's birthday.

It has a back to lean against and hold by, for the child will go over some very rough places, and might easily fall from

(continued on next page)

it; and then, you see, if she fell, it would be no easy matter to jump up again and climb back to her seat, for the little sled would have run away from her before she should have time to pick herself up. How could it run? Yes, that is the wonderful thing about it; for when her father made the sled he said to himself, "By the time this is finished, the two little brown dogs will be old enough to draw it, and Agoonack shall have them; for she is a princess, the daughter of a great chief."

Now you can see that, with two such brisk little dogs as the brown puppies harnessed to the sled, Agoonack must keep her seat firmly, that she may not roll over into the snow and let the dogs run away with it.

Now we will creep into the low house with the child and her mother, and see how they live.

Outside it is very cold, colder than you have ever known it to be in the coldest winter's day; but inside it is warm, even very hot; and the first thing Agoonack and her mother do is to take off their clothes, for here it is as warm as the place where the brown baby lives, who needs no clothes.

It is n't the sunshine that makes it warm, for you remember I told you it was as dark as night. There is no furnace in the cellar; indeed, there is no cellar, neither is there a stove, — but all this heat comes from a sort of lamp, with long wicks of moss, and plenty of walrus fat to burn. It warms the small house, which has but one room, and over it the mother hangs a shallow dish in which she cooks soup; but most of the meat is eaten raw, cut into long strips, and eaten much as one might eat a stick of candy.

They have no bread, no crackers, no apples, nor potatoes; nothing but meat, and sometimes the milk of the reindeer, for there are no cows in the far, cold northern countries.

(continued on next page)

There is some one else in the hut when Agoonack comes home; a little dark ball, rolled up on one corner of the stone platform which is built all around three sides of the house, serving for seats, beds, and table. This rolled-up ball unrolls itself, tumbles off the seat, and runs to meet them. It is Sip-su, the baby brother of Agoonack, a round little boy, who rides sometimes, when the weather is not too cold, in the hood of his mother's jumper, hanging at her back and peering out from his warm nestling-place over the long icy plain, to watch for his father's return from the bear-hunt.

When the men come home dragging the great Nannook, as they call the bear, there is a merry feast. They crowd together in the hut, bringing in a great block of snow, which they put over the lamp-fire to melt into water, and then they cut long strips of bear's meat, and laugh, and eat, and

B

sing as they tell the long story of the hunt of Nannook, and the seals they have seen, and the foot-tracks of the reindeer they have met in the long valley.

Perhaps while they are so merry there altogether a very great snow-storm will come and cover the little house, so that they cannot get out for several days. When the storm ends they dig out the low door-way, and creep again into the starlight ; and Agoonack slips into her warm clothes, and runs out for Jack Frost to kiss her cheeks, and leave roses wherever his lips touch. If it is very cold indeed, she must stay in, or Jack Frost will give her no roses, but a cold, frosty bite.

This is the way Agoonack lives through the long darkness. But I have to tell you more of her in another chapter, and you will find that it is not always dark in the cold northern countries.

LITTLE PRUDY, by Sophie May [pseudonym for Rebecca Sophia Clarke (1833–1906)]. Boston: Lee and Shepard (successors to Phillips, Sampson & Co.), 1864. 167 pages. 15½ cm.

"Genius comes in with 'Little Prudy.' Compared with her, all other book children are cold creations of literature only; she alone is the real thing."—*North American Review,* January, 1866

PRUDY IN THE PINES.—Page 51.

CHAPTER V.

PRUDY IN THE PINES.

"No, my dears," said grandma, "I couldn't consent to let you go strawberrying 'up by the Pines' as you call it. It is Mr. Judkins's mowing-field."

"But, grandma," said Grace, "Johnny Gordon went there yesterday, and there wasn't any fuss about it."

"Then you may be sure Mr. Judkins did not know it," said grandma. "If he should catch any children in his field, he would be sure to give them a severe scolding."

"Besides," chimed in aunt Madge, "Prudy isn't fit to walk so far—she isn't very well."

(continued on next page)

"No, she is quite out of sorts," said grandma. "So if you must go somewhere, you may take your little baskets and go out in the meadow on the other side of the corn-field. Only take good care of Prudy; now remember."

"Grandma always says that over," said Susy, as the three children were on their way to the meadow; "and aunt Madge always says it too—'take care of Prudy!' As if she were a little baby."

"That is all because she cries so much, I presume," said Grace, looking at poor Prudy rather sternly. "I did hope, Susy, that when Horace went down to the 'crick' fishing, you and I might go off by ourselves, and have a nice time for once. But here is 'little Pitcher' right at our heels. We never can have any peace. Little Miss Somebody thinks she must follow, of course."

"Yes, that's the way it is," said Susy. "Some folks are always round, you know."

"Now, Susy," said Prudy, forcing back her tears as well as she could, "I guess you don't love your little sister, or you wouldn't talk that way to me."

They gathered strawberries for a while in silence, Prudy picking more leaves than berries, and sometimes, in her haste to keep up with the others, pulling up grass by the roots.

"Well, I don't think much of this," said Grace; "there ain't more than ten straw-berries in this meadow, and those ain't bigger than peas."

"O, I know it," said Susy, in the tone of one who has made up her mind for the worst. "I suppose we've got to stay here, though. We could go up in the Pines now if it wasn't for Prudy, and they are real thick up there."

"Yes," said Grace, "but grandma knew we couldn't without she would be sure to follow. Do you think Mr. Judkins would be likely to scold, Susy?"

"No, indeed," said Susy, eating a dry strawberry. "He keeps sheep, and goes round talking to himself. I ain't a bit afraid of him. What could we little girls do to his grass, I'd like to know? It isn't as if we were great, rude boys, is it Grace?"

"No," said Grace, thoughtfully. "Now if we could only get rid of Prudy ——"

Little Prudy pushed back her "shaker," and looked up, showing a pair of flushed cheeks damp with tears.

"I don't think you are very polite to me," said the child. "Bime-by I shall go to heaven, and I shan't never come back any more, and then I guess you'll cry."

"What shall we do?" said Grace, looking

at Susy; "we musn't take her, and we can't go without her."

"Well, I'm a-goin' right straight home, right off — that's what I'm goin' to do," said Prudy, "and when I say my prayers, I shall just tell God how naughty you be!"

Prudy turned short about, and the girls went toward the Pines, feeling far from happy, for a "still, small voice" told them they were doing wrong.

They had got about half way up the hill, when, looking back, there was Prudy, puffing and running for dear life.

"I thought you had gone home," said Susy, quite vexed.

"Well, I didn't," said Prudy, who had got her smiles all back again; "I couldn't get home — 'cause — I got my feet 'most damp and some wet. I won't be no trouble, Susy."

4

(continued on next page)

So the girls made the best of it, and helped little "Mother Bunch" up the long, steep hill. Prudy had one hearty cry before the long walk was over. "Her nose fell on a rock," she said; but as it was only grazed a little, she soon forgot about it.

"This is something worth while, now," said Grace, after they had at last reached the field, and were seated in the tall grass. "The strawberries are as thick as spatter."

"Yes," said Susy, "and grandma and aunt Madge will be so glad to see our baskets full they'll certainly be glad we didn't stay in the meadow. Big as your thumb, ain't they?"

You see the girls were trying to stifle that still, small voice, and they tried to believe they were having a good time.

Grace and Susy had got their baskets nearly half full, and Prudy had covered the

bottom of hers with leaves, stems, and a few berries, when a man's voice was heard muttering, not far off.

"O Grace," whispered Susy, "that's Mr. Judkins!"

He carried a whetstone, on which he was sharpening his jackknife.

"Ah," said he, talking to himself, and not appearing to notice the girls, "I never would have thought that these little children — ah, would have come into my field — ah, and trampled down my grass! I shall hate — ah, to cut off their little ears — ah, and see the blood running down!"

I suppose it was not two minutes before the children had left that field, pulling the screaming Prudy through the bars as roughly as if she had been a sack of wool instead of flesh and blood, — their hair flying in the wind, and their poor little hearts pounding against their sides like trip-hammers. If the field had been on fire they could not have run faster, dragging helpless Prudy, who screamed all the way at the very top of her voice.

Susy and Prudy had thrown away their pretty little baskets. Grace had pushed hers up her arm, and her sleeve was soaking in the red juice of the bruised strawberries, while little streams of juice were trickling down her nice, buff-colored dress, ruining it entirely.

"You hadn't ought to have took me up there," sobbed Prudy, as soon as she could find her voice; and these were the first words spoken.

"O, hush, hush right up!" cried Susy, in terror. "He's after us, to take us to jail."

The family were really frightened when

the panting children rushed into the house in such a plight.

"It was a crazy drunk man," cried Prudy, "and he had a axe ——"

"No," said Grace, "it was that wicked Mr. Judkins, and it was his jackknife."

"And he snips off your ears and nose," broke in Prudy, "and blood comes a-runnin' down, and he kills you dead, and then he puts you in jail, and then he chased us — don't you hear him comin'?"

"What does all this mean?" cried grandma and aunt Madge in one breath. "Have you been in that mowing-field, children?"

Grace and Susy hung their heads.

"Yes, they did," said Prudy, "and I wasn't well, and they shouldn't have gone and took me up there, and 'twas 'cause they were naughty."

"What shall I do with children that

(continued on next page)

54 LITTLE PRUDY.

disobey me in this manner?" said grandma, much displeased.

"Worst of all," said aunt Madge, pulling off Prudy's shoes, "this child has got her feet wet, and is sure to be sick."

ON OPPOSITE PAGE:

ELSIE DINSMORE. By Martha Farquharson [pseudonym for Martha Farquharson Finley (1828–1909)]. New York: M. W. Dodd, 506 Broadway, 1867. 288 pages. 17½ cm.

The author, grouped with Susan Warner (*The Wide, Wide World*, 1850, and *Queechy*, 1852) and Maria Susanna Cummins (*The Lamplighter*, 1854) as the "lachrymose ladies," had a slight edge in literary regard over these contemporaries, though all came to be categorized as "scribblers." Their manner was unrelievedly one of dealing melodramatically with situations that brought forth tears and prayers from their sweet, humorless, and saintly heroines. Elsie's belief that breaking the Sabbath was a sin is illustrated here in a famous episode. In her consistent stand, Elsie on another occasion receives punishment for refusing to read a fairy tale to a younger child on the Sabbath.

(continued on next page)

ELSIE DINSMORE.

BY

MARTHA FARQUHARSON.

NEW YORK:

M. W. DODD, NO. 506 BROADWAY.

ELSIE DINSMORE *(continued from page 227)*

Chapter Tenth.

"If thou turn away thy foot from the Sabbath, from doing thy pleasure on my holy day, and call the Sabbath a Delight, the Holy of the Lord, Honorable, and shalt honor him, not doing thine own ways, nor finding thine own pleasure, nor speaking thine own words."—*Isaiah* lviii. 13.

"Whether it be right in the sight of God to hearken unto you, more than unto God, judge ye."—*Acts* iv. 19.

Quite a number of guests had dined at Roselands. They were nearly all gentlemen, and were now collected in the drawing-room, laughing, jesting, talking politics, and conversing with each other and the ladies upon various worldly topics, apparently quite forgetful that it was the Lord's day, which He has commanded to be kept holy in thought and word, as well as deed.

"May I ask what you are in search of, Mr. Eversham?" inquired Adelaide, as she noticed one of the guests glance around the room with a rather disappointed air.

"Yes, Miss Adelaide; I was looking for little Miss Elsie. Travilla has given me so very glowing an account of her precocious musical talent, that I have conceived a great desire to hear her play and sing."

"Do you hear that, Horace?" asked Adelaide, turning to her brother.

(continued on next page)

"Yes, and I shall be most happy to gratify you, Eversham," replied the young father, with a proud smile.

He crossed the room to summon a servant, but as he placed his hand upon the bell-rope, Mrs. Dinsmore arrested his movement.

"Stay, Horace," she said; "you had better not send for her."

"May I be permitted to ask *why*, madam?" he inquired in a tone of mingled surprise and annoyance.

"Because she will not sing," answered the lady, coolly.

"Pardon me, madam, but I think she will, if *I bid* her do it," he said with flashing eyes.

"No, she will not," persisted Mrs Dinsmore, in the same cold, quiet tone; "she will tell you she is wiser than her father, and that it would be a sin to obey him in this. Believe me, she will most assuredly defy your authority; so you had better take my advice and let her alone—thus sparing yourself the mortification of exhibiting before your guests your inability to govern your child."

Mr. Dinsmore bit his lip with vexation.

"Thank you," he said, haughtily, "but I prefer convincing you that that inability lies wholly in your own imagination; and I am quite at a loss to understand upon what you found your opinion, as Elsie has never yet made the very slightest resistance to my authority."

He had given the bell-rope a vigorous pull while

speaking, and a servant now appearing in answer to the summons, he sent him with a message to Elsie, requiring her presence in the drawing-room.

Then turning away from his step-mother, who looked after him with a gleam of triumph in her eye, he joined the group of gentlemen already gathered about the piano, where Adelaide had just taken her seat and begun a brilliant overture.

Yet, outwardly calm and self-satisfied as his demeanor may have been, Horace Dinsmore was even now regretting the step he had just taken; for remembering Elsie's conscientious scruples regarding the observance of the Sabbath—which he had for the moment forgotten—he foresaw that there would be a struggle, probably a severe one; and though, having always found her docile and yielding, he felt no doubt of the final result, he would willingly have avoided the contest, could he have done so without a sacrifice of pride; but, as he said to himself, with a slight sigh, he had now gone too far to retreat; and then he had all along felt that this struggle must come *some* time, and perhaps it was as well *now* as at any other.

Elsie was alone in her own room, spending the Sabbath afternoon in her usual manner, when the servant came to say that her papa wished to see her in the drawing-room. The little girl was a good deal alarmed at the summons, for the thought instantly flashed upon her, "He is going to bid me play and sing, or do something else which it is not right to do on the Sabbath day."

(continued on next page)

But remembering that he never had done so, she hoped he might not now; yet ere she obeyed the call she knelt down for a moment, and prayed earnestly for strength to do right, however difficult it might be.

"Come here, daughter," her father said as she entered the room. He spoke in his usual pleasant, affectionate tone, yet Elsie started, trembled, and turned pale; for catching sight of the group at the piano, and her Aunt Adelaide just vacating the music-stool, she at once perceived what was in store for her.

"Here, Elsie," said her father, selecting a song which she had learned during their absence, and sang remarkably well, "I wish you to sing this for my friends; they are anxious to hear it."

"Will not to-morrow do, papa?" she asked, in a low, tremulous tone.

Mrs. Dinsmore, who had drawn near to listen, now looked at Horace with a meaning smile, which he affected not to see.

"Certainly not, Elsie," he said; "we want it now. You know it quite well enough without any more practice."

"I did not want to wait for *that* reason, papa," she replied in the same low, trembling tones, "but you know this is the holy Sabbath day."

"Well, my daughter, and what of that? *I* consider this song perfectly proper to be sung to-day, and that ought to satisfy you that you will not be doing wrong to sing it: remember what I said to you some weeks ago; and now sit down and sing it at once, without any more ado."

"O papa! I *cannot* sing it to-day; *please* let me wait until to-morrow."

"Elsie," he said in his sternest tones, "sit down to the piano instantly, and do as I bid you, and let me have no more of this nonsense."

She sat down, but raising her pleading eyes, brimful of tears to his face, she repeated her refusal. "Dear papa, I *cannot* sing it to-day. I *cannot* break the Sabbath."

"Elsie, you *must* sing it," said he, placing the music before her. "I have told you that it will not be breaking the Sabbath, and that is sufficient; you must let me judge for you in these matters."

"Let her wait until to-morrow, Dinsmore; to-morrow will suit us quite as well," urged several of the gentlemen, while Adelaide good-naturedly said, "Let me play it, Horace; I have no such scruples, and presume I can do it nearly as well as Elsie."

"No," he replied, "when I give my child a command, it is to be obeyed; I have *said* she should play it, and play it she *must;* she is not to suppose that she may set up her opinion of right and wrong against mine."

Elsie sat with her little hands folded in her lap, the tears streaming from her downcast eyes over her pale cheeks. She was trembling, but though there was no stubbornness in her countenance, the expression

(continued on next page)

meek and humble, she made no movement toward obeying her father's order.

There was a moment of silent waiting: then he said in his severest tone, "Elsie, you shall sit there till you obey me, though it should be until to-morrow morning."

"Yes, papa," she replied in a scarcely audible voice, and they all turned away and left her.

"You see now that you had better have taken my advice, Horace," remarked Mrs. Dinsmore, in a triumphant aside; "I knew very well how it would end."

"Excuse me," said he, "but it has *not* ended; and ere it does, I think she will learn that she has a stronger will than her own to deal with."

Elsie's position was a most uncomfortable one; her seat high and uneasy, and seeming to grow more and more so as the weary moments passed slowly away. No one came near her or seemed to notice her, yet she could hear them conversing in other parts of the room, and knew that they were sometimes looking at her, and, timid and bashful as she was, it seemed hard to bear. Then, too, her little heart was very sad as she thought of her father's displeasure, and feared that he would withdraw from her the affection which had been for the last few months the very sunshine of her life. Besides all this, the excitement of her feelings, and the close and sultry air—for it was a very warm day—had brought on a nervous headache. She leaned forward and rested her head against the instrument, feeling in momentary danger of falling from her seat.

Thus two long hours had passed when Mr. Travilla came to her side, and said in a compassionate tone, "I am really very sorry for you, my little friend; but I advise you to submit to your papa. I see you are getting very weary sitting there, and I warn you not to hope to conquer him. I have known him for years, and a more determined person I never saw. Had you not better sing the song? it will not take five minutes, and then your trouble will be all over."

Elsie raised her head, and answered gently, "Thank you for your sympathy, Mr. Travilla, you are very kind; but I could not do it, because Jesus says, 'He that loveth father or mother more than me, is not worthy of me;' and I cannot disobey Him, even to please my own dear papa."

"But, Miss Elsie, why do you think it would be disobeying Him? Is there any verse in the Bible which says you must not sing songs on Sunday?"

"Mr. Travilla, it says the Sabbath is to be kept holy unto the Lord; that we are not to think our own thoughts, nor speak our own words, nor do our own actions; but all the day must be spent in studying God's word, or worshipping and praising Him: and there is no praise in that song; not one word about God or heaven."

"That is very true, Elsie, but still it is such a *very little* thing, that I cannot think there would be much

(continued on next page)

harm in it, or that God would be very angry with you for doing it."

"O Mr. Travilla!" she said, looking up at him in great surprise, "surely you know that there is no such thing as a *little sin;* and don't you remember about the man who picked up sticks on the Sabbath-day?"

"No; what was it?"

"God commanded that he should be stoned to death, and it was done. Would you not have thought *that* a very little thing, Mr. Travilla?"

"Yes, I believe I should," said he, turning away with a very grave face.

"Dinsmore," he said, going up to his friend, "I am sure that child is conscientious; had you not better give up to her in this instance?"

"*Never*, Travilla," he answered, with stern decision. "This is the first time she has rebelled against my authority, and if I let her conquer now, she will think she is always to have her own way. No; cost what it may, I *must* subdue her; she will have to learn that my will is law."

"Right, Horace," said the elder Mr. Dinsmore, approvingly, "let her understand from the first that you are to be master; it is always the best plan."

"Excuse me, Dinsmore," said Travilla; "but I must say that I think a parent has no right to coerce a child into doing violence to its conscience."

"Nonsense!" replied his friend, a little angrily;

"Elsie is entirely too young to set up her opinion against mine; she must allow me to judge for her in these matters for some years to come."

Eversham, who had been casting uneasy glances at Elsie all the afternoon, now drawing his chair near to Adelaide, said to her in an undertone, "Miss Adelaide, I am deeply sorry for the mischief I have unwittingly caused, and if you can tell me how to repair it you will lay me under lasting obligations."

Adelaide shook her head. "There is no moving Horace when he has once set his foot down," she said; "and as to Elsie, I doubt whether any power on earth can make her do what she considers wrong."

"Poor little thing!" said Eversham, sighing; "where in the world did she get such odd notions?"

"Partly from a pious Scotch woman, who had a good deal to do with her in her infancy, and partly from studying the Bible, I believe. She is always at it."

"Indeed!" and he relapsed into thoughtful silence.

Another hour passed slowly away, and then the tea-bell rang.

"Elsie," asked her father, coming to her side, "are you ready to obey me now? if so, we will wait a moment to hear the song, and then you can go to your tea with us."

"Dear papa, I cannot break the Sabbath," she replied, in a low, gentle tone, without lifting her head.

"Very well then, I cannot break my word; you

(continued on next page)

must sit there until you will submit; and until then you must fast. You are not only making yourself miserable by your disobedience and obstinacy, Elsie, but are mortifying and grieving *me* very much," he added in a subdued tone, that sent a sharp pang to the loving little heart, and caused some very bitter tears to fall, as he turned away and left her.

The evening passed wearily away to the little girl; the drawing-room was but dimly lighted, for the company had all deserted it to wander about the grounds, or sit in the portico enjoying the moonlight and the pleasant evening breeze, and the air indoors seemed insupportably close and sultry. At times Elsie could scarcely breathe, and she longed intensely to get out into the open air; every moment her seat grew more uncomfortable and the pain in her head more severe: her thoughts began to wander, she forgot where she was, everything became confused, and at length she lost all consciousness.

Several gentlemen, among whom were Mr. Horace Dinsmore and Mr. Travilla, were conversing together on the portico, when they were suddenly startled by a sound as of something falling.

Travilla, who was nearest the door, rushed into the drawing-room, followed by the others.

"A light! quick, quick, a light!" he cried, raising Elsie's insensible form in his arms; "the child has fainted."

One of the others, instantly snatching a lamp from a distant table, brought it near, and the increased light showed Elsie's little face, ghastly as that of a corpse, while a stream of blood was flowing from a wound in the temple, made by striking against some sharp corner of the furniture as she fell.

She was a pitiable sight indeed, with her fair face, her curls, and her white dress all dabbled in blood.

"Dinsmore, you're a brute!" exclaimed Travilla indignantly, as he placed her gently on a sofa.

Horace made no reply, but, with a face almost as pale as her own, bent over his little daughter in speechless alarm, while one of the guests, who happened to be a physician, hastily dressed the wound, and then applied restoratives.

It was some time ere consciousness returned, and the father trembled with the agonizing fear that the gentle spirit had taken its flight.

But at length the soft eyes unclosed, and gazing with a troubled look into his face, bent so anxiously over her, she asked, "Dear papa, are you angry with me?"

"No, darling," he replied in tones made tremulous with emotion, "not at all."

"What was it?" she asked in a bewildered way; "what did I do? what has happened?"

"Never mind, daughter," he said, "you have been ill; but you are better now, so don't think any more about it."

"She had better be put to bed at once," said the physician.

"There is blood on my dress," cried Elsie, in a startled tone; "where did it come from?"

(continued on next page)

"You fell and hurt your head," replied her father, raising her gently in his arms; "but don't talk any more now."

"Oh! I remember," she moaned, an expression of keen distress coming over her face; "papa—"

"Hush! hush! not a word more; we will let the past go," he said, kissing her lips. "I shall carry you to your room now, and see you put to bed."

He held her on his knee, her head resting on his shoulder, while Chloe prepared her for rest.

"Are you hungry, daughter?" he asked.

"No, papa; I only want to go to sleep."

"There, Aunt Chloe, that will do," he said, as the old nurse tied on the child's night-cap; and raising her again in his arms, he carried her to the bed and was about to place her on it.

"O papa! my prayers first, you know," she cried eagerly.

"Never mind them to-night," said he, "you are not able."

"Please let me, dear papa," she pleaded; "I cannot go to sleep without."

Yielding to her entreaties, he placed her on her knees, and stood beside her, listening to her murmured petitions, in which he more than once heard his own name coupled with a request that he might be made to love Jesus.

When she had finished, he again raised her in his arms, kissed her tenderly several times, and then laid her carefully on the bed, saying, as he did so, "Why did you ask, Elsie, that I might love Jesus?"

"Because, papa, I do so want you to love Him; it would make you so happy; and besides, you cannot go to heaven without; the Bible says so."

"Does it? and what makes you think I don't love Him?"

"Dear papa, please don't be angry," she pleaded, tearfully, "but you know Jesus says, 'He that keepeth my commandments, he it is that loveth me.'"

He stooped over her. "Good night, daughter," he said.

"Dear, *dear* papa," she cried, throwing her arm round his neck, and drawing down his face close to hers, "I do love you so very, *very* much!"

"Better than anybody else?" he asked.

"No, papa, I love Jesus best; you next."

He kissed her again, and with a half sigh turned away and left the room. He was not entirely pleased; not quite willing that she should love even her Saviour better than himself.

Elsie was very weary, and was soon asleep. She waked the next morning feeling nearly as well as usual, and after she had had her bath and been dressed by Chloe's careful hands, the curls being arranged to conceal the plaster that covered the wound on her temple, there was nothing in her appearance, except a slight paleness, to remind her friends of the last night's accident.

She was sitting reading her morning chapter

(continued on next page)

when her father came in, and taking a seat by her side, lifted her to his knee, saying, as he caressed her tenderly, "My little daughter is looking pretty well this morning; how does she feel?"

"Quite well, thank you, papa," she replied, looking up into his face with a sweet, loving smile.

He raised the curls to look at the wounded temple; then, as he dropped them again, he said, with a shudder, "Elsie, do you know that you were very near being killed last night?"

"No, papa, was I?" she asked with an awe-struck countenance.

"Yes, the doctor says if that wound had been made half an inch nearer your eye—I should have been childless."

His voice trembled almost too much for utterance as he finished his sentence, and he strained her to his heart with a deep sigh of thankfulness for her escape.

Elsie was very quiet for some moments, and the little face was almost sad in its deep thoughtfulness.

"What are you thinking of, darling?" he asked.

She raised her eyes to his face, and he saw that they were brimful of tears.

"O papa!" she said, dropping her head on his breast while the bright drops fell like rain down her cheeks, "would you have been so very sorry?"

"Sorry, darling! do you not know that you are more precious to me than all my wealth, all my friends and relatives put together? Yes, I would rather part with everything else than lose this one little girl," he said, kissing her again and again.

"Dear, *dear* papa! how glad I am that you love me so much!" she replied; and then relapsed into silence.

He watched her changing countenance for some time, then asked, "What is it, darling?"

"I was just thinking," she said, "whether I was ready to go to heaven, and I believe I was; for I know that I love Jesus; and then I was thinking how glad mamma would have been to see me; don't you think she would, papa?"

"I can't spare you to her yet," he replied with emotion, "and I think she loves me too well to wish it."

As Miss Day had not yet returned, Elsie's time was still pretty much at her own disposal, excepting when her papa gave her something to do; so, after breakfast, finding that he was engaged with some one in the library, she took her Bible, and seeking out a shady retreat in the garden, sat down to read.

The Bible was ever the book of books to her, and this morning the solemn, tender feelings naturally caused by the discovery of her recent narrow escape from sudden death made it even more than usually touching and beautiful in her eyes. She had been alone in the arbor for some time, when, hearing a step at her side, she looked up, showing a face all wet with tears.

It was Mr. Travilla who stood beside her.

(continued on next page)

"In tears, little Elsie! Pray, what may the book be that affects you so?" he asked, sitting down by her side and taking it from her hand. "The Bible, I declare!" he exclaimed in surprise. "What can there be in it that you find so affecting?"

"O Mr. Travilla!" said the little girl, "does it not make your heart ache to read how the Jews abused our dear, dear Saviour? and then to think that it was all because of our sins," she sobbed.

He looked half distressed, half puzzled; it seemed a new idea to him.

"Really, my little Elsie," he said, "you are quite original in your ideas. I suppose I *ought* to feel unhappy about these things, but indeed the truth is, I have never thought much about them."

"Then you don't love Jesus," she answered, mournfully. "Ah! Mr. Travilla, how sorry I am."

"Why, Elsie, what difference can it make to you whether I love Him or not?"

"Because, Mr. Travilla, the Bible says, 'If any man love not the Lord Jesus Christ, let him be anathema, maranatha,' accursed from God. Oh! sir, think how dreadful! You cannot be *saved* unless you love Jesus, and believe on Him. 'Believe on the Lord Jesus Christ, and thou shalt be saved.' That is what God says in His word."

She spoke with deep solemnity, and the tears trembling in her eyes. He was touched, but for a while sat perfectly silent.

Then he said, with an effort to speak lightly, "Ah!

well, my little friend, I certainly intend to repent and believe before I die, but there is time enough yet."

"Mr. Travilla," she said, laying her hand on his arm and looking earnestly into his face, "how do you know that there is time enough yet? *don't* put it off, I beg of you."

She paused a moment; then asked, "Do you know, Mr. Travilla, how near I came to being killed last night?"

He nodded.

"Well, suppose I had been killed, and had not loved Jesus; where would I be now?"

He put his arm round her, and giving her a kiss, said, "I don't think you would have been in any very bad place, Elsie; a sweet, amiable little girl, who has never harmed any one, would surely not fare very badly in another world."

She shook her head very gravely.

"Ah! Mr. Travilla, you forget the anathema, maranatha; if I had not loved Jesus, and had my sins washed away in His blood, I could not have been saved."

Just at this moment a servant came to tell Elsie that her papa wanted her in the drawing-room, and Mr. Travilla, taking her hand, led her into the house.

They found the company again grouped about the piano, listening to Adelaide's music.

Elsie went directly to her father and stood by his side, putting her hand in his with a gesture of confiding affection.

(continued on next page)

He smiled down at her, and kept fast hold of it until his sister had risen from the instrument, when putting Elsie in her place, he said, "Now, my daughter, let us have that song."

"Yes, papa," she replied, beginning the prelude at once, "I will do my very best."

And so she did. The song was both well played and well sung, and her father looked proud and happy as the gentlemen expressed their pleasure and asked for another and another.

Thus the clouds which had so suddenly obscured little Elsie's sky, seemed to have vanished as speedily as they had arisen.

Her father again treated her with all his wonted affection, and there even seemed to be a depth of tenderness in his love which it had not known before, for he could not forget how nearly he had lost her.

RAGGED DICK;

OR,

STREET LIFE IN NEW YORK

WITH THE BOOT-BLACKS.

BY

HORATIO ALGER, JR.,

AUTHOR OF "FRANK'S CAMPAIGN," "PAUL PRESCOTT'S CHARGE," "CHARLIE CODMAN'S CRUISE," "HELEN FORD."

LORING, Publisher,
319 WASHINGTON STREET,
BOSTON.

RAGGED DICK; or, Street Life in New York with the Boot-blacks by Horatio Alger, Jr. [1834–1899]. Boston, Loring, 1868. 296 pages. 18 cm. (Volume 1 of the Ragged Dick Series)

(continued on next page)

Described by Richard Nye as the "Homer" of juvenile fiction writers, and deplored by the discriminating for his shallow values and slipshod writing, Alger, a graduate of Harvard and an unsuccessful minister took up the writing of inspirational stories for boys partly *(continued from page 263)*

PREFACE.

"Ragged Dick" was contributed as a serial story to the pages of the Schoolmate, a well-known juvenile magazine, during the year 1867. While in course of publication, it was received with so many evidences of favor that it has been rewritten and considerably enlarged, and is now presented to the public as the first volume of a series intended to illustrate the life and experiences of the friendless and vagrant children who are now numbered by thousands in New York and other cities.

Several characters in the story are sketched from life. The necessary information has been gathered mainly from personal observation and conversations with the boys themselves. The author is indebted also to the excellent Superintendent of the Newsboys' Lodging House, in Fulton Street, for some facts of which he has been able to make use. Some anachronisms may be noted. Wherever they occur, they have been admitted, as aiding in the development of the story, and will prob-

vii

on the encouragement of William T. Adams, author of the Oliver Optic series. Alger's books soon became best sellers. The Ragged Dick series consisted of one basic plot (as did all his books)—the achievement of wealth by a poor boy, sometimes an orphan, sometimes the sole support of a widowed mother, through hard work or some deus ex machina, such as the timely rescue of a wealthy banker's daughter. His *Tattered Tom* (1871) tells of the adventures of an intrepid girl forced by unscrupulous adults to eke out a living in the streets.

(continued on next page)

ably be considered as of little importance in an unpretending volume, which does not aspire to strict historical accuracy.

The author hopes that, while the volumes in this series may prove interesting as stories, they may also have the effect of enlisting the sympathies of his readers in behalf of the unfortunate children whose life is described, and of leading them to co-operate with the praiseworthy efforts now making by the Children's Aid Society and other organizations to ameliorate their condition.

New York, April, 1868.

RAGGED DICK;

OR,

STREET LIFE IN NEW YORK.

CHAPTER I.

RAGGED DICK IS INTRODUCED TO THE READER.

"Wake up there, youngster," said a rough voice.

Ragged Dick opened his eyes slowly, and stared stupidly in the face of the speaker, but did not offer to get up.

"Wake up, you young vagabond!" said the man a little impatiently; "I suppose you'd lay there all day, if I hadn't called you."

"What time is it?" asked Dick.

"Seven o'clock."

"Seven o'clock! I oughter 've been up an hour ago. I know what 'twas made me so precious sleepy. I went to the Old Bowery last night, and didn't turn in till past twelve."

"You went to the Old Bowery? Where'd you get your money?" asked the man, who was a porter in the employ of a firm doing business on Spruce Street.

"Made it by shines, in course. My guardian don't allow me no money for theatres, so I have to earn it."

"Some boys get it easier than that," said the porter significantly.

"You don't catch me stealin', if that's what you mean," said Dick.

"Don't you ever steal, then?"

"No, and I wouldn't. Lots of boys does it, but I wouldn't."

"Well, I'm glad to hear you say that. I believe there's some good in you, Dick, after all."

"Oh, I'm a rough customer!" said Dick. "But I wouldn't steal. It's mean."

"I'm glad you think so, Dick," and the rough voice sounded gentler than at first. "Have you got any money to buy your breakfast?"

"No, but I'll soon get some."

While this conversation had been going on, Dick

had got up. His bedchamber had been a wooden box half full of straw, on which the young boot-black had reposed his weary limbs, and slept as soundly as if it had been a bed of down. He dumped down into the straw without taking the trouble of undressing. Getting up too was an equally short process. He jumped out of the box, shook himself, picked out one or two straws that had found their way into rents in his clothes, and, drawing a well-worn cap over his uncombed locks, he was all ready for the business of the day.

Dick's appearance as he stood beside the box was rather peculiar. His pants were torn in several places, and had apparently belonged in the first instance to a boy two sizes larger than himself. He wore a vest, all the buttons of which were gone except two, out of which peeped a shirt which looked as if it had been worn a month. To complete his costume he wore a coat too long for him, dating back, if one might judge from its general appearance, to a remote antiquity.

Washing the face and hands is usually considered proper in commencing the day, but Dick was above

(continued on next page)

such refinement. He had no particular dislike to dirt, and did not think it necessary to remove several dark streaks on his face and hands. But in spite of his dirt and rags there was something about Dick that was attractive. It was easy to see that if he had been clean and well dressed he would have been decidedly good-looking. Some of his companions were sly, and their faces inspired distrust; but Dick had a frank, straight-forward manner that made him a favorite.

Dick's business hours had commenced. He had no office to open. His little blacking-box was ready for use, and he looked sharply in the faces of all who passed, addressing each with, "Shine yer boots, sir?"

"How much?" asked a gentleman on his way to his office.

"Ten cents," said Dick, dropping his box, and sinking upon his knees on the sidewalk, flourishing his brush with the air of one skilled in his profession.

"Ten cents! Isn't that a little steep?"

"Well, you know 'taint all clear profit," said Dick, who had already set to work. "There's the

blacking costs something, and I have to get a new brush pretty often."

"And you have a large rent too," said the gentleman quizzically, with a glance at a large hole in Dick's coat.

"Yes, sir," said Dick, always ready to joke; "I have to pay such a big rent for my manshun up on Fifth Avenoo, that I can't afford to take less than ten cents a shine. I'll give you a bully shine, sir."

"Be quick about it, for I am in a hurry. So your house is on Fifth Avenue, is it?"

"It isn't anywhere else," said Dick, and Dick spoke the truth there.

"What tailor do you patronize?" asked the gentleman, surveying Dick's attire.

"Would you like to go to the same one?" asked Dick, shrewdly.

"Well, no; it strikes me that he didn't give you a very good fit."

"This coat once belonged to General Washington," said Dick, comically. "He wore it all through the Revolution, and it got torn some, 'cause he fit so hard. When he died he told his widder to give it to some smart young feller that hadn't got none of his own; so she gave it to me. But if you'd like it, sir, to remember General Washington by, I'll let you have it reasonable."

"Thank you, but I wouldn't want to deprive you of it. And did your pants come from General Washington too?"

"No, they was a gift from Lewis Napoleon. Lewis had outgrown 'em and sent 'em to me, — he's bigger than me, and that's why they don't fit."

"It seems you have distinguished friends. Now, my lad, I suppose you would like your money."

"I shouldn't have any objection," said Dick.

"I believe," said the gentleman, examining his pocket-book, "I haven't got anything short of twenty-five cents. Have you got any change?"

"Not a cent," said Dick. "All my money's invested in the Erie Railroad."

"That's unfortunate."

"Shall I get the money changed, sir?"

"I can't wait; I've got to meet an appointment immediately. I'll hand you twenty-five cents, and

you can leave the change at my office any time during the day."

"All right, sir. Where is it?"

"No. 125 Fulton Street. Shall you remember?"

"Yes, sir. What name?"

"Greyson, — office on second floor."

"All right, sir; I'll bring it."

"I wonder whether the little scamp will prove honest," said Mr. Greyson to himself, as he walked away. "If he does, I'll give him my custom regularly. If he don't, as is most likely, I shan't mind the loss of fifteen cents."

Mr. Greyson didn't understand Dick. Our ragged hero wasn't a model boy in all respects. I am afraid he swore sometimes, and now and then he played tricks upon unsophisticated boys from the country, or gave a wrong direction to honest old gentlemen unused to the city. A clergyman in search of the Cooper Institute he once directed to the Tombs Prison, and, following him unobserved, was highly delighted when the unsuspicious stranger walked up the front steps of the great stone building on Centre Street, and tried to obtain admission.

(continued on next page)

"I guess he wouldn't want to stay long if he did get in," thought Ragged Dick, hitching up his pants. "Leastways I shouldn't. They're so precious glad to see you that they won't let you go, but board you gratooitous, and never send in no bills."

Another of Dick's faults was his extravagance. Being always wide-awake and ready for business, he earned enough to have supported him comfortably and respectably. There were not a few young clerks who employed Dick from time to time in his professional capacity, who scarcely earned as much as he, greatly as their style and dress exceeded his. But Dick was careless of his earnings. Where they went he could hardly have told himself. However much he managed to earn during the day, all was generally spent before morning. He was fond of going to the Old Bowery Theatre, and to Tony Pastor's, and if he had any money left afterwards, he would invite some of his friends in somewhere to have an oyster stew; so it seldom happened that he commenced the day with a penny.

Then I am sorry to add that Dick had formed the habit of smoking. This cost him considerable, for

Dick was rather fastidious about his cigars, and wouldn't smoke the cheapest. Besides, having a liberal nature, he was generally ready to treat his companions. But of course the expense was the smallest objection. No boy of fourteen can smoke without being affected injuriously. Men are frequently injured by smoking, and boys always. But large numbers of the newsboys and boot-blacks form the habit. Exposed to the cold and wet they find that it warms them up, and the self-indulgence grows upon them. It is not uncommon to see a little boy, too young to be out of his mother's sight, smoking with all the apparent satisfaction of a veteran smoker.

There was another way in which Dick sometimes lost money. There was a noted gambling-house on Baxter Street, which in the evening was sometimes crowded with these juvenile gamesters, who staked their hard earnings, generally losing of course, and refreshing themselves from time to time with a vile mixture of liquor at two cents a glass. Sometimes Dick strayed in here, and played with the rest.

I have mentioned Dick's faults and defects,

2

because I want it understood, to begin with, that I don't consider him a model boy. But there were some good points about him nevertheless. He was above doing anything mean or dishonorable. He would not steal, or cheat, or impose upon younger boys, but was frank and straight-forward, manly and self-reliant. His nature was a noble one, and had saved him from all mean faults. I hope my young readers will like him as I do, without being blind to his faults. Perhaps, although he was only a boot-black, they may find something in him to imitate.

And now, having fairly introduced Ragged Dick to my young readers, I must refer them to the next chapter for his further adventures.

UNCLE REMUS, HIS SONGS AND HIS SAYINGS, The Folk-Lore of the Old Plantation by Joel Chandler Harris [1848–1908], with illustrations by Frederick S. Church and James H. Moser. New York: D. Appleton and Company, 1, 3, and 5 Bond Street, 1881. 231 pages. 19½ cm.

Included in this book are, according to the Contents page, legends of the old plantation, plantation proverbs, songs of Uncle Remus, a story of the war, sayings of Uncle Remus. The author writes that "with respect to the Folk-Lore societies, my purpose has been to preserve the

UNCLE REMUS

HIS SONGS AND HIS SAYINGS

THE FOLK-LORE OF THE OLD PLANTATION

BY JOEL CHANDLER HARRIS

WITH ILLUSTRATIONS BY FREDERICK S. CHURCH AND JAMES H. MOSER

NEW YORK
D. APPLETON AND COMPANY
1, 3, AND 5 BOND STREET
1881

legends themselves in their original simplicity, and to wed them permanently to the quaint dialect—if indeed, it can be called a dialect—through the medium of which they have become a part of the domestic history of every Southern family; and I have endeavored to give the whole a genuine flavor of the whole plantation."

Many plantation stories have a definite connection with African folklore, with Anansi the spider, the rabbit, and other well-known characters featured. One of the funniest and most famous, the Tar-Baby, is included here.

(continued on next page)

UNCLE REMUS AND HIS DECEITFUL JUG.

II.

THE WONDERFUL TAR-BABY STORY.

"DIDN'T the fox *never* catch the rabbit, Uncle Remus?" asked the little boy the next evening.

"He come mighty nigh it, honey, sho's you bawn—Brer Fox did. One day atter Brer Rabbit fool 'im wid dat calamus root, Brer Fox went ter wuk en got 'im some

tar, en mix it wid some turkentime, en fix up a contrapshun wat he call a Tar-Baby, en he tuck dish yer Tar-Baby en he sot 'er in de big road, en den he lay off in de bushes fer ter see wat de news wuz gwineter be. En he didn't hatter wait long, nudder, kaze bimeby here come Brer Rabbit pacin' down de road—lippity-clippity, clippity-lippity—dez ez sassy ez a jay-bird. Brer Fox, he lay low. Brer Rabbit come prancin' 'long twel he spy de Tar-Baby, en den he fotch up on his behime legs like he wuz 'stonished. De Tar-Baby, she sot dar, she did, en Brer Fox, he lay low.

"'Mawnin'!' sez Brer Rabbit, sezee—'nice wedder dis mawnin',' sezee.

"Tar-Baby ain't sayin' nuthin', en Brer Fox, he lay low.

"'How duz yo' sym'tums seem ter segashuate?' sez Brer Rabbit, sezee.

"Brer Fox, he wink his eye slow, en lay low, en de Tar-Baby, she ain't sayin' nuthin'.

"'How you come on, den? Is you deaf?' sez Brer Rabbit, sezee. 'Kaze if you is, I kin holler louder,' sezee.

"Tar-Baby stay still, en Brer Fox, he lay low.

"'Youer stuck up, dat's w'at you is,' says Brer Rabbit, sezee, 'en I'm gwineter kyore you, dat's w'at I'm a gwineter do,' sezee.

"Brer Fox, he sorter chuckle in his stummuck, he did, but Tar-Baby ain't sayin' nuthin'.

"'I'm gwineter larn you howter talk ter 'specttubble fokes ef hit's de las' ack,' sez Brer Rabbit, sezee. 'Ef you don't take off dat hat en tell me howdy, I'm gwineter bus' you wide open,' sezee.

"Tar-Baby stay still, en Brer Fox, he lay low.

"Brer Rabbit keep on axin' 'im, en de Tar-Baby, she keep on sayin' nuthin', twel present'y Brer Rabbit draw back wid his fis', he did, en blip he tuck 'er side er de

(continued on next page)

head. Right dar's whar he broke his merlasses jug. His fis' stuck, en he can't pull loose. De tar hilt 'im. But Tar-Baby, she stay still, en Brer Fox, he lay low.

"'Ef you don't lemme loose, I'll knock you agin,' sez Brer Rabbit, sezee, en wid dat he fotch 'er a wipe wid de udder han', en dat stuck. Tar-Baby, she ain't sayin' nuthin', en Brer Fox, he lay low.

"'Tu'n me loose, fo' I kick de natal stuffin' outen you,' sez Brer Rabbit, sezee, but de Tar-Baby, she ain't sayin' nuthin'. She des hilt on, en den Brer Rabbit lose de use er his feet in de same way. Brer Fox, he lay low. Den Brer Rabbit squall out dat ef de Tar-Baby don't tu'n 'im loose he butt 'er cranksided. En den he butted, en his head got stuck. Den Brer Fox, he sa'ntered fort', lookin' des ez innercent ez wunner yo' mammy's mockin'-birds.

"'Howdy, Brer Rabbit,' sez Brer Fox, sezee. 'You look sorter stuck up dis mawnin',' sezee, en den he rolled on de groun', en laft en laft twel he couldn't laff no mo'. 'I speck you'll take dinner wid me dis time, Brer Rabbit. I done laid in some calamus root, en I ain't gwineter take no skuse,' sez Brer Fox, sezee."

Here Uncle Remus paused, and drew a two-pound yam out of the ashes.

"Did the fox eat the rabbit?" asked the little boy to whom the story had been told.

"Dat's all de fur de tale goes," replied the old man. "He mout, en den agin he moutent. Some say Jedge B'ar come 'long en loosed 'im—some say he didn't. I hear Miss Sally callin'. You better run 'long."

2

DIDDIE, DUMPS, AND TOT, or Plantation Child-life by Louise-Clarke Pyrnelle. New York: Harper & Brothers, Franklin Square, 1882. 217 pages. 19½ cm.

The author, who grew up on a plantation, writes of her childhood and an idyllic relationship with Negroes in a defense of slavery. Christmas, a Negro wedding, old "uncles" and "mammies" who tell stories to the "lil" white "chillern" and their Negro companions (later to be their maids) are all affectionately depicted. The dialect-speaking, childlike Negro literary stereotype can be clearly seen in stories such as these.

(continued on next page)

DIDDIE, DUMPS, AND TOT

OR

PLANTATION CHILD-LIFE

BY

LOUISE-CLARKE PYRNELLE

ILLUSTRATED

NEW YORK
HARPER & BROTHERS, FRANKLIN SQUARE
1882

"YER'LL ALL BE HAVIN' DE CROUP NEXT."

CHAPTER XII.

HOW THE WOODPECKER'S HEAD AND THE ROBIN'S BREAST CAME TO BE RED.

"WELL," began Uncle Bob, "hit wuz all erlong er de jay bird, jes ez I wuz tellin' yer. Yer see, Mr. Jay Bird he fell'd in love, he did, 'long o' Miss Robin, an' he wuz er courtin' her, too; ev'y day de Lord sen', he'd be er gwine ter see her, an' er singin' ter her, an' er cyarin' her berries an' wums; but, somehow or udder, she didn't pyear ter tuck no shine ter him. She'd go er walkin' 'long 'im, an' she'd sing songs wid 'im, an' she'd gobble up de berries an' de wums wat he fotch, but den w'en hit come ter marry'n uv 'im, she wan't dar.

"Well, she wouldn't gib 'im no kin' er 'couragement, tell he got right sick at his heart, he did; an' one day, ez he wuz er settin' in his nes' an' er steddin how ter wuck on Miss Robin so's ter git her love, he hyeard somebody er laughin' an' talkin', an' he lookt out, he did, an' dar wuz Miss Robin er prumurradin' wid de Woodpecker. An' wen he seed dat, he got pow'ful mad, an' he 'low'd ter his-

(continued on next page)

se'f dat efn de Lord spar'd him, he inten' fur ter fix dat Woodpecker.

"In dem times de Woodpecker's head wuz right black, same ez er crow, an' he had er topknot on 'im like er rooster. Gemmun, he wuz er han'sum bird, too. See 'im uv er Sunday, wid his 'go-ter-meetin'' cloze on, an' dar wan't no bird could totch 'im fur looks.

"Well, he an' Miss Robin dey went on by, er laffin' an' er talkin' wid one ernudder; an' de Jay he sot dar, wid his head turnt one side, er steddin an' er steddin ter his-se'f; an' by'mby, atter he made up his min', he sot right ter wuck, he did, an' he fix him er trap.

"He got 'im some sticks, an' he nailt 'em cross'n 'is do' same ez er plank-fence, only he lef' space 'nuff twix' de bottum stick an' de nex' one fur er bird ter git thu; den, stid er nailin' de stick nex' de bottum, he tuck'n prope it up at one een wid er little chip fur ter hole it, an' den jes res' tudder een 'gins de side er de nes'. Soon's eber he done dat, he crawlt out thu de crack mighty kyeerful, I tell yer, caze he wuz fyeared he mout er knock de stick down, an' git his own se'f cotch in de trap; so yer hyeard me, mun, he crawlt thu mighty tick'ler.

"Atter he got thu, den he santer 'long, he did, fur ter hunt up de Woodpecker; an' by'mby he hyeard him peckin' at er log; an' he went up ter him kin' er kyeerless, an' he sez, 'Good-mornin',' sezee; 'yer pow'ful busy ter day.'

"Den de Woodpecker he pass de kempulmence wid 'im, des same ez any udder gemmun; an' atter dey talk er wile, den de Blue Jay he up'n sez, 'I wuz jes er lookin' fur yer,' sezee; 'I gwine ter hab er party ter-morrer night, an' I'd like fur yer ter come. All de birds'll be dar, Miss Robin in speshul,' sezee.

"An' wen de Woodpecker hyearn dat, he 'lowed he'd try fur ter git dar. An' den de Jay he tell him good-mornin', an' went on ter Miss Robin's house. Well, hit pyeart like Miss Robin wuz mo' cole dan uzhul dat day, an' by'mby de Jay Bird, fur ter warm her up, sez, 'Yer lookin' mighty hansum dis mornin',' sezee. An' sez she, 'I'm proud ter hyear yer say so; but, speakin' uv hansum,' sez she, 'hev yer seed Mr. Peckerwood lately?'

"Dat made de Blue Jay kint er mad; an' sezee, 'Yer pyear ter tuck er mighty intrus' in 'im.'

"'Well, I dunno 'bout'n dat,' sez Miss Robin, sez she, kinter lookin' shame. 'I dunno 'boutn dat; but, den I tink he's er mighty *hansum* bird,' sez she.

"Well, wid dat de Jay Bird 'gun ter git madder'n he wuz, an' he 'lowed ter hisse'f dat he'd ax Miss Robin ter his house, so's she could see how he'd fix de Peckerwood; so he sez,

"'Miss Robin, I gwine ter hab er party ter-morrer night; de Woodpecker'll be dar, an' I'd like fur yer ter come.'

(continued on next page)

"Miss Robin 'lowed she'd come, an' de Jay Bird tuck his leave.

"Well, de nex' night de Jay sot in 'is nes' er waitin' fur 'is cump'ny; an' atter er wile hyear come de Woodpecker. Soon's eber he seed de sticks ercross de do', he sez, 'Wy, pyears like yer ben er fixin' up,' sezee. 'Ain't yer ben er buildin'?'

"'Well,' sez de Jay Bird, 'I've jes put er few 'provemunce up, fur ter keep de scritch-owls outn my nes'; but dar's plenty room fur my frien's ter git thu; jes come in,' sezee; an' de Woodpecker he started thu de crack. Soon's eber he got his head thu, de Jay pullt de chip out, an' de big stick fell right crossn his neck. Den dar he wuz, wid his head in an' his feet out! an' de Jay Bird 'gun ter laff, an' ter make fun atn 'im. Sezee, 'I hope I see yer! Yer look like sparkin' Miss Robin now! hit's er gre't pity she can't see yer stretched out like dat; an' she'll be hyear, too, d'rectly; she's er comin' ter de party,' sezee, 'an' I'm gwine ter gib her er new dish; I'm gwine ter sot her down ter roas' Woodpecker dis ebenin'. An' now, efn yer'll 'scuse me, I'll lef' yer hyear fur ter sorter 'muse yerse'f wile I grin's my ax fur ten' ter yer.'

"An' wid dat de Jay went out, an' lef' de po' Woodpecker er lyin' dar; an' by'mby Miss Robin come erlong; an' wen she seed de Woodpecker, she axt 'im 'wat's he doin' down dar on de groun'?' an' atter he up an' tol' her, an' tol' her how de Jay Bird wuz er grin'in' his axe fur ter chop offn his head, den de Robin she sot to an' try ter lif' de stick offn him. She straint an' she straint, but her strengt' wan't 'nuff fur ter move hit den; an' so she sez, 'Mr. Woodpecker,' sez she, 's'posin' I cotch holt yer feet, an' try ter pull yer back dis way?' 'All right,' sez de Woodpecker; an' de Robin, she cotch er good grip on his feet, an' she brace herse'f up 'gins er bush, an' pullt wid all her might, an' atter er wile she fotch 'im thu; but she wuz bleeged fur ter lef' his topknot behin', fur his head wuz skunt des ez clean ez yer han'; an' 'twuz jes ez raw, honey, ez er piece er beef.

"An' wen de Robin seed dat, she wuz mighty 'stressed; an' she tuck his head an' helt it gins her breas' fur ter try an' cumfut him, an' de blood got all ober her breas', an' hit's red plum tell yit.

"Well, de Woodpecker he went erlong home, an' de Robin she nusst him tell his head got well; but de topknot wuz gone, an' it pyeart like de blood all settled in his head, caze fum *dat* day ter *dis* his head's ben red."

"An' did he marry the Robin?" asked Diddie.

"Now I done tol' yer all I know," said Uncle Bob. "I gun yer de tale jes like I hyearn it, an' I ain't er gwine ter make up *nuffin'*, an' tell yer wat I dunno ter be de truff. Efn dar's any mo' ter it, den I ain't neber hyearn

ZIG-ZAG
JOURNEYS
in INDIA

(continued on next page)

ZIGZAG JOURNEY IN INDIA; or, The Antipodes of the Far East. A Collection of the Zenänä Tales. By Hezekiah Butterworth [1839–1905]. Fully Illustrated. Boston: Estes and Lauriat [1887]. 320 pages. 22 cm.

The sumptuous format of the twelve quarto volumes in this best-seller series of the 1880's, one of which appeared before Christmas each year, plainly suggests "the gift book." Colored covers with pictures printed on paper over board or with gold stamping on a red cloth binding, pictorial end-paper spreads, and many illustrations throughout give a wholly luxurious look. Like Horace Scudder in his Bodley books, Butterworth mixed stories and history and fitted his texts to pictures supplied by his publisher. Just as the Bodleys were a more modern counterpart of the Rollo books, so the Zigzag books were recognized as an extension of the Bodley book principle, though Butterworth cared less than Scudder about style of writing. He was deeply interested in all folk literature; his inclusion of legends, ballads, and other poetry in his books contributed to their emphasis on the cultural contributions of different lands.

Of the Zigzags, Carl Sandburg remarked in his autobiography, *Always the Young Stranger,* "Even when I was older I liked rambling from one country to another with good old Hezekiah Butterworth."

RAJAH OF GWALIOR.

(continued on next page)

PREFACE.

HE "ZIGZAG JOURNEY IN INDIA" is a volume of the popular household or zenänä stories of India, so arranged as to give a view of the history of India and its present political condition and progress.

It was not the intention of the author to extend this series of books beyond eight volumes. But a quarter of a million copies of the "ZIGZAG" books have been sold, and are still greatly sought in families and schools as helps to the educational training of the young. They have been introduced into a great number of the schools of the country as collateral readings, and in many families have become a holiday annual. The author, therefore, yielding to the influence of the publishers, begins a new series. He is indebted to several friends for help in this work.

H. B.

ZIGZAG JOURNEY IN INDIA.

CHAPTER I.

BOMBAY.

A FAIRY TALE IN BOMBAY. — HOW THE ENGLISH OBTAINED INDIA. — SCENES IN BOMBAY.

SHALL never forget my first introduction into a zenänä. It was near Bombay. A dark-eyed Indian woman was swaying to and fro, and crying, —

"Ah, Oh, Ao, Ao,
Ring-a-ting,
Ah, Oh, Ao, Ao,
Ring-a-ting,
The king of the wood is dead."

"I should think that he was," I said. "Aunt Marie, what does this mean?"

"Wait! Seventee was about to tell a story to the children."

The dark Indian woman seemed offended by my interruption.

"Go on, Seventee," said Aunt Marie.

There was a brief silence, during which the dark eyes of Seventee glanced at the children and then furtively at me.

(continued on next page)

A FAIRY TALE IN BOMBAY.

"'Ah, Oh, Ao, Ao,
Ring-a-ting;'—

that was what the two cunning little jackals said when the lion was dead."

"What lion?" asked the children.

The question was evidently expected by Seventee.

"'Ah, Oh, Ao, Ao.'

[I was told afterwards that Seventee was mimicking the voice of the two cunning little jackals.]

"What lion? The great Rajah lion. He used to ro-ar, — ro-ar so loud that the little animals of the forest would fall down dead. That was the way he hunted. The animals fell down dead after he roared, and he would eat them.

"He roared until he had killed and eaten all the animals in the jungle except two little jackals. These were two cunning little jackals.

"A hard time of it they had. They ran hither and thither, and tried to keep beyond the sound of the lion's voice, that had been death to all other animals. One was a Rajah jackal, and the other a Rance jackal.

"Every day the little Rance jackal would say, 'Rajah, Rajah, I am afraid he will catch us to-day.'

"Then they would hear the lion roar, far away, like thunder.

"'Never fear, little wife,' the Rajah jackal would say; 'my wit will save you.'

"'Let us run,' the Rance would then say, 'quick, quick!'

"'Quick, quick!' said the Rajah, always.

"Then the two would run quick, quick, out of the hearing of the voice of the lion.

"But one day, when they thought the lion had left the jungle, they chanced to run right before the lion's eyes as he was returning home.

"'Oh, husband, husband, what shall we do?'

"'Be quiet, little wife, and trust me; wit will save us.'

"'Let us run quick, quick, before he roars, little wife, — quick, quick, right towards his den!'

"THE ANIMALS FELL DOWN DEAD AFTER HE ROARED."

(continued on next page)

"So the two cunning little jackals ran quick, quick, towards the lion's den.

"The lion was much astonished, and forgot to roar.

"'Quick, quick, little husband!'

"'Quick, quick, little wife, into the lion's den!'

"So the two little jackals ran quick, quick, into the lion's den.

"The lion came home after them.

"'Now, you little wretches, I have got you and will eat you. Come here, for I am hungry.'

"'Oh, Singh Rajah, listen! We know that you are our master; but there is a Rajah in the jungle that is greater than you.'

"'Greater, greater? There is no monarch of the jungle but me.

"'Oh, Rajah, Rajah, come with us and see. We will show him to you, for we know where he can be seen.'

"'Show me the Rajah, and I will save you and destroy him. I will be king alone.'

"The little jackals ran out of the den, followed by the lion. They came to a deep pool amid the rocks.

"And the full moon was shining.

"'There he is,' said the Rajah jackal. 'Quick, quick!'

"'There he is,' said the Rance jackal. 'Quick, quick!'

"'Look, look!' said both.

"The lion shook his mane, and looked over the cliff. He thought that he beheld another lion in a den below.

"'Don't roar,' said the Rajah jackal.

"'Don't roar,' said the Rance jackal.

"The lion's eyes blazed. He looked again, and he shook his head. The other lion shook his head. The lion's heart was now on fire, and he leaped into the pool.

"There was a splash and a gurgle; the moonbeams were broken in the water, and circled round and round. Then all was still; the pool became a mirror again.

"The full moon was shining, and the two cunning little jackals sang, —

'Ao, Ao,
Ring-a-ting,
Ring-a-ting,'

just like that, do you hear?

'Ring-a-ting.'"

(continued on next page)

(continued from page 293)

RIP VAN WINKLE. By Washington Irving [1783–1859]. Illustrated by Frank T. Merrill. Boston: S. E. Cassino, 1888. 49 pages. 30½ cm.

The copy from which these pages are reproduced is No. 141 in an elegant, gilt-edged limited edition of "Two Hundred and Fifty Copies for the United Kingdom."

The famous fairy tale, set in the Dutch colonial countryside of the Catskill Mountains up the Hudson River from New York City, is based on a German superstition about Emperor Frederick II. It appeared first in Irving's *Sketch Book* (1819) together with "The Legend of Sleepy Hollow" and other tales. As the complete text is readily available, only a few pages are reproduced here to show Frank Merrill's illustrations and give a general impression of this edition.

Frank Thayer Merrill, the Boston-trained artist, belongs chiefly to the period after 1880, his fame established with the 1880 edition of Louisa May Alcott's *Little Women* (Boston: Roberts Brothers). He was highly praised—for his "fertile fancy" by Miss Alcott herself and by a critic in *The Literary World* who commented that "rarely . . . an illustrator enters so heartily into the work of an author."

RIP VAN WINKLE.

A POSTHUMOUS WRITING OF DIEDRICH KNICKERBOCKER.

By Woden, God of Saxons,
From whence comes Wensday, that is Wodensday.
Truth is a thing that ever I will keep
Unto thylke day in which I creep into
My sepulchre —— CARTWRIGHT.

[The following Tale was found among the papers of the late Diedrich Knickerbocker, an old gentleman of New York, who was very curious in the

Dutch history of the province, and the manners of the descendants from its primitive settlers. His historical researches, however, did not lie so much

(continued on next page)

among books as among men; for the former are lamentably scanty on his favorite topics; whereas he found the old burghers, and still more their wives, rich in that legendary lore so invaluable to true history. Whenever, therefore, he happened upon a genuine Dutch family, snugly shut up in its low-roofed farmhouse, under a spreading sycamore, he looked upon it as a little clasped volume of black-letter, and studied it with the zeal of a book-worm.

The result of all these researches was a history of the province during the reign of the Dutch governors, which he published some years since. There have been various opinions as to the literary character of his work, and, to tell the truth, it is not a whit better than it should be. Its chief merit is its scrupulous accuracy, which indeed was a little questioned on its first appearance, but has since been completely established; and it is now admitted into all historical collections as a book of unquestionable authority.

The old gentleman died shortly after the publication of his work; and now that he is dead and gone, it cannot do much harm to his memory to say that his time might have been much better employed in weightier labors. He, however, was apt to ride his hobby his own way; and though it did now and then kick up the dust a little in the eyes of his neighbors, and grieve the spirit of some friends, for whom he felt the truest deference and affection, yet his errors and follies are remembered "more in sorrow than in anger," and it begins to be suspected that he never intended to injure or offend. But however his memory may be appreciated by critics, it is still held dear by many folk whose good opinion is well worth having; particularly by certain biscuit-bakers, who have gone so far as to imprint his likeness on their New-Year cakes; and have thus given him a chance for immortality, almost equal to the being stamped on a Waterloo Medal, or a Queen Anne's Farthing.]

WHOEVER has made a voyage up the Hudson must remember the Kaatskill mountains. They are a dismembered branch of the great Appalachian family, and are seen away to the west of the river, swelling up to a noble height, and lording it over the surrounding country. Every change of season, every change of weather, indeed, every hour of the day, produces some change in the magical hues and shapes of these mountains, and they are regarded by all the good wives, far and near, as perfect barometers. When the weather is fair and settled, they are clothed in blue and purple, and print their bold outlines on the clear evening sky; but sometimes, when the rest of the landscape is cloudless, they will gather a hood of gray vapors about their summits, which, in the last rays of the setting sun, will glow and light up like a crown of glory.

(continued on next page)

At the foot of these fairy mountains, the voyager may have descried the light smoke curling up from a village, whose shingle roofs gleam among the trees, just where the blue tints of the upland melt away into the fresh green of the nearer landscape. It is a little village of great antiquity, having been founded by some of the Dutch colonists in the early times of the province, just about the beginning of the government of the good Peter Stuyvesant (may he rest in peace!) and there were some of the houses of the original settlers standing within a few years, built of small yellow bricks brought from Holland, having latticed windows and gable fronts, surmounted with weathercocks.

In that same village, and in one of these very houses (which, to tell the precise truth, was sadly time-worn and weather-beaten), there lived many years since, while the country was yet a province of Great Britain, a simple, good-natured fellow, of the name of Rip Van Winkle. He was a descendant of the Van Winkles who figured so gallantly in the chivalrous days of Peter Stuyvesant, and accompanied him to the siege of Fort Christina. He inherited, however, but little of the martial character of his ancestors. I have observed that he was a simple, good-natured man; he was, moreover, a kind neighbor, and an obedient, hen-pecked husband. Indeed, to the latter circumstance might be owing that meekness of spirit which gained him such universal popularity; for those men are most apt to be obsequious and conciliating abroad who are under the discipline of shrews at home. Their tempers, doubtless, are rendered pliant and malleable in the fiery furnace of domestic tribulation, and a curtain-lecture is worth all the sermons in the world for teaching the virtues of patience and long-suffering. A termagant wife may, therefore, in some respects, be considered a tolerable blessing; and if so, Rip Van Winkle was thrice blessed.

Certain it is, that he was a great favorite among all the good wives of the village, who, as usual with the amiable sex, took his part in all family squabbles, and never failed, whenever they talked those matters over in their evening gossipings, to lay all the blame on Dame Van Winkle. The children of the village, too, would shout with joy whenever he approached. He assisted at their sports, made their playthings, taught them to fly kites and shoot marbles, and told

(continued on next page)

them long stories of ghosts, witches, and Indians. Whenever he went dodging about the village, he was surrounded by a troop of them, hanging on his skirts, clambering on his back, and playing a thousand tricks on him with impunity; and not a dog would bark at him throughout the neighborhood.

The great error in Rip's composition was an insuperable aversion to all kinds of profitable labor. It could not be from the want of assiduity or perseverance; for he would sit on a wet rock, with a rod as long and heavy as a Tartar's lance, and fish all day without a murmur, even though he should not be encouraged by a single nibble. He would carry a fowling-piece on his shoulder for hours together, trudging through woods and swamps, and up hill and down dale, to shoot a few squirrels or wild pigeons. He would never refuse to assist a neighbor even in the roughest toil, and was a foremost man at all country frolics for husking Indian corn, or building stone fences; the women of the village, too, used to employ him to run their errands, and to do such little odd jobs as their less obliging husbands would not do for them. In a word, Rip was ready to attend to anybody's

(See note on page 294)

(continued on next page)

always pretended to doubt the reality of it, and insisted that Rip had been out of his head, and that this was one point on which he always remained flighty. The old Dutch inhabitants, however, almost universally gave it full credit. Even to this day, they never hear a thunder-storm of a summer afternoon about the Kaatskill, but they say Hendrick Hudson and his crew are at their game of nine-pins; and it is a common wish of all henpecked husbands in the neighborhood, when life hangs heavy on their hands, that they might have a quieting draught out of Rip Van Winkle's flagon.

NOTE. — The foregoing tale, one would suspect, had been suggested to Mr. Knickerbocker by a little German superstition about the Emperor Frederick *der Rothbart* and the Kypphauser mountain; the subjoined note, however, which he had appended to the tale, shows that it is an absolute fact, narrated with his usual fidelity.

"The story of Rip Van Winkle may seem incredible to many, but nevertheless I give it my full belief, for I know the vicinity of our old Dutch settlements to have been very subject to marvellous events and appearances. Indeed, I have heard many stranger stories than this, in the villages along the Hudson; all of which were too well authenticated to admit of a doubt. I have even talked with Rip Van Winkle myself, who, when last I saw him, was a very venerable old man, and so perfectly rational and consistent on every other point, that I think no conscientious person could refuse to take this into the bargain; nay, I have seen a certificate on the subject taken before a country justice, and signed with a cross, in the justice's own handwriting. The story, therefore, is beyond the possibility of doubt."

(See note on page 294)

TWO LITTLE CONFEDERATES. By Thomas Nelson Page [1853–1922]. New York: C. Scribner's sons, 1888. 156 pages. 12½ cm.

In a partly autobiographical story that attempted to bring about a better understanding between the North and the South, the author, a Virginian, describes without bitterness his boyhood on a plantation during the Civil War. One of the illustrations (below) is shown here.

"LOOK! LOOK! THEY ARE RUNNING! THEY ARE BEATING OUR MEN!" EXCLAIMED THE BOYS.

THE LITTLE COLONEL By Annie Fellows-Johnston [1863–1931], author of "Big Brother." Illustrated by Etheldred B. Barry. "Cosy Corner Series." Boston: Joseph Knight Company, 1896. 102 pages. 18½ cm.

The Old South after the Civil War is described in this story of the reconciliation of a father and daughter who parted in bitterness on her marriage to a Northerner (a favorite theme in post-Civil War literature). The first of a series, this book depicts the agony of the time as well as the paternalistic treatment of Negroes as childlike individuals. The story ends happily due to the artless winsomeness of the Little Colonel in conquest of her grandfather. The title page is shown on the opposite page, followed by Chapter VII on pages 306–310.

"Cosy Corner Series"

THE LITTLE COLONEL

BY

ANNIE FELLOWS-JOHNSTON

AUTHOR OF "BIG BROTHER"

Illustrated by Etheldred B. Barry

BOSTON
JOSEPH KNIGHT COMPANY
1896

CHAPTER VIII.

THE first thing that greeted the Little Colonel's eyes when she opened them next morning was her mother's old doll. Maria had laid it on the pillow beside her.

It was beautifully dressed, although in a queer, old-fashioned style that seemed very strange to the child.

She took it up with careful fingers, remembering its great age. Maria had warned her not to waken her grandfather, so she admired it in whispers.

"Jus' think, Fritz," she exclaimed, "this doll has seen my gran'mothah Amanthis, an' it's named for her. My mothah wasn't any bigger'n me when she played with it. I think it is the loveliest doll I evah saw in my whole life."

Fritz gave a jealous bark.

"Sh!" commanded his little mistress. "Didn't you heah M'ria say, 'Fo' de Lawd's sake don't wake up ole Marse?' Why don't you mind?"

The Colonel was not in the best of humors after such a wakeful night, but the sight of her

happiness made him smile in spite of himself, when she danced into his room with the doll.

She had eaten an early breakfast and gone back upstairs to examine the other toys that were spread out in her room.

The door between the two rooms was ajar. All the time he was dressing and taking his coffee he could hear her talking to some one. He supposed it was Maria. But as he glanced over his mail he heard the Little Colonel saying, "May Lilly, do you know about Billy Goat Gruff? Do you want me to tell you that story?"

He leaned forward until he could look through the narrow opening of the door. Two heads were all he could see, — Lloyd's, soft-haired and golden, May Lilly's, covered with dozens of tightly braided little black tails.

He was about to order May Lilly back to the cabin, when he remembered the scene that followed the last time he had done so. He concluded to keep quiet and listen.

"Billy Goat Gruff was so fat," the story went on, "jus' as fat as gran'fathah."

The Colonel glanced up with an amused smile at the fine figure reflected in an opposite mirror.

"Trip-trap, trip-trap, went Billy Goat Gruff's little feet ovah the bridge to the giant's house."

Just at this point Walker, who was putting

(continued from page 305)

things in order, closed the door between the rooms.

"Open that door, you black rascal!" called the Colonel, furious at the interruption.

In his haste to obey, Walker knocked over a pitcher of water that had been left on the floor beside the washstand.

Then the Colonel yelled at him to be quick about mopping it up, so that by the time the door was finally opened, Lloyd was finishing her story.

The Colonel looked in just in time to see her put her hands to her temples, with her forefingers protruding from her forehead like horns. She said in a deep voice, as she brandished them at May Lilly, "With my two long speahs I'll poke yo' eyeballs through yo' yeahs."

The little darky fell back giggling. "That sut'n'y was like a billy-goat. We had one once that 'ud make a body step around mighty peart. It slip up behine me one mawnin' on the poach, an' fo' a while I thought my haid was buss open suah. I got up toreckly, though, an' I cotch him, and when I done got through, mistah Billy-goat feel po'ly moah'n a week. He sut'n'y did."

Walker grinned, for he had witnessed the scene.

Just then Maria put her head in at the door to say, "May Lilly, yo' mammy's callin' you."

Lloyd and Fritz followed her noisily downstairs. Then for nearly an hour it was very quiet in the great house.

The Colonel, looking out of the window, could see Lloyd playing hide-and-seek with Fritz under the bare locust trees.

When she came in her cheeks were glowing from her run in the frosty air. Her eyes shone like stars, and her face was radiant.

"See what I've found down in the dead leaves," she cried. "A little blue violet, bloomin' all by itself."

She brought a tiny cup from the next room, that belonged to the set of doll dishes, and put the violet in it.

"There!" she said, setting it on the table at her grandfather's elbow. "Now I'll put Amanthis in this chair, where you can look at her, an' you won't get lonesome while I'm playin' outdoors."

He drew her toward him and kissed her.

"Why, how cold your hands are!" he exclaimed. "Staying in this warm room all the time makes me forget it is so wintry outdoors. I don't believe you are dressed warmly enough. You ought not to wear sunbonnets this time of year."

(continued on next page)

Then for the first time he noticed her outgrown cloak and shabby shoes.

"What are you wearing these old clothes for?" he said impatiently. "Why didn't they dress you up when you were going visiting? It isn't showing proper respect to send you off in the oldest things you've got."

It was a sore point with the Little Colonel. It hurt her pride enough to have to wear old clothes without being scolded for it. Besides, she felt that in some way her mother was being blamed for what could not be helped.

"They's the best I've got," she answered, proudly choking back the tears. " don't need any new ones, 'cause maybe we'll be goin' away pretty soon."

"Going away!" he echoed blankly. "Where?"

She did not answer until he repeated the question. Then she turned her back on him, and started toward the door. The tears she was too proud to let him see were running down her face.

"We's goin' to the poah-house," she exclaimed defiantly, "jus' as soon as the money in the pocketbook is used up. It was nearly gone when I came away."

Here she began to sob, as she fumbled at the door she could not see to open.

"I'm goin' home to my mothah right now. She loves me if my clothes are old and ugly."

"Why, Lloyd," called the Colonel, amazed and distressed by her sudden burst of grief. "Come here to grandpa. Why didn't you tell me so before?"

The face, the tone, the outstretched arm, all drew her irresistibly to him. It was a relief to lay her head on his shoulder and unburden herself of the fear that had haunted her so many days.

With her arms around his neck, and the precious little head held close to his heart, the old Colonel was in such a softened mood that he would have promised anything to comfort her.

"There, there," he said soothingly, stroking her hair with a gentle hand, when she had told him all her troubles. "Don't you worry about that, my dear. Nobody is going to eat out of tin pans and sleep on straw. Grandpa just won't let them."

She sat up and wiped her eyes on her apron. "But Papa Jack would *die* befo' he'd take help from you," she wailed. "An' so would mothah. I heard her tell the doctah so."

The tender expression on the Colonel's face changed to one like flint, but he kept on stroking her hair.

"People sometimes change their minds," he said grimly. "I wouldn't worry over a little thing like that if I were you. Don't you want to run downstairs and tell M'ria to give you a piece of cake?"

"Oh, yes," she exclaimed, smiling up at him. "I'll bring you some too."

When the first train went into Louisville that afternoon, Walker was on board with an order in his pocket to one of the largest dry goods establishments in the city. When he came out again that evening, he carried a large box into the Colonel's room.

Lloyd's eyes shone as she looked into it. There was an elegant fur-trimmed cloak, a pair of dainty shoes, and a muff that she caught up with a shriek of delight.

"What kind of a thing is this?" grumbled the Colonel as he took out a hat that had been carefully packed in one corner of the box. "I told them to send the most stylish thing they had. It looks like a scare-crow," he continued, as he set it askew on the child's head.

She snatched it off to look at it herself. "Oh, it's jus' like Emma Louise Wyfo'd's!" she exclaimed. "You didn't put it on straight. See! This is the way it goes."

She climbed up in front of the mirror, and put it on as she had seen Emma Louise wear hers.

"Well, it's a regular Napoleon hat," exclaimed the Colonel, much pleased. "So little girls nowadays have taken to wearing soldier's caps, have they? It's right becoming to you with your short hair. Grandpa is real proud of his 'little Colonel.'"

She gave him the military salute he had taught her, and then ran to throw her arms around him. "Oh, gran'fathah!" she exclaimed between her kisses, "you'se jus' as good as Santa Claus, every bit."

The Colonel's rheumatism was better next day; so much better that toward evening he walked downstairs into the long drawing-room.

(continued on next page)

The room had not been illuminated in years as it was that night.

Every wax taper was lighted in the silver candelabra, and the dim old mirrors multiplied their lights on every side. A great wood fire threw a cheerful glow over the portraits and the frescoed ceiling. All the linen covers had been taken from the furniture.

Lloyd, who had never seen this room except with the chairs shrouded and the blinds down, came running in presently. She was bewildered at first by the change. Then she began walking softly around the room, examining everything.

In one corner stood a tall gilded harp that her grandmother had played in her girlhood. The heavy cover had kept it fair and untarnished through all the years it had stood unused. To the child's beauty-loving eyes it seemed the loveliest thing she had ever seen.

She stood with her hands clasped behind her as her gaze wandered from its pedals to the graceful curves of its tall frame. It shone like burnished gold in the soft firelight.

"Oh, gran'fathah!" she asked at last in a low, reverent tone, "where did you get it? Did an angel leave it heah fo' you?"

He did not answer for a moment. Then he said huskily as he looked up at a portrait over

the mantel, "Yes, my darling, an angel did leave it here. She always was one. Come here to grandpa."

He took her on his knee and pointed up to the portrait. The same harp was in the picture. Standing beside it, with one hand resting on its shining strings, was a young girl all in white.

"That's the way she looked the first time I ever saw her," said the Colonel dreamily. "A June rose in her hair, and another at her throat; and her soul looked right out through those great, dark eyes — the purest, sweetest soul God ever made! My beautiful Amanthis!"

"My bu'ful Amanthis!" repeated the child in an awed whisper.

She sat gazing into the lovely young face for a long time, while the old man seemed lost in dreams.

"Gran'fathah," she said at length, patting his cheek to attract his attention, and then nodding toward the portrait, "did *she* love my mothah like my mothah loves me?"

"Certainly, my dear," was the gentle reply.

It was the twilight hour, when the homesick feeling always came back strongest to Lloyd.

"Then I jus' know that if my bu'ful gran'mothah Amanthis could come down out of that

frame, she'd go straight and put her arms around my mothah an' kiss away all her sorry feelin's."

The Colonel fidgeted uncomfortably in his chair a moment. Then to his great relief the tea-bell rang.

III. The Magazines.
From the Colonial Period to 1900.

To PERUSE VOLUMES of the leading nineteenth-century American periodicals for children is to see as a panorama the work of the best-known American—and some other—writers and artists and to distinguish in it an interweaving of threads of American thought and culture.

From the appearance in Hartford, Connecticut, in 1789 of the first American children's magazine, *The Children's Magazine*—a modest, didactic venture—there came a widening flood of magazines too numerous to account for here. Those necessarily omitted range from the many Sunday School periodicals, such as the relatively long-lived American Sunday School Union's *The Youth's Friend and Scholar's Magazine* (1823–1864), comprising chiefly religious writings and anecdotes, to the boys' cheap weeklies of the blood-and-thunder dime-novel type, most of them having short duration. The small number of periodicals represented by the present selections typify the best quality of such publishing that was available at various periods.

The ever-continuing arguments of those who promoted reading for self-improvement and those who believed pleasure in itself to be a sufficient motive for reading had forceful policy statements by editors in their exercise of guardianship over the young. On the one side were the heavily moral exhortations of the Sunday School magazines, and on the other, those stressed particularly in its earlier years by that family magazine *The Youth's Companion* (1827–1929). Later *The Little Corporal* (1865–1874), which merged with *St. Nicholas,* immediately expressed editorial sentiments against such bad habits as swearing, tobacco, and drink, while it urged filial obedience. With different aims and purposes, the great magazines of the post-Civil War years—*St. Nicholas,* the *Riverside,* and *Harper's Young People*—provided genuine fun and tried to inspire an appreciation of art, as well as to foster a proper love of home and country and to reveal the changing world.

Literally building up a body of writing and illustrating for children, the creative editors of children's magazines searched for and promoted the work of new authors and artists whose later efforts with word and picture, in book form, were to receive the critical attention necessary for a thriving literature. Many of the editors and associate editors themselves contributed fiction as well as editorials and special features: Lydia Maria Child, Louisa May Alcott, John Townsend Trowbridge, Hezekiah Butterworth, Mary Mapes Dodge, Kirk Munroe, Frank R. Stockton, and Horace E. Scudder form a roster of famous contributors to this flowering of American literature for children.

Magazines for children of the nineteenth century, struggling for survival like those of today, had a constant need to renew subscription lists. Business conditions dictated a history of mergers and giveaway schemes to prolong solvency. The *Youth's Companion*'s system of offering premiums for new subscriptions was adopted in a lesser way by *The Little Corporal,* while the unsuccessful though brilliant *Riverside* offered a free reproduction of H. L. Stephens's "The Quack Doctor" for a full subscription to its 1869 issues.

Many have been the tributes later paid by readers as they came to recognize in retrospect the fun and values they had derived from reading of the "pleasure ground" (as Mary Mapes Dodge described her *St. Nicholas*).

JUVENILE MISCELLANY. Vols. 1–4, September 1826–July 1828; Vols. 1–6, September 1828–August 1831; third series, Vols. 1–6, [September ?] 1831–August 1834. Boston: J. Putnam, 1826–1834. 16 volumes, illustrated. 14½ cm. Bimonthly. Editors: Mrs. D. L. Child, 1826–1834; Mrs. S. J. Hale, 1834–1836.

A forerunner of magazines intended both to entertain and to instruct children, the *Juvenile Miscellany* under the editorship of Lydia Maria Francis (who soon married the abolitionist, David Child) was remarkable in its day for bringing the American scene to young people. Mrs. Child had received wide acclaim for writing the early novel *Hobomok* (1824). The *Miscellany* contained advice to the young; biographies of noted Americans and Europeans who fought in the Revolutionary War; excerpts from American history; factual pieces about Mount Vernon and other American landmarks; articles on scientific subjects; conundrums; verse; and notes on new and recommended books. Here, in 1830, first appeared Mrs. Sarah Josepha Hale's "Mary's Lamb" (see page 322).

In 1834, after the 1833 publishing of Mrs. Child's *An Appeal in Favor of That Class of Americans Called Africans,* subscriptions dropped off, and she was "compelled to bid a reluctant and most affectionate farewell to my little readers. . . ." The magazine continued under the editorship of Mrs. Hale until December 1836.

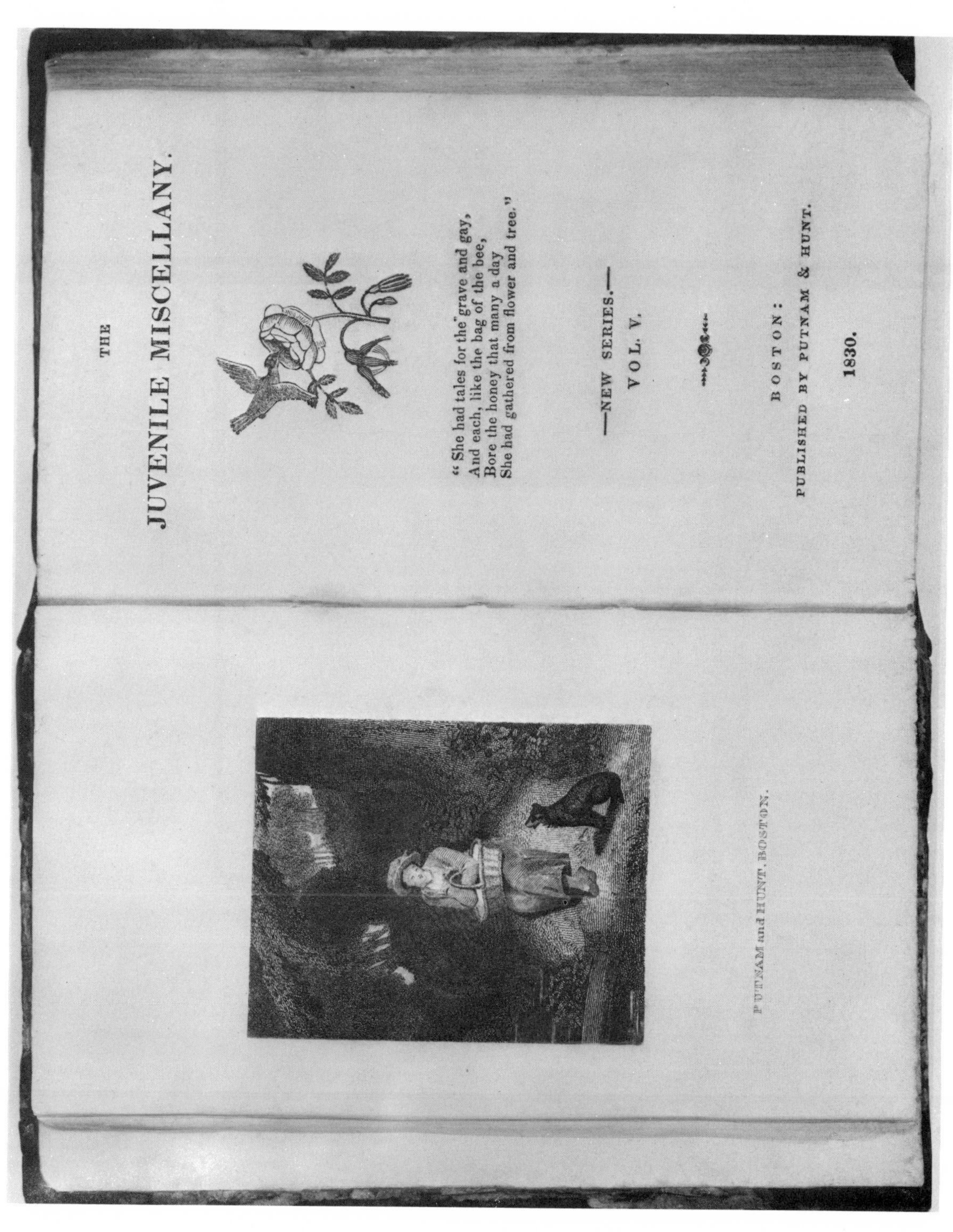

PUTNAM and HUNT. BOSTON.

THE

JUVENILE MISCELLANY.

"She had tales for the grave and gay,
And each, like the bag of the bee,
Bore the honey that many a day
She had gathered from flower and tree."

—NEW SERIES.—

VOL. V.

BOSTON:

PUBLISHED BY PUTNAM & HUNT.

1830.

(continued on next page)

64

MARY'S LAMB.

Mary had a little lamb,
Its fleece was white as snow,
And every where that Mary went
The lamb was sure to go;
He followed her to school one day—
That was against the rule,
It made the children laugh and play
To see a lamb at school.

And so the Teacher turned him out,
But still he lingered near,
And waited patiently about,
Till Mary did appear.
And then he ran to her and laid
His head upon her arm,
As if he said—"I'm not afraid—
You'll shield me from all harm."

"What makes the lamb love Mary so,"
The little children cry;
"O, Mary loves the lamb you know,
The Teacher did reply,
"And you each gentle animal
In confidence may bind,
And make them follow at your call,
If you are always *kind*."

S. J. H.

ANSWER TO CHARADE, Page 197.

Sea-son.

JUVENILE MISCELLANY *(continued from page 321)*

"Mary's Lamb," 1830, by Sarah Josepha Hale (1788–1879).

See pages 67, 163, and 164 for more information about this author and her work.

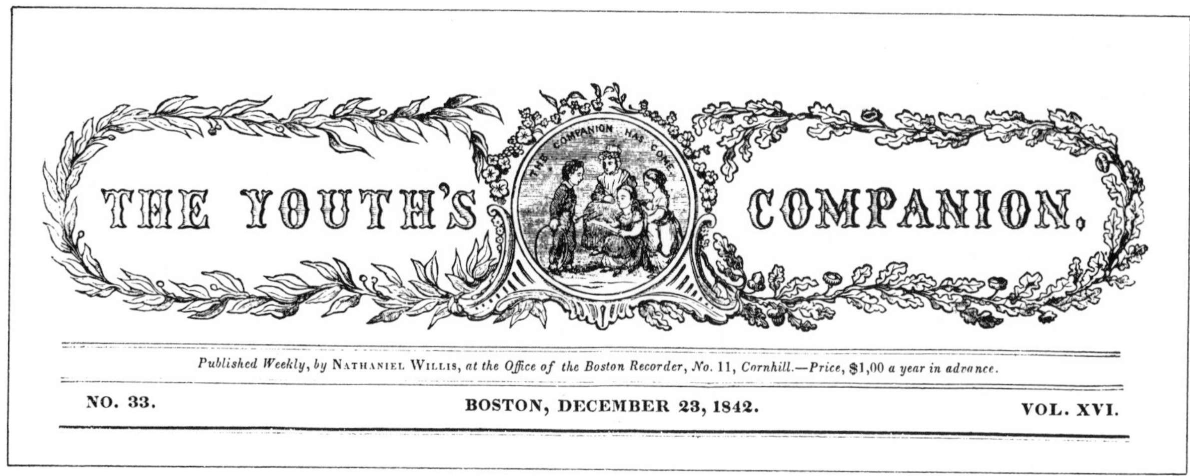
THE YOUTH'S COMPANION.
Published Weekly, by NATHANIEL WILLIS, at the Office of the Boston Recorder, No. 11, Cornhill.—Price, $1,00 a year in advance.
NO. 33. BOSTON, DECEMBER 23, 1842. VOL. XVI.

THE YOUTH'S COMPANION; for All the Family [subtitle varies]. Vols. 1–103, April 16, 1827–September 1929. Boston: Perry Mason Co. 42 cm. Weekly, 1827–August 1927; monthly, September 1827–1929. Editors: Nathaniel Willis, 1827–1857; Daniel Sharp Ford, 1857–1899. This magazine absorbed *Merry's Museum for Boys and Girls* in November 1872. It was merged into the *American Boy* in October 1929.

A folio, begun as a family newspaper, with special features for children in "The Children's Column," this Boston publication was the longest lived of all the young people's periodicals.

Shown here is the editorial from the opening issue. By the 1840's its subtitle overtly expressed the paper's moral aims: "A Family Paper Devoted to Piety, Morality, Brotherly Love—No Sectarianism, No Controversy." That it plainly objected to the theater can be seen from an editorial of April 27, 1865, covering the Lincoln assassination, where there appears: "We are sorry that he should have received his death-wound in a theatre."

The magazine attracted great names from the adult book world: Oliver Wendell Holmes and Mark Twain, as well as Rudyard Kipling and James M. Barrie, and other such celebrities as statesmen, scientists, and explorers. Every issue contained work by such noted poets as John Greenleaf Whittier, Walt Whitman, and Henry Wadsworth Longfellow. Anecdotes were used to break the columns. The juvenile author Hezekiah Butterworth served as assistant editor in the 1880's and 1890's, and Charles Asbury Stephens, acclaimed "star of the *Youth's Companion*," came to be a regular contributor from the 1870's to its last days, writing stories of Maine farm life.

By 1869 the magazine had grown from four to eight pages; in the 1880's to twelve pages, when circulation jumped to some four hundred thousand. By the time of its demise, the magazine had grown to sixteen pages, bound in covers with full-color pictures. Fiction began to supplant the sermonlike essay, but moral emphases continued. The miscellaneous short features, whether these were original or cuttings from other magazines and books, American or translated from foreign languages, were unsigned.

(continued on next page)

YOUTH's COMPANION.

Vol. I. BOSTON, APRIL 16, 1827. No. 1.

PROSPECTUS
OF THE
YOUTH'S COMPANION.

The Editors of the Boston Recorder propose to publish a paper for the special use of *Children* and *Youth*, entitled *Youth's Companion;* of which this sheet is intended as a *specimen*, both in respect to paper and type, and also the general quality of the matter it will contain. We have several reasons for making this proposal. We could about half fill the Recorder with interesting selections, adapted to our juvenile readers, from the various publications which we receive and peruse. Many of these are too valuable to be thrown by, and circulated no more; but we can by no means spare room to enlarge our Children's and Youth's Departments so as to admit one half of them. Yet they might be collected out of other publications, where they are embodied with other subjects, and placed together before the eye of the youthful reader. Another reason is, that the capacities of children, and the peculiar situation and duties of youth, require select and appropriate reading. And while adults have various periodical publications, which they consider highly valuable, the younger part of the community seem to require that the same means be prepared for their gratification and improvement. If to these we add one reason more, the propriety of the step we have taken will be apparent. *This is a day of peculiar care for Youth.* Christians feel that their children must be trained up for Christ. Patriots and philanthropists are making rapid improvements in every branch of education. Literature, science, liberty and religion are extending in the earth. The human mind is becoming emancipated from the bondage of ignorance and superstition. Our children are born to higher destinies than their fathers; they will be actors in a far advanced period of the church and the world. Let their minds be formed, their hearts prepared, and their characters moulded for the scenes and the duties of a brighter day.

The contents of the proposed work will be miscellaneous, though articles of a religious character will be most numerous. It will not take the form of discussion, or argument, and controversy will be entirely excluded. It will aim to inculcate truth by brief narratives, familiar illustrations, short biographies, and amusing anecdotes. It will attempt to excite attention to good things by entertaining matter; and yet every thing frivolous or injurious will be avoided. Its several departments will comprize religion, morals, manners, habits, filial duties, books, amusements, schools, and whatever may be thought truly useful, either in this life or the life to come. It will, of course, be a constant advocate, and we hope an efficient helper, of Sabbath Schools, Bible Classes, and the various means which are in operation for forming the characters of the rising generation on the standard of the Bible.

This publication, so far as we know, is of a new kind. There are Tract and Sabbath School Magazines, very useful for youth, as well as others; but confined to their appropriate spheres. There are Literary Magazines for youth, which exclude religious topics; and others for mere amusement, whose influence is unfavorable to religion and morals. There are publications, devoted to the subject of education; but intended more for the parent and teacher, than for the child and pupil. Any or all of these occupy only in part the ground which we propose to take. A small weekly journal, which should entertain their children and insensibly instruct them; which should occupy leisure hours, and turn them to good account; which should sanction and aid parental counsel and pulpit admonition; which should, in an easy and familiar manner, warn against the ways of transgression, error and ruin, and allure to those of virtue and piety; a journal of this description has long been desired by anxious Christian parents—or at least they have felt the wants which this is intended to supply. The little they have had in this way, in the Recorder and other publications, has excited their wishes for more; and those to whom our present plan has been named, have hailed it with much satisfaction.

If the publication proceeds, we shall hope to receive aid from such friends as can write feelingly for children and youth, and bring their language to their capacities. For ourselves, as editors, we can only say that we are fathers, and we hope Christian fathers, who know practically the anxieties of parents; that we have access to many sources of supply for such a paper; and that we trust our manner of conducting the Recorder has been such, as to inspire a good degree of confidence in the minds of our readers, that what few talents we may have will be faithfully applied to the direction of the Youth's Companion.

We do not intend that our new engagements shall interfere with our present editorial duties, or diminish our attention to the Recorder. If the new paper is encouraged, we shall procure whatever assistance may be necessary, that both may receive full attention. The Children's and Youth's Departments will be continued in the Recorder; and no article will ever appear in both papers, unless, very rarely, it be one of peculiar importance, or occasionally a paragraph of very interesting intelligence. The new paper will contain no advertisements, and no secular news.

With these remarks we introduce the *Youth's Companion* to our young friends and to their parents. If it shall prove an acceptable associate at their firesides, or in their social circles, we shall be happy to send it forth on weekly visits, and trust that none will have occasion to regret its appearance among them.

CONDITIONS.

I. The Youth's Companion will be published weekly, at the office of the Boston Recorder, in the folio form, on a sheet of the same size as this specimen.

II. The terms will be, $2, 00 a volume, payable at the end of the year: or $1, 50 in advance. Agents who pay in advance for 8 copies, $1, 25.

III. No subscription taken for less than a year. Subscriptions considered permanent, unless they are expressly limited.

IV. The next number will be published on the first week in June next, provided sufficient patronage is obtained.

V. If persons at a distance send their names by the last Wednesday in May, and their payments any time in June, they will be entitled to the paper at the *advance* price.

These terms cannot be considered high, in comparison with the Recorder and other papers, if it be remembered that we may not at first expect so large a list of subscribers, and that no profit will be derived from advertisements. If an extensive subscription should be obtained, the price will be reduced.

WILLIS & RAND.

REVIEW.

Nina, *an Icelandic Tale. By a Mother. Author of "Always Happy," &c. &c,* Boston, Munroe & Francis.

"The following story," says the Preface, "was written as one of an intended series of Tales, illustrative of the customs, productions, &c. &c. of different countries. Thus in the guise of fiction, to make children familiar with facts." In other words, this little book, which contains only a hundred short pages, presents to our young friends a good deal of information concerning the distant and unfrequented country of Iceland, and yet connects it with an entertaining story. It tells of the short summers, the long, drear winters, the deep snows, and severe storms of that northern latitude. It speaks of the Aurora Borealis, or Northern Light, which we sometimes see in this country, but which is very different in Iceland. It describes the volcano which rises from Mount Hecla, and a great earthquake which took place before one of its violent eruptions. The island is more than half as large as all New England, but does not contain so many inhabitants as the city of Boston. Here we read of the customs, manners, possessions, and supplies, or rather poverty and wants of the inhabitants. Our children and youth would not believe they could exist, if they were fed on such food, and were lodged in such cabins, and were exposed to such tempestuous weather. But even *there*

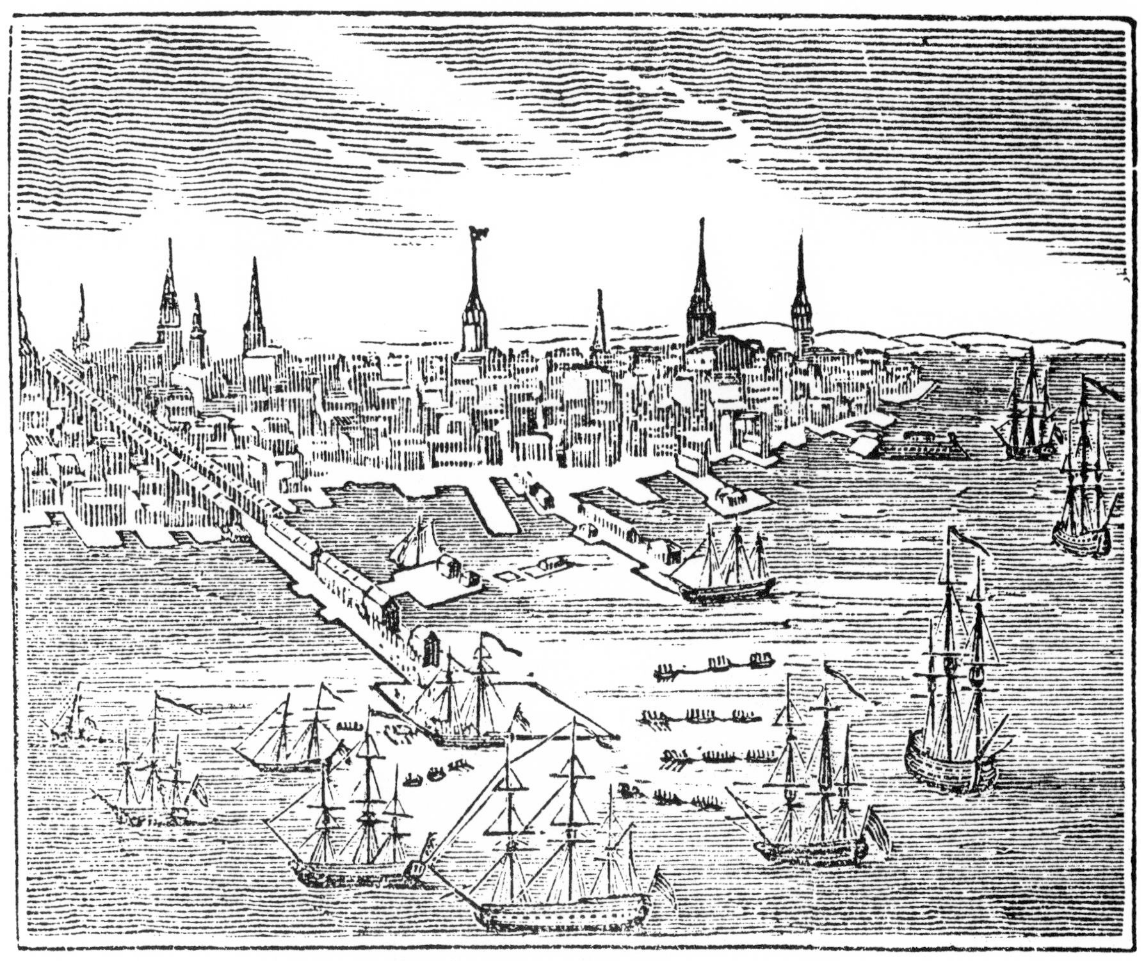

"Siege of Boston," 1844

ON FOLLOWING PAGE:

"Recollections of My Childhood," 1888, by Louisa May Alcott (1832–1888).

Miss Alcott, who of all American writers for the young needs least introduction here, wrote for many of the children's magazines and saw her stories later gathered into book form as collections of short tales or full-length novels from serialized magazine publication. She wrote prolifically from 1840 to 1888 and reflected in stories for children her warm childhood family experiences in Concord, Massachusetts, as the daughter of the philosopher-educator Bronson Alcott and near neighbor of Ralph Waldo Emerson.

For the Companion.

RECOLLECTIONS OF MY CHILDHOOD.

By Louisa M. Alcott.

One of my earliest memories is of playing with books in my father's study. Building towers and bridges of the big dictionaries, looking at pictures, pretending to read, and scribbling on blank pages whenever pen or pencil could be found. Many of these first attempts at authorship still exist, and I often wonder if these childish plays did not influence my after life, since books have been my greatest comfort, castle-building a never-failing delight, and scribbling a very profitable amusement.

Another very vivid recollection is of the day when running after my hoop I fell into the Frog Pond and was rescued by a black boy, becoming a friend to the colored race then and there, though my mother always declared that I was an abolitionist at the age of three.

During the Garrison riot in Boston the portrait of George Thompson was hidden under a bed in our house for safe-keeping, and I am told that I used to go and comfort "the good man who helped poor slaves" in his captivity. However that may be, the conversion was genuine, and my greatest pride is in the fact that I have lived to know the brave men and women who did so much for the cause, and that I had a very small share in the war which put an end to a great wrong.

Being born on the birthday of Columbus I seem to have something of my patron saint's spirit of adventure, and running away was one of the delights of my childhood. Many a social lunch have I shared with hospitable Irish beggar children, as we ate our crusts, cold potatoes and salt fish on voyages of discovery among the ash heaps of the waste land that then lay where the Albany station now stands.

Many an impromptu picnic have I had on the dear old Common, with strange boys, pretty babies and friendly dogs, who always seemed to feel that this reckless young person needed looking after.

On one occasion the town-crier found me fast asleep at nine o'clock at night, on a door-step in Bedford Street, with my head pillowed on the curly breast of a big Newfoundland, who was with difficulty persuaded to release the weary little wanderer who had sobbed herself to sleep there.

I often smile as I pass that door, and never forget to give a grateful pat to every big dog I meet, for never have I slept more soundly than on that dusty step, nor found a better friend than the noble animal who watched over the lost baby so faithfully.

My father's school was the only one I ever went to, and when this was broken up because he introduced methods now all the fashion, our lessons went on at home, for he was always sure of four little pupils who firmly believed in their teacher, though they have not done him all the credit he deserved.

I never liked arithmetic or grammar, and dodged these branches on all occasions; but reading, composition, history and geography I enjoyed, as well as the stories read to us with a skill which made the dullest charming and useful.

"Pilgrim's Progress," Krummacher's "Parables," Miss Edgeworth, and the best of the dear old fairy tales made that hour the pleasantest of our day. On Sundays we had a simple service of Bible stories, hymns, and conversation about the state of our little consciences and the conduct of our childish lives which never will be forgotten.

Walks each morning round the Common while in the city, and long tramps over hill and dale when our home was in the country, were a part of our education, as well as every sort of housework, for which I have always been very grateful, since such knowledge makes one independent in these days of domestic tribulation with the help who are too often only hindrances.

Needle-work began early, and at ten my skilful sister made a linen shirt beautifully, while at twelve I set up as a doll's dress-maker, with my sign out, and wonderful models in my window. All the children employed me, and my turbans were the rage at one time to the great dismay of the neighbors' hens, who were hotly hunted down, that I might tweak out their downiest feathers to adorn the dolls' head-gear.

Active exercise was my delight from the time when a child of six I drove my hoop round the Common without stopping, to the days when I did my twenty miles in five hours and went to a party in the evening.

I always thought I must have been a deer or a horse in some former state, because it was such a joy to run. No boy could be my friend till I had beaten him in a race, and no girl if she refused to climb trees, leap fences and be a tomboy.

My wise mother, anxious to give me a strong body to support a lively brain, turned me loose in the country and let me run wild, learning of nature what no books can teach, and being led, as those who truly love her seldom fail to be,

"Through nature up to nature's God."

I remember running over the hills just at dawn one summer morning, and pausing to rest in the silent woods saw, through an arch of trees, the sun rise over river, hill and wide green meadows as I never saw it before.

Something born of the lovely hour, a happy mood, and the unfolding aspirations of a child's soul seemed to bring me very near to God, and in the hush of that morning hour I always felt that I "got religion" as the phrase goes. A new and vital sense of His presence, tender and sustaining as a father's arms, came to me then, never to change through forty years of life's vicissitudes, but to grow stronger for the sharp discipline of poverty and pain, sorrow and success.

Those Concord days were the happiest of my life, for we had charming playmates in the little Emersons, Channings, Hawthornes and Goodwins, with the illustrious parents and their friends to enjoy our pranks and share our excursions.

PLAYING HORSE.

Plays in the barn were a favorite amusement, and we dramatized the fairy tales in great style. Our giant came tumbling off a loft when Jack cut down the squash vine running up a ladder to represent the immortal bean. Cinderella rolled away in a vast pumpkin, and a long, black pudding was lowered by invisible hands to fasten itself on the nose of the woman who wasted her three wishes.

Little pilgrims journeyed over the hills with scrip and staff and cockle-shells in their hats; elves held their pretty revels among the pines, and "Peter Wilkins'" flying ladies came swinging down on the birch tree-tops. Lords and ladies haunted the garden, and mermaids splashed in the bath-house of woven willows over the brook.

People wondered at our frolics, but enjoyed them, and droll stories are still told of the adventures of those days. Mr. Emerson and Margaret Fuller were visiting my parents one afternoon, and the conversation having turned to the ever interesting subject of education, Miss Fuller said:

"Well, Mr. Alcott, you have been able to carry out your methods in your own family, and I should like to see your model children."

She did in a few moments, for as the guests stood on the door steps a wild uproar approached, and round the corner of the house came a wheelbarrow holding baby May arrayed as a queen; I was the horse, bitted and bridled and driven by my elder sister Anna, while Lizzie played dog and barked as loud as her gentle voice permitted.

All were shouting and wild with fun which, however, came to a sudden end as we espied the stately group before us, for my foot tripped, and down we all went in a laughing heap, while my mother put a climax to the joke by saying with a dramatic wave of the hand:

"Here are the model children, Miss Fuller."

My sentimental period began at fifteen when I fell to writing romances, poems, a "heart journal," and dreaming dreams of a splendid future.

Browsing over Mr. Emerson's library I found "Goethe's Correspondence with a Child," and was at once fired with the desire to be a second Bettine, making my father's friend my Goethe. So I wrote letters to him, but was wise enough never to send them, left wild flowers on the door-steps of my "Master," sung Mignon's song in very bad German under his window, and was fond of wandering by moonlight, or sitting in a cherry-tree at midnight till the owls scared me to bed.

The girlish folly did not last long, and the letters were burnt years ago, but Goethe is still my favorite author, and Emerson remained my beloved "Master" while he lived, doing more for me, as for many another young soul, than he ever knew, by the simple beauty of his life, the truth and wisdom of his books, the example of a good, great man untempted and unspoiled by the world which he made nobler while in it, and left the richer when he went.

The trials of life began about this time, and my happy childhood ended. Money is never plentiful in a philosopher's house, and even the maternal pelican could not supply all our wants on the small income which was freely shared with every needy soul who asked for help.

Fugitive slaves were sheltered under our roof, and my first pupil was a very black George Washington whom I taught to write on the hearth with charcoal, his big fingers finding pen and pencil unmanageable.

Motherless girls seeking protection were guarded among us; hungry travellers sent on to our door to be fed and warmed, and if the philosopher happened to own two coats the best went to a needy brother, for these were practical Christians who had the most perfect faith in Providence, and never found it betrayed.

In those days the prophets were not honored in their own land, and Concord had not yet discovered her great men. It was a sort of refuge for reformers of all sorts whom the good natives regarded as lunatics, harmless but amusing.

My father went away to hold his classes and conversations, and we women folk began to feel that we also might do something. So one gloomy November day we decided to move to Boston and try our fate again after some years in the wilderness.

My father's prospect was as promising as a philosopher's ever is in a money-making world, my mother's friends offered her a good salary as their missionary to the poor, and my sister and I hoped to teach. It was an anxious council, and always preferring action to discussion, I took a brisk run over the hill and then settled down for "a good think" in my favorite retreat.

It was an old cart-wheel, half hidden in grass under the locusts where I used to sit to wrestle with my sums, and usually forget them scribbling verses or fairy tales on my slate instead. Perched on the hub I surveyed the prospect and found it rather gloomy, with leafless trees, sere grass, leaden sky and frosty air, but the hopeful heart of fifteen beat warmly under the old red shawl, visions of success gave the gray clouds a silver lining, and I said defiantly, as I shook my fist at fate embodied in a crow cawing dismally on the fence near by,—

"I *will* do something by-and-by. Don't care what, teach, sew, act, write, anything to help the family; and I'll be rich and famous and happy before I die, see if I won't!"

Startled by this audacious outburst the crow flew away, but the old wheel creaked as if it began to turn at that moment, stirred by the intense desire of an ambitious girl to work for those she loved and find some reward when the duty was done.

I did not mind the omen then, and returned to the house cold but resolute. I think I began to shoulder my burden then and there, for when the free country life ended the wild colt soon learned to tug in harness, only breaking loose now and then for a taste of beloved liberty.

My sisters and I had cherished fine dreams of a home in the city, but when we found ourselves in a small house at the South End with not a tree in sight, only a back yard to play in, and no money to buy any of the splendors before us, we all rebelled and longed for the country again.

Anna soon found little pupils, and trudged away each morning to her daily task, pausing at the corner to wave her hand to me in answer to my salute with the duster. My father went to his classes at his room down town, mother to her all-absorbing poor, the little girls to school, and I was left to keep house, feeling like a caged sea-gull as I washed dishes and cooked in the basement kitchen where my prospect was limited to a procession of muddy boots.

Good drill, but very hard, and my only consolation was the evening reunion when all met with such varied reports of the day's adventures, we could not fail to find both amusement and instruction.

Father brought news from the upper world, and the wise, good people who adorned it; mother, usually much dilapidated because she *would* give away her clothes, with sad tales of suffering and sin from the darker side of life; gentle Anna a modest account of her success as teacher, for even at seventeen her sweet nature won all who knew her, and her patience quelled the most rebellious pupil.

My reports were usually a mixture of the tragic and the comic, and the children poured their small joys and woes into the family bosom where comfort and sympathy were always to be found.

Then we youngsters adjourned to the kitchen for our fun, which usually consisted of writing, dressing and acting a series of remarkable plays. In one I remember I took five parts and Anna four, with lightning changes of costume, and characters varying from a Greek prince in silver armor to a murderer in chains.

It was good training for memory and fingers, for we recited pages without a fault, and made every sort of property from a harp to a fairy's spangled wings. Later we acted Shakespeare, and Hamlet was my favorite hero, played with a gloomy glare and a tragic stalk which I have never seen surpassed.

But we were now beginning to play our parts on a real stage, and to know something of the pathetic side of life with its hard facts, irksome duties, many temptations and the daily sacrifice of self. Fortunately we had the truest, tenderest of guides and guards, and so learned the sweet uses of adversity, the value of honest work, the beautiful law of compensation which gives more than it takes, and the real significance of life.

At sixteen I began to teach twenty pupils, and for ten years learned to know and love children. The story writing went on all the while with the usual trials of beginners. Fairy tales told the Emersons made the first printed book, and "Hospital Sketches" the first successful one.

Every experience went into the chauldron to come out as froth, or evaporate in smoke, till time and suffering strengthened and clarified the mixture of truth and fancy, and a wholesome draught for children began to flow pleasantly and profitably.

So the omen proved a true one, and the wheel of fortune turned slowly, till the girl of fifteen found herself a woman of fifty with her prophetic dream beautifully realized, her duty done, her reward far greater than she deserved.

November 22.

For the Companion.

PRISON MUSIC.

At the Western Penitentiary in Pennsylvania there is a nightly concert given by what is probably the largest orchestra in the world. It is composed of at least three hundred players, who never see one another. The music begins precisely at six o'clock every evening, and ends at the stroke of seven. Within that hour the convicts are permitted to make, each independently, as much music or discord as he pleases.

This prison is, perhaps, the only one in the United States where the inmates are allowed to cultivate the art of music, and the privilege is deeply appreciated by them. Just before six o'clock they may be seen by the officials, sitting with their instruments in readiness. As the hour strikes, they begin to play, and rattle off tune after tune during the appointed time.

As may be imagined, with several hundred instruments playing at once, it is impossible to distinguish any one of them from the rest, or to tell one tune from another. As the waves of sound rise and mingle, the listener can only be reminded of a wind howling in the distance.

"They look forward to this hour with great pleasure," said one of the keepers to a reporter. "Music is the only thing that varies the monotony of their lives, and taking an instrument away from a prisoner is about the severest punishment we can inflict."

As they were talking, there was a moment's silence. It was a few minutes before seven, and a man began playing "Home, Sweet Home" on a violin.

His neighbor accompanied him on a guitar, and in a short time they were joined by a flute, cornet

(continued from page 325)

THE YOUTH'S COMPANION.
1888
1888
THANKSGIVING NUMBER.

PARLEY'S MAGAZINE. Vol. 1, March 16, 1833–1845. New York: C. S. Francis. 18 cm. Biweekly, 1833–1835; monthly, 1836–1845.

MERRY'S MUSEUM FOR BOYS AND GIRLS. Vols. 1–62, February 1841–November 1872. Boston: H. B. Fuller, 1841–1872. 20–23 cm. The title of this magazine varies: from 1841 to 1850 it was called *Robert Merry's Museum;* from 1832–1860, *Merry's Musuem and Parley's Magazine;* from 1862–1866, *Merry's Museum, Parley's Magazine, Woodworth's Cabinet* and the *Schoolfellow;* in 1867, *Merry's Museum and Woodworth's Cabinet;* and from 1870–1872 *Merry's Museum for Boys and Girls.* Founded by S. C. Goodrich. Absorbed *Parley's Magazine,* August 1845; *Playmate,* July 1848.

WOODWORTH'S YOUTH'S CABINET, May 1857; and the *Schoolfellow,* October 1857. Merged into *Youth's Companion,* 1872.

Samuel Goodrich, editor of *Parley's Magazine* for only one year before he sold it, was glad to lend his name to a children's magazine. In 1841 he said of *Merry's Museum for Boys and Girls* that he was pleased to do this, but "I cannot undertake to become its editor, as you desire, for my quill is nearly worn to the stump." Under the pen name of Robert Merry he noted in an "address to the reader" in the first issue, February 1841: "I have a variety of matters and things on hand, anecdotes, adventures, tales, travels, rhymes, riddles, songs &c—some glad and some sad, some to make you laugh and some to weep. My only trouble is to select among such variety. . . ." Others took over, including Louisa May Alcott, who assumed the editorship in 1867 and stayed with the magazine until she went abroad in 1870. In her "Journal" she wrote:

> *September, 1867.* "Niles, partner of Roberts, asked me to write a girls' book. Said I'd try. F. asked me to be the editor of 'Merry's Museum.' Said I'd try. Began at once on both new jobs; but didn't like either."
>
> *October.* "Agreed with F. to be editor for $500 a year. Read manuscripts, write one story each month and an editorial. On the strength of this engagement went to Boston, took a room—No. 6 Hayward Place—furnished it, and set up housekeeping for myself."
>
> *January, 1868.* Gamp's Garret, Hayward Place, Boston. "F. pays me $500 a year for my name and some editorial work on Merry's Museum; 'The Youth's Companion' pays $20 for two short tales each month; L. $50 and $100 for all I will send him; and others take anything I have."

The magazine's varied and attractively set-forth contents had a bright cover and always a frontispiece and title-page vignette. Luminaries of the day—Longfellow, Hawthorne, and Holmes—appeared here along with many others. The year 1866 saw an appraisal of "The Silver Skates" (with pictures by Nast) advertised thus as "written by M. E. D. (sic), so well known to the Museum. It is one of the most interesting books of the year. We give an extract from it, and commend it to all our readers." Louisa May Alcott's *An Old-Fashioned Girl* was serialized July to December 1869. The department entitled "Merry's Monthly Chat with His Friends" contained the editor's message to young readers, letters from them (some with answers appended), other chitchat from the house, and puzzles, enigmas, charades, and further similar offerings for fun. The excerpt shown on pages 330–331 is dated 1853.

(continued on next page)

THE OLD HEN AND THE PHILOSOPHER: A FABLE.

PART I.

REFLECTIONS OF A HEN WITH CHICKENS DURING AN ECLIPSE OF THE SUN.

"Craw * * * craw * * * craw! What's the matter with my eyes? It looks very dark, for a clear summer's day. I must be getting old, for it aint more than 10 o'clock, and it seems exactly like sundown. Craw * * * craw * * * craw! Why, it's getting cold. It seems as chill as evening. Cut, cut, cudawcut! What can be the matter? Why, the sun is going to bed before it's fairly got up. Cur—r-r-r-r-r! Well, after all, it may be only a fit of the vapors—or my gizzard may be put out of order by that toad I ate yesterday. I thought, then, I should pay dear for it. Cur—r-r-r-r-r! Here chicks—come under my wings! I'm going to take a nap. Come along—Nip, Dip, Pip, Rip—come into your feather-bed, my little dearies! There! Don't stick your noses out—be still now—I'm going to sing a song.

Hush, my chickies—don't you peep—
Hush, my children—go to sleep!
Now the night is dark and thick—
Go to sleep each little chick!

* * * * *

Fiddle-de-dee—I can't sleep, and the chickens are as lively as bed-bugs. Cut—cut—cu—daw—cut! What on airth is the matter! The sun has got put out, right up there in the sky, just like a candle. Well—never did I see or hear of such a thing afore! And now it's night in the middle of the day! What will come next? Why, I expect I shall walk on my head, and fly with my claws! It aint half fair, to shave an old hen and chickens out of their dinner and supper in this way. However, it's too dark for decent people to be abroad. So, my chicks, we must get into the coop and go to rest. Cur—r-r-r-r--it's very queer—indeed. How thankful I am that I don't make day and night, and get the world into such a scrape as this. Come in! Come in, chicks! It aint our affair. Come along—there—you rowdies! You aint sleepy, and I don't wonder at it. But hens and chickens must go to bed when the lamp is put out. Cur—r-r-r-r-r.

PART II.

REFLECTIONS OF A PHILOSOPHER UPON A BLADE OF GRASS.

Here is a leaf, which we call a blade of grass There are myriads like it in this field; it seems a trifle; it seems insignificant. But let me look at it with my glass. How wonderful is its texture! It seems woven like net-work, and nothing can exceed the beauty of its structure. And yet every blade of grass is like this. It exceeds all human art in the delicacy of its fabric, yet it grows here out of the ground. *Grows!* What does that mean? What makes it grow? Has it life? It must have life, or it could not grow. And what is that life? It cannot think; it cannot walk; who makes it grow then? Who made this blade of grass? It was not man; it is not the beast of the field. It is God who made it! And is God here in the field, all around me—in every blade of grass, in every leaf, and stem, and flower?

It must be so, indeed. How full of instruction is every thing around us, if we use the powers we possess!

Moral.—Some people believe, that birds and beasts have minds and souls as well as human beings; but we see that the most stupendous wonder of nature excited in one of the most intelligent and civilized of birds, only a queer sort of surprise, expressed in the words cut—cut—cu—dawcut! At the same time it appears that a single blade of grass opens to the philosopher a sublime strain of thought, teaching the profound lesson that God is everywhere!

Is there not a gulf as wide as eternity, between the human soul and animal instinct?

All the children. Bravo, Bravo—John!

Merry. Well, John—that'll do for a boy. I shan't insert it as my own, you know; people will say, it's good for John Smith, only fourteen years old; but for Robert Merry—why, it's too ridiculous, altogether. At any rate—John—the moral is good—and if people do laugh at the article, you just say to 'em—*keep your tongue between your teeth, till you*

"The Old Hen and the Philosopher: A Fable," 1853

do better, and you won't speak for a year! There's nothing like showing a proper spirit upon occasions of importance.

And now my friends, good night.

I insert the following with pleasure, though I cannot possibly find out what the conundrum means. I hope the writer will excuse the delay of the insertion. If I ever get to Centreville, I shall find him out.

Winton, Nov. 4.

Mr. Merry:

I have had a great deal of pleasure in reading your Museum, but have been disappointed in not finding any puzzles in the last number. I send you a conundrum which was written for me by a friend, which I suppose your subscribers will not find very difficult to solve.

My first, is a word which we commonly use
When we taste what we like; or commend
A pithy expression: nor would we refuse,
To prefix it, before the word friend.

My second, to be, is the ardent desire
Of all who this world highly prize;
Altho', my young friends, I trust you'll aspire
To what is more worthy your sighs.

My whole is a name which o'er all girls and boys
A magical power must wield,
As leading them on to taste of the joys
Cull'd from wisdom and virtue's fair field.

When I was at Baltimore last, I went to see an exhibition of canary birds which I thought very curious.

There were one hundred of them, and they cut a great many funny capers, but I thought they acted the death of Marshal Ney better than any thing else. They were dressed in marshals' uniform, with military caps and cloaks, and mounted on toy-horses. The little bird which acted Napoleon, was the most inquisitive little bird you ever saw, and kept turning his head about as if giving orders, while the others sat as if listening most attentively to them. A very small cannon was brought out, and a little post set up with a stick balanced on it, just above the touch-hole of the cannon. One end of this stick was set on fire, and a little bird representing the gunner, upon receiving the order jumped upon the stick, which caused it to fall on the touch-hole, and made the cannon go off with a loud report, while Marshal Ney fell as if killed. Two of them stood on a pistol while it was shot off, and never moved. They suffered themselves to be put in little coffins, with lighted torches around them, and did not stir until the flames came very near them. They did a great many other things of which I have not time to tell you.

That little girl's letter from Paris was very interesting, and I should like her to write again. She must have felt rather flat when the donkey threw her over his head. If I had been in her place I should have been very much frightened.

We hope you will not stop with Billy Bump, for we want very much to see how he got on at the gold-diggings.

I am the same little boy, Mr. Merry, who wrote to you last May telling you that I was then only nine years old. I shall be ten on Christmas-day. I always look forward to that day with a great deal of pleasure.

I should like very much if you ever come to Baltimore, to have you visit Centreville on the eastern shore of Maryland, which was the former residence of Mr. R——n, now a pastor in Boston, who says he is acquainted with you. If you should come there, we should certainly invite you to Winton, where you would meet with a most cordial reception.

Your friend and admirer,

R. T. E.

Memphis. Dec. 10. 1849.

Mr. Merry:

Dear Sir—My brother Thomas has been a subscriber to your Museum for several years past, and I have been an occasional reader of it myself. Last night he left home by stage for Jackson, Tenn., to commence his studies in the West Tennessee College, located in that town, and he has left all the back numbers to me, and I have taken his place in father's store. I now feel able to set up for myself a little, and I want to become a subscriber to your Museum, so will you direct me one every month next year. Direct it to R. A. P——r, jr., Memphis, Tennessee.

OUR YOUNG FOLKS. An Illustrated magazine for Boys and Girls. Vols. 1–9, 1865–1873. Boston: Ticknor and Fields. Editors: J. T. Trowbridge, Gail Hamilton [pseudonym of Mary A. Dodge], Lucy Larcom, 1865–1867; J. T. Trowbridge, Lucy Larcom, 1868–1873. Merged into *St. Nicholas* in January 1874.

In 1865 the magazine presented a different look in periodicals, emerging in the great new period of children's books when children's literature became recognized as desirable for recreation, though often still with an expressed educational purpose. Witness the change in illustration, and the unadulterated humor and gaiety of such contributors as Lucretia Hale and Thomas Bailey Aldrich, whose *The Story of a Bad Boy* was serialized in the same year as installments of the *Peterkin Papers*. Poetry had its place, too, with Celia Thaxter's famous "The Sandpiper" and Henry Wadsworth Longfellow's "Christmas Bells."

The editors had strong purposes: John Townsend Trowbridge contributed much story material (his most famous book, *Cudjo's Cave,* and others) which always reflected slavery problems; Gail Hamilton, an active member of the antislavery party; and Lucy Larcom, whose moral views were strongly expressed in articles and poems appearing in almost every issue.

Although the magazine did not have an English edition, it contained British contributions, including Charles Dickens's *Holiday Romance* (1868), later titled *The Magic Fishbone.*

THE SANDPIPER.

ACROSS the lonely beach we flit,
One little sandpiper and I,
And fast I gather, bit by bit,
The scattered drift-wood, bleached and dry.
The wild waves reach their hands for it,
The wild wind raves, the tide runs high,
As up and down the beach we flit,
One little sandpiper and I.

Above our heads the sullen clouds
Scud, black and swift, across the sky:
Like silent ghosts in misty shrouds
Stand out the white light-houses high.
Almost as far as eye can reach
I see the close-reefed vessels fly,
As fast we flit along the beach,
One little sandpiper and I.

I watch him as he skims along,
Uttering his sweet and mournful cry;
He starts not at my fitful song,
Nor flash of fluttering drapery.
He has no thought of any wrong,
He scans me with a fearless eye;
Stanch friends are we, well tried and strong,
The little sandpiper and I.

Comrade, where wilt thou be to-night,
When the loosed storm breaks furiously?
My drift-wood fire will burn so bright!
To what warm shelter canst thou fly?
I do not fear for thee, though wroth
The tempest rushes through the sky;
For are we not God's children both,
Thou, little sandpiper, and I?

C. T.

THE PORTRAIT.

THEY were a family that had long outlived their grandeur, — the Fotheringtons. And though the last generation had been kept alive with traditions of it, the present one knew those traditions only as vague dreams that might or might not be true, and which, either way, had nothing at all to do with their absolute want of bread and butter, other than as having fostered past pride they had hindered honest labor. Of all those great colonial possessions, nothing remained to them but the rambling old house and its well-worn hereditaments; and though various parts even of the old mansion itself had been sold and moved away, still much more room remained than was needed by the mother and her five children, — the mother, whose woful condition had brought her to an utter contempt of the ancestral Fotheringtons, the children, who yet preserved a certain happiness in the midst of their poverty in remembering that at their great-grandfather's wedding a hundred guests were entertained for a week in the house after princely fashion. Not that the Fotheringtons of to-day did not present a decent appearance; — gowns were turned, and ribbons were pressed, and laces were darned till there was nothing left of them; nobody knew exactly how poor they were, which perhaps made it all the harder. The eldest daughters had been quite comfortably educated before everything was gone; the elder son had pushed his own way through college with but small debt, and was now studying his profession at home, finding much reason for unhappiness, and vexed out of patience by little Sarah's troublesome tongue and fingers, and young Tommy's musical fancy, which occasioned him opportunity of exercising his lungs and his shrill little voice all day long and sometimes half the night. It was hard work for poor Frederick Fotherington to try and bury himself in the dismal profundities of his law-books, and the quirks and catches of their citations, when little Sarah had been planted at one end of the great, lumbering cradle in which the first Fotherington might have been rocked, — planted there to be entertained by Tommy, who, inserting himself at the other end,

"The Sandpiper," 1865, by Celia Thaxter (1835–1894).

A New England poet, noticeably inspired by the sea which surrounded her Isles of Shoals home. Her *Poems for Children* appeared in 1884, and *Stories and Poems for Children* in 1895.

CHRISTMAS BELLS.

I HEARD the bells on Christmas Day
Their old, familiar carols play,
And wild and sweet
The words repeat
Of peace on earth, good-will to men!

And thought how, as the day had come,
The belfries of all Christendom
Had rolled along
The unbroken song
Of peace on earth, good-will to men!

Till, ringing, singing on its way,
The world revolved from night to day
A voice, a chime,
A chant sublime
Of peace on earth, good-will to men!

Then from each black, accursed mouth,
The cannon thundered in the South,
And with the sound
The carols drowned
Of peace on earth, good-will to men!

It was as if an earthquake rent
The hearth-stones of a continent,
And made forlorn
The households born
Of peace on earth, good-will to men!

And in despair I bowed my head;
"There is no peace on earth," I said;
"For hate is strong
And mocks the song
Of peace on earth, good-will to men!"

Then pealed the bells more loud and deep:
"God is not dead; nor doth he sleep!
The Wrong shall fail,
The Right prevail,
With peace on earth, good-will to men!"

Henry W. Longfellow.

"Christmas Bells," 1865, by Henry Wadsworth Longfellow (1807–1882).

Published in many of the children's magazines, the poems of this Cambridge poet were kept alive for twentieth-century children in *The Children's Own Longfellow* and other volumes.

OUR YOUNG FOLKS.

An Illustrated Magazine

FOR BOYS AND GIRLS.

VOL. I. JULY, 1865. No. VII.

FREDDY'S NEW-YEAR'S DINNER.

A STORY FOR SMALL YOUNG FOLKS.

FREDDY LINCOLN was the son of a widow, and, because he was born on the First of January, she called him her New Year's Present. A charming present he was, the bright, loving little fellow! His mother was not very well. She was not strong enough to earn much money. But Freddy grew stout on boiled potatoes, and good sweet bread and milk. His clothes were patched; but he liked them, because mother mended them so nicely. He had no money to buy playthings; but he did not need any. He could amuse himself all day with chips and shavings, and his little frisky kitten, and a tin cow that he picked up in the street. The cow had her feet broken off, but his mother bored four holes in a piece of wood, and put the cow's legs into the holes, and then she stood as well as any cow in the barn-yard; but she could not give any milk, you know, because she was made of tin. Kitty was a live thing, that would n't break, and Freddy liked her much better than anything made of tin or wood. She was a white kitten,—all white, except a little black spot on her nose. That black spot made her look as if she had been smelling of crocky kettles. When boys peeped in through the open fence, they called her Smutty Nose. Freddy

"Freddy's New-Year's Dinner," 1865, by Lydia Maria Child (1802–1880).

See pages 164, 165, and 320 for more information about this author and her work.

(continued on next page)

did not like to have them laugh at his kitten. One day he took a basin of water and a piece of sponge, and tried to wash the black spot off. The kitten cried, "Miou!" and kicked her hind legs very hard against his wrists. But he held her tight, and scrubbed poor kitty's nose till he almost rubbed the skin off. Perhaps he would have rubbed the skin quite off, if his mother had not called him. But as soon as he heard her sweet voice calling, "Freddy dear!" he ran to see what was wanted. His mother said to him, "Here is Bobby Spring come to see you. He is going to have a Christmas party, and he wants you to come." "O mother, do let me go!" exclaimed Freddy; and when mother said he might go, he jumped up and down, and shook his elbows, and laughed out loud, he was so glad. When kitty saw him jumping about, she began to jump too. She ran round and round, after her own tail; but she did n't catch it; for the tail ran round as fast as she did. "What a little fool!" said Bobby Spring. "She don't know that her tail is tied on." Freddy clapped his hands, and laughed to see how fast the kitten ran round. "So it *is* tied on," said he; "and kitty don't know it. She thinks she can catch it, but she can't *never* catch it. Mother, when *is* Christmas? Is it to-night? May I wear my blue jacket?"

When he was told that the next night would be Christmas Eve, he thought it was a long time to wait. All the next day he kept asking, every hour, how long it would be before sunset. The sun went down at last, and Freddy went to the Christmas party. There he saw wonderful things. There was an evergreen tree on the table, lighted up with little candles; and dogs, and dolls, and birds, and all sorts of pretty things, were on the branches. Every little girl and boy had something from the tree. Freddy had a small flag with stars and stripes on it, and on the top was a bright gilded eagle and a yellow tassel. And he had a paper full of sugared almonds, and a book full of pretty pictures. He jumped round with a little black-eyed girl, and called it dancing. Mrs. Spring played on the piano, and they had a merry time.

When Freddy's mother came for him, he could not believe it was nine o'clock, though he never sat up so late before. His mother told him it was time his little peepers were shut. But his peepers were open for two hours afterward; and when he fell asleep, he went to the Christmas party again. He dreamed that he saw his white kitten up in the Christmas tree, stretching her paw down to catch the dolls, that were dancing on the branches to the tune of Yankee Doodle. He remembered it when he woke up, and talked to his mother about it. When she told him the kitten did not go to the party, he said, "Yes, she *was* there, mother, for I did see her." Then he turned to puss, who was sleeping on the hearth-rug, and said, "Kitty, you know you was there. I did see you trying to catch the dolls." The kitten winked her eyes sleepily, and did n't seem to remember anything about the Christmas tree. But Freddy always thought that puss was at the party, though she could n't talk about it. He talked it over to *her* ever so many times.

A week after the party it was New Year's Day. Freddy came down stairs barefoot, his little toes all red with the cold. He jumped and skipped about, for he was never still. And he hugged and kissed his mother, and said, "I woke up first! I did wish you a happy New Year first! Did n't I, dear mother?" Then, looking at his cup of milk and crust of bread, he began to think of the nice things at the Christmas party. And he said, "Mother, I don't think that is a very good breakfast for New Year's Day. It 's my birthday, too. All the boys have things New Year's Day. Bobby Spring said he was going to have lots of things. His father, and his mother, and his grandfather, and his grandmother are all going to give him something."

Freddy's mother kissed him, and said, "My little boy has no father, and no grandfather, and no grandmother; and mother is not well, and can't earn much money to buy things. But she has made her dear little son a nice cap, just such a one as he wanted. See! it is like a soldier's cap. There are two bright buttons and a tassel. Is n't that a pretty New Year's present?"

Freddy seized it with both hands, pushed it down on his head, and began to march about the room. His mother smiled to see how tall he felt. "I wish I had a feather in it," said he.

"Well, here is the cockerel's feather you picked up; I will put that in," said his mother.

Freddy was delighted to have it, and as soon as it was fastened in, he began to march about again.

"But is n't my little son going to give mother a New Year's present?" said she.

He stopped marching at once, and said, sorrowfully, "I don't know what to give you, dear mother. I have n't got anything. I am sorry I did eat up all my sugared almonds."

His mother kissed him, and said, "*You* are my New Year's present, sonny. Give mother a kiss. She will like that better than sugared almonds."

When they had kissed each other many times, his mother said, "Now my little boy must be dressed, and eat his breakfast."

Freddy jumped down and looked out of the window. "It did snow while I was asleep," said he. "Let me have on my copper-toed shoes, and go out in the snow."

"But you must eat your breakfast first," said his mother.

Freddy nibbled away at the crust; then he laid it down, and, looking up coaxingly in his mother's face, he said, "You know once, when I did look into the baker's window, he *comed* out and did give me a gingerbread rabbit, with two black currants for eyes. *Praps*, if I wish the baker a happy New Year, he will give me another gingerbread rabbit. May I go and wish the baker a happy New Year? Do let me go, dear mother."

She smiled, and said, "You may go and wish Mr. Wheaton a happy New Year, my son; but you must n't ask him for a gingerbread rabbit. If he gives you a cake, make a bow, and say, I thank you, sir; and if he does not give you a cake, make a bow and say, Good morning, sir, and come right away, like a little man."

"But, mother, if the baker don't give me a cake," said Freddy, "I should like to stop outside one little minute, just to look into the window and see the gingerbread rabbits. I won't ask him for a rabbit. I will only look at 'em."

(continued on next page)

"Well, you may look at them, darling," said his mother. "But drink your cup of milk before you go."

He took the tin cup with both his little plump hands, and held back his head, and poured every drop into his mouth, and then set the cup down, smacking his lips. "Now, mother," said he, "please put on my coat, and my new cap, with the brass buttons and the cockerel's feather; and I 'll take my little flag, and then I shall look like a soldier." When his coat and cap were on, he gave his mother a smacking kiss, and said, "If the baker gives me a gingerbread rabbit, I will give you half of it." And away he went, saying, "March! March!"

His mother looked after him with a smile, but the tears were in her eyes; for Freddy was her darling boy, and she felt sad because she had no New Year's cake to give him. It was a beautiful winter morning. There was snow on the ground, and a sprinkling of snow on the trees, and bright sparkles of frost in the air. Freddy went marching along, making the snow fly with his little copper-toed shoes. His eyes were blue as the sky, his cheeks were rosy with cold, and the curls of his soft yellow hair blew about in the wind. He felt very tall, with a flag on his shoulder and a feather in his cap. He saw a man coming toward him dressed in a blue coat, with bright brass things on his cap. But he did n't mind that. He kept marching along. When the man came up to him, he stopped and said, "What are you doing, my fine little fellow?"

"Playing soldier, sir," said Freddy, looking up into the man's face with his clear blue eyes.

The man caught him up in his strong arms, and hugged him and kissed him. "Bless your heart, I wish you were my little boy," said the man. "Your eyes are just like my little Lucy's. Whose boy are you?"

"I 'm Mrs. Lincoln's boy. Whose boy are you?" said Freddy, with a roguish smile. His mother had taught him to say so, for fun; and he said it to the stranger man because he thought he would think it funny.

The man did think it was funny. He laughed, and chucked Freddy under the chin, saying, "You little rogue! I 'm one of *Mister* Lincoln's boys." He said that because he was a soldier in President Lincoln's army.

"Please let me get down," said Freddy. "I 'm going to the baker's, to wish him happy New Year; and *praps* he will give me a gingerbread rabbit. He did give me a gingerbread rabbit once."

"You had better come with me," said the soldier. "I will give you a cake. You will see ever so many soldiers, and they will play Yankee Doodle for you on the drum and the fife."

"I would like to see the soldiers, and hear the drum and the fife," said Freddy. "Is it a great ways? Will you bring me back? I don't want to go a great ways from my mother."

"I will bring you safely back, my boy," said he. "So come with me and see the soldiers." He kissed him again, and set him down on the ground very tenderly.

Freddy liked this new friend very much. Sometimes he looked up in his face and smiled; and the soldier smiled to see him marching along by his side, with his little copper-toed shoes, and the flag on his shoulder, and the feather in his cap. Freddy felt very safe and very grand, marching along with a real live soldier. He thought it was a great deal better than playing with tin soldiers at the Christmas party. When his friend asked him if he had ever been to see the soldiers, he said he had played with a whole company of tin soldiers. Then he told him all about the Christmas party, how he danced with a little girl, and how Santa Claus put a little flag, and a picture-book, and some sugared almonds, in the tree for him.

"I should like to see you dance with my little Lucy," said the soldier. "She has great blue eyes and curly yellow hair, just like you. She is a pretty little puss, and I love her dearly."

"Is she a kitten?" asked Freddy.

"No indeed. She is my little girl," said the soldier. "What made you think she was a kitten?"

"Because you did call her a pretty little puss; and that is what mother calls my kitten," said Freddy. Then he began to tell about his kitten; how she was all white, except a smutty spot on her nose, that he could n't wash off.

The big soldier was as much pleased with his prattle as if he himself had been a little boy. It sounded very pleasantly in his ears, for his own dear little Lucy at home was just such a chatterbox. They had not walked very far before they came to a large building, and in front of it there were a great many men wearing blue coats and soldiers' caps. Some were singing, some talking, and some cleaning their guns. Freddy had never seen so many men together before. He began to wish his mother was with him. He nestled close up to his new friend, and took hold of his coat.

"You need n't be afraid," said the man. "These are all Mr. Lincoln's boys, and they 'll all be glad to see you. Come with me. I 'll take good care of you."

"Hilloa, Sergeant!" shouted one of the soldiers, "who is this?"

(continued on next page)

"He is a little boy I found in the street," said the Sergeant. "I brought him here to see the soldiers. He wants to hear you play Yankee Doodle on the drum and the fife."

"That we will!" said the drummer. "Come here, my little fellow."

"Wish you happy New Year! Wish you happy New Year!" said the soldiers.

"It 's my birthday, too," said Freddy, who began to feel that he was among friends.

They gave him apples and peanuts, and told him about the little girls and boys they had left at home. Then they began to play Yankee Doodle, with a big drum and a little drum, and a big fife and a little fife; and some of the soldiers sang Yankee Doodle, and snapped their fingers to the music; and one of the men danced, and another made up droll faces. All this made Freddy so merry, he did n't know what to do with himself. He jumped up and down, and rolled over in the snow, and laughed, and laughed. Then he got up and marched about with his little flag, and tried to sing Yankee Doodle. He forgot all about the baker, and the gingerbread rabbit, and his little white kitten, and everything. The soldiers thought he was a charming little fellow, and he thought they were charming great fellows; and they had all manner of fun together.

Presently there was the rolling sound of a big drum, and somebody called out that dinner was ready. Then little Freddy stopped jumping about, and said, "I must go right home to my mother."

But his friend the Sergeant said, "You could n't find the way home, my boy. Come and eat dinner with us, and as soon as I have done dinner, I will carry you home."

"I don't want to be carried," said Freddy. "I am a great, large boy, and I can walk home alone."

"What a big tail our kitten's got!" said one of the soldiers.

"Where *is* the kitty?" asked Freddy.

When the soldiers saw him looking all round for a kitten, they laughed; but Freddy did n't know what they were laughing at.

An officer came up and told the soldiers to form into a line. So they marched, two and two, to the dinner-tables; and Freddy took hold of the friendly Sergeant's hand, and marched along, with the cockerel's feather in his cap, and the little flag on his shoulder. The drums and the fifes sounded so merrily, that he wanted to jump and skip; but the Sergeant told him he must march like a little soldier, because he had the flag to carry. So he marched along very steadily, and his little copper-toed shoes made marks on the snow exactly alongside of the sergeant's big shoes. Freddy felt as if he was a man.

The ladies of the town had sent the soldiers a great many good things for a New Year's dinner. They all seemed to think that Freddy was king of the feast. They mounted him on a tall box, so that he was as high as any of them. They put on his plate a slice of roasted turkey, and squash, and potato, and gravy. He was in a hurry to have his friend the Sergeant cut up the turkey for him; for he had never had roasted turkey but twice before in his life. It tasted wonderfully good; but when he had eaten two or three mouthfuls, he stopped, and, looking up in the Sergeant's face, he said, "If you please, sir, I should like to put this nice dinner in a paper, and carry it home to my mother. My mother is n't very well, and she don't get much money to buy good things."

"That 's right! Always be good to your mother, my brave boy," said the Sergeant. "But you may eat the turkey on your plate. I will give you another slice to carry home to your mother."

Then Freddy ate his turkey with a good appetite. And when he had eaten it, they gave him a slice of plum-pudding with sweet sauce. He looked at the big raisins, and laughed, and began to sing,

"Little Jack Horner sat in a corner,
Eating Christmas pie;
He put in his thumb and pulled out a plum,
And cried, What a *great* boy am I!"

He wanted to pull out a plum; but the pudding looked so good, he said, "If you please, I would like to put this in a paper and carry it home to my mother."

"Eat your pudding, my boy," said one of the soldiers. "I will go out presently and buy a basket, and we will fill it full of nice things for your mother."

So he ate his pudding, and all the sweet sauce on his plate. Then he took a little tin cup of water with both hands, and drank it all, and said he had had dinner enough.

The soldier went out and bought a basket, as large as he thought such a little boy could lift, and they filled it full of nice things. Then Freddy was in a great hurry to go home to show his mother what a New Year's present the soldiers had sent her. His friend the Sergeant put a bow of ribbon in his cap, red, white, and blue, with a bright gilt eagle in the middle. The long ends of the ribbon hung down about his ears, and mixed with his yellow curls; and it all looked as pretty as a picture. Freddy was in a great hurry to go and show it to his mother; but the soldiers all wanted to kiss him. It took a long while to go round among them all; and his friend the Sergeant said, "Make haste. The boy ought to go home. His mother will think he is lost."

Freddy hurried through his kissing, and heaved a big sigh when he said, "Good by, Mr. Lincoln's boys. I wish I could come again to-morrow."

"We are going to march away to-morrow," said the men; "and we don't know whether we shall ever see little Freddy again. Good by. Remember Mr. Lincoln's boys."

Some of them felt tears coming in their eyes, for they were thinking of their own dear little children at home.

"Good by," said Freddy. "Thank you for my nice dinner, and for the nice things you have sent my mother."

"Good by, Good by, Good by," they all said; and Freddy did not see them more.

(continued on next page)

He felt sorry they were going away; but when the Sergeant began to whistle Yankee Doodle, he became merry again; and as they walked along, he shook his little head to the music, till the cockerel's feather in his cap, and the red and white and blue ribbons, and the yellow curls, all seemed to be dancing a jig. There never was a little boy so happy as Freddy was that day.

When they came in sight of his mother's house, the Sergeant said, "Now *you* can carry the basket the rest of the way. Good by, dear little fellow." He took him up in his arms, and looked in his face, and kissed his mouth, and both his cheeks, and both his eyes. When he sat him down on the ground, tears fell on his yellow curls, for the kind soldier was thinking of his own little blue-eyed Lucy at home.

Freddy did not see the tears, and he did not know what his friend was thinking of when he kissed him so many times. He was in a great hurry to show his mother the present he had brought her, and he tugged the basket along as fast as he could. His mother opened the door and said, "Why Freddy! Where *have* you been all this while?"

He was all out of breath, but as soon as he could speak, he said, "O mother, I did have such a darling New Year's Day! I did see such a many, many soldiers! And they did give me roast turkey, and they did give me plum-pudding; and they did send a New Year's present to you."

"But, Freddy," said his mother, "you have been naughty. Poor mother has been much troubled about you. She thought her little boy was lost."

"*Was* I naughty?" said Freddy, sorrowfully. "I did n't know I was naughty."

"Why only think how long you have been gone!" said his mother. "You went away at breakfast-time, and now it is after dinner."

"So I did!" said Freddy. He was very much surprised. He did not know where the day had gone to, it had gone so quick. When his mother told him she had been frightened about him, he felt sorry, and began to make up a lip to cry.

But his mother patted him on the head and said, "Don't cry. You did n't *mean* to be a naughty boy. You did n't *mean* to stay away from poor mother so long; did you? How was it? Tell me all about it."

But Freddy was busy unpacking the basket. "O mother," said he, "see what lots of things the soldiers did send you! Here is a great piece of mince-pie, and a great piece of apple-pie, and a great piece of plum-pudding, and a great piece of turkey, and four red apples; and see this great, big, *large* orange!"

His mother smiled, and said, "But where is the gingerbread rabbit you went out to get this morning?"

Freddy laid down the big orange, and seemed very much surprised again. "Why, mother," said he, "I did forget all about the gingerbread rabbit! How funny! But I did have a darling New Year's Day."

"You have not told me where you have been," said his mother. "Come, sit in my lap, and tell me all about it."

Then he began to tell how he met a soldier, who took him up in his arms and kissed him, and told him he looked like his little blue-eyed Lucy at home. And how he asked him to go and see the soldiers; and how they played Yankee Doodle on a great drum and a little drum, and a big fife, and a little fife. How his tongue did run! It seemed as if he could never go to sleep that night. And when at last his peepers were shut, his mother saw him smiling in his sleep. He was dreaming about the soldier that made such funny faces. He was awake bright and early in the morning, and the first words he said were, "Hark, mother! Don't you hear the drums and fifes? I guess the soldiers are marching away. O mother, let me get up and be dressed, and march a little way with 'em."

She put her arm round him and said, "My little boy don't want to go away and leave his poor mother all alone, does he?"

"No, dear mother, I don't." He nestled close up to her, and began to tell her over again all the wonderful things he had seen and heard. Freddy was a chatterbox.

When the winter passed away, something else happened. A lady in the country invited his mother to come and stay at her house; for she thought the fresh air and the smell of the new hay would be good for her. Freddy was delighted to go. He was always delighted with everything. The lady had a neighbor, whose little blue-eyed daughter was named Lucy; and they lived alone, because Lucy's father had gone to be a soldier.

One day, when Lucy was picking up chips, Freddy helped her to fill her little basket; and when it was full, he took hold of one side of the handle, and she took hold of the other, and they carried it into the house to her mother. The lady asked him whose little boy he was; and when he told her he was Mrs. Lincoln's boy, she smiled, and asked him if he did n't go to see *Mr.* Lincoln's boys on New Year's Day. Freddy began to tell about the charming time he had with the soldiers. The lady took him up in her lap and kissed him, and told him her husband was the soldier who met him in the street. "And is that his little Lucy?" asked Freddy. "Yes, that is his little Lucy," said the lady. Then Freddy felt as if he was very well acquainted with the little girl. They played together every day. He told her, over and over again, what great times he had on Christmas Eve and New Year's Day; and he told her all about his white kitten with a smutty nose; and she told him all about her chickens and her lambs. They made houses of cobs, and rode seesaw on the boards. He called her Sissy, and she called him Bubby. They had very pleasant times together.

When summer was gone, he did not want to go back to the city. He said, "I shall have nobody to play with me, mother. I wish Lucy would go with me. I wish she *was* my Sissy." "I wish so, too," said his mother. "But Lucy must not leave her mother all alone, you know. And we must go home now, and see what has become of puss." "O yes," said Freddy, "I want to see puss again."

He found that she had grown to be a great puss; and he told his mother he did not like her half so well as he did little Lucy.

L. Maria Child.

1868.] *About Elizabeth Eliza's Piano.* 391

ABOUT ELIZABETH ELIZA'S PIANO.

ELIZABETH Eliza had a present of a piano, and she was to take lessons of the postmaster's daughter.

They decided to have the piano set across the window in the parlor, and the carters brought it in, and went away. After they had gone, the family all came in to look at the piano; but they found the carters had placed it with its back turned towards the middle of the room, standing close against the window.

How could Elizabeth Eliza open it? How could she reach the keys to play upon it?

Solomon John proposed that they should open the window, which Agamemnon could do with his long arms. Then Elizabeth Eliza should go round upon the piazza and open the piano. Then she could have her music-stool on the piazza, and play upon the piano there.

So they tried this; and they all thought it was a very pretty sight to see Elizabeth Eliza playing on the piano, while she sat on the piazza with the honeysuckle vines behind her.

It was very pleasant, too, moonlight evenings. Mr. Peterkin liked to take a doze on his sofa in the room; but the rest of the family liked to sit on the piazza. So did Elizabeth Eliza, only she had to have her back to the moon.

All this did very well through the summer; but, when the fall came, Mr. Peterkin thought the air was too cold from the open window, and the family did not want to sit out on the piazza.

Elizabeth Eliza practised in the mornings with her cloak on; but she was obliged to give up her music in the evenings, the family shivered so.

One day, when she was talking with the lady from Philadelphia, she spoke of this trouble.

The lady from Philadelphia looked surprised, and then said, "But why don't you turn the piano round?"

One of the little boys pertly said, "It is a square piano."

But Elizabeth Eliza went home directly, and, with the help of Agamemnon and Solomon John, turned the piano round.

"Why did not we think of that before?" said Mrs. Peterkin. "What shall we do when the lady from Philadelphia goes home again?"

Lucretia P. Hale.

"About Elizabeth Eliza's Piano," 1868, by Lucretia Peabody Hale (1820–1900).

A sister of Edward Everett Hale and Susan Hale, this Boston author saw her series of stories about the Peterkins published both in *Our Young Folks* and in *St. Nicholas.* The *Peterkin Papers* appeared in book form in 1880, and *The Last of the Peterkins* in 1886.

OUR YOUNG FOLKS.

An Illustrated Magazine

FOR BOYS AND GIRLS.

Vol. V. APRIL, 1869. No. IV.

THE STORY OF A BAD BOY.

CHAPTER VII.

ONE MEMORABLE NIGHT.

TWO months had elapsed since my arrival at Rivermouth, when the approach of an important celebration produced the greatest excitement among the juvenile population of the town.

There was very little hard study done in the Temple Grammar School the week preceding the Fourth of July. For my part, my heart and brain were so full of fire-crackers, Roman-candles, rockets, pin-wheels, squibs, and gunpowder in various seductive forms, that I wonder I did n't explode under Mr. Grimshaw's very nose. I could n't do a sum to save me; I could n't tell, for love or money, whether Tallahassee was the capital of Tennessee or of Florida; the present and the pluperfect tenses were inextricably mixed in my memory, and I did n't know a verb from an adjective when I met one. This was not alone my condition, but that of every boy in the school.

Mr. Grimshaw considerately made allowances for our temporary distraction, and sought to fix our interest on the lessons by connecting them directly or indirectly with the coming Event. The class in arithmetic, for instance, was requested to state how many boxes of fire-crackers, each box measuring sixteen inches square, could be stored in a room of such and such dimensions. He gave us the Declaration of Independence for

"The Story of a Bad Boy," 1869, by Thomas Bailey Aldrich (1836–1907).

These semiautobiographical stories based on the author's boyhood experiences in New Hampshire were collected and published in book form in 1870. They appeared first serialized in *Our Young Folks,* from which the following material is taken.

(continued on next page)

a parsing exercise, and in geography confined his questions almost exclusively to localities rendered famous in the Revolutionary war.

"What did the people of Boston do with the tea on board the English vessels?" asked our wily instructor.

"Threw it into the river!" shrieked the boys, with an impetuosity that made Mr. Grimshaw smile in spite of himself. One luckless urchin said, "Chucked it," for which happy expression he was kept in at recess.

Notwithstanding these clever stratagems, there was not much solid work done by anybody. The trail of the serpent (an inexpensive but dangerous fire-toy) was over us all. We went round deformed by quantities of Chinese crackers artlessly concealed in our trousers-pockets; and if a boy whipped out his handkerchief without proper precaution, he was sure to let off two or three torpedoes.

Even Mr. Grimshaw was made a sort of accessory to the universal demoralization. In calling the school to order, he always rapped on the table with a heavy ruler. Under the green baize table-cloth, on the exact spot where he usually struck, a certain boy, whose name I withhold, placed a fat torpedo. The result was a loud explosion, which caused Mr. Grimshaw to look queer. Charley Marden was at the water-pail, at the time, and directed general attention to himself by strangling for several seconds and then squirting a slender thread of water over the blackboard.

Mr. Grimshaw fixed his eyes reproachfully on Charley, but said nothing. The real culprit (it was n't Charley Marden, but the boy whose name I withhold) instantly regretted his badness, and after school confessed the whole thing to Mr. Grimshaw, who heaped coals of fire upon the nameless boy's head by giving him five cents for the Fourth of July. If Mr. Grimshaw had caned this unknown youth, the punishment would not have been half so severe.

On the last day of June, the Captain received a letter from my father, enclosing five dollars "for my son Tom," which enabled that young gentleman to make regal preparations for the celebration of our national independence. A portion of this money, two dollars, I hastened to invest in fireworks; the balance I put by for contingencies. In placing the fund in my possession, the Captain imposed one condition that dampened my ardor considerably,— I was to buy no gunpowder. I might have all the snapping-crackers and torpedoes I wanted; but gunpowder was out of the question.

I thought this rather hard, for all my young friends were provided with pistols of various sizes. Pepper Whitcomb had a horse-pistol nearly as large as himself, and Jack Harris, though he to be sure was a big boy, was going to have a real old-fashioned flint-lock musket. However, I did n't mean to let this drawback destroy my happiness. I had one charge of powder stowed away in the little brass pistol which I brought from New Orleans, and was bound to make a noise in the world once, if I never did again.

It was a custom observed from time immemorial for the towns-boys to have a bonfire on the Square on the midnight before the Fourth. I did n't ask the Captain's leave to attend this ceremony, for I had a general idea that he would n't give it. If the Captain, I reasoned, does n't forbid me, I break no orders by going. Now this was a specious line of argument, and the mishaps that befell me in consequence of adopting it were richly deserved.

On the evening of the 3d I retired to bed very early, in order to disarm suspicion. I did n't sleep a wink, waiting for eleven o'clock to come round; and I thought it never would come round, as I lay counting from time to time the slow strokes of the ponderous bell in the steeple of the Old North Church. At length the laggard hour arrived. While the clock was striking I jumped out of bed and began dressing.

My grandfather and Miss Abigail were heavy sleepers, and I might have stolen down stairs and out at the front door undetected; but such a commonplace proceeding did not suit my adventurous disposition. I fastened one end of a rope (it was a few yards cut from Kitty Collins's clothes-line) to the bedpost nearest the window, and cautiously climbed out on the wide pediment over the hall door. I had neglected to knot the rope; the result was, that, the moment I swung clear of the pediment, I descended like a flash of lightning, and warmed both my hands smartly. The rope moreover was four or five feet too short; so I got a fall that would have proved serious had I not tumbled into the middle of one of the big rose-bushes growing on either side of the steps.

I scrambled out of that without delay, and was congratulating myself on my good luck, when I saw by the light of the setting moon the form of a man leaning over the garden gate. It was one of the town watch, who had probably been observing my operations with curiosity. Seeing no chance of escape, I put a bold face on the matter and walked directly up to him.

"What on airth air you a doin'?" asked the man, grasping the collar of my jacket.

"I live here, sir, if you please," I replied, "and am going to the bonfire. I did n't want to wake up the old folks, that 's all."

The man cocked his eye at me in the most amiable manner, and released his hold.

"Boys is boys," he muttered. He did n't attempt to stop me as I slipped through the gate.

Once beyond his clutches, I took to my heels and soon reached the Square, where I found forty or fifty fellows assembled, engaged in building a pyramid of tar-barrels. The palms of my hands still tingled so that I could n't join in the sport. I stood in the doorway of the Nautalis Bank, watching the workers, among whom I recognized lots of my schoolmates. They looked like a legion of imps, coming and going in the twilight, busy in raising some infernal edifice. What a Babel of voices it was, everybody directing everybody else, and everybody doing everything wrong!

When all was prepared, somebody applied a match to the sombre pile. A fiery tongue thrust itself out here and there, then suddenly the whole fabric burst into flames, blazing and crackling beautifully. This was a signal for the boys to join hands and dance around the burning barrels, which they did

(continued on next page)

shouting like mad creatures. When the fire had burnt down a little, fresh staves were brought and heaped on the pyre. In the excitement of the moment I forgot my tingling palms, and found myself in the thick of the carousal.

Before we were half ready, our combustible material was expended, and a disheartening kind of darkness settled down upon us. The boys collected together here and there in knots, consulting as to what should be done. It yet lacked four or five hours of daybreak, and none of us were in the humor to return to bed. I approached one of the groups standing near the town-pump, and discovered in the uncertain light of the dying brands the figures of Jack Harris, Phil Adams, Harry Blake, and Pepper Whitcomb, their faces streaked with perspiration and tar, and their whole appearance suggestive of New Zealand chiefs.

"Hullo! here 's Tom Bailey!" shouted Pepper Whitcomb; "he 'll join in!"

Of course he would. The sting had gone out of my hands, and I was ripe for anything, — none the less ripe for not knowing what was on the *tapis*. After whispering together for a moment, the boys motioned me to follow them.

We glided out from the crowd and silently wended our way through a neighboring alley, at the head of which stood a tumble-down old barn, owned by one Ezra Wingate. In former days this was the stable of the mail-coach that ran between Rivermouth and Boston. When the railroad superseded that primitive mode of travel, the lumbering vehicle was rolled into the barn, and there it stayed. The stage-driver, after prophesying the immediate downfall of the nation, died of grief and apoplexy, and the old coach followed in his wake as fast as it could by quietly dropping to pieces. The barn had the reputation of being haunted, and I think we all kept very close together when we found ourselves standing in the black shadow cast by the tall gable. Here, in a low voice, Jack Harris laid bare his plan, which was to burn the ancient stage-coach.

"The old trundle-cart is n't worth twenty-five cents," said Jack Harris, "and Ezra Wingate ought to thank us for getting the rubbish out of the way. But if any fellow here does n't want to have a hand in it, let him cut and run, and keep a quiet tongue in his head ever after."

With this he pulled out the staples that held the rusty padlock, and the big barn-door swung slowly open. The interior of the stable was pitch-dark, of course. As we made a movement to enter, a sudden scrambling, and the sound of heavy bodies leaping in all directions, caused us to start back in terror.

"Rats!" cried Phil Adams.

"Bats!" exclaimed Harry Blake.

"Cats!" suggested Jack Harris. "Who 's afraid?"

Well, the truth is, we were all afraid; and if the pole of the stage had not been lying close to the threshold, I don't believe anything on earth would have induced us to cross it. We seized hold of the pole-straps and succeeded with great trouble in dragging the coach out. The two fore wheels had rusted to the axle-tree, and refused to revolve. It was the merest skeleton of a coach. The cushions had long since been removed, and the leather hangings had crumbled away from the worm-eaten frame. A load of ghosts and a span of phantom horses to drag them would have made the ghastly thing complete.

Luckily for our undertaking, the stable stood at the top of a very steep hill. With three boys to push behind, and two in front to steer, we started the old coach on its last trip with little or no difficulty. Our speed increased every moment, and, the fore wheels becoming unlocked as we arrived at the foot of the declivity, we charged upon the crowd like a regiment of cavalry, scattering the people right and left. Before reaching the bonfire, to which some one had added several bushels of shavings, Jack Harris and Phil Adams, who were steering, dropped on the ground, and allowed the vehicle to pass over them, which it did without injuring them ; but the boys who were clinging for dear life to the trunk-rack behind fell over the prostrate steersmen, and there we all lay in a heap, two or three of us quite picturesque with the nose-bleed.

The coach, with an intuitive perception of what was expected of it, plunged into the centre of the kindling shavings, and stopped. The flames sprung up and clung to the rotten woodwork, which burned like tinder. At this moment a figure was seen leaping wildly from the inside of the blazing coach. The figure made three bounds towards us, and tripped over Harry Blake. It was Pepper Whitcomb, with his hair somewhat singed, and his eyebrows completely scorched off!

Pepper had slyly ensconced himself on the back seat before we started, intending to have a neat little ride down hill, and a laugh at us afterwards. But the laugh, as it happened, was on our side, or would have been, if half a dozen watchmen had not suddenly pounced down upon us, as we lay scrambling on the ground, weak with our mirth over Pepper's misfortune. We were collared and marched off before we well knew what had happened.

The abrupt transition from the noise and light of the Square to the silent, gloomy brick room in the rear of the Meat Market seemed like the work of enchantment. We stared at each other aghast.

"Well," remarked Jack Harris, with a sickly smile, "*this* is a go!"

"No go, I should say," whimpered Harry Blake, glancing at the bare brick walls and the heavy iron-plated door.

"Never say die," muttered Phil Adams, dolefully.

The bridewell was a small, low-studded chamber built up against the rear end of the Meat Market, and approached from the Square by a narrow passage-way. A portion of the room was partitioned off into eight cells, numbered, each capable of holding two persons. The cells were full at the time, as we presently discovered by seeing several hideous faces leering out at us through the gratings of the doors.

A smoky oil-lamp in a lantern suspended from the ceiling threw a flickering light over the apartment, which contained no furniture excepting a couple

(continued on next page)

of stout wooden benches. It was a dismal place by night, and only little less dismal by day, for the tall houses surrounding "the lock-up" prevented the faintest ray of sunshine from penetrating the ventilator over the door, — a long narrow window opening inward and propped up by a piece of lath.

As we seated ourselves in a row on one of the benches, I imagine that our aspect was anything but cheerful. Adams and Harris looked very anxious, and Harry Blake, whose nose had just stopped bleeding, was mournfully carving his name, by sheer force of habit, on the prison-bench. I don't think I ever saw a more "wrecked" expression on any human countenance than Pepper Whitcomb's presented. His look of natural astonishment at finding himself incarcerated in a jail was considerably heightened by his lack of eyebrows. As for me, it was only by thinking how the late Baron Trenck would have conducted himself under similar circumstances that I was able to restrain my tears.

None of us were inclined to conversation. A deep silence, broken now and then by a startling snore from the cells, reigned throughout the chamber. By and by, Pepper Whitcomb glanced nervously towards Phil Adams and said, "Phil, do you think they will — *hang us?*"

"Hang your grandmother!" returned Adams, impatiently; "what I 'm afraid of is that they 'll keep us locked up until the Fourth is over."

"You ain't smart ef they do!" cried a voice from one of the cells. It was a deep bass voice that sent a chill through me.

"Who are you?" said Jack Harris, addressing the cells in general; for the echoing qualities of the room made it difficult to locate the voice.

"That don't matter," replied the speaker, putting his face close up to the gratings of No. 3, "but ef I was a youngster like you, free an' easy outside there, with no bracelets * on, this spot would n't hold *me* long."

"That 's so!" chimed several of the prison-birds, wagging their heads behind the iron lattices.

"Hush!" whispered Jack Harris, rising from his seat and walking on tiptoe to the door of cell No. 3. "What would you do?"

"Do? Why, I 'd pile them 'ere benches up agin that 'ere door, an' crawl out of that 'ere winder in no time. That 's my adwice."

"And wery good adwice it is, Jim," said the occupant of No. 5, approvingly.

Jack Harris seemed to be of the same opinion, for he hastily placed the benches one on the top of another under the ventilator, and, climbing up on the highest bench, peeped out into the passage-way.

"If any gent happens to have a ninepence about him," said the man in cell No. 3, "there 's a sufferin' family here as could make use of it. Smallest favors gratefully received, an' no questions axed."

This appeal touched a new silver quarter of a dollar in my trousers-pocket; I fished out the coin from a mass of fireworks, and gave it to the prisoner. He appeared to be such a good-natured fellow that I ventured to ask what he had done to get into jail.

* Handcuffs.

"Intirely innocent. I was clapped in here by a rascally nevew as wishes to enjoy my wealth afore I 'm dead."

"Your name, sir?" I inquired, with a view of reporting the outrage to my grandfather and having the injured person reinstated in society.

"Git out, you insolent young reptyle!" shouted the man, in a passion. I retreated precipitately, amid a roar of laughter from the other cells.

"Can't you keep still?" exclaimed Harris, withdrawing his head from the window.

A portly watchman usually sat on a stool outside the door day and night; but on this particular occasion, his services being required elsewhere, the bridewell had been left to guard itself.

"All clear," whispered Jack Harris, as he vanished through the aperture and dropped gently on the ground outside. We all followed him expeditiously, — Pepper Whitcomb and myself getting stuck in the window for a moment in our frantic efforts not to be last.

"Now, boys, everybody for himself!"

CHAPTER VIII.

THE ADVENTURES OF A FOURTH.

THE sun cast a broad column of quivering gold across the river at the foot of our street, just as I reached the doorstep of the Nutter House. Kitty Collins, with her dress tucked about her so that she looked as if she had on a pair of calico trousers, was washing off the sidewalk.

"Arrah, you bad boy!" cried Kitty, leaning on the mop-handle, "the Capen has jist been askin' for you. He 's gone up town, now. It 's a nate thing you done with my clothes-line, and it 's me you may thank for gettin' it out of the way before the Capen come down."

The kind creature had hauled in the rope, and my escapade had not been discovered by the family; but I knew very well that the burning of the stage-coach, and the arrest of the boys concerned in the mischief, were sure to reach my grandfather's ears sooner or later.

"Well, Thomas," said the old gentleman, an hour or so afterwards, beaming upon me benevolently across the breakfast-table, "you did n't wait to be called this morning."

"No, sir," I replied, growing very warm, "I took a little run up town to see what was going on."

I did n't say anything about the little run I took home again!

"They had quite a time on the Square last night," remarked Captain Nutter, looking up from the "Rivermouth Barnacle," which was always placed beside his coffee-cup at breakfast.

I felt that my hair was preparing to stand on end.

"Quite a time," continued my grandfather. "Some boys broke into Ezra Wingate's barn and carried off the old stage-coach. The young rascals! I do believe they 'd burn up the whole town if they had their way."

(continued on next page)

With this he resumed the paper. After a long silence he exclaimed, "Hullo!" — upon which I nearly fell off the chair.

"'Miscreants unknown,'" read my grandfather, following the paragraph with his forefinger; "'escaped from the bridewell, leaving no clew to their identity, except the letter H, cut on one of the benches.' 'Five dollars reward offered for the apprehension of the perpetrators.' Sho! I hope Wingate will catch them."

I don't see how I continued to live, for on hearing this the breath went entirely out of my body. I beat a retreat from the room as soon as I could, and flew to the stable with a misty intention of mounting Gypsy and escaping from the place. I was pondering what steps to take, when Jack Harris and Charley Marden entered the yard.

"I say," said Harris, as blithe as a lark, "has old Wingate been here?"

"Been here?" I cried. "I should hope not!"

"The whole thing 's out, you know," said Harris, pulling Gypsy's forelock over her eyes and blowing playfully into her nostrils.

"You don't mean it!" I gasped.

"Yes, I do, and we 're to pay Wingate three dollars apiece. He 'll make rather a good spec out of it."

"But how did he discover that we were the — the miscreants?" I asked, quoting mechanically from the "Rivermouth Barnacle."

"Why, he saw us take the old ark, confound him! He 's been trying to sell it any time these ten years. Now he has sold it to us. When he found that we had slipped out of the Meat Market, he went right off and wrote the advertisement offering five dollars reward; though he knew well enough who had taken the coach, for he came round to my father's house before the paper was printed to talk the matter over. Was n't the governor mad, though! But it 's all settled, I tell you. We 're to pay Wingate fifteen dollars for the old go-cart, which he wanted to sell the other day for seventy-five cents, and could n't. It 's a downright swindle. But the funny part of it is to come."

"O, there 's a funny part to it, is there?" I remarked bitterly.

"Yes. The moment Bill Conway saw the advertisement, he knew it was Harry Blake who cut that letter H on the bench; so off he rushes up to Wingate — kind of him, was n't it? — and claims the reward. 'Too late, young man,' says old Wingate, 'the culprits has been discovered.' You see Sly-boots had n't any intention of paying that five dollars."

Jack Harris's statement lifted a weight from my bosom. The article in the "Rivermouth Barnacle" had placed the affair before me in a new light. I had thoughtlessly committed a grave offence. Though the property in question was valueless, we were clearly wrong in destroying it. At the same time Mr. Wingate *had* tacitly sanctioned the act by not preventing it when he might easily have done so. He had allowed his property to be destroyed in order that he might realize a large profit.

Without waiting to hear more, I went straight to Captain Nutter, and, laying my remaining three dollars on his knee, confessed my share in the previous night's transaction.

The Captain heard me through in profound silence, pocketed the bank-notes, and walked off without speaking a word. He had punished me in his own whimsical fashion at the breakfast-table, for, at the very moment he was harrowing up my soul by reading the extracts from the "Rivermouth Barnacle," he not only knew all about the bonfire, but had paid Ezra Wingate his three dollars. Such was the duplicity of that aged impostor!

I think Captain Nutter was justified in retaining my pocket-money, as additional punishment, though the possession of it later in the day would have got me out of a difficult position, as the reader will see further on.

I returned with a light heart and a large piece of punk to my friends in the stable-yard, where we celebrated the termination of our trouble by setting off two packs of fire-crackers in an empty wine-cask. They made a prodigious racket, but failed somehow to fully express my feelings. The little brass pistol in my bedroom suddenly occurred to me. It had been loaded I don't know how many months, long before I left New Orleans, and now was the time, if ever, to fire it off. Muskets, blunderbusses, and pistols were banging away lively all over town, and the smell of gunpowder, floating on the air, set me wild to add something respectable to the universal din.

When the pistol was produced, Jack Harris examined the rusty cap and prophesied that it would not explode. "Never mind," said I, "let 's try it."

I had fired the pistol once, secretly, in New Orleans, and, remembering the noise it gave birth to on that occasion, I shut both eyes tight as I pulled the trigger. The hammer clicked on the cap with a dull, dead sound. Then Harris tried it; then Charley Marden; then I took it again, and after three or four trials was on the point of giving it up as a bad job, when the obstinate thing went off with a tremendous explosion, nearly jerking my arm from the socket. The smoke cleared away, and there I stood with the stock of the pistol clutched convulsively in my hand, — the barrel, lock, trigger, and ramrod having vanished into thin air.

"Are you hurt?" cried the boys, in one breath.

"N—no," I replied, dubiously, for the concussion had bewildered me a little.

When I realized the nature of the calamity, my grief was excessive. I can't imagine what led me to do so ridiculous a thing, but I gravely buried the remains of my beloved pistol in our back garden, and erected over the mound a slate tablet to the effect that "Mr. Barker, formerly of new orleans, was Killed accidentally on the Fourth of july, 18— in the 2nd year of his Age." * Binny Wallace, arriving on the spot just after the disaster, and Charley Marden (who enjoyed the obsequies immensely), acted with me as chief mourners. I, for my part, was a very sincere one.

As I turned away in a disconsolate mood from the garden, Charley Marden remarked that he should n't be surprised if the pistol-but took root and grew into a mahogany-tree or something. He said he once planted an old musket-stock, and shortly afterwards a lot of *shoots* sprung up!

* This inscription is copied from a triangular-shaped piece of slate, still preserved in the garret of the Nutter House, together with the pistol-but itself, which was subsequently dug up for a *post-mortem* examination.

(continued on next page)

Jack Harris laughed; but neither I nor Binny Wallace saw Charley's wicked joke.

We were now joined by Pepper Whitcomb, Fred Langdon, and several other desperate characters, on their way to the Square, which was always a busy place when public festivities were going on. Feeling that I was still in disgrace with the Captain, I thought it politic to ask his consent before accompanying the boys. He gave it with some hesitation, advising me to be careful not to get in front of the firearms. Once he put his fingers mechanically into his vest-pocket and half drew forth some dollar-bills, then slowly thrust them back again as his sense of justice overcame his genial disposition. I guess it cut the old gentleman to the heart to be obliged to keep me out of my pocket-money. I know it did me. However, as I was passing through the hall, Miss Abigail, with a very severe cast of countenance, slipped a bran-new quarter into my hand. We had silver currency in those days, thank Heaven!

Great were the bustle and confusion on the Square. By the way, I don't know why they called this large open space a square, unless because it was an oval, — an oval formed by the confluence of half a dozen streets, now thronged by crowds of smartly dressed towns-people and country folks; for Rivermouth on the Fourth was the centre of attraction to the inhabitants of the neighboring villages.

On one side of the Square were twenty or thirty booths arranged in a semicircle, gay with little flags, and seductive with lemonade, ginger-beer, and seed-cakes. Here and there were tables at which could be purchased the smaller sort of fireworks, such as pin-wheels, serpents, double-headers, and punk warranted not to go out. Many of the adjacent houses made a pretty display of bunting, and across each of the streets opening on the Square was an arch of spruce and evergreen, blossoming all over with patriotic mottoes and paper roses.

It was a noisy, merry, bewildering scene as we came upon the ground. The incessant rattle of small arms, the booming of the twelve-pounder firing on the Mill Dam, and the silvery clangor of the church-bells ringing simultaneously, — not to mention an ambitious brass-band that was blowing itself to pieces on a balcony, — were enough to drive one distracted. We amused ourselves for an hour or two, darting in and out among the crowd and setting off our crackers. At one o'clock the Hon. Hezekiah Elkins mounted a platform in the middle of the Square and delivered an oration, to which his fellow-citizens did n't pay much attention, having all they could do to dodge the squibs that were set loose upon them by mischievous boys stationed on the surrounding house-tops.

Our little party, which had picked up recruits here and there, not being swayed by eloquence, withdrew to a booth on the outskirts of the crowd, where we regaled ourselves with root-beer at two cents a glass. I recollect being much struck by the placard surmounting this tent: —

ROOT BEER

SOLD HERE.

It seemed to me the perfection of pith and poetry. What could be more terse? Not a word to spare, and yet everything fully expressed. Rhyme and rhythm faultless. It was a delightful poet who made those verses. As for the beer itself, — that, I think, must have been made from the root of all evil! A single glass of it insured an uninterrupted pain for twenty-four hours. The influence of my liberality working on Charley Marden, — for it was I who paid for the beer, — he presently invited us all to take an ice-cream with him at Pettingil's saloon. Pettingil was the Delmonico of Rivermouth. He furnished ices and confectionery for aristocratic balls and parties, and did n't disdain to officiate as leader of the orchestra at the same; for Pettingil played on the violin, as Pepper Whitcomb described it, "like Old Scratch."

Pettingil's confectionery store was on the corner of Willow and High Streets. The saloon, separated from the shop by a flight of three steps leading to a door hung with faded red drapery, had about it an air of mystery and seclusion quite delightful. Four windows, also draped, faced the side-street, affording an unobstructed view of Marm Hatch's back yard, where a number of inexplicable garments on a clothes-line were always to be seen careering in the wind.

There was a lull just then in the ice-cream business, it being dinner-time, and we found the saloon unoccupied. When we had seated ourselves around the largest marble-topped table, Charley Marden in a manly voice ordered twelve sixpenny ice-creams, "strawberry and verneller mixed."

It was a magnificent sight, those twelve chilly glasses entering the room on a waiter, the red and white custard rising from each glass like a church-steeple, and the spoon-handle shooting up from the apex like a spire. I doubt if a person of the nicest palate could have distinguished, with his eyes shut, which was the vanilla and which the strawberry; but, if I could at this moment obtain a cream tasting as that did, I would give five dollars for a very small quantity.

We fell to with a will, and so evenly balanced were our capabilities that we finished our creams together, the spoons clinking in the glasses like one spoon.

"Let 's have some more!" cried Charley Marden, with the air of Aladdin ordering up a fresh hogshead of pearls and rubies. "Tom Bailey, tell Pettingil to send in another round."

Could I credit my ears? I looked at him to see if he were in earnest. He meant it. In a moment more I was leaning over the counter giving directions for a second supply. Thinking it would make no difference to such a gorgeous young sybarite as Marden, I took the liberty of ordering nine-penny creams this time.

On returning to the saloon, what was my horror at finding it empty!

There were the twelve cloudy glasses, standing in a circle on the sticky marble slab, and not a boy to be seen. A pair of hands letting go their hold on the window-sill outside explained matters. I had been made a victim.

I could n't stay and face Pettingil, whose peppery temper was well known among the boys. I had n't a cent in the world to appease him. What

(continued on next page)

should I do? I heard the clink of approaching glasses, — the ninepenny creams. I rushed to the nearest window. It was only five feet to the ground. I threw myself out as if I had been an old hat.

Landing on my feet, I fled breathlessly down High Street, through Willow, and was turning into Brierwood Place when the sound of several voices, calling to me in distress, stopped my progress.

"Look out, you fool! the mine! the mine!" yelled the warning voices.

Several men and boys were standing at the head of the street, making insane gestures to me to avoid something. But I saw no mine, only in the middle of the road in front of me was a common flour-barrel, which, as I gazed at it, suddenly rose into the air with a terrific explosion. I felt myself thrown violently off my feet. I remember nothing else, excepting that, as I went up, I caught a momentary glimpse of Ezra Wingate leering though his shop window like an avenging spirit.

For an account of what followed, I am indebted to hearsay, for I was insensible when the people picked me up and carried me home on a shutter borrowed from the proprietor of Pettingil's saloon. I was supposed to be killed, but happily (happily for me, at least) I was merely stunned. I lay in a semi-unconscious state until eight o'clock that night, when I attempted to speak. Miss Abigail, who watched by the bedside, put her ear down to my lips and was saluted with these remarkable words: —

"Root Beer
Sold Here!"

T. B. Aldrich.

"At this moment a figure was seen leaping wildly from the inside of the blazing coach."

DRAWN BY S. EYTINGE, JR.]

[See THE STORY OF A BAD BOY, page 209.

WIDE AWAKE. Vols. 1–37, 1875–August 1893. Boston: D. Lothrop & Co. 25½ cm. Monthly. Editors: Ella F. Pratt, C. S. Pratt. *Wide Awake* absorbed *Sunshine* [Cal.] and *The Little Pilgrim* in 1878. It was merged with *St. Nicholas* in 1893.

Published first in 1875, two years after the beginning of *St. Nicholas,* this popular monthly resembled it in numerous ways, having much illustration, a regular page in larger print for younger children, and occasional contributions from England. As well as serializing the famous *Five Little Peppers and How They Grew* (1881) by Margaret Sidney (the pseudonym of Harriet Mulford Stone, who became Mrs. Lothrop when she married her publisher), the magazine offered first appearances also of works by other popular authors, including Edward Everett Hale, Mrs. A. D. T. Whitney, Sophie May, Sarah Orne Jewett, Hezekiah Butterworth, and James Whitcomb Riley. The title varied slightly, sometimes being shown as *Wide Awake Pleasure Book.* A colorful cover of one of these volumes is reproduced on page 318 of this book.

ON OPPOSITE PAGE:
"Five Little Peppers; and How They Grew," 1880, by Margaret Sidney [pseudonym of Harriet Mulford Stone Lothrop (1844–1924)].

The first of the family stories in this author's popular series appeared in book form in 1881 as *Five Little Peppers and How They Grew.* It was serialized in the same year in *Wide Awake,* and it is from this periodical that the material on the following pages is taken. It was followed in 1892 by *The Five Little Peppers Midway,* in 1893 by *The Five Little Peppers Grown-Up,* and in 1897 by *Phronsie Pepper.*

FIVE LITTLE PEPPERS; AND HOW THEY GREW.

BY MARGARET SIDNEY.

CHAPTER I.

A HOME VIEW.

THE little old kitchen had quieted down from the bustle and confusion of mid-day; and now, with its afternoon manners on, presented a holiday aspect, that as the principal room in the brown house it was eminently proper it should have. It was just on the edge of the twilight; and the little Peppers, all except Ben, the oldest of the flock, were taking a "breathing spell" as their mother called it, which meant some quiet work suitable for the hour. All the "breathing spell" they could remember however, poor things; for times were always hard with them now-a-days; and since the father died, when Phronsie was a baby, Mrs. Pepper had had hard work to scrape together money enough to put bread into her children's mouths, and to pay the rent of the little brown house.

But she had met life too bravely to be beaten down now. So with a stout heart and a cheery face, she had worked away day after day at making coats, and tailoring and mending of all descriptions; and she had seen with pride that couldn't be concealed, her noisy, happy brood growing up around her, and filling her heart with comfort, and making the little brown house fairly ring with jollity and fun.

"Poor things!" she would say to herself, "they haven't had any bringing up; they've just scrambled up!" And then she would set her lips together tightly, and fly at her work faster than ever. "I must get learnin' for 'em someway, but I don't see *how!*"

Once or twice she had thought, "now the time's comin'!" but it never did; for winter shut in very cold, and it took so much more to feed and warm them, that the money went faster than ever. And then, when the way seemed clear again, the store changed hands, so that for a long time she failed to get her usual supply of sacks and coats to make; and that made sad havoc in the quarters and half dollars laid up as her nest egg. But —— "Well, it'll come *some* time," she would say to herself; "because it *must!*" And so at it again she would fly, brisker than ever.

"To help mother," was the great ambition of all the children, older and younger; but in Polly's and Ben's souls, the desire grew so overwhelmingly great as to absorb all lesser things. Many and vast were their secret plans, by which they were to astonish her at some future day, which they would only confide — as they did everything else — to one another. For this brother and sister were everything to each other, and stood loyally together through thick and thin.

Polly was ten, and Ben one year older; and the younger three of the "Five Little Peppers," as they were always called, looked up to them with the intensest admiration and love. What *they* failed to do, *couldn't* very well be done by *any* one!

"Oh dear!" exclaimed Polly as she sat over in the corner by the window helping her mother pull out basting threads from a coat she had just finished, and giving an impatient twitch to the sleeve, "I do wish we could ever have any light — just as much as we want!"

"You don't need any light to see *these* threads," said Mrs. Pepper, winding up hers carefully, as she spoke, on an old spool. "Take care, Polly, you broke that; thread's dear now."

"I couldn't help it," said Polly, vexedly; "it snapped; everything's dear now, seems to me! I wish we could have — oh! ever an' ever so many candles; as many we wanted! I'd light 'em all, so

(continued on next page)

there! and have it light here *one* night, anyway!"

"Yes, and go dark all the rest of the year, like as anyway," observed Mrs. Pepper, stopping to untie a knot. "Folks who do so never have *no* candles," she added, sententiously.

"How many'd you have, Polly?" asked Joel, curiously, laying down his hammer, and regarding her with the utmost anxiety.

"Oh, two hundred!" said Polly, decidedly. "I'd have two hundred, all in a row!"

"*Two hundred candles!*" echoed Joel, in amazement. "My whockety! what a lot!"

"Don't say such dreadful words, Joel," put in Polly, nervously, stopping to pick up her spool of basting thread that was racing away all by itself; "'tisn't nice."

"'Tain't worse 'n to wish you'd got things you hain't," retorted Joel. "I don't believe you'd light 'em all at once," he added, incredulously.

"Yes, I would too!" replied Polly, recklessly; "two hundred of 'em, if I had a chance; all at once, so there, Joey Pepper!"

"Oh," said little Davie, drawing a long sigh. "Why, 'twould be just like heaven, Polly! but wouldn't it cost money though!"

"I don't care," said Polly, giving a flounce in her chair, which snapped another thread; "oh dear me! I didn't mean to, mamma; well, I wouldn't care how much money it cost, we'd have as much light as we wanted, for once; so!"

"Mercy!" said Mrs. Pepper, "you'd have the house afire! Two hundred candles! who ever heard of such a thing!"

"Would they burn?" asked Phronsie, anxiously, getting up from the floor where she was crouching with David, overseeing Joel nail on the cover of an old box; and going to Polly's side she awaited her answer patiently.

"Burn?" said Polly. "There, that's done now, mamsie dear!" And she put the coat, with a last little pat into her mother's lap. "I guess they *would*, Phronsie pet." And Polly caught up the little girl, and spun round and round the old kitchen till they were both glad to stop.

"Then," said Phronsie, as Polly put her down, and stood breathless after her last glorious spin, "I do so wish we might, Polly; oh, just this very one minute!" And Phronsie clasped her fat little hands in rapture at the thought.

"Well," said Polly, giving a look up at the old clock in the corner; "mercy me! it's half-past five; and most time for Ben to come home!"

Away she flew to get supper. So for the next few moments nothing was heard but the pulling out of the old table into the middle of the floor, the laying the cloth, and all the other bustle attendant upon the being ready for Ben. Polly went skipping around, cutting the bread, and bringing dishes; only stopping long enough to fling some scraps of reassuring nonsense to the two boys, who were thoroughly dismayed at being obliged to remove their traps into a corner.

Phronsie still stood just where Polly left her. *Two hundred candles!* oh! what *could* it mean! She gazed up to the old beams overhead, and around the dingy walls, and to the old black stove, with the fire nearly out, and then over everything the kitchen contained, trying to think how it would seem. To have it bright and winsome and warm! to suit Polly — "*oh!*" she screamed.

"Goodness!" said Polly, taking her head out of the old cupboard in the corner, "how you scat me, Phronsie!"

"Would they *never* go out?" asked the child, gravely, still standing where Polly left her.

"What?" asked Polly, stopping with a dish of cold potatoes in her hand. "What, Phronsie?"

"Why, the candles," said the child, "the ever-an'-ever so many pretty lights!"

"Oh, my senses!" cried Polly, with a little laugh, "haven't you forgotten that! Yes — no, that is, Phronsie, if we could have 'em at all, we wouldn't *ever* let 'em go out!"

"Not once?" asked Phronsie, coming up to Polly with a little skip, and nearly upsetting her, potatoes and all — "not once, Polly, truly?"

"No, not forever-an'-ever," said Polly; "take care Phronsie! there goes a potato; no, we'd keep 'em always!"

"No, you don't want to," said Mrs. Pepper, coming out of the bedroom in time to catch the last words; "they won't be good to-morrow; better have 'em to-night, Polly."

"Ma'am!" said Polly, setting down her potato-dish on the table, and staring at her mother with all her might — "have *what*, mother?"

"Why, the potatoes, to be sure," replied Mrs. Pepper; "didn't you say you better keep 'em, child?"

"'Twarn't potatoes — at all," said Polly, with a little gasp; "'twas — oh, mercy! here's Ben!" For the door opened, and Phronsie, with a scream of delight, bounded into Ben's arms.

"It's just jolly," said Ben, coming in, his chubby face all aglow, and his big blue eyes shining so honest and true; "it's just jolly to get home! supper ready, Polly?"

"Yes," said Polly; "that is — all but — " and she dashed off for Phronsie's eating apron.

"Sometime," said Phronsie, with her mouth half full, when the meal was nearly over, "we're going to be *awful* rich; we are, Ben, truly!"

"No?" said Ben, affecting the most hearty astonishment; "you don't say so, Chick!"

"Yes," said Phronsie, shaking her yellow head very wisely at him, and diving down into her cup of very weak milk and water to see if Polly *had* put any sugar in by mistake — a proceeding always expectantly observed. "Yes, we are really, Bensie, very dreadful rich!"

"I wish we could be rich now then," said Ben, taking another generous slice of the brown bread; "in time for mamsie's birthday," and he cast a sorrowful glance at Polly.

"I know," said Polly; "oh dear! if we only *could* celebrate it!"

"I don't want no other celebration," said Mrs.

"MOTHER'S RICH ENOUGH!"

Pepper, beaming on them so that a little flash of sunshine seemed to hop right down on the table, "than to look round on you all; I'm rich now, and that's a fact!"

"Mamsie don't mind her five bothers," cried Polly jumping up and running to hug her mother; thereby producing a like desire in all the others, who immediately left their seats and followed her example.

"Mother's rich enough," ejaculated Mrs. Pepper; her bright, black eyes glistening with delight, as the noisy troop filed back to their bread and potatoes; "if we can only keep together, dears, and grow up good, so that the little brown house won't be ashamed of us, that's all I ask."

"Well," said Polly, in a burst of confidence to Ben, after the table had been pushed back against the wall, the dishes nicely washed, wiped, and set up neatly in the cupboard, and all traces of the meal cleared away; "I don't care; let's *try* and get a celebration, somehow, for mamsie!"

"How you goin' to do it?" asked Ben, who was of a decidedly practical turn of mind, and thus couldn't always follow Polly in her flights of imagination.

(continued on next page)

"I don't know," said Polly; "but we *must* some way."

"Phoh! that's no good," said Ben, disdainfully; then seeing Polly's face, he added kindly: "let's think though; and p'raps there'll be some way."

"Oh, I know," cried Polly, in delight; "I know the very thing, Ben! let's make her a cake; a big one, you know, and ——"

"She'll see you bake it," said Ben; "or else she'll smell it, and that 'd be just as bad."

"No, she won't either," replied Polly. "Don't you know she's goin' to help Mrs. Henderson to-morrow; so there!"

"So she is," said Ben; "good for you, Polly, you always think of everything!"

"And then," said Polly, with a comfortable little feeling at her heart at Ben's praise, "why we can have it all out of the way perfectly splendid when she comes home—and besides, Grandma Bascom 'll tell me how. You know we've only got brown flour, Ben; I mean to go right over and ask her now."

"Oh, no, you musn't," cried Ben, catching hold

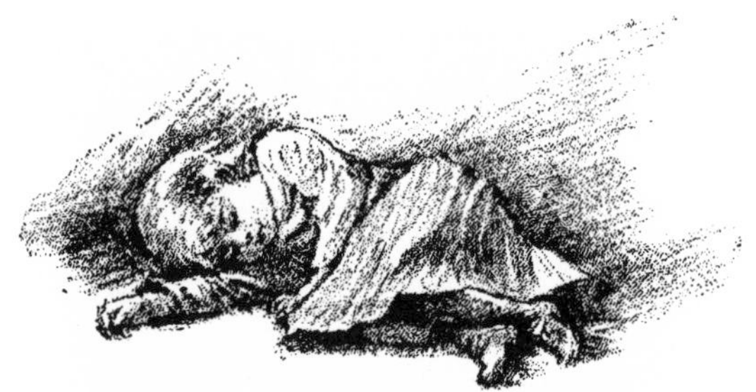

PHRONSIE THINKS SHE WANTS TO GO TO BED.

of her arm as she was preparing to fly off. "Mammy'll find it out; better wait till to-morrow; and besides Polly ——" and Ben stopped, unwilling to dampen this propitious beginning. "The stove'll act like everything, to-morrow! I know 'twill; then what'll you do!"

"It *sha'n't*!" said Polly, running up to look it in the face; "if it does, I'll shake it; the mean old thing!"

The idea of Polly's shaking the lumbering old black affair, sent Ben into such a peal of laughter that it brought all the other children running to the spot; and nothing would do, but they must one and all, be told the reason. So Polly and Ben took them into confidence, which so elated them that half an hour after, when long past her bedtime, Phronsie declared, "I'm not going to bed! I want to sit up like Polly!"

"Don't tease her," whispered Polly to Ben, who thought she ought to go; so she sat straight up on her little stool, winking like everything to keep awake.

At last, as Polly was in the midst of one of her liveliest sallies, over tumbled Phronsie, a sleepy little heap, right onto the floor.

"I want — to go — to bed!" she said; "take me — Polly!"

"I thought so," laughed Polly, and bundled her off into the bedroom.

CHAPTER II.

MAKING HAPPINESS FOR MAMSIE.

And so, the minute her mother had departed for the minister's house next morning, and Ben had gone to his day's work, chopping wood for Deacon Blodgett, Polly assembled her force around the old stove, and proceeded to business. She and the children had been up betimes that morning to get through with the work; and now, as they glanced around with a look of pride on the neatly swept floor, the dishes all done, and everything in order, the moment their mother's back was turned they began to implore Polly to hurry and begin.

"It's most 'leven o'clock," said Joel, who, having no work to do outside, that day, was prancing around, wild to help along the festivities; "it's most 'leven o'clock, Polly Pepper! you won't have it done."

"Oh, no; 'taint either, Jo;" said Polly, with a very flushed face, and her arms full of kindlings, glancing up at the old clock as she spoke; "'taint but quarter of nine; there, take care, Phronsie! you can't lift off the cover; do help her, Davie."

"No; let me!" cried Joel, springing forward; "it's my turn; Dave got the shingles; it's my turn, Polly."

"So 'tis," said Polly; "I forget; there," as she flung in the wood, and poked it all up in a nice little heap coaxingly. "It can't help *but* burn; *what* a cake we'll have for mamsie!"

"It'll be so big," cried Phronsie, hopping around on one toe, "that mamsie won't know what to do, will she, Polly?"

"No, I don't believe she will," said Polly, gaily, stuffing in more wood; "oh, *dear!* there goes Ben's putty; it's all fell out!"

"So it has," said Joel, going around back of the

stove to explore; and then he added cheerfully, "it's bigger'n ever; oh! it's an awful big hole, Polly!"

"Now, whatever *shall* we do!" said Polly, in great distress; "that *hateful* old crack! and Ben's clear off to Deacon Blodgett's!"

"I'll run an' get him," cried Joel, briskly; "I'll bring him right home in ten minutes."

"Oh, no, you must not, Joe," cried Polly in alarm; "it wouldn't never be right to take him off from his work; mamsie wouldn't like it."

"What *will* you do then?" asked Joel, pausing on way to the door.

"I'm sure I don't know," said Polly, getting down on her knees to examine the crack; "I shall have to stuff it with paper, I s'pose."

"'Twon't stay in," said Joel, scornfully; "don't you know you stuffed it before, last week?"

"I know," said Polly, with a small sigh; and sitting down on the floor, she remained quite still for a minute, with her two black hands stuck out straight before her.

"Can't you fix it?" asked Davie, soberly, coming up; "then we can't have the cake."

"Oh, mercy!" exclaimed Polly, springing up quickly; "don't be afraid; we're going to *have* that cake! There, you ugly old thing, you! (this to the stove) see what you've done!" as two big tears flew out of Phronsie's brown eyes, at the direful prospect; and the sorrowful faces of the two boys looked up into Polly's own, for comfort. "I can fix it, I most know; do get some paper, Joe, as quick as you can."

"Don't know where there is any," said Joel, rumaging around; "it's all tore up; 'xcept the almanac; can't I take that?"

"Oh, mercy, no!" cried Polly; "put it right back, Joe; I guess there's some in the wood-shed."

"There ain't either," said little Davie, quickly; "Joel and me took it to make kites with."

"Oh dear," groaned Polly; "I don't know what we *shall* do; unless," as a bright thought struck her, "you let me have the kites, boys."

"Can't," said Joel; "they've all flew away; and tore up."

"Well, now children," said Polly, turning round impressively upon them, the effect of which was heightened by the extremely crocky appearance she had gained in her explorations, "we *must* have some paper, or *something* to stop up that old hole with—some way, *there!*"

"I know," said little Davie, "where we'll get it! it's up-stairs;" and without another word he flew out of the room, and in another minute he put into Polly's hand an old leather boot-top, one of his most treasured possessions. "You can chip it," he said, "real fine, and then 'twill go in."

"So we can," said Polly; "and you're a real good boy, Davie, to give it; that's a splendid present to help celebrate for mamsie!"

"I'd a-give a boot-top," said Joel, looking grimly at the precious bit of leather which Polly was rapidly stripping into little bits; "if I'd a-had it; I don't have nothin'!"

"I know you would, Joey," said Polly, kindly; "there now, you'll stay, I guess!" as with the united efforts of the two boys, cheered on by Phronsie's enthusiastic little crow of delight, the leather was crammed into place, and the fire began to burn.

"Now boys," said Polly, getting up, and drawing a long breath, "I'm agoin' over to Grandma Bascom's to get her to tell me how to make the cake; and you must stay and keep house."

"I'm goin' to nail," said Joel; "I've got lots to do."

"All right," said Polly, tying on her hood; "Phronsie'll love to watch you; I won't be gone long," and she was off.

"Grandma Bascom" wasn't really the children's grandmother; only everybody in the village called her so by courtesy. Her cottage was over across the lane, and just a bit around the corner; and Polly flew along and up to the door, fully knowing that now she would be helped out of her difficulty. She didn't stop to knock, as the old lady was so deaf she knew she wouldn't hear her, but opened the door and walked in. Grandma was sweeping up the floor, already as neat as a pin; when she saw Polly coming, she stopped, and leaned on her broom.

"How's your ma?" she asked, when Polly had said "good morning," and then hesitated.

"Oh, mammy's pretty well," shouted Polly into the old lady's ear; "and to-morrow's her birthday!"

"To-morrow'll be a bad day!" said grandma.

"Oh, don't never say that."

"You mustn't borrow trouble, child."

"I didn't," said Polly; "I mean—it's her *birthday*, grandma!" this last so loud that grandma's cap-border vibrated perceptibly.

"The land's sakes 'tis!" cried Mrs. Bascom, delightedly; "you don't say so!"

(continued on next page)

"Yes," said Polly, skipping around the old lady, and giving her a small hug; "and we're agoin' to give her a surprise."

"What is the matter with her eyes?" asked grandma, sharply, turning around and facing her; "she's been a sewin' too stiddy, hain't she?"

"A *surprise!*" shouted Polly, standing upon tiptoe, to bring her mouth on a level with the old lady's ear; "a *cake*, grandma, a big one!"

"A *cake!*" exclaimed grandma, dropping the broom to settle her cap, which Polly in her extreme endeavors to carry on the conversation, had knocked slightly awry; "well, that'll be fine."

"Yes," said Polly, picking up the broom, and flinging off her hood at the same time; "and, oh! won't you please tell me how to make it, grandma!"

"To be sure; to be sure;" cried the old lady, delighted beyond measure to give advice; "I've got splendid receets; I'll go get 'em right off," and she ambled to the door of the pantry.

"And I'll finish sweeping up," said Polly, which grandma didn't hear; so she took up the broom, and sent it energetically, and merrily flying away to the tune of her own happy thoughts.

"Yes, they're right in here," said grandma, waddling back with an old tin teapot in her hand; — "goodness, child! what a dust you've kicked up! that ain't the way to sweep," and she took the broom out of Polly's hand, who stood stock still in mortification. "There," she said, drawing it mildly over the few bits she could scrape together, and gently coaxing them into a little heap; "that's the way; and then they don't go all over the room."

"I'm sorry," began poor Polly.

"'Tain't any matter," said Mrs. Bascom, kindly, catching sight of Polly's discomfited face; "'tain't a mite of matter; you'll sweep better next time; now let's go to the cake;" and putting the broom into the corner, she waddled back again to the table, followed by Polly, and proceeded to turn out the contents of the teapot, in search of just the right "receet."

But the right one didn't seem to appear; not even after the teapot was turned upside down and shaken by both grandma's and Polly's anxious hands. Every other "receet" seemed to tumble out gladly, and stare them in the face — little dingy rolls of yellow paper, with an ancient odor of spice still clinging to them; but all efforts to find this particular one failed utterly.

"Won't some other one do?" asked Polly, in the interval of fruitless searching, when grandma bewailed and lamented, and wondered, "where I could a-put it!"

"No, no child," answered the old lady; "now, where *do* you s'pose 'tis!" and she clapped both hands to her head, to see if she could possibly remember; "no, no child," she repeated. "Why, they had it down to my niece Mirandy's weddin' — 'twas just elegant! light as a feather; and 'twan't rich either," she added; "no eggs, nor ——"

"Oh, I couldn't have *eggs;*" cried Polly, in amazement at the thought of such luxury; "and we've only brown flour, grandma, you know."

"Well, you can make it of brown," said Mrs. Bascom, kindly; "when the raisins is in 'twill look quite nice."

"Oh, we haven't any raisins," answered Polly.

"*Haven't any raisins!*" echoed grandma, looking at her over her spectacles; "what *are* you goin' to put in?"

"Oh — cinnamon," said Polly, briskly; "we've got plenty of that, and — it'll be good, I guess, grandma!" she finished, anxiously; "anyway, we *must* have a cake; there ain't any other way to celebrate mamsie's birthday."

"Well, now," said grandma, bustling around; "I shouldn't be surprised if you had real good luck, Polly! and your ma'll set ever so much by it; now, if we only could find that receet!" and returning to the charge she commenced to fumble among her bits of paper again; "I never shall forget how they eat on it; why, there wasn't a crumb left, Polly!"

"Oh, dear," said Polly, to whom "Mirandy's wedding cake" now became the height of her desires; "if you only *can* find it! can't I climb up and look on the pantry shelves?"

"Maybe 'tis there," said Mrs. Bascom, slowly; "you might try; sometimes I do put things away, so's to have 'em safe."

So Polly got an old wooden chair, according to direction, and then mounted up on it, with grandma below to direct, she handed down bowl after bowl, interspersed at the right intervals with cracked tea-cups and handleless pitchers. But at the end of these explorations, "Mirandy's wedding cake" was further off than ever!

"'Tain't a mite o' use," at last said the old lady, sinking down in dispair, while Polly perched on the top of the chair and looked at her; "I must a-give it away."

"Can't I have the next best one, then?" asked Polly, despairingly, feeling sure that "Mirandy's wedding cake" would have celebrated the day just right; "and I must hurry right home, please," she added, getting down from the chair, and tying on her hood; "or Phronsie won't know what to do."

So another "receet" was looked over, and selected; and with many charges, and bits of advice not to let the oven get too hot, etc., etc., Polly took the precious bit in her hand, and flew over home.

"Now, we've got to ——" she began, bounding in merrily, with dancing eyes; but her delight had a sudden stop, as she brought up so suddenly at the sight within, that she couldn't utter another word. Phronsie was crouching, a miserable little heap of woe, in one corner of the mother's big calico-covered rocking-chair, and crying bitterly, while Joel hung over her in the utmost concern.

"*What's the matter?*" gasped Polly. Flinging the "receet" on the table, she rushed up to the old chair and was down on her knees before it, her arms around the little figure. Phronsie turned, and threw herself into Polly's protecting arms, who gathered her up, and sitting down in the depths of the chair, comforted her as only *she* could.

"What is it?" she asked of Joel, who was nervously begging Phronsie not to cry; "now, tell me all that's happened."

"I was a-nailin'," began Joel; "oh dear! don't cry, Phronsie! do stop her, Polly."

"*Go on*," said Polly, hoarsely.

"I was a-nailin'," began Joel, slowly; "and — and — Davie's gone to get the peppermint," he added, brightening up.

"Tell me, Joe," said Polly, "all that's been a-goin' on!" and she looked sternly into his face; "or I'll get Davie to," as little Davie came running back, with a bottle of castor oil, which in his flurry he had mistaken for peppermint. This he presented with a flourish to Polly, who was too excited to see it.

"Oh, no!" cried Joel, in intense alarm; "Davie ain't a-goin' to! I'll tell, Polly; I will truly."

"Go on, then," said Polly; "tell at *once*;" feeling as if somebody didn't tell pretty quick, she should tumble over.

"Well," said Joel, gathering himseif up with a fresh effort, "the old hammer was a-shakin', and Phronsie stuck her foot in the way — and — I couldn't help it, Polly —— no, I just couldn't, Polly."

Quick as a flash, Polly tore off the little old shoe, and well-worn stocking, and brought to light Phronsie's fat little foot. Tenderly taking hold of the white toes, the boys clustering around in the greatest anxiety, she worked them back and forth, and up and down. "'Taint nothin' broke," she said at last, and drew a long breath.

"It's there," said Phronsie, through a rain of tears; "and it hurts, Polly;" and she began to wiggle the big toe, where around the nail was settling a small black spot.

"Poor little toe," began Polly, cuddling up the suffering foot. Just then, a small and peculiar noise struck her ear; and looking up she saw Joel, with a very distorted face, making violent efforts to keep from bursting out into a loud cry. All his attempts, however, failed; and he flung himself into Polly's lap in a perfect torrent of tears. "I didn't — mean to — Polly," he cried; "'twas the — ugly, old hammer! *oh dear!*"

"There, there, Joey dear," said Polly, gathering him up in the other corner of the old chair, close to her side; "don't feel bad; I know you didn't mean to," and she dropped a kiss on his stubby brown head.

When Phronsie saw that anybody else *could* cry, she stopped immediately, and leaning over Polly, put one little fat hand on Joel's neck. "Don't cry," she said; "does *your* toe ache?"

At this, Joel screamed louder than ever; and Polly was at her wit's end to know what to do; for the boy's heart was almost broken. That he should have hurt Phronsie! the baby, and pet of the whole house, upon whom all their hearts centered — it was too much. So for the next few moments, Polly had all she could do by way of comforting and consoling him. Just as she had succeeded, the door opened, and Grandma Bascom walked in.

"Settin' down?" said she; "I hope your cake ain't in, Polly," looking anxiously at the stove, "for I've found it;" and she waved a small piece of paper triumphantly towards the chair as she spoke.

"Do tell her," said Polly to little David, "what's happened; for I can't get up."

So little Davie went up to the old lady, and standing on tiptoe, screamed into her ear all the particulars he could think of, concerning the accident that had just happened.

"Hey?" said grandma, in a perfect bewilderment;

(continued on next page)

"what's he a-sayin', Polly? — I can't make it out."

"You'll have to go all over it again, David," said Polly, despairingly; "she didn't hear one word, I don't believe."

So David tried again; this time with better success. And then he got down from his tiptoes, and escorted grandma to Phronsie, in flushed triumph.

"Land alive!" said the old lady, sitting down in the chair which he brought her; "you got pounded, did you?" looking at Phronsie, as she took the little foot in her ample hand.

"Yes'm," said Polly, quickly; "'twarn't no one's fault; what'll we do for it, grandma?"

"Wormwood," said the old lady, adjusting her spectacles in extreme deliberation, and then examining the little black and blue spot, which was spreading rapidly, "is the very best thing; and I've got some to home — you run right over," she said, turning round on David, quickly, "an' get it; it's a-hangin' by the chimbley."

"Let me! let me!" cried Joel, springing out of the old chair, so suddenly that grandma's spectacles nearly dropped off in fright; "oh! I want to do it for Phronsie!"

"Yes, let Joel, please," put in Polly; "he'll find it, grandma."

So Joel departed with great speed; and presently returned, with a bunch of dry herbs, which dangled comfortingly by his side, as he came in.

"Now I'll fix it," said Mrs. Bascom, geiting up and taking off her shawl; "there's a few raisins for you, Polly; I don't want 'em, and they'll make your cake go better," and she placed a little parcel on the table as she spoke. "Yes, I'll put it to steep; an' after it's put on real strong, and tied up in an old cloth, Phronsie won't know as she's got *any* toes!" and grandma broke up a generous supply of the herb, and put it into an old tin cup, which she covered up with a saucer, and placed on the stove.

"Oh!" said Polly; "I *can't* thank you! for the raisins and all — you're *so* good!"

"They're awful hard," said Joel, investigating into the bundle with Davie, which, however, luckily the old lady didn't hear.

"There, don't try," she said cheerily; "an' I found cousin Mirandy's weddin' cake receet, for ——"

"*Did* you?" cried Polly; "oh! I'm *so* glad!" feeling as if that was comfort enough for a good deal.

"Yes, 'twas in my Bible," said Mrs. Bascom; "I remember now; I put it there to be ready to give John's folks when they come in; they wanted it; so you'll go all straight now; and I must get home, for I left some meat a-boilin'." So grandma put on her shawl, and waddled off, leaving a great deal of comfort behind her.

"Now, says I," said Polly to Phronsie, when the little foot was snugly tied up in the wet wormwood, "you've got to have on one of mamsie's old slippers."

"Oh, ho," laughed Phronsie; "won't that be funny, Polly!"

"I should think it *would*," laughed Polly, back again, pulling on the big black cloth slipper, which Joel produced from the bed-room, the two boys joining uproariously, as the old black thing flapped dismally up and down, and showed strong symptoms of flying off. "We shall have to tie it on."

"It looks like a pudding bag," said Joel, as Polly tied it securely through the middle with a bit of twine; "an old black pudding bag!" he finished.

"IT LOOKS LIKE A PUDDING BAG."

"Old black pudding bag!" echoed Phronsie, with a merry little crow; and then all of a sudden she grew very sober, and looked intently at the foot stuck out straight before her, as she still sat in the chair.

"What is it, Phronsie?" asked Polly, who was bustling around, making preparations for the cake-making.

"Can I *ever* wear my new shoes again?" asked the child, gravely, looking dismally at the black bundle before her.

"Oh, yes; my goodness, yes!" cried Polly; "as

quick again as ever; you'll be around again as smart as a cricket in a week — see if you ain't!"

"Will it go on?" asked Phronsie, still looking incredulously at the bundle, "and button up?"

"Yes, indeed!" cried Polly, again; "button into every one of the little holes, Phronsie Pepper; just as elegant as ever!"

"Oh!" said Phronsie; and then she gave a sigh of relief, and thought no more of it, because Polly said so.

(TO BE CONTINUED.)

THE SISTERS.

RIVERSIDE MAGAZINE FOR YOUNG PEOPLE. An illustrated monthly. Vols. 1–4, January 1867–December 1870. New York: Hurd and Houghton. 25 cm. Editor: Horace E. Scudder, 1867–1870. Merged into *Scribner's Monthly*, 1870.

Launched under the discriminating editorship of Horace Scudder, this magazine offered its readers both "imagination and homely fact." His monthly editorial, "Books for Young People," addressed to adults, contained much that is of value today about book selection, the responsibility of parents for their children's reading, and the importance of offering the child the best. Like Mary Mapes Dodge, a few years later, Scudder urged that books for children be judged by the same standard as those for their elders.

The *Riverside*'s contents were varied—poetry, biography, science, games, and puzzles, as well as stories—from such writers as Frank R. Stockton, Sarah Orne Jewett, Christopher Pearse Cranch, Jacob Abbott, Hezekiah Butterworth, Sophie May, and Lucretia Hale. In the "Programme of The Riverside Magazine for Young People for 1869," the editor proudly announced: "First of all, Hans Christian Andersen, the most eminent living writer for the young, has consented to be a regular contributor to the *Riverside*. Hereafter, all his new stories will be introduced to the American public through the *Riverside*, in advance of their publication in Denmark, Germany, and England. . . ."

Horace Scudder spared no pains to make his magazine an aesthetic delight and sought out leading artists of the day to work for him. Among these were John La Farge, F. O. C. Darley, Henry L. Stephens, and Thomas Nast—"the best that can be procured." He boasted with some justification that *The New York Times* had pronounced the *Riverside* "the handsomest magazine in America."

A victim of an economic depression, the *Riverside* was taken over by *Scribner's Monthly*. Volume 1 of the latter (December 1870) announces on page 212: "We open broadly our arms to receive the charming RIVERSIDE and extend to its readers our heartiest greetings." Horace E. Scudder did not lose his interest in children's reading although he never edited another magazine for children. He later became literary adviser for Houghton Mifflin Company, responsible for the Riverside Literature Series for Young People. A number of the contributors to the *Riverside* ultimately worked for *Harper's Young People* and *St. Nicholas;* one such writer, Frank R. Stockton, became Mary Mapes Dodge's assistant editor when her magazine began in 1873.

ON OPPOSITE PAGE:

"The Doings of the Bodley Family," 1867, by Horace E. Scudder (1838–1902).

The Bodley books were issued as bright quarto annuals, one of which appeared before Christmas each year: five in the first series (1875–1880), and three in the second series (1882–1885). Scudder was more famous, however, for his *Children's Book; a Collection of the Best and Most Famous Stories and Poems in the English Language* (1881). From 1890 to 1898 he served as editor of the *Atlantic Monthly*.

THE

RIVERSIDE MAGAZINE

FOR YOUNG PEOPLE.

Vol. I. — APRIL, 1867. — No. IV.

THE DOINGS OF THE BODLEY FAMILY.

MOVING INTO THE COUNTRY.

THE sun was shining brightly one morning in April and in such good-natured fashion that he was warming both rogues and honest men, and not only spreading his light and warmth over the fields that lay stretched out waiting for him, but hunting through the narrow, high-walled streets of the city, in search of cold and damp places, and travelling just as far from one side of the street to the other as the houses would let him. It was pleasant to see what he was doing in Asylum Street, for he had sought out the orphan-house, and now its whole red front was glowing; and it seemed as if the sun were trying his best to work through the thick walls and get at the children with his gigantic smile. The windows let him in, and about them were the children clustered, with some drowsy flies, too, that had just begun to wake from their winter's nap and were stumbling over the panes; though some more discreet had sat down on the sill, and were first rubbing their sleepy heads with their fore-legs.

And now, not satisfied with shining here, the sun resolved to get across the street to the dingy house opposite, and look in there with his round face. He set out on his travels, and by noon was looking in at the attic windows, but all was deserted there; then he clambered down and looked in at the next story, and, much wondering, got fairly down to the sidewalk. Positively he could find nothing; in fact, every thing had been taken out of the house, and it could do without sunshine; and to get over here he had been obliged to leave the orphan-house, which now stood blank and dark. What a pity! But the sun had a happy thought, and going slyly he crept round behind, and peeped in at the back windows.

The flies had been too sleepy, but the children had watched out of the front while the sun was journeying, and they had seen what was going on opposite. The windows and doors were wide open, and three long carts stood in the street. They were furniture-wagons, and men were busy stowing in them the contents of the house. The side-walk was lively with pieces of furniture that had never come so near each other before. There stood the pompous *étagère* from the parlor, swelling out grandly; and yet a towel-horse, standing on two legs only, was rearing up against it. The oil portrait of the great-grandfather, with white neck-handkerchief and his head set on one side

(continued on next page)

like a robin's, was sitting in a lowly rocking-chair hauled up from the kitchen, which gave a thumping sound in its lower part whenever rocked in. The sofa stood against the wall, stretching its arms out; and it was very improper, but a hat-tub had sat down in it. Things were put on the cart, not in order of merit but as they happened to fit in best; though to be sure the parlor furniture was wrapped up in pieces of old carpet, but how different that was from having one's feet on the best carpet.

The children could see the pieces come down-stairs and out of doors, and it was great fun to watch each make its way into the street: one man first appearing, staggering backward and looking anxiously over his shoulder, while a chest of drawers thumped into him at every step, till his hat was tipped forward and he could not see where he was going to; and then after the chest the other man, peeping over the top and clinging to it as if he did not want it to go down at all. Then one man would come along, lugging a great mattress, twice as big as himself, around which he pryed to see his way down the steps; and just behind, another carrying a clock in his arms as if it were a child. Then what a work it was to get the piano out! Six men, two behind, two in front, and two in the middle, stumbled to the doorway, and then the two middle men had to squeeze past, and they had nothing to take hold of; and then the children thought it was going to fall, but it did not, and it was safely lodged in the cart, and the men came down again, triumphantly bringing the legs and the piano-stool and the swell. They all took off their hats after that and wiped their heads, and then went up again after the bedsteads. There was one huge book-case that came apart in the middle, and had looking-glass doors above: it was a great feat to get that out; and behind it came an ancient secretary, which also took to pieces in a wonderful manner, and was covered with dust behind.

Now as the orphans looked, they saw three children run down the steps, and at that they became very lively.

"That is Nathan!" cried one of the boys; "he has got a bow-gun in his hand."

"And there is Phippy," said a little girl; "she does n't stand still a minute. I should n't think those piano men would like to have her climbing up on the cart."

"Lucy is carrying her kitten," said a third. "It is that very same black-and-white kitten that she brought here one day."

"Yes, and she let me play with it," said a little black girl, named Ebby. "Oh, how sorry I am they are all going away."

"There, the carts have all gone. There were twelve loads; I counted," said the one who had spoken first. Still the children seemed to be waiting for something. Nathan marched solemnly up the street with his gun on his shoulder, and looked round the corner, but came back shaking his head. Lucy sat down on the upper step holding Kitty in her lap and humming to her; while Philippa did nothing but run up and down the steps and race to the corner and back. Their mother was in the house, hunting through every room to see that nothing was left behind, and collecting all the stray articles into a little heap on the parlor floor. But at last she heard the children shout, —

"Mamma, it has come!" shouted Philippa. "There is the carryall!" and she hopped up and down on the sidewalk. A bay horse with a white nose was drawing the carryall, and inside sat Martin the man.

"Whoa!" said Nathan to carryall, horse, and man. Martin laughed and jumped out of the carriage. "You stopped him that time — you did, Master Nathan," said he; "but don't fire your gun at him."

"I am going to fire a salute to the orphans," said Nathan, who had been thinking about it a good deal, and before any body could say no, or he could get his gun quite straight, he pulled the trigger and away went an arrow right over to the orphan-house.

"Oh, you 've shot the orphans! You 've shot the orphans!" cried Philippa, as she saw the arrow go through one of the windows.

"It ought to have gone straight up," said Nathan, very much frightened, "and come right down again."

"I must go over at once," said Mrs. Bodley. "Nathan, how could you?" and she hurried away alarmed, but almost laughing too. The matron met her at the door.

"Is any one hurt?" she asked quickly.

"No," said the matron, "though it is a wonder, for the children were all crowded about, but its force was nearly spent on the glass, and it fell down inside, scattering the glass about."

"I am truly sorry," said Mrs. Bodley. "My little boy was very foolish. He meant to fire a salute, as he said, to the children," and she smiled; "for we are all sorry to leave their pleasant faces. We ought to bid them good-by, Mrs. Keeper;" and so saying, she beckoned to the children in the carriage.

"Come here, children," said she. Philippa and Lucy came slowly over, — Lucy crying and hugging her kitten, and Phippy looking very solemn and very red; but Nathan was on the back seat of the carryall, with his head buried in the cushion, calling to Martin to drive off as fast as he could, for he had killed an orphan. His mother came hurrying over, and opening the door, called out, —

"Nathan, nobody is hurt. It was very careless in you; but you must come over and bid the children good-by, and tell Mrs. Keeper how sorry you are."

Nathan got out, very much tumbled up, and holding on to his mother's hand walked gravely across the street. The orphan children were all in the entry or on the staircase, and Phippy and Lucy were saying good-by. Nathan hung back a little, and then said:

"Mrs. Keeper, I did not wish to kill any one. I am very sorry; I meant to give a salute, but the arrow went the wrong way. I would give you the bow-gun," he added seriously, "but we are going into the country, and I suppose I shall need it there. There may be Indians. I can get another arrow," but still he looked somewhat wistfully toward the arrow which Mrs. Keeper held.

"My little boy must pay for the new glass," said Mrs. Bodley, "and for any other mischief which he has done."

"Indeed, there is little," said Mrs. Keeper, good-naturedly, "and he may have his arrow again; but I hope you will take better aim, Nathan, when you shoot Indians." The orphan children all huddled together at this, and looked with awe on their little neighbor, who now began to feel more grand.

"Good-by, children," said he, loftily waving his arrow toward them, and marching across the street, with his bow-gun on his shoulder, followed by his mother and sisters.

"Nathan, you deserve a good, sound whipping," said Mrs. Bodley, "but how few get their deserts," she added to herself. And now at length the carryall with its load was off, Nathan and Phippy being on the front seat with Martin, while Lucy and her mother were behind. All the way up Asylum Street, the children flung out their good-byes, putting their heads out on one side and the other. Mrs. Batterman's house, a one-story shed with tar roof, stood next their own.

"Good-by, Mrs. Batterman," shouted Nathan, shaking his hand at it. "You won't think our water leaks into your house again. You ought to see old Ma'am Batterman, Martin," and he began to tell him about her; but just then they passed the place where he had been run over by Mr. Wilkins's milk-cart, and he must tell about that; and Phippy and he kept up a great clatter, shaking their hands at the people and laughing with glee, while their mother hushed at them, and Martin clucked at the horse, as if they were a grand procession such as never had passed up the street before and must do it now in fine style. The horse jogged along leisurely, and seemed to think it a very ordinary occasion.

"This is a pretty good horse of ours, Martin," said Nathan, now that they were out of the street and fairly away.

"Well, yes," laughed Martin. "He 's a bit of a weaver."

"A weaver?" said Mrs. Bodley.

(continued on next page)

"Yes, ma'am; but Mr. Bodley, he said it would n't make much matter, you see."

"A weaver!" said Nathan. "Why, I thought a weaver was a man, like — like" — and he tried to think of a weaver.

"Like Bottom," suggested Mrs. Bodley. "Bottom was a weaver."

"Yes, like Bottom," said Nathan, who had never heard of him before.

"Well," said Martin, "when your Mr. Bottom weaves, he just pushes the shuttle from one side to the other and moves along with it; and so when a horse in his stall moves his head back and forth along the crib, we say he is a weaver."

"What is his name?" asked Mrs. Bodley.

"The last folks that had him called him Peter, ma'am," said Martin.

"But what is his last name?" asked Philippa. "Peter what?"

"That I never heard," said Martin.

"I know what it is," said Nathan, who already felt himself master of the horse; "it's Bottom, because he's like the man that mother knows. Get up, Peter Bottom."

Mr. Bottom wagged along with the party, and the farther they went the more excited were the children, who had not yet seen the place where they were to live, and who only knew that it was a brick-house in the country, three miles from Asylum Street. The street they were driving on became wider and the houses more rare. They left the city behind, but had not yet come to green fields.

"Now we are on General Street," said Mrs. Bodley, and the children, knowing that their new home was on that street, became very much excited.

"This must be the place," cried Nathan. "Stop, Mr. Bottom. Stop, Martin. Whoa!"

"Oh, how nice!" said Phippy; "there is a garden in front." But it was not the place, only a poor sunburnt brick-house with a patch of ground squeezed in between it and the street. As they drove on, the street became freer and the houses more scattered. But though they had pleasant gardens about them, they were nearly all built of wood. They passed by a cliff of rocks where men were at work, drilling; and then on the other side of the way, as they went up the hill, they saw a stone-castle, as Lucy said, — a real stone-castle with a tower, — and she was pretty sure people shot out of the windows.

"Only let them shoot at us!" said Nathan, bravely, and he tried to get at his bow-gun, which was on the bottom of the carryall. But they were at the top of the hill, and Mrs. Bodley's — "Now then, children!" made them all put their heads out and peer excitedly about.

"I see it, I see it!" said Phippy, jumping out of her seat and almost falling over on to Mr. Bottom.

"That!" said Nathan. "That is not it; it is not near the street at all. Our house is near the street." But Martin, who had been here before, suddenly turned a corner and drove through a gate-way up an avenue.

"Oh, here we are!" laughed Lucy, and then she stooped over and told Kitty.

"No, we 're not at all," said the obstinate little Nathan; "our house is on the street. This is not a street. What are you going up here for, Martin?"

"Well, Master Nathan, I 'm just going to put Peter Bottom up in the barn, and put you up in the house."

"Is it the house, mother?" persisted Nathan. But she only laughed and said that Mr. Bottom lived here, at any rate.

"Well, not my Mr. Bottom," said Nathan. "Your Mr. Bottom, the real weaver."

"O Nathan, do stop!" cried Phippy. "Just see! Is n't it splendid? And there's the barn, and oh! I can see the hay."

"And there are chickens," said Lucy, putting her little head out and calling to them.

The avenue up which they had driven wound through a pleasant field up to the house. It was bordered by narrow flower-beds, and in the beds stood flowering shrubs and young trees, which would some day grow to be large and arch over the road, but now they hardly shut out from light the field on the left, where a dozen stout cherry-trees grew; and that on the right, which was a grassy plat stretching up a little hill, and disappearing whither they could not say on the other side of the rising. At the end of the avenue stood the house. It was not a very splendid house, but it was a good one to live in. Two locust-trees stood in front of it, and in the corner, where the wooden-shed was joined to the house, was a graceful elm. The house had a red, good-natured face, looking as if it had set itself down squarely in this open country, where it could draw a long breath, and not be too crowded for elbow-room. It had windows that leaned out on the roof, and looked off — one way over the hills, the other toward the sea.

The children, who entered with their parents, went into all the rooms, and came at last into the upper story of all. What a splendid place that was; for there was one great room covering the entire floor, and the six windows, three on each side, were the windows that looked off so far. A window-seat was below the middle one on each side, and climbing up on one, they could see over the garden and into the pasture, and beyond among the rocks and trees that were about May Pond, and still farther the blue hills that rolled along in gentle line beneath the blue sky. Then from the other side, at foot was the barn and the little houses that straggled about it, for pig and cow and hens; the kitchen-garden, the currant-bushes, the apple-orchard; and farther off the bay, which opened into the broad sea; and away off, as far as one could look, were white-winged ships, sailing out of sight beyond the edge of the sky and water, or coming nearer to draw up to the great city, the houses of which could also be seen, and the bells, when they rang sent their sounds up to the house and into the children's play-room.

The sun when it rose looked in at the windows on one side, and saw the children's playthings; and when it had gone its round and could look into the opposite windows, perhaps it would see the children at play, — but this was only in winter, for on sunny days in summer they were always in the garden or in the pasture. But in winter it could see them; and perhaps just as it went down behind the earth in the west, it stopped to take one more look at three little children nestled together on the cushioned window-seat, chattering to one another, or two little children playing cats-cradle or checkers, or one little child reading a book spread out on her lap. How could the sun be willing to set at all!

Now from time to time let us learn what the children of the Bodley family see and hear and do and say in the house and garden and pasture.

H. E. S.

ON FOLLOWING PAGE:
"Ting-a-Ling," 1867, by Frank R. Stockton (1834–1902).

A prolific inventor of fanciful tales, as well as assistant editor of *St. Nicholas* to which he regularly contributed these, Stockton was to see his magazine work appear in book form in subsequent collections: *The Floating Prince and Other Fairy Tales* (1881); *Ting-a-ling Tales* (1882); *The Bee-Man of Orn and Other Fanciful Tales* (1887); and other later titles.

TING-A-LING:

A MAKE-BELIEVE FAIRY TALE.

In a far country of the East, in a palace, surrounded by orange groves, where the nightingales sang, and by silvery lakes, where the soft fountains plashed, there lived a fine old king. For many years he had governed, with great comfort to himself, and to the tolerable satisfaction of his subjects. His queen being dead, his whole affection was given to his only child, the Princess Aufalia; and, whenever he happened to think of it, he paid great attention to her education. She had the best masters of embroidery and in the language of flowers, and she took lessons on the zithar three times a week.

A suitable husband, the son of a neighboring monarch, had been selected for her when she was about two hours old, thus making it unnecessary for her to go into society, and she consequently passed her youthful days in almost entire seclusion. She was now, when our story begins, a woman, more beautiful than the roses of the garden, more musical than the nightingales, and far more graceful than the plashing fountains.

One balmy day in spring, when the birds were singing lively songs on the trees, and the crocuses were coaxing the jonquils almost off their very stems with their pretty ways, Aufalia went out to take a little promenade, followed by two grim

slaves. Closely veiled, she walked in the secluded suburbs of the town, where she was generally obliged to take her lonely exercise. To-day, however, the slaves being impelled by a sweet tooth, which each of them possessed, thought it would be no harm if they went a little out of their way to procure some sugared cream-beans, which were made most excellently by a confectioner near the outskirts of the city. While they were in the shop, bargaining for the sugar-beans, a young man who was passing thereby stepped up to the Princess, and asked her if she could tell him the shortest road to the baths, and if there was a good eating-house in the neighborhood. Now as that was the first time in her life that the Princess had been addressed by a young man, it is not surprising that she was too much astonished to speak, especially as this youth was well dressed, extremely handsome, and of proud and dignified manners, — although, to be sure, a little travel-stained and tired-looking.

When she had somewhat recovered from her embarrassment, she raised her veil, (as if it was necessary to do so in speaking to a young man,) and told him that she was sure she had not the slightest idea where any place in the city was, — she very seldom went into the city, and never thought about the way to any place when she did go, — she wished she knew where those places were that he mentioned, for she would very much like to tell him, especially if he was hungry, which she knew was not pleasant, and no doubt he was not used to it, but indeed she had n't any idea about the way anywhere, but —

There is no knowing how long the Princess might have run on thus (and her veil up all the time) had not the two slaves at that moment emerged from the sugar-bean shop. The sight of the Princess actually talking to a young man in the broad daylight so amazed them, that they stood for a moment dumb in the door. But, recovering from their surprise, they drew their cimeters, and ran toward the Prince (for such his very action proclaimed him to be). When this high-born personage saw them coming with drawn blades, his countenance flushed, and his eyes sparkled with rage. Drawing his flashing sword, he shouted, — " Crouch, varlets! Lie with the dust, ye dogs!" and sprang furiously upon them.

The impetuosity of the onslaught caused the two men to pause, and in a few minutes they fell back some yards, so fast and heavy did the long sword clash upon their upraised cimeters. This contest was soon over, for, unaccustomed to such a vigorous way of attacking, the slaves turned and fled, and the Prince pursued them down a long street, and up an alley, and over a wall, and through a garden, and under an arch, and over a court-yard, and through a gate, and down another street, and up another alley, and through a house, and up a long staircase, and out upon a roof, and over several abutments, and down a trap-door, and down another pair of stairs, and through an-

other house, into another garden, and over another wall, and down a long road, and over a field, clear out of sight.

When the Prince had performed this feat, he sat down to rest, but, suddenly bethinking himself of the maiden, he rose and went to look for her.

"I have chased away her servants," said he, "how will she ever find her way anywhere?"

If this was difficult for her, the Prince found that it was no less so for himself, and he spent much time in endeavoring to reach again the northern suburbs of the city. At last, after con-

siderable walking, he got into the long street into which he had first chased the slaves, and, seeing a line of children eagerly devouring a line of sugared cream-beans, he remembered seeing these confections dropping from the pockets of the slaves as he pursued them, and following up the clew, soon reached the shop, and found the Princess sitting under a tree before the door. The shop-keeper, knowing her to be the Princess, had been afraid to speak to her, and was working away inside, making believe that he had not seen her, and that he knew nothing of the conflict which had taken place before his door.

Up jumped Aufalia. "Oh! I am so glad to see you again! I have been waiting here ever so long. But what have you done with my slaves?"

"I am your slave," said the Prince, bowing to the ground.

"But you don't know the way home," said she, "and I am dreadfully hungry."

Having ascertained from her that she was the King's daughter, and lived at the palace, the Prince reflected for a moment, and then entering the shop, dragged forth the maker of sugared cream-beans, and ordered him to lead the way to the presence of the King. The confectioner, crouching to the earth, immediately started off, and the Prince and Princess side by side, followed over what seemed to them a very short road to the palace. The Princess talked a great deal, but the Prince was rather quiet. He had a great many things to think about. He was the younger son of a king who lived far away to the north, and had been obliged to flee the kingdom on account of the custom of only allowing one full-grown heir to the throne to live in the country.

"Now," thought he, "this is an excellent commencement of my adventures. Here is a truly lovely Princess whom I am conducting to her anxious parent. He will be overwhelmed with gratitude, and will doubtless bestow upon me the government of a province — or — perhaps he will make me his Vizier — no, I will not accept that, — the province will suit me better." Having settled this little matter to his mind, he gladdened the heart of the Princess with the dulcet tones of his gentle voice.

On reaching the palace they went directly to the grand hall, where the King was giving audience. Justly astounded at perceiving his daughter (now veiled) approaching under the guidance of a crouching sugar-bean maker, and a strange young man, he sat in silent amazement, until the Prince, who was used to court life, had made his manners, and related his story. When the King had heard it, he clapped his hands three times, and in rushed twenty-four eunuchs.

"Take," said the monarch, "this bird to her bower." And they surrounded the Princess and hurried her off to the women's apartments.

Then he clapped his hands twice, and in rushed twenty-four armed guards from another door.

"Bind me this dog!" quoth the King, point-

(continued on next page)

ing to the Prince. And they bound him in a twinkling.

"Is this the way you treat a stranger?" cried the Prince.

"Aye," said the King, merrily. "We will treat you royally. You are tired. To-night and to-morrow you shall be lodged and feasted daintily, and the day after we will have a celebration, when you shall be beaten with sticks, and shall fight a tiger, and be tossed by a bull, and be bowstrung, and beheaded, and drawn, and

quartered, and we will have a nice time. Bear him away to his soft couch."

The guards then led the Prince away to be kept a prisoner until the day for the celebration. The room to which he was conducted was comfortable, and he soon had a plenteous supper laid out before him, of which he partook with great avidity. Having finished his meal, he sat down to reflect upon his condition, but feeling very sleepy, and remembering that he would have a whole day of leisure, to-morrow, for such reflections, he concluded to go to bed. Before doing so, however, he wished to make all secure for the night. Examining the door, he found there was no lock to it, and being unwilling to remain all night liable to intrusion, after pondering the matter for some minutes, he took up a wide and very heavy stool, and, having partially opened the door, he put the stool up over it, partly resting it on the door and partly on the surrounding woodwork, so that if any one tried to come in, and pushed the door open, the stool would fall down and knock the intruder's head off. Having arranged this to his satisfaction, the Prince went to bed.

That evening the Princess Aufalia was in great grief, for she had heard of the sentence pronounced upon the Prince, and felt herself the cause of it. What other reason she had to grieve over the Prince's death, need not be told. Her handmaidens fully sympathized with her; and one of them, Nerralina, the handsomest and most energetic of them all, soon found, by proper inquiry, that the Prince was confined in the fourth story of the "Tower of Tears." So they devised a scheme for his rescue. Every one of the young ladies contributed their scarfs, and when they were all tied together, the conclave decided that they made a rope plenty long enough to reach from the Prince's window to the ground.

Thus much settled, it but remained to get this means of escape to the prisoner. This the lady Nerralina volunteered to do. Waiting until the dead of night, she took off her slippers, and with the scarf-rope rolled up into a ball under her arm, she silently stepped past the drowsy sentinels, and, reaching the Prince's room, pushed open the door, and the stool fell down and knocked her head off. Her body lay in the doorway, but her head rolled into the middle of the room.

Notwithstanding the noise occasioned by this

accident, the Prince did not awake; but in the morning, when he was up and nearly dressed, he was astonished at seeing a lady's head in the middle of the room.

"Hallo!" said he. "Here 's somebody's head."

Picking it up, he regarded it with considerable interest. Then seeing the body in the doorway, he put the head and it together, and, finding they fitted, came to the conclusion that they belonged to each other, and that the stool had done the mischief. When he saw the bundle of scarfs lying by the body, he unrolled it, and soon imagined the cause of the lady's visit.

"Poor thing!" said he; "doubtless the Princess sent her here with this, and most likely with a message also, which now I shall never hear. But these poor women! what do they know? This rope will not bear a man like me. Well! well! this poor girl is dead. I will pay respect to her."

And so he picked her up, and put her on his bed, thinking at the time that she must have fainted when she heard the stool coming, for no blood had flowed. He fitted on the head, and then he covered her up with the sheet; but, in pulling this over her head, he uncovered her feet, which he now perceived to be slipperless.

"No shoes! Ah me! Well, I will be polite to a lady, even if she is dead."

And so he drew off his own yellow boots, and put them on her feet, which was easily done, as they were a little too big for her. He had hardly done this, and dressed himself, when he heard some one approaching. So, hastily removing the fallen stool, he got behind the door just as a fat old fellow entered with a broadsword in one hand, and a pitcher of hot water and some towels in the other. Glancing at the bed, and seeing the yellow boots sticking out, he muttered: "Gone to bed with his clothes on, eh? Well, I 'll let him sleep!" And so, putting down the pitcher and the towels, he walked out again. But not alone, for the Prince silently stepped after him, and by keeping close behind him, followed without being heard, — his politeness having been the fortunate cause of his being in his stocking-feet. For some distance they walked together thus, the Prince intending to slip off at the first cross passage he came to. It was quite dusky in the long passage, there being no windows, and when the guard, at a certain place, made a very wide step, taking hold of a rod by the side of the wall as he did so, the Prince, not perceiving this, walked straight on, and popped right down an open trap-door.

Nerralina not returning, the Princess was in great grief, not knowing at first whether she had eloped with the Prince, or had met with some misfortune on the way to his room. In the morning, however, the ladies ascertained that the rope was not hanging from the Prince's window, and as the guards reported that he was comfortably sleeping in his bed, it was unanimously concluded that Nerralina had been discovered in her attempt, and had come to grief. Sorrowing bitterly, somewhat for the unknown mishap of her maid of honor, but still more for the now certain fate of him she loved, Aufalia went into the garden, and, making her way through masses of rose-trees and jasmines, to the most secluded part of the grounds, threw herself upon a violet bank and wept unrestrainedly, the tears rolling one by one from her eyes, like a continuous string of pearls.

Now it so happened that this spot was the pleasure ground of a company of fairies, who had a colony near by. These fairies were about an inch and a half high, beautifully formed, and of the most respectable class. They had not been molested for years by any one coming to this spot, but as they knew perfectly well who the Princess was, they were not at all alarmed at her appearance. In fact, the sight of her tears rolling so prettily down into the violet cups, and over the green leaves, seemed to please them much, and many of the younger ones took up a tear or two upon their shoulders to take home with them.

There was one youth, the handsomest of them all, named Ting-a-ling, who had a beautiful little sweetheart called Ling-a-ting.

[To be concluded in the next number.]

(continued on next page)

TING-A-LING:

A MAKE-BELIEVE FAIRY TALE.

[Concluded.]

EACH one of these lovers, when they were about to return to their homes, picked up the prettiest tear they could find. Ting-a-ling put his tear upon his shoulder, and walked along as gracefully as an Egyptian woman with her water-jug; while little Ling-a-ting, with her treasure borne lightly over her head, skipped by her lover's side, as happy as happy could be.

"Don't walk out in the sun, my dearest," said Ting-a-ling. "Your shin-shiney wili burst."

"Burst! Oh no, Tingy darling, no it won't. See how nice and big it is getting, and so light

Look!" cried she, throwing back her head; "I can see the sky through it; and oh! what pretty colors, — blue, green, pink, and" — And the tear burst, and poor little Ling-a-ting sunk down on the grass, drenched and drowned.

Horror-stricken, Ting-a-ling dropped his tear and wept. Clasping his hands above his head, he fell on his knees beside his dear one, and raised his eyes to the blue sky in bitter anguish. But when he cast them down again, little Ling-a-ting was all soaked into the grass. Then sterner feelings filled his breast, and revenge stirred up the depths of his soul.

"This thing shall end!" he said, hissing the words between his teeth. "No more of us shall die like Ling-a-ting!"

So he ran quickly, and with his little sword cut down two violets, and of the petals he made two little soft bundles, and, tying them together with his garters, he slung them over his shoulder. Full of his terrible purpose, he then ran to the Princess, and going behind her, clambered up her dress until he stood on her shoulder, and, getting on the top of her head, he loosened a long hair, and lowered himself down with it, until he stood upon the under lashes of her left eye. Now, his intention was evident. Those violet bundles were to "end this thing." They were to be crammed into the source of those fatal tears, to the beauty of which poor Ling-a-ting had fallen a victim.

"Now we shall see," said he, "if some things cannot be done as well as others!" and, kneeling down, he took one bundle from his shoulder, and prepared to put it in her eye. It is true, that, occupying the position he did, he, in some measure, obstructed the lady's vision; but as her eyes had been so long dimmed with tears, and her heart overshadowed with sorrow, she did not notice it.

Just as Ting-a-ling was about to execute his purpose, he happened to look before him, and saw to his amazement another little fairy on his knees, right in front of him. Starting back he dropped the bundle from his hand, and the other from his shoulder. Then, upon his hands and knees, he stared steadfastly at the little man opposite to him, who immediately imitated him. And there they knelt with equal wonder in each of their countenances, bobbing at each other every time the lady winked. Then did Ting-a-ling get very red in the face, and standing erect he took strong hold of the Princess's upper eyelash, to steady himself, resolved upon punishing the saucy fairy, when, to his dismay, the eyelash came out, he lost his balance, and at the same moment a fresh shower of tears burst from her eyes, which washed Ting-a-ling senseless into her lap.

When he recovered he was still sticking to her silk apron, all unobserved, as she sat in her own room talking to one of her maids, who had just returned from a long visit into the country. Slipping down to the floor, Ting-a-ling ran, all shivering to the window, to the seat of which he climbed, and getting upon a chrysanthemum that was growing in a flower-pot in the sunshine, he took off his shoes and stockings, and, hanging them on a branch to dry, lay down in the warm blossom; and while he was drying, listened to the mournful tale that Aufalia was telling her maid, about the poor Prince that was to die tomorrow. The more he heard, the more was his tender heart touched with pity, and, forgetting all his resentment against the Princess, he only felt the deepest sympathy for her misfortunes, and those of her lover. When she had finished, Ting-a-ling had resolved to assist them, or die in the attempt!

But, as he could not do much himself, he intended instantly to lay their case before a Giant of his acquaintance, whose good-humor and benevolence were proverbial. So he put on his shoes and stockings, which were not quite dry, and hastily descended to the garden by means of a vine which grew upon the wall. The distance to the Giant's castle was too great for him to think of walking; so he hurried around to a friend of his who kept a livery-stable. When he reached this place he found his friend sitting in his stable-door, and behind him Ting-a-ling could see the long rows of stalls, with all the butterflies on one side, and the grasshoppers on the other.

"How do you do?" said Ting-a-ling, seating himself upon a horse-block, and wiping his face. "It is a hot day, is n't it?"

"Yes, sir," said the livery-stable man, who was rounder and shorter than Ting-a-ling. "Yes, it is very warm. I have n't been out to-day."

"Well, I should n't advise you to go," said Ting-a-ling. "But I must to business, for I 'm in a great hurry. Have you a fast butterfly that you can let me have right away?"

"Oh yes, two or three of them, for that matter."

"Have you that one," asked Ting-a-ling, "that I used to take out last summer?"

"That animal," said the livery-stable man, rising and clasping his hands under his coat-tail, "I am sorry to say, you can't have. He 's foundered."

(continued on next page)

"That 's bad," said Ting-a-ling, "for I always liked him."

"I can let you have one just as fast," said the stable-keeper. "By the way, how would you like a real good grasshopper?"

"Too hot a day for the saddle," said Ting a-ling; "and now please harness up, for I 'm in a dreadful hurry."

"Yes, sir, right away. But I don't know exactly what wagon to give you. I have two first-rate new pea-pods, but they are both out. However, I can let you have a nice easy Johnny-jump-up, if you say so."

"Any thing will do," said Ting-a-ling, dusting his boots with his handkerchief, "only get it out quick."

In a very short time a butterfly was brought out, and harnessed to a first-class Johnny-jump-up. The vehicles used by these fairies were generally a cup-like blossom, or something of that nature, furnished, instead of wheels, with little bags filled with a gas resembling that used to inflate balloons. Thus the vehicle was sustained in the air while the steed drew it rapidly along.

As soon as Ting-a ling heard the sound of the approaching equipage, he stood upon the horse-block, and when the wagon was brought up to it, he quickly jumped in and took the reins from the hostler. "Get up!" said he, and away they went.

It was a long drive, and it was at least three in the afternoon when Ting-a-ling reached the Giant's castle. Drawing up before the great gates, he tied his animal to a hinge, and walked in himself under the gate. Going boldly into the hall, he went up-stairs, or rather, he ran up the top rail of the banisters, for it would have been hard work for him to have clambered up each separate step. As he expected, he found the Giant (whose name I forgot to say was Tur-il-i-ra) in his dining-room. He had just finished his dinner, and was sitting in his arm-chair by the table, fast asleep. This Giant was about as large as two mammoths. It was useless for Ting a-ling to stand on the floor, and endeavor to make himself heard above the roaring of the snoring, which sounded to him louder than the thunders of a cataract. So, climbing upon one of the Giant's boots, he ran up his leg, and hurried over the waistcoat so fast, that, slipping on one of the brass buttons, he came down upon his knees with great force.

"Whew!" said he, "that must have hurt him! after dinner too!"

Jumping up quickly, he ran easily over the bosom, and getting on his shoulder, clambered up into his ear. Standing up in the opening of this immense cavity, he took hold of one side with his outstretched arms, and shouted with all his might, —

"*Tur*-il-i! *Tur*-il-i! *Tur*-il-i-RA!"

Startled at the noise, the Giant clapped his hand to his ear with such force, that had not Ting-a-ling held on very tightly, he would have been shot up against the tympanum of this mighty man.

"Don't do that again!" cried the little fellow. "Don't do that again! It 's only me — Ting-a-ling. Hold your finger."

Recognizing the voice of his young friend, the Giant held out his forefinger, and Ting-a-ling mounting it, was carried round before the Giant's face, where he proceeded to relate the misfortunes of the two lovers, in his most polished and affecting style.

The Giant listened with great attention, and when he had done, said: "Ting-a-ling, I feel a great interest in all young people, and will do what I can for this truly unfortunate couple. But I must finish my nap first, otherwise I could not do any thing. So, just jump down on the table and eat something, while I go to sleep for a little while."

So saying, he put Ting-a-ling gently down upon the table. But this young gentleman having a dainty appetite, did not see much that he thought he would like: so, cutting a grain of rice in two, he ate one half of it, and then lay down on a napkin and went to sleep.

When Tur-il-i-ra awoke, he remembered that it was time to be off, and waking Ting-a-ling, he took out his great purse, and placed the little fairy in it, where he had very comfortable quarters, as there was no money there to hurt him.

"Don't forget my wagon when you get to the gate," said Ting-a-ling, sleepily, rolling himself up for a fresh nap, as the Giant closed the purse with a snap. Tur-il-i-ra, having put on his hat, went down-stairs, and crossed the court-yard in a very few steps. When he had closed the great gates after him, he bethought himself of Ting-a-ling's turn-out, which the fairy had mentioned as being tied to the hinge. Not being able to see any thing so minute at the distance of his eyes from the ground, he put on his spectacles, and getting upon his hands and knees, peered closely about the hinges.

"Oh! here you are," said he, and picking up the butterfly and wagon, he put them in his vest pocket — that is, all excepting the butterfly's head. That remained fast to the hinge, as the Giant forgot he was tied. Then our lofty friend set off at a smart pace for the King's castle, but notwithstanding his haste, it was dark when he reached it.

"Come now, young man," said he, opening his purse, "wake up, and let us get to work. Where is that Prince you were talking about?"

"Well, I'm sure I don't know," said Ting-a-ling, rubbing his eyes. "But just put me up to that window which has the vine growing beneath it. That is the Princess's room, and she can tell us all about it."

So the Giant took him on his finger, and put him in the window. There, in the lighted room, Ting-a-ling beheld a sight which greatly moved him. Although she had slept but little the night before, the Princess was still up, and was sitting in an easy-chair, weeping profusely. Near her stood a maid-of-honor, who continually handed her fresh handkerchiefs from a great basketful by her side. As fast as the Princess was done with one, she threw it behind her, and the great pile there showed that she must have been weeping nearly all day. Getting down upon the floor, Ting-a-ling clambered up the Princess's dress, and reaching, at last, her ear, shouted into it, —

"Princess! Princess! Stop crying, for I'm come!"

The Princess was very much startled; but she did not, like the Giant, clap her hand to her ear, for, if she had, she would have ruined the beautiful curls which stood out so nicely on each side. So Ting-a-ling implored her to be quiet, and told her how that the Giant had come to assist her, and they wanted to know where the Prince was confined.

"I will tell you! I will show you!" cried the Princess quickly, and, jumping up, she ran to the window with Ting-a-ling still at her ear. "O you good Giant," she cried, "are you there? If you will take me, I will show you the tower, the cruel tower, where my Prince is confined."

"Fear not!" said the good Giant. "Fear not! I soon will release him. Let me take you in my hands, and do you show me where to go."

"Are you sure you can hold me?" said the Princess, standing timidly upon the edge of the window.

"I guess so," said the Giant. "Just get into my hands."

And, taking her down gently, he set her on his arm, and then he took Ting-a-ling from her hair, and placed him on the tip of his thumb. Thus they proceeded to the Tower of Tears.

"Here is the place," said the Princess. "Here is the horrid tower where my beloved is. Please put me down a minute, and let me cry."

"No, no," said the Giant; "you have done enough of that, my dear, and we have no time to spare. So, if this is your Prince's tower, just get in at the window, and tell him to come out quickly, and I will take you both away without making any fuss."

"That is the window — the fourth-storey one. Lift me up," said the Princess.

But though the Giant was very large, he was not quite tall enough for this feat, for they built their towers very high in those days. So, putting Ting-a-ling and the Princess into his pocket, he looked around for something to stand on. Seeing a barn near by, he picked it up, and placed it underneath the window. He put his foot on it to see if it would bear him, and, finding it would, (for in those times barns were very strong,) he stood upon it, and looked in the fourth-storey window. Taking his little friends out of his pocket, he put them on the window-sill, where Ting-a-ling remained to see what would happen, but the Princess jumped right down on the floor. As there was a lighted candle on the table, she saw that there was some one covered up in the bed.

"Oh, there he is!" said she. "Now I will wake him up, and hurry him away." But, just at that moment, as she was going to give the sleeper a gentle shake, she happened to perceive the yellow boots sticking out from under the sheet.

"Oh dear!" said she in a low voice, "if he has n't gone to bed with his boots on! And if I wake him, he will jump right down on the floor, and make a great noise, and we shall be found out."

So she went to the foot of the bed and pulled them off very gently.

"White stockings!" said she. "What does this mean? I know the Prince wore green stockings, for I took particular notice how well they looked with his yellow boots. There must be something wrong, I declare! Let me run to the other end of the bed, and see how it is there. Oh my! oh my!" cried she, turning down the sheet. "A woman's head! Wrong both ways! Oh what shall I do?"

Letting the sheet drop, she accidentally touched the head, which immediately rolled off on to the floor.

"Loose! Loose!! Loose!!!" she screamed in bitter agony, clasping her hands above her head. "What shall I ever do? Oh misery! misery

(continued on next page)

me! Some demon has changed him, all but his boots. Oh Despair! Despair!"

And, without knowing what she did, she rushed frantically out of the room, and along the dark passage, and popped right down through the open trap.

"What's up?" said the Giant, putting his face to the window. "What's all this noise about?"

"Oh I don't know," said Ting-a-ling, almost crying, "but somebody's head is off; and it's a lady — all but the boots — and the Princess has run away! oh dear! oh dear!"

"Come now!" said Tur-il-i-ra. "Ting-a-ling, get into my pocket. I must see into this myself, for I can't be waiting here all night, you know."

So the Giant, still standing on the barn, lifted off the roof of the tower, and threw it to some distance. He then, by the moonlight, examined the upper storey, but finding no Prince or Princess, brushed down the walls until he came to the floor, and, taking it up, he looked carefully over the next storey. This he continued, until he had torn down the whole tower, and found no one but servants and guards, who ran away in all directions, like ants when you destroy their hills. He then kicked down all those walls which connected the tower with the rest of the palace, and, when it was all level with the ground, he happened to notice, almost at his feet, a circular opening like an entrance to a vault, from which arose a very pleasant smell as of something good to eat. Stooping down to see what it was that caused this agreeable perfume, he perceived that at the distance of a few yards the aperture terminated in a huge yellow substance, in which, upon a closer inspection, he saw four feet sticking up — two with slippers, and two with only green stockings.

"Why, this is strange!" said he, and, stooping down, he .felt the substance, and found it was quite soft and yielding. He then loosened it by passing his hand around it, and directly lifted it out almost entire.

"By the beard of the Prophet!" he cried, "but this is a cheese!" and, turning it over, he saw on the other side two heads, one with short black hair, and the other covered with beautiful brown curls.

"Why, here they are! As I'm a living Giant! these must be the Prince and Princess, stowed away in a cheese!" And he laughed until the very hills cracked.

When he ot a little over his merriment, he asked the imprisoned couple how they got there, and if they felt comfortable. They replied that they had fallen down a trap, and had gone nearly through this cheese where they had stuck fast, and that was all they had known about it, and if the blood did not run down into their heads so, they would be pretty comfortable, thank him — which last remark the Giant accounted for by the fact, that, when lovers are near each other, they do not generally pay much attention to surrounding circumstances.

"This, then," said he, rising, "is where the King hardens his cheeses, is it? Well, well, it's a jolly go!" And he laughed some more.

"O Tur-il-i-ra," cried Ting-a-ling, looking out from the vest-pocket, "I'm so glad you've found them."

"Well, so am I," said the Giant.

Then Tur-il-i-ra, still holding the cheese, walked away for a little distance, and sat down on a high bank, intending to wait there until morning, when he would call on the King, and confer with him in relation to his new-found treasure. Leaning against a great rock, the Giant put the cheese upon his knees in such a manner as not to injure the heads and feet of the lovers, and dropped into a very comfortable sleep.

"Don't I wish I could get my arms out!" whispered the Prince.

"Oh my!" whispered the Princess.

Ting-a-ling, having now nothing to occupy his mind, and desiring to stretch his legs, got out of the vest pocket where he had remained so safely during all the disturbance, and descended to the ground to take a little walk. He had not gone far before he met a friend of his, who was running along as fast as he could.

"Hallo! Ting-a-ling," cried the other. "Is that you? Come with me, and I will show you the funniest thing you ever saw in your life."

"Is it far?" said Ting-a-ling, "for I must be back here by daylight."

"Oh no! come on. It won't take you long, and I tell you, it's fun!"

So away they ran, merrily vaulting over the hickory-nuts, or acorns, that happened to be in their way, in mere playfulness, as if they were nothing. They soon came to a large, open space, so brightly lighted by the moon, that every object was as visible as if it were daylight. Scattered over the smooth green were thousands of fairies of Ting-a-ling's nation, the most of whom were standing gazing intently at a very wonderful sight.

Seated on a stone, under a great tree that stood all alone in the centre of this plain, was a woman without any head. She moved her hands rapidly about over her shoulders, as if in search of the missing portion of herself, and encountering nothing but mere air, she got very angry, and stamped her feet, and shrugged her shoulders, which amused the fairies very much, and they all set up a great laugh, and seemed to be enjoying the fun amazingly. On one side, down by a little brook, was a great crowd of fairies, who appeared to be washing something therein. Scattered all around were portions of the Tower of Tears, much of which had fallen hereabouts.

Ting-a-ling and his friend had not gazed long upon this scene before the sound of music was heard, and, in a few moments there appeared from out the woods a gorgeous procession. First came a large band of music, ringing blue-bells and blowing honeysuckles. Then came an array of courtiers, magnificently dressed ; and, after them, the Queen of the fairies, riding in a beautiful water-lily, drawn by six royal purple butterflies, and surrounded by a brilliant body of lords and ladies.

This procession halted at a short distance in front of the lady-minus-a-head, and formed itself into a semicircle, with the Queen in the centre. Then the crowd at the brook were seen approaching, and on the shoulders of the multitude was borne a head. They hurried as fast as their heavy load would permit, until they came to the tree under which sat the headless Nerralina, who, bed and all, had fallen here, when the Giant tore down the tower. Then quickly attaching a long rope (that they had put over a branch directly above the lady) to the hair of the head, they all took hold of the other end, and, pulling with a will, soon hoisted the head up until it hung at some distance above the neck to which it had previously belonged. Then they began to lower it slowly, and the Queen stood up with her wand raised ready to utter the magic word which should unite the parts when they touched. A deep silence spread over the plain, and even the lady seemed conscious that something was about to happen, for she sat perfectly still.

There was but one person there who did not feel pleasure at the approaching event, and that was a dwarf about a foot high, very ugly and wicked, who, by some means or other, had got into this goodly company, and who was now seated in a crotch of the tree, very close to the rope by which the crowd was lowering the lady's head. No one perceived him, for he was very much the color of the tree, and there he sat alone, quivering with spite and malice.

At the moment the head touched the ivory neck, the Queen, uttering the magic word, dropped the end of the wand, and immediately the head adhered as firmly as of old.

But a wild shout of horror rang through all the plain ! For, at the critical moment, the dwarf had reached out his hand, and twisted the rope, so that when the head was joined, it was wrong side foremost — face back !

Just then the little villain stuck his head out from behind the branch, and, giving a loud and mocking laugh of triumph, dropped from the tree. With a yell of anger the whole crowd, Queen, courtiers, common people, and all, set off in a mad chase after the dwarf, who fled like a stag before the hounds.

All were gone but little Ting-a-ling, and when he saw the dreadful distress of poor Nerralina, who jumped up, and twisted around, and ran backward both ways, screaming for help, he stopped not a minute, but ran to where he had left the Giant, and told him, as fast as his breathing would allow, the sad story.

Rubbing his eyes, Tur-il-i-ra perceived that it was nearly day, and concluded to commence operations. So he put Ting-a-ling on his shirt-frill, where he could see what was going on, and, taking about eleven strides, he came to where poor Nerralina was jumping about, and, picking her

(continued on next page)

up, put her carefully into his coat-tail pocket. Then with the cheese in his hand, he walked slowly toward the palace.

When he arrived there, he found the people running about, and crowding around the ruins of the Tower of Tears. He passed on, however, to the great Audience Chamber, and, looking in, saw the King sitting upon his throne behind a velvet-covered table, holding an early morning coun-

cil, and receiving the reports of his officers concerning the damage. As this Hall, and the doors thereof, were of great size, the Giant walked in, stooping a little as he entered.

He marched right up to the King, and held the cheese down before him.

"Here, your Majesty, is your daughter, and the young Prince, her lover. Does your Majesty recognize them?"

"Well, I declare!" cried the King. "If that is n't my great cheese, that I had put in the vault-flue to harden! And my daughter and that young man in it! What does this mean? What have you been doing, Giant?"

Then Tur-il-i-ra related the substance of the whole affair in a very brief manner, and concluded by saying that he hoped to see them made man and wife, as he considered them under his protection, and intended to see them safely through this affair. And he held them up so that all the people who thronged into the Hall could see.

The people all laughed, but the King cried "Silence!" and said to the Giant, "If the young man is of as good blood as my daughter, I have no desire to separate them. In fact, I don't think I am separating them. I think it 's the cheese!"

"Come! come!" said the Giant, turning very red in the face, "none of your trifling, or I 'll knock your house down over your eyes!"

And, putting the cheese down close to the table, he broke it in half, and let the lovers drop out on the velvet covering, when they immediately rushed into each other's arms, and remained thus clasped for a length of time.

They then slowly relinquished their hold upon each other, and were exchanging looks of supreme tenderness, when the Prince, happening to glance at his feet, sprang back so that he almost fell off the long table, and shouted, —

"Blood! Fire! Thunder! Where 's my boots? Boots! Slaves! Hounds! Get me my boots! boots!! boots!!!"

"Oh! he 's a Prince!" cried the King, jumping up. "I want no further proof. He 's a Prince. Give him boots. And blow, horners, blow! Beat your drums, drummers! Join hands all! Clear the floor for a dance!"

And in a trice the floor was cleared, and about five thousand couples stood ready for the first note from the band.

"Hold up!" cried the Giant. "Hold up! here is one I forgot," and he commenced feeling in his pockets. "I know I have got her somewhere. Oh yes, here she is!" And taking the Lady Nerralina from his coat-tail pocket, he put her carefully upon the table.

Every face in the room was in an instant the picture of horror, — all but that of the little girl whose duty it was to fasten Nerralina's dress every morning, — who got behind the door, and jumping up, and clapping her hands and heels, exclaimed, "Good! good! Now she can fasten her own frock behind!"

The Prince was the first to move, and, with tears in his eyes, he approached the luckless lady, who was sobbing piteously.

"Poor thing!" said he, and putting his arm around her, he kissed her. What joy thrilled through Nerralina! She had never been kissed by a man before, and it did for her what such things have done for many a young lady since — it turned her head!

"Blow, horners, blow!" shouted the King. "Join hands all!"

Seizing Nerralina's hand, and followed by the Prince and Princess, who sprang from the table, he led off the five thousand couples in a grand gallopade.

The Giant stood, and laughed heartily, until, at last, being no longer able to restrain himself, he sprang into the midst of them, and danced away royally, trampling about twenty couples under foot at every jump.

"Dance away, old fellow!" shouted the King, from the other end of the room. "Dance away! my boy, and never mind the people."

And the music blew louder, and round they all went faster and faster, until the building shook and trembled from the cellar to the roof.

At length, perfectly exhausted, they all stopped, and Ting-a-ling, slipping down from the Giant's frill, went out of the door.

"Oh!" said he, wiping the tears of laughter from his eyes, "it was all so funny, and every body was so happy — that — that I almost forgot my bereavement."

FOURTH OF JULY NIGHT.

"The Pied Piper of Hamelin," 1868, by Robert Browning (1812–1889). Illustrated by John La Farge (1835–1910).

The well-known American landscape painter and muralist illustrated Browning's classic.

ON OPPOSITE PAGE:
"The Court Cards," 1869, by Hans Christian Andersen (1805–1875).

A lesser-known Andersen story which has survived only in complete collections of the storyteller's tales, this is one of a series secured by Horace Scudder for first publication in his magazine.

THE

RIVERSIDE MAGAZINE

FOR YOUNG PEOPLE.

Vol. III. — JANUARY, 1869. — No. XXV.

THE COURT CARDS.

BY HANS CHRISTIAN ANDERSEN.

How many beautiful things may be cut out of and pasted on paper! Thus a castle was cut out and pasted, so large that it filled a whole table, and it was painted as if it were built of red stones. It had a shining copper roof, it had towers and a draw-bridge, water in the canals just like plate-glass, for it was plate-glass, and in the highest tower stood a wooden watchman. He had a trumpet, but he did not blow it.

The whole belonged to a little boy, whose name was William. He raised the draw-bridge himself and let it down again, made his tin soldiers march over it, opened the castle gate and looked into the large and elegant drawing-room, where all the court cards of a pack — Hearts, Diamonds, Clubs, and Spades — hung in frames on the walls, like pictures in real drawing-rooms. The kings held each a sceptre, and wore crowns; the queens wore veils flowing down over their shoulders, and in their hands they held a flower or a fan; the knaves had halberds and nodding plumes.

One evening the little boy peeped through the open castle gate, to catch a glimpse of the court cards in the drawing-room, and it seemed to him that the kings saluted him with their sceptres, that the Queen of Spades swung the golden tulip which she held in her hand, that the Queen of Hearts lifted her fan, and that all four queens graciously recognized him. He drew a little nearer, in order to see better, and that made him hit his head against the castle so that it shook. Then all the four knaves of Hearts, Diamonds, Clubs, and Spades, raised their halberds, to warn him that he must not try to get in that way.

The little boy understood the hint, and gave a friendly nod; he nodded again, and then said: "Say something!" but the knaves did not say a word. However, the third time he nodded, the Knave of Hearts sprang out of the card, and placed himself in the middle of the floor.

"What is your name?" the knave asked the little boy. "You have clear eyes and good teeth, but your hands are dirty: you do not wash them often enough!"

Now this was rather coarse language, but, of course, not much politeness can be expected from a knave. He is only a common fellow.

"My name is William," said the little boy, "and the castle is mine, and you are my Knave of Hearts!"

"No, I am not. I am my king's and my queen's knave, not yours!" said the Knave of Hearts. "I am not obliged to stay here. I can get down off the card, and out of the frame too, and so can my gracious king and queen, even more easily than I. We can go out into the wide world, but that is such a wearisome march; we have grown tired of it; it is more convenient, more easy, more agreeable, to be sitting in the cards, and just to be ourselves!"

"Have all of you really been human beings once?" asked little William.

(continued on next page)

"Human beings!" repeated the Knave of Hearts. "Yes, we have; but not so good as we ought to have been! Please now light a little wax candle (I like a red one best, for that is the color of my king and queen); then I will tell the lord of the castle — I think you said you were the lord of the castle, did you not? — our whole history; but for goodness' sake, don't interrupt me, for if I speak, it must be done without any interruption whatever. I am in a great hurry! Do you see my king, I mean the King of Hearts? He is the oldest of the four kings there, for he was born first, — born with a golden crown and a golden apple. He began to rule at once. His queen was born with a golden fan; that she still has. They both were very agreeably situated, even from infancy. They did not have to go to school, they could play the whole day, build castles, and knock them down, marshal tin soldiers for battle, and play with dolls. When they asked for buttered bread, then there was butter on both sides of the bread, and powdered brown sugar, too, nicely spread over it. It was the good old time, and was called the Golden Age; but they grew tired of it, and so did I. Then the King of Diamonds took the reins of government!"

The knave said nothing more. Little William waited to hear something further, but not a syllable was uttered; so presently he asked, — "Well, and then?"

The Knave of Hearts did not answer; he stood up straight, silent, bold, and stiff, his eyes fixed upon the burning wax candle. Little William nodded; he nodded again, but no reply. Then he turned to the Knave of Diamonds; and when he had nodded to him three times, up he sprang out of the card, in the middle of the floor, and uttered only one single word, —

"Wax candle!"

Little William understood what he meant, and immediately lighted a red candle, and placed it before him. Then the Knave of Diamonds presented arms, for that is a token of respect, and said: —

"Then the King of Diamonds succeeded to the throne! He was a king with a pane of glass on his breast; also the queen had a pane of glass on her breast, so that people could look right into her. For the rest, they were formed like other human beings, and were so agreeable and so handsome, that a monument was erected in honor of them, which stood for seven years without falling. Properly speaking, it should have stood forever, for so it was intended; but from some unknown reasons, it fell." Then the Knave of Diamonds presented arms, out of respect for his king, and he looked fixedly on his red wax candle.

But now at once, without any nod or invitation from little William, the Knave of Clubs stepped out, grave and proud, like the stork that struts with such a dignified air over the green meadow. The black clover-leaf in the corner of the card flew like a bird beyond the knave, and then flew back again, and stuck itself where it had been sticking before. And without waiting for his wax candle, the Knave of Clubs spoke: —

"Not all get butter on both sides of the bread, and brown powdered sugar on that. My king and queen did not get it. They had to go to school, and learn what they had not learnt before. They also had a pane of glass on their breasts, but nobody looked through it, except to see if there was not something wrong with their works inside, in order to find, if possible, some reason for giving them a scolding! I know it; I have served my king and queen all my life-time; I know every thing about them, and obey their commands. They bid me say nothing more to-night. I keep silent, therefore, and present arms!"

But little William was a kind-hearted boy, so he lighted a candle for this knave also, a shining white one, white like snow. No sooner was the candle lighted, than the Knave of Spades appeared in the middle of the drawing-room. He came hurriedly; yet he limped, as if he had a sore leg. Indeed, it had once been broken, and he had had, moreover, many ups and downs in his life. He spoke as follows: —

"My brother knaves have each got a candle, and I shall also get one; I know that. But if we poor knaves have so much honor, our kings and queens must have thrice as much. Now, it is proper that my King of Spades and my Queen of Spades, should have *four* candles to gladden them. An additional honor ought to be conferred upon them. Their history and trials are so doleful, that they have very good reason to wear mourning, and to have a grave-digger's spade on their coat of arms. My own fate, poor knave that I am, is deplorable enough. In one game at cards, I have got the nickname of '*Black Peter!*' * But alas! I have got a still uglier

* *Black Peter* is the name of a game in Denmark, where it is called "*Sorte Peer,*" the word *sorte* denoting black. When the cards are dealt, he who happens to get the Knave of Spades is all the evening nicknamed Black Peter by his fellow players, who paint his face black.

name, which, indeed, it is hardly the thing to mention aloud," and then he whispered, — "In another game, I have been nicknamed '*Dirty Mads!*' * I, who was once the King of Spades' Lord Chamberlain! Is not this a bitter fate? The history of my royal master and queen I will not relate; they don't wish me to do so! Little lord of the castle, as he calls himself, may guess it himself if he chooses, but it is very lamentable, — oh, no doubt about that! Their circumstances have become very much reduced, and are not likely to change for the better, until we are all riding on the red horse higher than the skies, where there are no haps and mishaps!"

Little William now lighted, as the Knave of Spades had said was proper, three candles for each of the kings, and three for each of the queens; but for the King and Queen of Spades he lighted four candles apiece, and the whole drawing-room became as light and transparent as the palace of the richest emperor, and the illustrious kings and queens bowed to each other serenely and graciously. The Queen of Hearts made her golden fan bow; and the Queen of Spades swung her golden tulip in such a way, that a stream of fire issued from it. The royal couples alighted from the cards and frames, and moved in a slow and graceful minuet up and

* *Dirty Mads* is another Danish game. *Mads* is a name almost exclusively in use amongst the peasantry.

(continued on next page)

down the floor. They were dancing in the very midst of flames, and the knaves were dancing too.

But alas! the whole drawing-room was soon in a blaze; the devouring element roared up through the roof, and all was one crackling and hissing sheet of fire; and in a moment little William's castle itself was enveloped in flames and smoke. The boy became frightened, and ran off, crying to his father and mother, — "Fire, fire, fire! my castle is on fire!" He grew pale as ashes, and his little hands trembled like the aspen-leaf. The fire continued sparkling and blazing, but in the midst of this destructive scene, the following words were uttered in a singing tone: —

"Now we are riding on the red horse, higher than the skies! This is the way for kings and queens to go, and this is the way for their knaves to go after them!"

Yes! that was the end of William's castle, and of the court cards. William did not perish in the flames; he is still alive, and he washed his small hands, and said: "I am innocent of the destruction of the castle." And, indeed, it was not his fault that the castle was burnt down.

ON OPPOSITE PAGE:
"Father Gander's Rhymes About the Animals," 1870, by Christopher Pearse Cranch (1813–1892).

See page 197 for more information about this author and his work.

FATHER GANDER'S RHYMES ABOUT THE ANIMALS.

FOR MIDDLE-SIZED CHILDREN.

BY C. P. CRANCH.

FATHER GANDER'S PREFACE.

OLD MOTHER GOOSE has had her say,
Some simple things she taught you, —
Light baby-rhymes for Christmas times, —
Such were the themes she brought you.

Good Mother Goose, she sang her songs,
More than you now can number;
Oft did they make young tears and ache
Turn into golden slumber.

It was a pretty thing to see
How oft you stopped and listened,
And checked your cries and wiped your eyes,
That opened wide and glistened,

While your dear mother o'er and o'er
Beguiled you with her singing, —
How Jack and Jill went up the hill,
How Banbury bells went ringing,

How Horner ate his Christmas pie,
Cock Robin was assaulted,
How young Bo-peep lost all her sheep,
How moonstruck Mooley vaulted.

How in a huge shoe sat the dame,
By countless children worried,
While breadless broth and blows, when wroth,
She gave them, bedward hurried.

How piper's sons stole countless pigs,
How blackbirds sang while baking, —
Such were the rhymes, in those young times,
Heard between sleep and waking.

Good Mother Goose a helper was,
Whom we will never slander;
But now you care no more for her,
Listen to Father Gander.

You left the nursery long ago,
You need good books — not nurses.
So may our pages suit your ages,
And may you like our verses.

THE BEAR AND THE SQUIRRELS.

To the tune of "Heigh ho! says Anthony Rowley."

THERE was an old Bear that lived near a wood
(His name it was Growly, Growly),
Where two little Squirrels gathered their food,
With a ramble, scramble, chittery tit!
O, a terrible fellow was Growly!

The two little Squirrels they lived in a tree,
Growly, Growly, Growly!
They were so merry, and happy, and free,
With a ramble, scramble, chittery tit, —
"Don't come near me," says Growly.

The Squirrels were rather afraid of the Bear,
Growly, Growly, Growly,
With his claws, and his teeth, and his shaggy hair;
For their ramble, scramble, chittery tit,
Made too much noise for Growly.

So whenever the Bear came into the wood,
Growly, Growly, Growly!
The Squirrels ran, and dropped their food,
With a ramble, scramble, chittery tit;
"Those nuts are all mine," says Growly.

One day old Bruin lay down in the shade,
Growly, Growly, Growly, —
Under the tree where the Squirrels played,
With a ramble, scramble, chittery tit!
"I'll just take a nap," says Growly.

Old Bruin then began to snore,
Growly, Growly, Growly;
Said the Squirrels, — "We'd rather hear that than a roar;
With a ramble, scramble, chittery tit,
We'll wake you up, old Growly!"

So, plump on his nose a nut they dropped,
Growly, Growly, Growly!
When all of a sudden the snoring stopped,
With a ramble, scramble, chittery tit, —
"Plague take the flies!" — says Growly.

(continued on next page)

So he turned him round to sleep again,
Growly, Growly, Growly,
When down came the nuts like a patter of rain,
With a ramble, scramble, chittery tit!
"It's hailing!" — says Sir Growly.

"No matter," says Bruin, "I'll have my nap!"
Growly, Growly, Growly;
So he slept again, when tap, tap, tap,
With a ramble, scramble, chittery tit, —
They pelted him well, — old Growly.

Then up he sprang and looked all around,
Growly, Growly, Growly;
But nothing he saw, and he heard no sound
But a ramble, scramble, chittery tit, —
"Why, what can it be?" — says Growly.

At last he looked up into the tree,
Growly, Growly, Growly!
And there the little rogues saw he,
With a ramble, scramble, chittery tit!
"Why, what's the matter, old Growly?

"You often have made the poor Squirrels run,
Growly, Growly, Growly!
So now we thought *we* would have some fun,
With a ramble, scramble, chittery tit!"
"It served me right," — says Growly.

And so the old fellow he saw the joke,
Growly, Growly, Growly!
And began to laugh till they thought he'd choke
With a ramble, scramble, Ha, ha, ha!
"What a capital joke!" says Growly.

Sir Bruin then grew gentle and mild,
Growly, Growly, Growly!
And played with the squirrels like a child
With a ramble, scramble, chittery tit,
And lost the name of Growly.

ST. NICHOLAS; a Monthly Magazine for Boys and Girls [subtitle varies]. Vols. 1–70, November 1873–June 1943. New York: issues for November 1873–June 1881 published by Scribner's; issues for July 1881–May 1930 by Century Company. 25–30 cm. Editor: Mary Mapes Dodge (1873–1905). Absorbed *Our Young Folks* in January 1874; the *Children's Hour* in July 1874; the *Little Corporal,* and the *Schoolday Magazine* in May 1875; *Wide Awake* in September 1893. Publication suspended March 1940–February 1943.

The most famous of the American magazines for children which enlivened the nineteenth century, this had its success largely secured by the creative editorship of Mrs. Dodge, famous also as the author of *Hans Brinker: or, The Silver Skates* (1865). The writer Frank R. Stockton became her assistant, and his stories a notable contribution to the magazine. Editorial skill accounted for the magazine's sustained lighthearted quality. Mrs. Dodge had expressed in *Scribner's Magazine* in 1873 her intent to make it "a child's pleasure ground."

Beginning as an octavo of forty-eight pages, the periodical grew to double that number of pages, attracting the first rank of writers and artists and having an English edition as well (1872–1917). Thus there were pictures by Arthur Rackham, and stories by Rudyard Kipling, which were later to appear in his *Jungle Books* and *Just-So Stories.* In England the works of Charles E. Carryl, Frances Hodgson Burnett, and Susan Coolidge serialized here were to have a book life equally as long as they have had in the United States. Some of *St. Nicholas*'s most prolific contributors—Howard Pyle, Palmer Cox, Laura E. Richards, and Frank R. Stockton—sent their work to other children's magazines as well.

So, from the earliest issues onward, *St. Nicholas* presented the best of American literature for children, not only serialized novel after novel, but also successions of short stories, later also to become classics, folktales, poetry, and art. In addition, the issues had for variety regular features for children's participation including, from 1898 the famous "St. Nicholas League" to which the young sent their own contributions. *(continued on next page)*

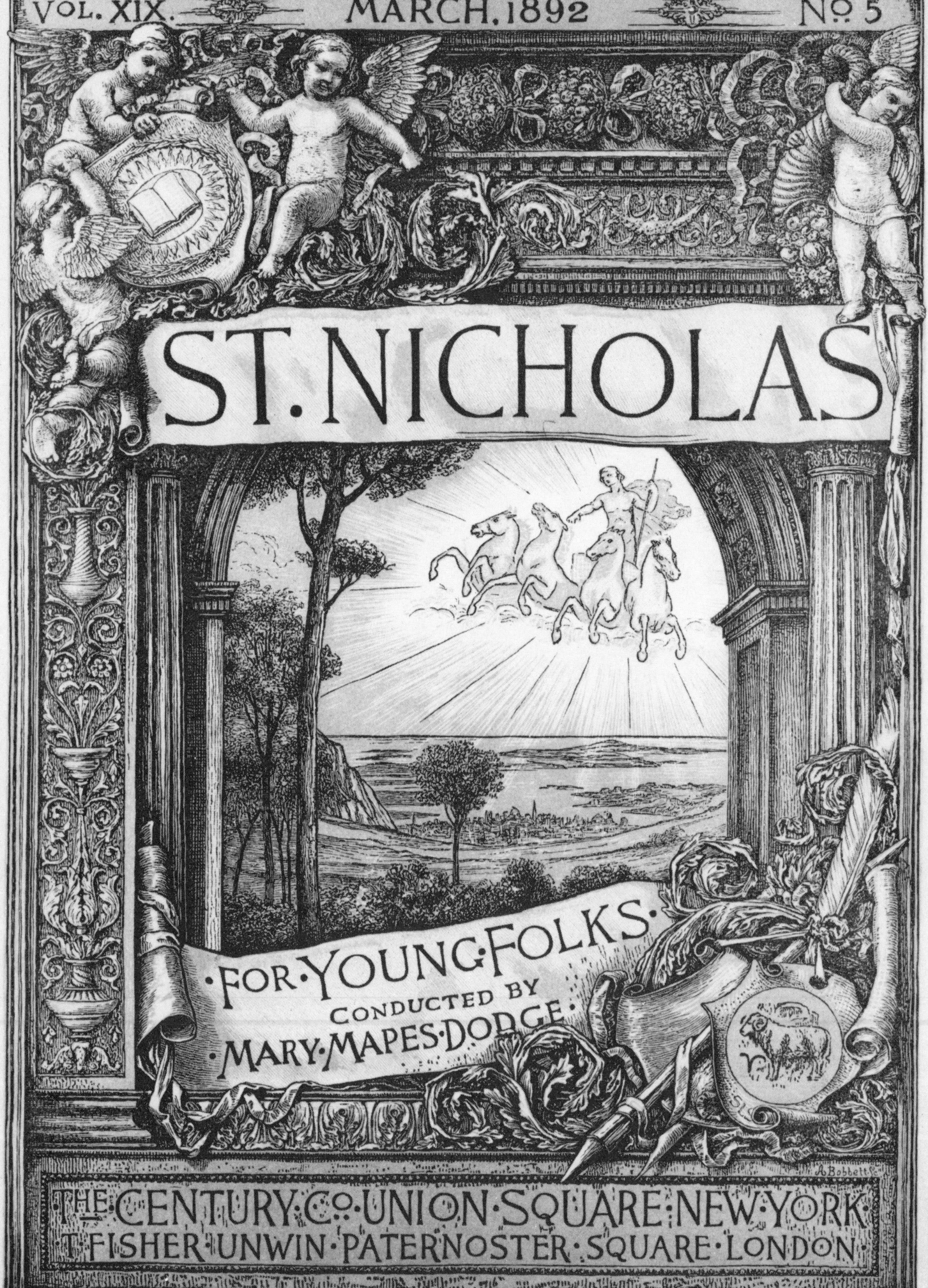

VOL. XIX.
MARCH, 1892
No. 5
ST. NICHOLAS
·FOR·YOUNG·FOLKS·
CONDUCTED BY
·MARY·MAPES·DODGE·
THE CENTURY·CO·UNION·SQUARE·NEW·YORK·
·T·FISHER·UNWIN·PATERNOSTER·SQUARE·LONDON·
COPYRIGHT, 1892, BY THE CENTURY CO. · ENTERED AT THE POST OFFICE AT NEW-YORK AS SECOND-CLASS MAIL MATTER

THE STORY OF THE LITTLE RED HEN.

ABOUT twenty-five years ago my mother told me the story of the little red hen. She told it often to me at that time; but I have never heard it since. So I shall try to tell it to you now from memory:

There was once a little red hen. She was scratching near the barn one day, when she found a grain of wheat.

She said, "Who will plant this wheat?" The rat said, "I wont;" the cat said, "I wont;" the dog said, "I wont;" the duck said, "I wont;" and the pig said, "I wont." The little red hen said, "I will, then." So she planted the grain of wheat. After the wheat grew up and was ripe, the little red hen said, "Who will reap this wheat?" The rat said, "I wont;" the cat said, "I wont;" the dog said, "I wont;" the duck said, "I wont;" and the pig said, "I wont." The little red hen said, "I will, then." So she reaped the wheat. Then she said, "Who will take this wheat to mill to be ground into flour?" The rat said, "I wont;" the cat said, "I wont;" the dog said, "I wont;" the duck said, "I wont:" and the pig said, "I wont." The little red hen said, "I will, then." So she took the wheat to mill. When she came back with the flour, she said, "Who will make this into bread?" The rat said, "I wont;" the cat said, "I wont;" the dog said, "I wont;" the duck said, "I wont;" and the pig said,

"The Story of the Little Red Hen," 1874 (anonymous).

This is one of the simple stories provided on *St. Nicholas*'s regular large-print page for younger children.

(continued on next page)

"I wont." The little red hen said, "I will, then." So she made it into bread. Then she said, "Who will bake this bread?" The rat said, "I wont;" the cat said, "I wont;" the dog said, "I wont;" the duck said, "I wont;" and the pig said, "I wont." The little red hen said, "I will, then." When the bread was baked, the little red hen said, "Who will EAT this bread?" The rat said, "I WILL;" the cat said, "I WILL;" the dog said, "I WILL;" the duck said, "I WILL;" and the pig said, "I WILL." The little red hen said, "No, you WONT, for I am going to do that myself." And she picked up the bread and ran off with it.

WHEN the moon is shining brightly,
And the dew is on the ground,
Then 's the time, you know, that nightly,
Cruel foxes are around.

Oh, but how the mischief thickens
When they prowl among the hens!
Sucking eggs and taking chickens
To their damp and dismal dens.

THE STORY OF THE LITTLE RED HEN *(continued from page 395)*

THE QUEEN OF THE ORKNEY ISLANDS.

By Laura E. Richards.

Oh, the Queen of the Orkney Islands,
She 's traveling over the sea;
She 's bringing a cuttle-fish with her,
To play with my baby and me.

Oh, his head is three miles long, dear;
His tail is three miles short;
And when he goes out, he wriggles his snout
In a way that no cuttle-fish ought.

"The Queen of the Orkney Islands," 1876, by Laura E. Richards (1850–1943).

See page 185 for more information about the author.

THE QUEEN OF THE ORKNEY ISLANDS.

Oh, the Queen of the Orkney Islands,
  She rides on a sea-green whale.
He takes her a mile, with an elegant smile,
  At every flip of his tail.

Oh, the Queen of the Orkney Islands,
  She dresses in wonderful taste;
The sea-serpent coils, all painted in oils,
  Around her bee-yutiful waist.

Oh, her gown is made of the green sea-kale,
  And though she knows nothing of feet,
She can manage her train, with an air of disdain,
  In a way that is perfectly sweet.

Oh, the Queen of the Orkney Islands,
  She 's traveling over the main;
So we 'll hire a hack, and send her right back
  To her beautiful islands again.

THE OWL, THE EEL AND THE WARMING-PAN.

THE owl and the eel and the warming-pan,
They went to call on the soap-fat man.
The soap-fat man, he was not within;
He 'd gone for a ride on his rolling-pin;
So they all came back by the way of the town,
And turned the meeting-house upside down.

"The Owl, the Eel, and the Warming Pan," 1876, by Laura E. Richards (1850–1943).

(See also pages 185 and 397.)

TOINETTE AND THE ELVES.

(A Christmas Story.)

By Susan Coolidge.

THE winter sun was nearing the horizon's edge. Each moment the tree-shadows grew longer in the forest; each moment the crimson light on the upper boughs became more red and bright. It was Christmas Eve, or would be in half-an-hour, when the sun should be fairly set; but it did not feel like Christmas, for the afternoon was mild and sweet, and the wind in the leafless boughs sang, as it moved about, as though to imitate the vanished birds. Soft trills and whistles, odd little shakes and twitters;—it was astonishing what pretty noises the wind made, for it was in good humor, as winds should be on the Blessed Night; all its storm-tones and bass-notes were for the moment laid aside, and gently, as though hushing a baby to sleep, it cooed and rustled and brushed to and fro in the leafless woods.

Toinette stood, pitcher in hand, beside the well. "Wishing Well" the people called it, for they believed that if any one standing there, bowed to the East, repeated a certain rhyme and wished a wish, the wish would certainly come true. Unluckily, nobody knew exactly what the rhyme should be. Toinette did not; she was wishing that she did, as she stood with her eyes fixed on the bubbling water. How nice it would be! she thought. What beautiful things should be hers, if it were only to wish and to have! She would be beautiful, rich, good—oh, so good! The children should love her dearly, and never be disagreeable. Mother should not work so hard—they should all go back to France—which mother said was *si belle*. Oh, dear, how nice it would be! Meantime, the sun sank lower, and mother at home was waiting for the water, but Toinette forgot that.

Suddenly she started. A low sound of crying met her ear, and something like a tiny moan. It seemed close by, but she saw nothing.

Hastily she filled her pitcher, and turned to go. But again the sound came, an unmistakable sob, right under her feet. Toinette stopped short.

"What *is* the matter?" she called out bravely. "Is anybody there; and if there is, why don't I see you?"

A third sob—and all at once, down on the ground beside her, a tiny figure became visible, so small that Toinette had to kneel and stoop her head to see it plainly. The figure was that of an odd little man. He wore a garb of green, bright and glancing as the scales of a beetle. In his mite of a hand was a cap, out of which stuck a long-pointed feather. Two specks of tears stood on his cheeks, and he fixed on Toinette a glance so sharp and so sad, that it made her feel sorry and frightened and confused all at once.

"Why, how funny this is!" she said, speaking to herself out loud.

"Not at all," replied the little man, in a voice as dry and crisp as the chirr of a grasshopper. "Anything but funny. I wish you would n't use such words. It hurts my feelings, Toinette."

"Do you know my name, then?" cried Toinette, astonished. "That 's strange! But what is the matter? Why are you crying so, little man?"

"I 'm not a little man. I 'm an elf," responded the dry voice; "and I think you 'd cry if you had an engagement out to tea, and found yourself spiked on a great bayonet, so that you could n't move an inch. Look!" He turned a little as he spoke, and Toinette saw a long rose-thorn sticking through the back of the green robe. The little man could by no means reach the thorn, and it held him fast prisoner to the place.

"Is that all? I 'll take it out for you," she said.

"Be careful—oh, be careful!" entreated the little man. "This is my new dress, you know—my Christmas suit, and it 's got to last a year. If there is a hole in it, Peascod will tickle me, and Bean Blossom tease till I shall wish myself dead." He stamped with vexation at the thought.

"Now, you must n't do that," said Toinette, in a motherly tone, "else you 'll tear it yourself, you know." She broke off the thorn as she spoke, and gently drew it out. The elf anxiously examined the stuff. A tiny puncture only was visible, and his face brightened.

"You 're a good child," he said. "I 'll do as much for you some day, perhaps."

"I would have come before if I had seen you," remarked Toinette, timidly. "But I did n't see you a bit."

"No, because I had my cap on," replied the elf. He placed it on his head as he spoke, and,

"Toinette and the Elves," 1876, by Susan Coolidge (pseudonym of Sarah Chauncey Woolsey, 1835–1905).

This author's most popular books—the celebrated Katy stories—also had magazine publication. They appeared in book form as *What Katy Did* (1872), *What Katy Did at School* (1873), and *What Katy Did Next* (1886). Katy is still alive, both in America and abroad.

(continued on next page)

hey, presto! nobody was there, only a voice which laughed and said: "Well—don't stare so. Lay your finger on me now."

"Oh!" said Toinette, with a gasp. "How wonderful! What fun it must be to do that! The children would n't see me. I should steal in and surprise them; they would go on talking, and never guess that I was there! I should so like it! Do elves ever lend their caps to anybody? I wish you 'd lend me yours. It must be so nice to be invisible!"

"Ho!" cried the elf, appearing suddenly again. "Lend my cap, indeed! Why, it would n't stay on the very tip of your ear, it 's so small. As for nice, that depends. Sometimes it is, and sometimes it is n't. No, the only way for mortal people to be invisible is to gather the fern-seed and put it in their shoes."

"Gather it? Where? I never saw any seed to the ferns," said Toinette, staring about her.

"Of course not—we elves take care of that," replied the little man. "Nobody finds the fern-seed but ourselves. I 'll tell you what, though. You were such a nice child to take out the thorn so cleverly, that I 'll *give* you a little of the seed. Then you can try the fun of being invisible to your heart's content."

"Will you really? How delightful! May I have it now?"

"Bless me! do you think I carry my pocket stuffed with it?" said the elf. "Not at all. Go home, say not a word to anybody, but leave your bedroom window open to-night, and you 'll see what you 'll see."

He laid his finger on his nose as he spoke, gave a jump like a grasshopper, clapping on his cap as he went, and vanished. Toinette lingered a moment, in hopes that he might come back, then took her pitcher and hurried home. The woods were very dusky by this time; but, full of her strange adventure, she did not remember to feel afraid.

"How long you have been!" said her mother. "It 's late for a little maid like you to be up. You must make better speed another time, my child."

Toinette pouted, as she was apt to do when reproved. The children clamored to know what had kept her, and she spoke pettishly and crossly; so that they too became cross, and presently went away into the outer kitchen to play by themselves. The children were apt to creep away when Toinette came. It made her angry and unhappy at times that they should do so, but she did not realize that it was in great part her own fault, and so did not set herself to mend it.

"Tell me a 'tory," said baby Jeanneton, creeping to her knee a little later. But Toinette's head was full of the elf; she had no time to spare for Jeanneton.

"Oh, not to-night!" she replied. "Ask mother to tell you one."

"Mother 's busy," said Jeanneton, wistfully.

Toinette took no notice, and the little one crept away disconsolately.

Bed-time at last. Toinette set the casement open, and lay a long time waiting and watching; then she fell asleep. She waked with a sneeze and jump, and sat up in bed. Behold, on the coverlet stood her elfin friend, with a long train of other elves beside him, all clad in the beetle-wing green, and wearing little pointed caps! More were coming in at the window; outside a few were drifting about in the moon-rays, which lit their sparkling robes till they glittered like so many fire-flies. The odd thing was, that though the caps were on, Toinette could see the elves distinctly, and this surprised her so much, that again she thought out loud, and said:

"How funny!"

"You mean about the caps," replied her special elf, who seemed to have the power of reading thoughts. "Yes, you can see us to-night, caps and all. Spells lose their value on Christmas Eve always. Peascod, where is the box? Do you still wish to try the experiment of being invisible, Toinette?"

"Oh, yes—indeed I do!"

"Very well—so let it be!"

As he spoke he beckoned, and two elves, puffing and panting like men with a heavy load, dragged forward a droll little box about the size of a pumpkin-seed. One of them lifted the cover.

"Pay the porter, please ma'am," he said, giving Toinette's ear a mischievous tweak with his sharp fingers.

"Hands off, you bad Peascod!" cried Toinette's elf. "This is my girl. She sha' n't be pinched." He dealt Peascod a blow with his tiny hand as he spoke, and looked so brave and warlike, that he seemed at least an inch taller than he had before. Toinette admired him very much; and Peascod slunk away with an abashed giggle, muttering that Thistle need n't be so ready with his fist.

Thistle—for thus, it seemed, Toinette's friend was named—dipped his fingers in the box, which was full of fine brown seeds, and shook a handful into each of Toinette's shoes, as they stood, toes together, by the bedside.

"Now you have your wish," he said, "and can go about and do what you like, no one seeing. The charm will end at sunset. Make the most of it while you can; but if you want to end it sooner, shake the seeds from the shoes, and then you are just as usual."

"Oh, I sha' n't want to," protested Toinette; "I 'm sure I sha' n't."

"Good-bye," said Thistle, with a mocking little laugh.

"Good-bye, and thank you ever so much," replied Toinette.

"Good-bye, good-bye," replied the other elves, in shrill chorus. They clustered together, as if in consultation; then straight out of the window they flew like a swarm of gauzy-winged bees, and melted into the moonlight. Toinette jumped up and ran to watch them; but the little men were gone —not a trace of them was to be seen; so she shut the window, went back to bed, and presently, in the midst of her amazed and excited thoughts, fell asleep.

She waked in the morning with a queer, doubtful feeling. Had she dreamed, or had it really happened? She put on her best petticoat, and laced her blue bodice; for she thought the mother would perhaps take them across the wood to the little chapel for the Christmas service. Her long hair smoothed and tied, her shoes trimly fastened, downstairs she ran. The mother was stirring porridge over the fire. Toinette went close to her, but she did not move or turn her head.

"How late the children are!" she said at last, lifting the boiling pot on the hob. Then she went to the stair-foot, and called, "Marc, Jeanneton, Pierre, Marie! Breakfast is ready, my children. Toinette—but where, then, is Toinette? She is used to be down long before this."

"Toinette is n't upstairs," said Marie, from above. "Her door is wide open, and she is n't there."

"That is strange!" said the mother. "I have

THE ELVES VISIT TOINETTE.

(continued on next page)

been here an hour, and she has not passed this way since." She went to the outer door and called, "Toinette! Toinette!"—passing close to Toinette as she did so, and looking straight at her with unseeing eyes. Toinette, half-frightened, half-pleased, giggled low to herself. She really was invisible then! How strange it seemed, and what fun it was going to be!

The children sat down to breakfast, little Jeanneton, as the youngest, saying grace. The mother distributed the hot porridge, and gave each a spoon, but she looked anxious.

"Where can Toinette have gone?" she said to herself.

Toinette was conscience-pricked. She was half inclined to dispel the charm on the spot. But just then she caught a whisper from Pierre to Marc, which so surprised her as to put the idea out of her head.

"Perhaps a wolf has eaten her up—a great big wolf, like the 'Capuchon Rouge,' you know." This was what Pierre said; and Marc answered, unfeelingly:

"If he has, I shall ask mother to let me have her room for my own!"

Poor Toinette! her cheeks burnt and her eyes filled with tears at this. Did n't the boys love her a bit, then? Next she grew angry, and longed to box Marc's ears, only she recollected in time that she was invisible. What a bad boy he was! she thought.

The smoking porridge reminded her that she was hungry; so brushing away the tears, she slipped a spoon off the table, and whenever she found the chance, dipped it into the bowl for a mouthful. The porridge disappeared rapidly.

"I want some more," said Jeanneton.

"Bless me, how fast you have eaten!" said the mother, turning to the bowl.

This made Toinette laugh, which shook her spoon, and a drop of the hot mixture fell right on the tip of Marie's nose, as she sat with up-turned face waiting her turn for a second helping. Marie gave a little scream.

"What is it?" said the mother.

"Hot water! Right in my face!" spluttered Marie.

"Water!" cried Marc. "It 's porridge."

"You spattered with your spoon. Eat more carefully, my child," said the mother; and Toinette laughed again as she heard her. After all, there was some fun in being invisible!

The morning went by. Constantly the mother went to the door, and, shading her eyes with her hand, looked out, in hopes of seeing a little figure come down the wood-path, for she thought, perhaps, the child went to the spring after water, and fell asleep there. The children played happily, meanwhile. They were used to doing without Toinette, and did not seem to miss her, except that now and then baby Jeanneton said: "Poor Toinette gone—not here—all gone!"

"Well, what if she has?" said Marc at last, looking up from the wooden cup he was carving for Marie's doll. "We can play all the better."

Marc was a bold, outspoken boy, who always told his whole mind about things.

"If she were here," he went on, "she 'd only scold and interfere. Toinette almost always scolds. I like to have her go away It makes it pleasanter."

"It *is* rather pleasanter," admitted Marie, "only I 'd like her to be having a nice time somewhere else."

"Bother about Toinette!" cried Pierre. "Let's play 'My godmother has cabbage to sell.'"

I don 't think Toinette had ever felt so unhappy in her life, as when she stood by unseen, and heard the children say these words. She had never meant to be unkind to them, but she was quick-tempered, dreamy, wrapped up in herself. She did not like being interrupted by them, it put her out, and then she spoke sharply and was cross. She had taken it for granted that the others must love her, by a sort of right, and the knowledge that they did not grieved her very much. Creeping away, she hid herself in the woods. It was a sparkling day, but the sun did not look so bright as usual. Cuddled down under a rose-bush, Toinette sat, sobbing as if her heart would break at the recollection of the speeches she had overheard.

By and by a little voice within her woke up and began to make itself audible. All of us know this little voice. We call it conscience.

"Jeanneton missed me," she thought. "And, oh dear! I pushed her away only last night and would n't tell her a story. And Marie hoped I was having a pleasant time somewhere. I wish I had n't slapped Marie last Friday. And I wish I had n't thrown Marc's ball into the fire that day I was angry with him. How unkind he was to say that—but I was n't always kind to him. And once I said that I wished a bear would eat Pierre up. That was because he broke my cup. Oh dear, oh dear! What a bad girl I 've been to them all!"

"But you could be better and kinder if you tried, could n't you?" said the inward voice. "I think you could." And Toinette clasped her hands tight and said out loud: "I could. Yes—and I will."

The first thing to be done was to get rid of the fern-seed, which she now regarded as a hateful thing. She untied her shoes and shook it out in the grass. It dropped and seemed to melt into the air, for it instantly vanished. A mischievous laugh sounded close behind, and a beetle-green coat-tail was visible, whisking under a tuft of rushes. But Toinette had had enough of the elves, and tying her shoes, took the road toward home, running with all her might.

"Where have you been all day, Toinette?" cried the children, as, breathless and panting, she flew in at the gate. But Toinette could not speak. She made slowly for her mother, who stood in the door-way, flung herself into her arms, and burst into a passion of tears.

"Ma chérie, what is it, whence hast thou come?" asked the good mother, alarmed. She lifted Toinette into her arms as she spoke, and hastened indoors. The other children followed, whispering and peeping, but the mother sent them away, and, sitting down by the fire with Toinette in her lap, she rocked and hushed and comforted, as though Toinette had been again a little baby. Gradually the sobs ceased. For awhile Toinette lay quiet, with her head on her mother's breast. Then she wiped her wet eyes, put her arms around her mother's neck, and told her all from the very beginning, keeping not a single thing back. The dame listened with alarm.

"Saints protect us," she muttered. Then feeling Toinette's hands and head, "Thou hast a fever," she said. "I will make thee a *tisane*, my darling, and thou must at once go to bed." Toinette vainly protested; to bed she went, and perhaps it was the wisest thing, for the warm drink threw her into a long, sound sleep, and when she woke she was herself again, bright and well, hungry for dinner, and ready to do her usual tasks.

Herself,—but not quite the same Toinette that she had been before. Nobody changes from bad to better in a minute. It takes time for that, time and effort and a long struggle with evil habits and tempers. But there is sometimes a certain minute or day in which people *begin* to change, and thus it was with Toinette. The fairy lesson was not lost upon her. She began to fight with herself, to watch her faults and try to conquer them. It was hard work; often she felt discouraged, but she kept on. Week after week and month after month, she grew less selfish, kinder, more obliging than she used to be. When she failed, and her old fractious temper got the better of her, she was sorry, and begged every one's pardon so humbly, that they could not but forgive. The mother began to think that the elves really had bewitched her child. As for the children, they learned to love Toinette as never before, and came to her with all their pains and pleasures, as children should to a kind older sister. Each fresh proof of this, each kiss from Jeanneton, each confidence from Marc, was a comfort to Toinette, for she never forgot Christmas-day, and felt that no trouble was too much to wipe out that unhappy recollection. "I *think* they like me better than they did then," she would say, but then the thought came, "Perhaps if I were invisible again, if they did not know I was there, I might hear something to make me feel as badly as I did that morning." These sad thoughts were part of the bitter fruit of the fairy fern-seed.

So with doubts and fears the year went by, and again it was Christmas Eve. Toinette had been asleep some hours, when she was roused by a sharp tapping at the window pane. Startled and only half-awake, she sat up in bed, and saw by the moonlight, a tiny figure outside, which she recognized. It was Thistle, drumming with his knuckles on the glass.

"Let me in," cried the dry little voice. So Toinette opened the casement, and Thistle flew in and perched, as before, on the coverlet.

"Merry Christmas, my girl," he said, "and a Happy New Year when it comes! I've brought you a present;" and, dipping into a pouch tied round his waist, he pulled out a handful of something brown. Toinette knew what it was in a moment.

"Oh, no!" she cried, shrinking back. "Don't give me any fern-seeds. They frighten me. I don't like them."

"Now, don't be silly," said Thistle, his voice sounding kind this time, and earnest. "It was n't pleasant being invisible last year, but perhaps this year it will be. Take my advice and try it. You'll not be sorry."

"Sha' n't I?" said Toinette, brightening. "Very well then, I will." She leaned out of bed, and watched Thistle strew the fine, dust-like grains in each shoe.

"I'll drop in to-morrow night, and just see how you like it," he said. Then, with a nod, he was gone.

The old fear came back when she woke in the morning, and she tied on her shoes with a tremble at her heart. Down-stairs she stole. The first thing she saw was a wooden ship standing on her plate. Marc had made the ship, but Toinette had no idea that it was for her.

The little ones sat round the table with their eyes on the door, watching till Toinette should come in, and be surprised.

"I wish she'd hurry," said Pierre, drumming on his bowl with a spoon.

"We all want Toinette, don't we?" said the mother, smiling as she poured the hot porridge.

"It will be fun to see her stare," declared Marc. "Toinette is jolly when she stares. Her eyes look big, and her cheeks grow pink. Andre Brugen

(continued on next page)

thinks his sister Aline is prettiest, but I don't. Our Toinette is ever so pretty."

"She is ever so nice, too," said Pierre. "She's as good to play with as—as—a boy!" he finished, triumphantly.

"Oh, I wish my Toinette *would* come!" said Jeanneton.

Toinette waited no longer, but sped upstairs with glad tears in her eyes. Two minutes, and

THE ELVES' SUPPER.

down she came again, visible this time. Her heart was light as a feather.

"Merry Christmas!" clamored the children. The ship was presented, Toinette was duly surprised, and so the happy day began.

That night Toinette left the window open, and lay down in her clothes; for she felt, as Thistle had been so kind, she ought to receive him politely. He came at midnight, and with him all the other little men in green.

"Well, how was it?" asked Thistle.

"Oh, I liked it this time," declared Toinette, with shining eyes. "And I thank you so much!"

"I'm glad you did," said the elf. "And I'm glad you are thankful, for we want you to do something for us."

"What can it be?" inquired Toinette, wondering.

"You must know," went on Thistle, "that there is no dainty in the world which we elves enjoy like a bowl of fern-seed broth. But it has to be cooked over a real fire, and we dare not go near fire, you know, lest our wings scorch. So we seldom get any fern-seed broth. Now, Toinette—will you make us some?"

"Indeed I will," cried Toinette, "only you must tell me how."

"It is very simple," said Peascod; "only seed and honey dew, stirred from left to right with a sprig of fennel. Here's the seed and the fennel, and here's the dew. Be sure and stir from the left; if you don't, it curdles, and the flavor will be spoiled."

Down into the kitchen they went, and Toinette, moving very softly, quickened the fire, set on the smallest bowl she could find, and spread the doll's table with the wooden saucers which Marc had made for Jeanneton to play with. Then she mixed and stirred as the elves bade, and when the soup was done, served it to them smoking hot. How they feasted! No bumble-bee, dipping into a flower-cup, ever sipped and twinkled more rapturously than they.

When the last drop was eaten, they made ready to go. Each, in turn, kissed Toinette's hand, and said a little word of farewell. Thistle brushed his feathered cap over the door-post as he passed.

"Be lucky, house," he said, "for you have received and entertained the luck-bringers. And be lucky, Toinette. Good temper *is* good luck, and sweet words and kind looks and peace in the heart are the fairest of fortunes. See that you never lose them again, my girl." With this, he, too, kissed Toinette's hand, waved his feathered cap and—whirr! they all were gone, while Toinette, covering the fire with ashes, and putting aside the little cups, stole up to her bed a happy child.

AMERICA'S BIRTHDAY-PARTY.

BY FRANK R. STOCKTON.

I SUPPOSE there is scarcely an American boy or girl who has not heard of the great party which is to be given on the occasion of the one-hundredth birthday of our country—a party which will last six months, and to which the whole world is invited.

It is probable that this "Centennial Exhibition" will be the grandest affair of the kind that the world has ever known. In ancient times, it was impossible to have such celebrations, as the different countries of the world had very little to do with each other when they were not fighting; and although we have had several "World's Fairs" in our day, it must be remembered that this is more than an "International Exhibition,"—it is the celebration of a nation's birthday, and so it will not be surprising if it excites, even in foreigners, much more interest and enthusiasm than the great exhibitions at London, Vienna, and other cities.

One thing is certain, and that is, it will excite interest and enthusiasm enough in the people of the United States. I suppose there is scarcely a person in this country old enough to care about such things, who will not go to the Centennial—or want to go.

The United States is not a very old country—Iceland recently celebrated its one thousandth birthday. But then we have done so much more in one hundred years than Iceland has done in its thousand, that we feel very proud about our birthday, and proud that all the world is coming to help us celebrate it. Even England, who did not want us to have our first birthday, and who fought so hard to prevent us ever becoming a nation at all, is among the first to accept our invitation, and seems to take almost as much interest in the matter as if she had been fighting on our side all through the Revolution.

And we are happier to have England come than any one else. For we can never forget that she is our mother-country, that her language is our language, and that, in great part, her blood is our blood. The British lion is a noble beast, and we welcome him warmly when he comes to us in jolly good-humor, wagging his tail with gladness to see us. This is very different from the way he came growling and roaring a hundred years ago. He is a terrible animal to fight. I doubt if any national bird or beast, except the American eagle, could have torn itself away from the British lion, as our bird did in the last century.

From almost every land the people will come—from countries that have always been our friends,

"America's Birthday-Party," 1876, by Frank R. Stockton (1834–1902).

See pages 373 and 393 for more information about this author.
(continued on next page)

and from countries that have only recently made our acquaintance. Even Japan, who for thousands of years has shut herself up from the rest of the world, and who, only twenty years ago, would not think of such a thing as allowing commerce or intercourse between her people and the rest of mankind, has sent architects and carpenters to build a house for her people on our Centennial grounds.

Europe, Asia, Africa, and Oceanica will send to America their representatives, who will come laden with specimens of the products of their soil, their labor, and their ingenuity; so that at our great birthday celebration we can see gathered together the productions and manufactures of every land, as well as the people who dwell therein.

And now we will take a glance at the preparations we are making for this Birthday-party.

and smooth, wide roads, and lovely shady walks, and through the whole of it runs the placid river Schuylkill.

More than two hundred acres of this park have been appropriated for the Centennial buildings and for Exhibition purposes generally.

There are five principal buildings on the grounds, the largest of which is the Main Exhibition Building, which is truly immense. It is difficult to make any one, who has not seen this building, understand how large it really is. It is 1,880 feet long and 464 feet wide. Three such buildings, set end to end, would extend over a mile. Boys and girls who live in the country will appreciate its size when I tell them it covers a space of over twenty acres, all in one room! Twenty acres in some parts of the country is considered a snug little farm; and when you think of the whole of

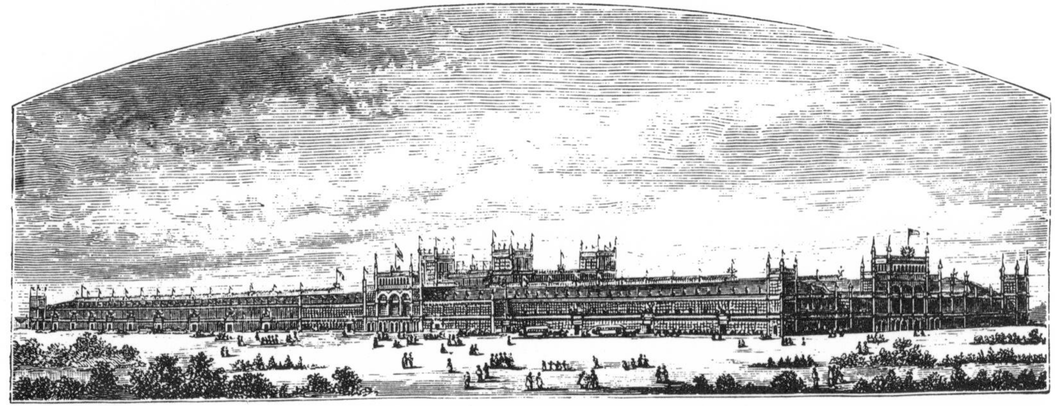

THE MAIN EXHIBITION BUILDING.

Philadelphia was wisely selected as the most fitting place for the celebration, for in that city the nation truly had its birthplace. There, as soon as the Declaration of Independence was signed in the Old State House, the little baby "United States of America" opened its eyes, and began to cry and kick. It was not a very strong little baby at first, but it cried pretty loud and kicked pretty hard, and very soon let the world know that it was alive, and intended to live. "Faneuil Hall" in Boston is called "The Cradle of Liberty," and it is true that our baby was well rocked and cared for there, and that from North to South he received the greatest support and attention until he grew up to be a stout fellow. But he was born in Philadelphia, and so there his birthday is to be celebrated.

On the outskirts of Philadelphia is a magnificent park called Fairmount Park, which contains about three thousand acres of land. There are meadows and grassy hills, and beautiful groves,

such a farm,—house, barns, barn-yard, wagon-houses, vegetable garden, lawn, wheat-field, corn-field, potato-patch, pasture-lot, and everything under one roof,—you can imagine a pretty big house.

If you live in the city, in an ordinary four-story house, the comparative size of your house and this main building may be inferred from these two black marks:

The little mark is your house; the large one is the Main Centennial Building.

This great house is constructed almost entirely of iron and glass, and when the sun shines it is nearly as light inside as it is out of doors. There are rows of iron pillars running up and down the building to support the roof, but these are so slender and so far apart that they do not interfere with the view of the interior. When I last saw the building, it was just finished; and as I stood at one end and looked over the immense, smooth, and vacant floor, I could see that off in the distance the roof was higher, and there were great entrance-doors to the right and the left; beyond that there did not seem to be much. In reality, however, that higher portion was the center of the building, and beyond it was a vast stretch of floor as great as that which I was looking over. But that distant half of the building was so far away that the central portion seemed to be the end of the building.

In this great hall will be exhibited goods and manufactures of every possible kind, from all quarters of the world. There will be wide passage-ways up and down the building, and cross-ways intersecting these, and all the rest of the space will be filled with the curious, beautiful, and wonderful things that man's ingenuity has taught him to make or adapt to his needs. If a person were determined to see everything in this main building, and would therefore walk up one side of every passage and avenue and down the other (and that would be the only way of seeing everything), he would have to walk at least ten miles!

Near this building is another, very much like it, but not so large, covering over fourteen acres, which is called Machinery Hall. In this will be exhibited all kinds of machines, the greater part of which will be in operation, so that visitors can see what work they do, and how they do it. Steam-boilers and engines are to be set up in this hall to provide the power to set all this machinery going.

I expect there will be machinery in this hall which will do almost everything under the sun that a machine can possibly be made to do. I will not try to imagine, in advance, what will be there, for the reality will be far more astonishing than any one's imagination is likely to be. Just think of fourteen acres of machinery, all in motion at once! There you will see printing, weaving, grinding, sawing, pounding, rolling, stamping, with the buzz and the whirr and the clash and the clatter of thousands of wheels and belts and levers and arms of every kind—of iron and steel and brass hard at work doing all sorts of things and making all sorts of things.

MEMORIAL HALL, OR ART GALLERY.

At a short distance from the Main Building, which stands on a line with the machinery building, is a beautiful edifice, quite different from either of these. This is Memorial Hall, or the Art Gallery. It is an imposing structure of granite, which cost a million and a half dollars, and is intended to remain always as a memento of the Great Exhibition, and to serve as a permanent art gallery. It covers an acre and a half of ground, and is built entirely of stone and iron, so that it is absolutely fire-proof. It would not do to have a building in which will be placed so many valuable paintings and statues, exposed to any danger from fire.

Over the center of this structure, which is of a higher order of architecture than any of the other buildings, most of which are temporary and intended to be taken down when the Great Exhibition is over, is a magnificent dome one hundred and fifty feet high. On the highest point of this dome stands a colossal statue of Columbia.

In this great hall will be collected together thousands of the finest pictures and statues that the artists of the world can produce. The building itself, with its galleries and halls and pavilions and arcades, will be a grand sight in itself. It is estimated that eight thousand people can assemble in this building at one time, but I hope that when

(continued on next page)

you and I are there to look at the pictures and statues, there will be not quite so many spectators present.

To the northward of the three buildings we have already seen, and separated from them by a beautiful little valley with a romantic little stream running through it, stands a very peculiar edifice, built in the Moorish style. This is of marble, iron, and glass, and is called Horticultural Hall.

In the other buildings will be exhibited the wonders of man's art; here we may see the wonders of nature.

Here there will be fruits, flowers, trees, shrubs, and plants from every part of the world. Growing in a climate as soft and mild as that of their native land, may be seen oranges, lemons, palms, and all manner of luxuriant tropical plants; while in parts of the great building will be the most delicious and lovely fruits and flowers, filling the air with their fragrance. In the central portion are four large garden-beds, which are to be filled with the loveliest things that gardeners know how to cultivate; and these gardens can be dug, and raked, and hoed, and weeded, and enjoyed in all weathers; for they are under roof, and protected from all rain and storm. There are many boys and girls, I think, who would consider it a grand thing to have a large garden in the house; one in which they could work at any time in the year, and in all weathers.

Horticultural Hall, like the Art Gallery, is a permanent building, and will be maintained as a grand public conservatory for the citizens of Philadelphia.

The last of the five great buildings is Agricultural Hall. This covers over ten acres of ground, and will be filled with everything that relates to farmers' work all over the world. We know that people in other countries farm in many peculiar ways—different from each other, and from our plans of working. And even in the various sections of our country farm-work and farm products are so entirely different, that it will be of great interest to the people from Maine to see how sugar and cotton are grown, and what they look like in their various stages. There are things, too, which grow in the North which will be quite novel to the people of the South. And we shall all be interested in the farm products of China, Persia, Tunis, Siam, Hawaii, and other far-away countries. We are familiar with the productions of some of these countries, but only in the condition in which they are ready for our use.

This building looks like a great cathedral, or four or five churches crowded into one, and is one of the most peculiar structures on the ground.

Besides these five principal buildings, there are many others, large and imposing in themselves, though inferior in size and appearance to those that we have described.

The United States Government has erected a building which covers more than an acre of ground, in which a great many things appertaining especially to our National Government will be exhibited. There will be, of course, a large collection of materials of war; and already there stands near one entrance of this building a great cannon into which a small boy could easily creep. It is about long enough to accommodate a moderate-sized infant-class.

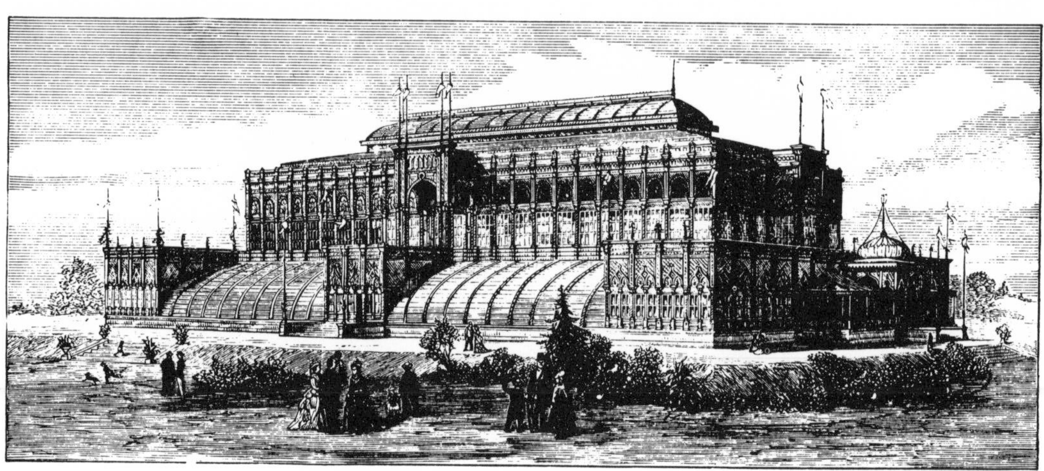

HORTICULTURAL HALL.

Then there will be a Woman's Pavilion, where all sorts of things, illustrating the work that the women of the world are doing, will be shown.

Buildings have been erected by Great Britain

and other countries for the use of the Commissioners who have been sent over to attend to their interests, and many of our States will have separate houses for their officers.

One of the most curious edifices on the ground is one erected for Japan. This has been built entirely by Japanese workmen, and in its construction not a nail or a screw has been used. The boards and timbers are all fitted together in such a way that they need not be screwed or nailed; and yet the building is as firm and strong as any other frame-house, and the joints are all very tight and neat.

It was a curious sight to see the Japanese carpenters at work. They did everything in their own style, just as they were accustomed to work at home. In Japan they do not *push* a plane or a saw, but the workman pulls them toward himself. So these carpenters, when they used American saws, tied cloths around the lower end of the saw-blade, and held the saw by that end, so that the saw-teeth would cut into the wood as they pulled it toward them. They seemed to do everything hind-part foremost. I suppose that if they had used nails they would have driven them in heads first.

AGRICULTURAL BUILDING.

There will also be buildings for photographers, carriage-builders, and many other exhibitors who desire separate accommodations. Six large restaurants will be put up on the grounds, and in some of these we shall have a chance of seeing how the French and other foreign nations cook and serve meals. It is supposed that there will be over two hundred buildings in all, making quite a little town out in Fairmount Park.

Just outside of the Exhibition grounds, a tall observatory, one hundred and fifty feet high, has been erected. Visitors can go to the top of this in an elevator, and then they can see the whole Exhibition spread out before them, and have, besides, a view of the city of Philadelphia and all the beautiful scenery round about.

There are a great many other preparations, either completed or nearly so, for this great Birthday-party which our country is about to give; but I cannot begin to tell you all about them now. It is expected that millions of people will visit these grounds and buildings during the Exhibition, which will continue from the tenth of May until the tenth of November.

The most extensive arrangements have been made for accommodating these vast crowds from all parts of the world. A company has been formed to find board and lodgings in private houses for all visitors who do not want to go to hotels, and a person living in Constantinople or Rio Janeiro, or any other city of the world accessible by railroads or steam-vessels, can buy tickets furnished by this company, which will take him to Philadelphia, where he will be met on the cars, just before he reaches the city, by a messenger, who will conduct him with his baggage to a comfortable room in a house where his meals and lodging will be provided for him for as long a time as he has bargained for.

Of course, it is expected that a great deal of money will be made by those who supply all these people with what they need. Thousands and thousands of dollars have been paid for the privilege of setting up eating-houses, &c., on the grounds, and one man paid seven thousand dollars just for the privilege of selling pop-corn during the Exhibition!

Apart from the vast number of curious and interesting things which may be seen at this Centennial Exhibition, it will be a wonderful thing to

(continued on next page)

see the great multitude of people of all nations which will be collected together there.

To those of us who are not able to travel in foreign countries, it will seem as if those foreign countries had come to us. And surely this is the next best thing to traveling one's self.

And there will be more to see for people who live outside the city of Philadelphia than the great crowds and the great Exhibition. For there, in the city itself, is the Old State House in which Independence was declared, and there is the very room in which the Declaration was signed, and around the room the very chairs in which the signers sat, and on the walls their portraits are hanging. There is the table on which the great paper was signed, and there is the old silver ink-stand which was then used by John Adams, who wrote his name so boldly, and by Stephen Hopkins, whose hand trembled—on account of palsy, not fear—so that he could scarcely write at all, and by all the rest of those brave men. In another room of that Old State House may be seen all sorts of relics of our forefathers: Letters written by Washington, furniture and china and glass-ware used by him; clothes worn by the patriots of the Revolution, and swords and guns carried and used by them, and many other things of the kind, which carry one back to those old days better than the pages of the best book of history that ever was written.

There, too, is to be seen the Old Liberty Bell which was rung when our nation was born, to "proclaim liberty throughout all the land to all the inhabitants thereof."

It is well worth seeing, this grand old bell. It will never ring again, for it is broken; but it has done its duty. We do not need it now, for liberty *is* proclaimed to all the land.

But I cannot tell you about all the curious and interesting things, some belonging to old times and some to new times, that may be seen in Philadelphia. There is one thing, however, that I must mention, because every boy and girl will care to know something about it.

This is the Zoological Garden, where all kinds of animals are to be seen, not shut up in narrow cages, but many of them in such commodious and extensive quarters that their condition must seem to them to be the next best thing to being free. To be sure, the lions and tigers and other savage beasts are in cages; but then they have very large cages, where they can run and jump around and have a good time.

In one of the cages is a large leopard, who is named Commodore Perry, because for three days he commanded the Chesapeake. The "Chesapeake" in this case was a schooner in which the leopard was brought from Africa. He got loose while the ship was lying in the Delaware River, on its arrival at Philadelphia, and everybody speedily departed from the vessel, leaving him in sole command. The schooner was towed out into the middle of the river and anchored. Every plan was tried to coax the leopard on deck and into a cage, but he would not go. Boats rowed around the ship night and day, to kill the animal if he jumped overboard and tried to swim ashore. For three days he held the vessel, but, at last, another vessel was brought near the Chesapeake, and a cage containing a little pig was put on board. The Commodore was very hungry by this time, and, hearing the pig squeak, he bounced on deck and into the cage, the door of which was immediately pulled shut by persons on the other vessel. I do not know whether or not the little pig was jerked out of the cage before the leopard reached it, but I hope it was.

Besides all the wild beasts in the various houses—and most of these have out-door accommodations in warm weather—there are many animals who live altogether in yards in the open air. Five or six big buffaloes roam about in a half-acre lot, and there is even an inclosed stream where the beavers live and where they have built a dam. In another place, with a wire fence around it, is a whole colony of prairie dogs. It is amusing to see these little fellows, sitting up on their hind-legs at the entrances of their underground dwellings, the doors to which are always at the top of a little mound like an enormous ant-hill. In other large inclosures are beautiful deer and antelopes; and there are three great stone pits for the bears, who climb up posts which are planted in the middle of the pits. Then they seem quite near you, but they can't jump from the posts to the edge of the pit.

But if I go on telling about all the things that are to be seen here, there will not be room for anything else in the magazine.

If possible, you must all attend America's Birthday-party. You are all invited, you know. And it will be a hundred years before there is such another celebration.

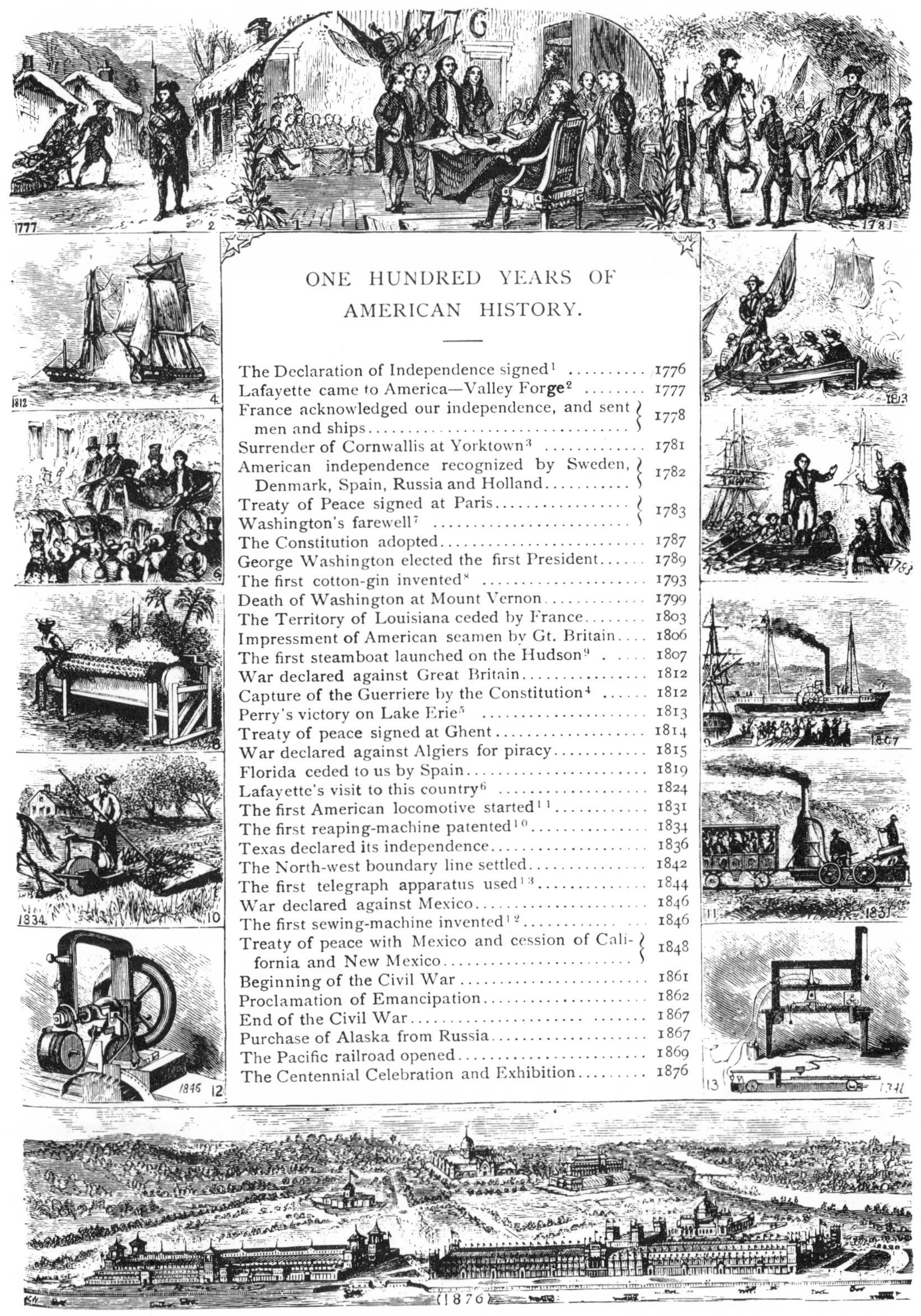

ONE HUNDRED YEARS OF AMERICAN HISTORY.

The Declaration of Independence signed[1]	1776
Lafayette came to America—Valley Forge[2]	1777
France acknowledged our independence, and sent men and ships	1778
Surrender of Cornwallis at Yorktown[3]	1781
American independence recognized by Sweden, Denmark, Spain, Russia and Holland	1782
Treaty of Peace signed at Paris / Washington's farewell[7]	1783
The Constitution adopted	1787
George Washington elected the first President	1789
The first cotton-gin invented[8]	1793
Death of Washington at Mount Vernon	1799
The Territory of Louisiana ceded by France	1803
Impressment of American seamen by Gt. Britain	1806
The first steamboat launched on the Hudson[9]	1807
War declared against Great Britain	1812
Capture of the Guerriere by the Constitution[4]	1812
Perry's victory on Lake Erie[5]	1813
Treaty of peace signed at Ghent	1814
War declared against Algiers for piracy	1815
Florida ceded to us by Spain	1819
Lafayette's visit to this country[6]	1824
The first American locomotive started[11]	1831
The first reaping-machine patented[10]	1834
Texas declared its independence	1836
The North-west boundary line settled	1842
The first telegraph apparatus used[13]	1844
War declared against Mexico	1846
The first sewing-machine invented[12]	1846
Treaty of peace with Mexico and cession of California and New Mexico	1848
Beginning of the Civil War	1861
Proclamation of Emancipation	1862
End of the Civil War	1867
Purchase of Alaska from Russia	1867
The Pacific railroad opened	1869
The Centennial Celebration and Exhibition	1876

SARA CREWE; OR, WHAT HAPPENED AT MISS MINCHIN'S.*

BY FRANCES HODGSON BURNETT.

IN the first place, Miss Minchin lived in London. Her home was a large, dull, tall one, in a large, dull square, where all the houses were alike, and all the sparrows were alike, and where all the door-knockers made the same heavy sound, and on still days — and nearly all the days were still — seemed to resound through the entire row in which the knock was knocked. On Miss Minchin's door there was a brass plate. On the brass plate there was inscribed in black letters,

MISS MINCHIN'S
SELECT SEMINARY FOR YOUNG LADIES.

Little Sara Crewe never went in or out of the house without reading that door-plate and reflecting upon it. By the time she was twelve, she had decided that all her trouble arose because, in the first place, she was not "Select," and in the second, she was not a "Young Lady." When she was eight years old, she had been brought to Miss Minchin as a pupil, and left with her. Her papa had brought her all the way from India. Her mamma had died when she was a baby, and her papa had kept her with him as long as he could. And then, finding the hot climate was making her very delicate, he had brought her to England and left her with Miss Minchin, to be part of the Select Seminary for Young Ladies. Sara, who had always been a sharp little child, who remembered things, recollected hearing him say that he had not a relative in the world whom he knew of, and so he was obliged to place her at a boarding-school, and he had heard Miss Minchin's establishment spoken of very highly. The same day, he took Sara out and bought her a great many beautiful clothes,—clothes so grand and rich that only a very young and inexperienced man would have bought them for a mite of a child who was to be brought up in a boarding-school. But the fact was that he was a rash, innocent young man, and very sad at the thought of parting with his little girl, who was all he had left to remind him of her beautiful mother, whom he had dearly loved. And he wished her to have everything the most fortunate little girl could have; and so, when the polite saleswomen in the shops said, "Here is our very latest thing in hats, the plumes are exactly the same as those we sold to Lady Diana Sinclair yesterday," he immediately bought what was offered to him, and paid whatever was asked. The consequence was that Sara had a most extraordinary wardrobe. Her dresses were silk and velvet and India cashmere, her hats and bonnets were covered with bows and plumes, her small undergarments were adorned with real lace, and she returned in the cab to Miss Minchin's with a doll almost as large as herself, dressed quite as grandly as herself, too.

Then her papa gave Miss Minchin some money and went away, and for several days Sara would neither touch the doll, nor her breakfast, nor her dinner, nor her tea, and would do nothing but crouch in a small corner by the window and cry. She cried so much, indeed, that she made herself ill. She was a queer little child, with old-fashioned ways and strong feelings, and she had adored her papa, and could not be made to think that India and an interesting bungalow were not better for her than London and Miss Minchin's Select Seminary. The instant she had entered the house, she had begun promptly to hate Miss Minchin, and to think little of Miss Amelia Minchin, who was smooth and dumpy, and lisped, and was evidently afraid of her older sister. Miss Minchin was tall, and had large, cold, fishy eyes, and large, cold hands, which seemed fishy, too, because they were damp and made chills run down Sara's back when they touched her, as Miss Minchin pushed her hair off her forehead and said:

"A most beautiful and promising little girl, Captain Crewe. She will be a favorite pupil; *quite* a favorite pupil, I see."

For the first year she was a favorite pupil; at least she was indulged a great deal more than was good for her. And when the Select Seminary went walking, two by two, she was always decked out in her grandest clothes, and led by the hand, at the head of the genteel procession, by Miss

"Sara Crewe," 1887, by Frances Hodgson Burnett (1849–1924).

Mrs. Burnett, who came to the United States from England, had a close association with *St. Nicholas* and with the artist Reginald Birch. Her stories appeared early in book form as well as in the magazine,

Minchin herself. And when the parents of any of the pupils came, she was always dressed and called into the parlor with her doll; and she used to hear Miss Minchin say that her father was a distinguished Indian officer, and she would be heiress to a great fortune. That her father had inherited a great deal of money, Sara had heard before; and also that some day it would be hers, and that he would not remain long in the army, but would come to live in London. And every time a letter came, she hoped it would say he was coming, and they were to live together again.

But about the middle of the third year a letter came bringing very different news. Because he was not a business man himself, her papa had given his affairs into the hands of a friend he trusted. The friend had deceived and robbed him. All the money was gone, no one knew exactly where, and the shock was so great to the poor, rash young officer, that, being attacked by jungle fever shortly afterward, he had no strength to rally, and so died, leaving Sara with no one to take care of her.

Miss Minchin's cold and fishy eyes had never looked so cold and fishy as they did when Sara went into the parlor, on being sent for, a few days after the letter was received.

No one had said anything to the child about mourning, so, in her old-fashioned way, she had decided to find a black dress for herself, and had picked out a black velvet she had outgrown, and came into the room in it, looking the queerest little figure in the world, and a sad little figure, too. The dress was too short and too tight, her face was white, her eyes had dark rings around them, and her doll, wrapped in a piece of old black crape, was held under her arm. She was not a pretty child. She was thin, and had a weird, interesting little face, short black hair, and very large green-gray eyes fringed all around with heavy black lashes.

"I am the ugliest child in the school," she had said once, after staring at herself in the glass for some minutes.

But there had been a clever, good-natured little French teacher who had said to the music-master:

"Zat leetle Crewe. Vat a child! A so ogly beauty! Ze so large eyes; ze so little spirituelle face. Waid till she grow up. You shall see!"

This morning, however, in the tight, small black frock, she looked thinner and odder than ever, and her eyes were fixed on Miss Minchin with a queer steadiness as she slowly advanced into the parlor, clutching her doll.

"Put your doll down!" said Miss Minchin.

"No," said the child, "I won't put her down; I want her with me. She is all I have. She has stayed with me all the time since my papa died."

She had never been an obedient child. She had had her own way ever since she was born, and there was about her an air of silent determination under which Miss Minchin had always felt secretly uncomfortable. And that lady felt even now that perhaps it would be as well not to insist on her point. So she looked at her as severely as possible.

"You will have no time for dolls in future," she said; "you will have to work and improve yourself, and make yourself useful."

Sara kept the big odd eyes fixed on her teacher and said nothing.

"Everything will be very different now," Miss Minchin went on. "I sent for you to talk to you and make you understand. Your father is dead. You have no friends. You have no money. You have no home and no one to take care of you."

The little pale olive face twitched nervously, but the green-gray eyes did not move from Miss Minchin's, and still Sara said nothing.

"What are you staring at?" demanded Miss Minchin sharply. "Are you so stupid you don't understand what I mean? I tell you that you are quite alone in the world, and have no one to do anything for you, unless I choose to keep you here."

The truth was, Miss Minchin was in her worst mood. To be suddenly deprived of a large sum of money yearly and a show pupil, and to find herself with a little beggar on her hands, was more than she could bear with any degree of calmness.

"Now listen to me," she went on, "and remember what I say. If you work hard and prepare to make yourself useful in a few years, I shall let you stay here. You are only a child, but you are a sharp child, and you pick up things almost without being taught. You speak French very well, and in a year or so you can begin to help with the younger pupils. By the time you are fifteen you ought to be able to do that much at least."

"I can speak French better than you, now," said Sara; "I always spoke it with my papa in India." Which was not at all polite, but was painfully true; because Miss Minchin could not speak French at all, and, indeed, was not in the least a clever person. But she was a hard, grasping business woman, and, after the first shock of disappointment, had seen that at very little expense to herself she might prepare this clever, determined child to be very useful to her and save her the necessity of paying large salaries to teachers of languages.

"Don't be impudent, or you will be punished," she said. "You will have to improve your manners if you expect to earn your bread. You are not a parlor boarder now. Remember, that if you don't please me, and I send you away, you have no home but the street. You can go now."

Sara turned away.

and are still widely read. *Sara Crewe; or, What Happened at Miss Minchin's* (1888) was later dramatized and then rewritten, with added characters, as *A Little Princess. Little Lord Fauntleroy* appeared in the magazine in 1885–1886, and as a book in 1886; *The Secret Garden* was published in 1911.

(continued on next page)

"Stay," commanded Miss Minchin, "don't you intend to thank me?"

Sara turned toward her. The nervous twitch was to be seen again in her face, and she seemed to be trying to control it.

"What for?" she said.

"For my kindness to you," replied Miss Minchin. "For my kindness in giving you a home."

Sara went two or three steps nearer to her. Her thin little chest was heaving up and down, and she spoke in a strange, unchildish voice.

"You are not kind," she said. "You are not kind." And she turned again and went out of the room, leaving Miss Minchin staring after her strange, small figure in stony anger.

The child walked up the staircase, holding tightly to her doll; she meant to go to her bedroom, but at the door she was met by Miss Amelia.

"You are not to go in there," she said. "That is not your room now."

"Where is my room?" asked Sara.

"You are to sleep in the attic next to the cook."

Sara walked on. She mounted two flights more, and reached the door of the attic room, opened it and went in, shutting it behind her. She stood against it and looked about her. The room was slanting-roofed and whitewashed; there was a rusty grate, an iron bedstead, and some odd articles of furniture, sent up from better rooms below, where they had been used until they were considered to be worn out. Under the skylight in the roof, which showed nothing but an oblong piece of dull gray sky, there was a battered old red footstool.

Sara went to it and sat down. She was a queer child, as I have said before, and quite unlike other children. She seldom cried. She did not cry now. She laid her doll, Emily, across her knees, and put her face down upon her, and her arms around her, and sat there, her little black head resting on the black crape, not saying one word, not making one sound.

From that day her life changed entirely. Sometimes she used to feel as if it must be another life altogether, the life of some other child. She was a little drudge and outcast; she was given her lessons at odd times and expected to learn without being taught; she was sent on errands by Miss Minchin, Miss Amelia, and the cook. Nobody took any notice of her except when they ordered her about. She was often kept busy all day and then sent into the deserted school-room with a pile of books to learn her lessons or practice at night. She had never been intimate with the other pupils, and soon she became so shabby that, taking her queer clothes together with her queer little ways, they began to look upon her as a being of another world than their own. The fact was that, as a rule, Miss Minchin's pupils were rather dull, matter-of-fact young people, accustomed to being rich and comfortable; and Sara, with her elfish cleverness, her desolate life, and her odd habit of fixing her eyes upon them and staring them out of countenance, was too much for them.

"She always looks as if she was finding you out," said one girl, who was sly and given to making mischief. "I am," said Sara, promptly, when she heard of it. "That 's what I look at them for. I like to know about people. I think them over afterward."

She never made any mischief herself or interfered with any one. She talked very little, did as she was told, and thought a great deal. Nobody knew, and in fact nobody cared, whether she was unhappy or happy, unless, perhaps, it was Emily, who lived in the attic and slept on the iron bedstead at night. Sara thought Emily understood her feelings, though she was only wax and had a habit of staring herself. Sara used to talk to her at night.

"You are the only friend I have in the world," she would say to her. "Why don't you say something? Why don't you speak? Sometimes I 'm sure you could, if you would try. It ought to make you try, to know you are the only thing I have. If I were you, I should try. Why don't you try?"

It really was a very strange feeling she had about Emily. It arose from her being so desolate. She did not like to own to herself that her only friend, her only companion, could feel and hear nothing. She wanted to believe, or to pretend to believe, that Emily understood and sympathized with her, that she heard her even though she did not speak in answer. She used to put her in a chair sometimes and sit opposite to her on the old red footstool, and stare at her and think and pretend about her until her own eyes would grow large with something which was almost like fear, particularly at night, when the garret was so still, when the only sound that was to be heard was the occasional squeak and skurry of rats in the wainscot. There were rat-holes in the garret, and Sara detested rats, and was always glad Emily was with her when she heard their hateful squeak and rush and scratching. One of her "pretends" was that Emily was a kind of good witch and could protect her. Poor little Sara! everything was "pretend" with her. She had a strong imagination; there was almost more imagination than there was Sara, and her whole forlorn, uncared-for child-life was made up of imaginings. She imagined and pretended things until she almost believed them, and she would scarcely have been surprised at any remarkable thing that could have happened. So she insisted to herself

"SHE SLOWLY ADVANCED INTO THE PARLOR, CLUTCHING HER DOLL."

that Emily understood all about her troubles and was really her friend.

"As to answering," she used to say, "I don't answer very often. I never answer when I can help it. When people are insulting you, there is nothing so good for them as not to say a word —

(continued on next page)

just to look at them and *think*. Miss Minchin turns pale with rage when I do it, Miss Amelia looks frightened, so do the girls. They know you are stronger than they are, because you are strong enough to hold in your rage and they are not, and they say stupid things they wish they had n't said, afterward. There 's nothing so strong as rage, except what makes you hold it in — that 's stronger. It 's a good thing not to answer your enemies. I scarcely ever do. Perhaps Emily is more like me than I am like myself. Perhaps she would rather not answer her friends, even. She keeps it all in her heart."

But though she tried to satisfy herself with these arguments, Sara did not find it easy. When, after a long, hard day, in which she had been sent here and there, sometimes on long errands, through wind and cold and rain; and, when she came in wet and hungry, had been sent out again because nobody chose to remember that she was only a child, and that her thin little legs might be tired, and her small body, clad in its forlorn too small finery, all too short and too tight, might be chilled; when she had been given only harsh words and cold, slighting looks for thanks; when the cook had been vulgar and insolent; when Miss Minchin had been in her worst moods, and when she had seen the girls sneering at her among themselves and making fun of her poor, outgrown clothes,— then Sara did not find Emily quite all that her sore, proud, desolate little heart needed as the doll sat in her old chair and stared.

One of these nights, when she came up to the garret cold, hungry, tired, and with a tempest raging in her small breast, Emily's stare seemed so vacant, her sawdust legs and arms so limp and inexpressive, that Sara lost all control over herself.

"I shall die presently!" she said at first.

Emily stared.

"I can't bear this!" said the poor child, trembling. "I know I shall die. I 'm cold, I 'm wet, I 'm starving to death. I 've walked a thousand miles to-day, and they have done nothing but scold me from morning until night. And because I could not find that last thing they sent me for, they would not give me any supper. Some men laughed at me because my old shoes made me slip down in the mud. I 'm covered with mud now. And they laughed! Do you *hear?*"

She looked at the staring glass eyes and complacent wax face, and suddenly a sort of heart-broken rage seized her. She lifted her little savage hand and knocked Emily off the chair, bursting into a passion of sobbing.

"You are nothing but a Doll!" she cried. "Nothing but a Doll — Doll — Doll! You care for nothing. You are stuffed with sawdust. You never had a heart. Nothing could ever make you feel. You are a *Doll!*" Emily lay upon the floor, with her legs ignominiously doubled up over her head, and a new flat place on the end of her nose; but she was still calm, even dignified.

Sara hid her face on her arms and sobbed. Some rats in the wall began to fight and bite each other, and squeak and scramble. But, as I have already intimated, Sara was not in the habit of crying. After a while she stopped, and when she stopped, she looked at Emily, who seemed to be gazing at her around the side of one ankle, and actually with a kind of glassy-eyed sympathy. Sara bent and picked her up. Remorse overtook her.

"You can't help being a doll," she said, with a resigned sigh, "any more than those girls downstairs can help not having any sense. We are not all alike. Perhaps you do your sawdust best."

None of Miss Minchin's young ladies were very remarkable for being brilliant; they were Select, but some of them were very dull, and some of them were fond of applying themselves to their lessons. Sara, who snatched her lessons at all sorts of untimely hours from tattered and discarded books, and who had a hungry craving for everything readable, was often severe upon them in her small mind. They had books they never read; she had no books at all. If she had always had something to read, she would not have been so lonely. She liked romances and history and poetry; she would read anything. There was a sentimental housemaid in the establishment who bought the weekly penny papers, and subscribed to a circulating library, from which she got greasy volumes containing stories of marquises and dukes who invariably fell in love with orange-girls and gypsies and servant-maids, and made them the proud brides of coronets; and Sara often did parts of this maid's work, so that she might earn the privilege of reading these romantic histories. There was also a fat, dull pupil, whose name was Ermengarde St. John, who was one of her resources. Ermengarde had an intellectual father who, in his despairing desire to encourage his daughter, constantly sent her valuable and interesting books, which were a continual source of grief to her. Sara had once actually found her crying over a big package of them.

"What is the matter with you?" she asked her, perhaps rather disdainfully.

And it is just possible she would not have spoken to her, if she had not seen the books. The sight of books always gave Sara a hungry feeling, and she could not help drawing near to them if only to read their titles.

"What is the matter with you?" she asked.

"My papa has sent me some more books,"

answered Ermengarde wofully, "and he expects me to read them."

"Don't you like reading?" said Sara.

"I hate it!" replied Miss Ermengarde St. John. "And he will ask me questions when he sees me; he will want to know how much I remember; how would *you* like to have to read all those?"

"I'd like it better than anything else in the world," said Sara.

Ermengarde wiped her eyes to look at such a prodigy.

"Oh, gracious!" she exclaimed.

Sara returned the look with interest. A sudden plan formed itself in her sharp mind.

"Look here!" she said. "If you'll lend me those books, I'll read them and tell you everything that's in them afterward, and I'll tell it to you so that you will remember it. I know I can. The A B C children always remember what I tell them."

"Oh, goodness!" said Ermengarde. "Do you think you could?"

"I know I could," answered Sara. "I like to read, and I always remember. I'll take care of the books, too; they will look just as new as they do now, when I give them back to you."

Ermengarde put her handkerchief in her pocket.

"If you'll do that," she said, "and if you'll make me remember, I'll give you — I'll give you some money."

"I don't want your money," said Sara, "I want your books — I want them." And her eyes grew big and queer, and her chest heaved once.

"Take them, then," said Ermengarde; "I wish I wanted them, but I am not clever, and my father is, and he thinks I ought to be."

Sara picked up the books and marched off with them. But when she was at the door, she stopped and turned round.

"What are you going to tell your father?" she asked.

"Oh," said Ermengarde, "he need n't know; he'll think I've read them."

Sara looked down at the books; her heart really began to beat fast.

"I won't do it," she said rather slowly, "if you are going to tell him lies about it — I don't like lies. Why can't you tell him I read them and then told you about them?"

"But he wants me to read them," said Ermengarde.

"He wants you to know what is in them," said Sara; "and if I can tell it to you in an easy way and make you remember, I should think he would like that."

"He would like it better if I read them myself," replied Ermengarde.

"He will like it, I dare say, if you learn anything in any way," said Sara. "I should, if I were your father."

And though this was not a flattering way of stating the case, Ermengarde was obliged to admit it was true, and, after a little more argument, gave in. And so she used afterward always to hand over her books to Sara, and Sara would carry them to her garret and devour them; and after she had read each volume, she would return it and tell Ermengarde about it in a way of her own. She had a gift for making things interesting. Her imagination helped her to make everything rather like a story, and she managed this matter so well that Miss St. John gained more information from her books than she would have gained if she had read them three times over by her poor stupid little self. When Sara sat down by her and began to tell some story of travel or history, she made the travelers and historical people seem real; and Ermengarde used to sit and regard her dramatic gesticulations, her thin little flushed cheeks and her shining odd eyes, with amazement.

"It sounds nicer than it seems in the book," she would say. I never cared about Mary, Queen of Scots, before, and I always hated the French Revolution, but you make it seem like a story."

"It is a story," Sara would answer. "They are all stories. Everything is a story — everything in this world. You are a story — I am a story — Miss Minchin is a story. You can make a story out of anything."

"I can't," said Ermengarde.

Sara stared at her a minute reflectively.

"No," she said at last. "I suppose you could n't. You are a little like Emily."

"Who is Emily?"

Sara recollected herself. She knew she was sometimes rather impolite in the candor of her remarks, and she did not want to be impolite to a girl who was not unkind — only stupid. Notwithstanding all her sharp little ways, she had the sense to wish to be just to everybody. In the hours she spent alone, she used to argue out a great many curious questions with herself. One thing she had decided upon was, that a person who was clever ought to be clever enough not to be unjust or deliberately unkind to any one. Miss Minchin was unjust and cruel, Miss Amelia was unkind and spiteful, the cook was malicious and hasty-tempered — they all were stupid, and made her despise them, and she desired to be as unlike them as possible. So she would be as polite as she could to people who in the least deserved politeness.

"Emily is — a person — I know," she replied.

"Do you like her?" asked Ermengarde.

"Yes, I do," said Sara.

Ermengarde examined her queer little face and

(continued on next page)

figure again. She did look odd. She had on, that day, a faded blue plush skirt, which barely covered her knees, a brown cloth sacque, and a pair of olive-green stockings which Miss Minchin had made her piece out with black ones, so that they would be long enough to be kept on. And yet Ermengarde was beginning slowly to admire her. Such a forlorn, thin, neglected little thing as that, who could read and read and remember and tell you things so that they did not tire you all out! A child who could speak French, and who had learned German, no one knew how! One could not help staring at her and feeling interested, particularly one to whom the simplest lesson was a trouble and a woe.

"Do you like *me?*" said Ermengarde, finally, at the end of her scrutiny.

Sara hesitated one second, then she answered:

"I like you because you are not ill-natured—I like you for letting me read your books—I like you because you don't make spiteful fun of me for what I can't help. It 's not your fault that——"

She pulled herself up quickly. She had been going to say, "that you are stupid."

"That what?" asked Ermengarde.

"That you can't learn things quickly. If you can't, you can't. If I can, why, I can—that 's all." She paused a minute, looking at the plump face before her, and then, rather slowly, one of her wise, old-fashioned thoughts came to her.

"Perhaps," she said, "to be able to learn things quickly, is n't everything. To be kind is worth a good deal to other people. If Miss Minchin knew everything on earth, which she does n't, and if she was like what she is now, she 'd still be a detestable thing, and everybody would hate her. Lots of clever people have done harm and been wicked. Look at Robespierre——"

She stopped again, and examined her companion's countenance.

"Do you remember about him?" she demanded. "I believe you 've forgotten."

"Well, I don't remember *all* of it," admitted Ermengarde.

"Well," said Sara with courage and determination, "I 'll tell it to you over again."

And she plunged once more into the gory records of the French Revolution, and told such stories of it, and made such vivid pictures of its horrors, that Miss St. John was afraid to go to bed afterward, and hid her head under the blankets when she did go, and shivered until she fell asleep. But afterward she preserved lively recollections of the character of Robespierre, and did not even forget Marie Antoinette and the Princess de Lamballe.

"You know they put her head on a pike and danced around it," Sara had said; "and she had beautiful blonde hair; and when I think of her, I never see her head on her body, but always on a pike, with those furious people dancing and howling."

Yes, it was true, to this imaginative child everything was a story; and the more books she read, the more imaginative she became. One of her chief entertainments was to sit in her garret, or walk about it, and "suppose" things. On a cold night, when she had not had enough to eat, she would draw the red footstool up before the empty grate, and say in the most intense voice:

"Suppose there was a great, wide steel grate here, and a great glowing fire—a *glowing* fire—with beds of red-hot coal and lots of little dancing, flickering flames. Suppose there was a soft, deep rug, and this was a comfortable chair, all cushions and crimson velvet; and suppose I had a crimson velvet frock on, and a deep lace collar, like a child in a picture; and suppose all the rest of the room was furnished in lovely colors, and there were bookshelves full of books, which changed by magic as soon as you had read them; and suppose there was a little table here, with a snow-white cover on it, and little silver dishes, and in one there was hot, hot soup, and in another a roast chicken, and in another some raspberry-jam tarts with criss-cross on them, and in another some grapes; and suppose Emily could speak, and we could sit and eat our supper, and then talk and read; and then suppose there was a soft, warm bed in the corner, and when we were tired, we could go to sleep, and sleep as long as we liked."

Sometimes, after she had supposed things like these for half an hour, she would feel almost warm, and would creep into bed with Emily and fall asleep with a smile on her face.

"What large, downy pillows!" she would whisper. "What white sheets and fleecy blankets!" And she almost forgot that her real pillows had scarcely any feathers in them at all, and smelled musty, and that her blankets and coverlid were thin and full of holes.

At another time she would "suppose" she was a princess, and then she would go about the house with an expression on her face which was a source of great secret annoyance to Miss Minchin, because it seemed as if the child scarcely heard the spiteful, insulting things said to her, or, if she heard them, did not care for them at all. Sometimes, while she was in the midst of some harsh and cruel speech, Miss Minchin would find the odd, unchildish eyes fixed upon her with something like a proud smile in them. At such times she did not know that Sara was saying to herself:

"You don't know that you are saying these

"SHE LAID HER DOLL, EMILY, ACROSS HER KNEES, AND PUT HER FACE DOWN UPON HER, AND HER ARMS AROUND HER, AND SAT THERE, HER LITTLE BLACK HEAD RESTING ON THE BLACK CRAPE, NOT SAYING ONE WORD, NOT MAKING ONE SOUND."

(continued on next page)

things to a princess, and that if I chose, I could wave my hand and order you to execution. I only spare you because I *am* a princess, and you are a poor, stupid, old, vulgar thing, and don't know any better."

This used to please and amuse her more than anything else; and, queer and fanciful as it was, she found comfort in it, and it was not a bad thing for her. It really kept her from being made rude and malicious by the rudeness and malice of those about her.

"A princess must be polite," she said to herself. And so when the servants, who took their tone from their mistress, were insolent and ordered her about, she would hold her head erect, and reply to them sometimes in a way which made them stare at her, it was so quaintly civil.

"I am a princess in rags and tatters," she would think, "but I am a princess, inside. It would be easy to be a princess if I were dressed in cloth-of-gold; it is a great deal more of a triumph to be one all the time when no one knows it. There was Marie Antoinette: when she was in prison, and her throne was gone, and she had only a black gown on, and her hair was white, and they insulted her and called her the Widow Capet,—she was a great deal more like a queen then than when she was so gay and had everything grand. I like her best then. Those howling mobs of people did not frighten her. She was stronger than they were, even when they cut her head off."

Once when such thoughts were passing through her mind, the look in her eyes so enraged Miss Minchin that she flew at Sara and boxed her ears.

Sara wakened from her dream, started a little, and then broke into a laugh.

"What are you laughing at, you bold, impudent child!" exclaimed Miss Minchin.

It took Sara a few seconds to remember she was a princess. Her cheeks were red and smarting from the blows she had received.

"I was thinking," she said.

"Beg my pardon immediately," said Miss Minchin.

"I will beg your pardon for laughing, if it was rude," said Sara; "but I won't beg your pardon for thinking."

"What were you thinking?" demanded Miss Minchin. "How dare you think? What were you thinking?"

This occurred in the school-room, and all the girls looked up from their books to listen. It always interested them when Miss Minchin flew at Sara, because Sara always said something queer, and never seemed in the least frightened. She was not in the least frightened now, though her boxed ears were scarlet, and her eyes were as bright as stars.

"I was thinking," she answered gravely and quite politely, "that you did not know what you were doing."

"That I did not know what I was doing!" Miss Minchin fairly gasped.

"Yes," said Sara, "and I was thinking what would happen, if I were a princess and you boxed my ears—what I should do to you. And I was thinking that if I were one, you would never dare to do it, whatever I said or did. And I was thinking how surprised and frightened you would be if you suddenly found out ——"

She had the imagined picture so clearly before her eyes, that she spoke in a manner which had an effect even on Miss Minchin. It almost seemed for the moment to her narrow unimaginative mind that there must be some real power behind this candid daring.

"What?" she exclaimed; "found out what?"

"That I really was a princess," said Sara, "and could do anything—anything I liked."

"Go to your room," cried Miss Minchin breathlessly, "this instant. Leave the school-room. Attend to your lessons, young ladies."

Sara made a little bow.

"Excuse me for laughing, if it was impolite," she said, and walked out of the room, leaving Miss Minchin in a rage and the girls whispering over their books.

"I should n't be at all surprised if she did turn out to be something," said one of them. "Suppose she should!"

(To be continued.)

After Sara's banishment to the attic of Miss Minchin's School, she suffered many hardships. But, fortunately, the "Indian Gentleman" next door, with whose servant she had become friendly, discovered her plight, and this led to the revelation that Sara's father had, indeed, not lost all his money.

This famous story is still in print under the title of *A Little Princess*—from J. B. Lippincott, with Tasha Tudor's illustrations, and as a paperback, illustrated by Ethel Franklin Betts, from Scribner's—with the subtitle, *Being the Whole Story of Sara Crewe Now Told for the First Time.* This is Frances Hodgson Burnett's longer version (1905), based on her play of that title, with added characters. As *Sara Crewe,* the story is in print as a Scholastic paperback.

ON OPPOSITE PAGE:

"The Admiral's Caravan," 1891, by Charles E. Carryl (1841–1920).

Inspired by Mother Goose, Lewis Carroll, and his own children, Carryl produced *The Admiral's Caravan* with its ebullient verses

By Charles E. Carryl.

CHAPTER I.

DOROTHY AND THE ADMIRAL.

The Blue Admiral Inn stood on the edge of the shore, with its red brick walls, and its gabled roof, and the old willow-trees that overhung it, all reflected in the quiet water as if the harbor had been a great mirror lying upon its back in the sun. This made it a most attractive place to look at. Then there were crisp little dimity curtains hanging in the windows of the coffee-room and giving great promise of tidiness and comfort within, and this made it a most delightful place to think about. And then there was a certain suggestion of savory cooking in the swirl of the smoke that came out of the chimneys, and this made it a most difficult place to stay away from. In fact, if any ships had chanced to come into the little harbor, I believe everybody on board of them, from the captains down to the cabin-boys, would have scrambled into the boats the moment the anchors were down and pulled away for the Blue Admiral Inn.

But, so far as ships were concerned, the harbor was as dead as a door-nail, and poor old Uncle Porticle, who kept the inn, had long ago given up all idea of expecting them, and had fallen into a melancholy habit of standing in the little porch that opened on the village street, gazing first to the right and then to the left, and lastly at the opposite side of the way, as if he had a faint hope that certain seafaring men were about to steal a march upon him from the land-side of the town. And Dorothy, who was a lonely little child, with no one in the world to care for but Uncle Porticle, had also fallen into a habit of sitting on

88

illustrated here. It appeared in book form in 1891. Earlier, this New York stockbroker had written *Davy and the Goblin* (1884), also serialized in *St. Nicholas.*

(continued on next page)

the step of the porch by way of keeping him company; and here they passed many quiet hours together, with the big robin hopping about in his cage, and with the Admiral himself, on his pedestal beside the porch, keeping watch and ward over the fortunes of the inn.

THE ADMIRAL.

Now the Admiral was only a yard high, and was made of wood into the bargain; but he was a fine figure of a man for all that, dressed in a snug blue coat (as befitted his name) and canary-colored knee-breeches, and wearing a fore-and-aft hat rakishly perched on the back of his head. On the other hand, he had sundry stray cracks in the calves of his legs and was badly battered about the nose; but, after all, this only gave him a certain weather-beaten appearance as if he had been around the world any number of times; and for as long as Dorothy could remember he had been standing on his pedestal beside the porch, enjoying the sunshine and defying the rain, as a gallant officer should, and earnestly gazing at the opposite side of the street through a spy-glass.

Now, what the Admiral was staring at was a mystery. He might, for instance, have been looking at the wooden Highlander that stood at the door of Mr. Pendle's instrument-shop, for nothing more magnificent than this particular Highlander could possibly be imagined. His clothes were of every color of the rainbow, and he had silver buckles on his shoes, and he was varnished to such an extent that you could hardly look at him without winking; and, what was more, he had been standing for years at the door of the shop, proudly holding up a preposterous wooden watch that gave half-past three as the correct time at all hours of the day and night. In fact, it would have been no great wonder if the Admiral had stared at him to the end of his days.

Then there was Sir Walter Rosettes, a long-bodied little man in a cavalier's cloak, with a ruff about his neck and enormous rosettes on his shoes, who stood on a pedestal at old Mrs. Peevy's garden gate, offering an imitation tobacco-plant, free of charge, as it were, to any one who would take the trouble of carrying it home. This bold device was intended to call attention to the fact that Mrs. Peevy kept a tobacco-shop in the front parlor of her little cottage behind the hollyhock bushes, the announcement being backed up by the spectacle of three pipes arranged in a tripod in the window, and by the words "Smokers' Emporium" displayed in gold letters on the glass. Dorothy knew perfectly well who *this* little man was, as somebody had taken the trouble of writing his name with a lead-pencil on his pedestal just below the toes of his shoes.

THE HIGHLANDER.

And lastly there was old Mrs. Peevy herself, who might be seen at any hour of the day, sitting at the door of her cottage, fast asleep in the shade of her big cotton umbrella with the Chinese mandarin for a handle. She was n't much to look at, perhaps, but there was no way of getting at the Admiral's taste in such matters, so he stared through his spy-glass year in and year out, and nobody was any the wiser.

Now from sitting so much in the porch,

Dorothy had come to know the Admiral and the Highlander and Sir Walter Rosettes as well as she could possibly know people who did n't

SIR WALTER ROSETTES.

know her and who could n't have spoken to her if they *had* known her; but nothing came of the acquaintance until a certain Christmas eve. Of course, nobody knew better than Dorothy what Christmas eve should be like. The snow should be falling softly, and just enough should come down to cover up the pavements and make the streets look beautifully white and clean, and to edge the trees and the lamp-posts and the railings as if they were trimmed with soft lace; and just enough to tempt children to come out, and not so much as to keep grown people at home — in fact, just enough for Christmas eve, and not a bit more. Then the streets should be full of people hurrying along and all carrying plenty of parcels; and the windows should be very gay with delightful wreaths of greens and bunches of holly with plenty of scarlet berries on them, and the greengrocers should have little forests of assorted hemlock-trees on the sidewalks in front of their shops, and everything should be cheerful and bustling. And, if you liked, there might be just a faint smell of cooking in the air, but this was not important by any means.

Well, all these good old-fashioned things came to pass on this particular Christmas eve except the snow; and in place of that there came a soft, warm rain which was all very well in its way, except that, as Dorothy said, "It did n't belong on Christmas eve." And just at nightfall she went out into the porch to smell the rain, and to see how Christmas matters generally were getting on in the wet; and she was watching the people hurrying by, and trying to fancy what was in the mysterious-looking parcels they were carrying under their umbrellas, when she suddenly noticed that the toes of the Admiral's shoes were turned sideways on his pedestal, and looking up at him she saw that he had tucked his spy-glass under his arm and was gazing down backward at his legs with an air of great concern. This was so startling that Dorothy almost jumped out of her shoes, and she was just turning to run back into the house when the Admiral caught sight of her and called out excitedly, "Cracks in my legs!" — and then

"THE ADMIRAL MADE A DESPERATE ATTEMPT TO GET A VIEW OF HIS LEGS THROUGH HIS SPY-GLASS."

(continued on next page)

stared hard at her as if demanding some sort of an explanation.

Dorothy was dreadfully frightened, but she was a very polite little girl, and would have answered the town pump if it had spoken to her; so she swallowed down a great lump that had come up into her throat, and said, as respectfully as she could, "I 'm very sorry, sir. I suppose it must be because they are so very old."

"Old!" exclaimed the Admiral, making a desperate attempt to get a view of his legs through his spy-glass. "Why, they 're no older than *I* am"; and, upon thinking it over, this seemed so very true that Dorothy felt quite ashamed of her remark and stood looking at him in a rather foolish way.

"Try again," said the Admiral, with a patronizing air.

"No," said Dorothy, gravely shaking her head. "I 'm sure I don't know any other reason; only it seems rather strange, you know, that you 've never even seen them before."

"If you mean my legs," said the Admiral, "of course I 've seen them before — lots of times. But I 've never seen 'em behind. That is," he added by way of explanation, "I 've never seen 'em behind before."

"But I mean the cracks," said Dorothy, with a faint smile. You see she was beginning to feel a little acquainted with the Admiral, and the conversation did n't seem to be quite so solemn as it had been.

"Then you should say 'seen 'em before *behind*,'" said the Admiral. "That 's where they 've always been, you know."

Dorothy did n't know exactly what reply to make to this remark; but she thought she ought to say something by way of helping along the conversation, so she began, "I suppose it 's kind of——" and here she stopped to think of the word she wanted.

"Kind of what?" said the Admiral severely.

"Kind of — cripplesome, is n't it?" said Dorothy rather confusedly.

"Cripplesome?" exclaimed the Admiral. "Why, that 's no word for it. It 's positively decrepitoodle——" here he paused for a moment and got extremely red in the face, and then finished up with "——loodlelarious," and stared hard at her again, as if inquiring what she thought of *that*.

"Goodness!" said Dorothy, drawing a long breath, "what a word!"

"Well, it *is* rather a word," said the Admiral with a very satisfied air. "You see, it means about everything that can happen to a person's legs——" but just here his remarks came abruptly to an end, for as he was strutting about on his pedestal he suddenly slipped off the edge of it and came to the ground flat on his back. Dorothy gave a little scream of dismay; but the Admiral, who did n't appear to be in the least disturbed by this accident, sat up and gazed about with a complacent smile. Then, getting on his feet, he took a pipe out of his pocket, and lit it with infinite relish, and having turned up his coat-collar by way of keeping the rest of his clothes dry, he started off down the street without another word. The people going by had all disappeared in the most unac-

"THE ADMIRAL SAT UP AND GAZED ABOUT WITH A COMPLACENT SMILE."

countable manner, and Dorothy could see him quite plainly as he walked along, tacking from one side of the street to the other with a strange rattling noise, and blowing little puffs of smoke into the air like a shabby little steam-tug going to sea in a storm.

Now all this was extremely exciting, and Dorothy, quite forgetting the rain, ran down the street a little way so as to keep the Admiral in sight. "It 's *precisely* like a doll going traveling all by itself," she exclaimed as she ran along. "How he rattles! I suppose *that* 's his little cracked legs — and goodness gracious, how he smokes!" she added, for by this time the Admiral had fired up, so to speak, as if he were bound on a long journey, and was blowing out such clouds of smoke that he presently quite shut himself out from view. The smoke smelt somewhat like burnt feathers, which, of course, was not very agreeable, but the worst of it was that when Dorothy turned to run home again she discovered that she could n't see her way back to the porch, and she was feeling about for it with her hands stretched out when the smoke suddenly cleared away and she found that the inn, and Mr. Pendle's shop, and Mrs. Peevy's cottage, had all disappeared like a street in a pantomime, and that she was standing quite alone before a strange little stone house.

CHAPTER II.

THE FERRY TO NOWHERE.

THE rain had stopped and the moon was shining through the breaking clouds, and as Dorothy looked up at the little stone house she saw that it had an archway through it with "FERRY" in large letters on the wall above it. Of course she had no idea of going by herself over a strange ferry; but she was an extremely curious little girl, and so she immediately ran through the archway to see what the ferry was like and where it took people, but to her surprise she came out into a strange, old-fashioned looking street lined on both sides by tall houses with sharply peaked roofs looming up against the evening sky.

There was no one in sight but a stork. He was a very tall stork with red legs, and wore a sort of paper bag on his head with "FERRYMAN" written across the front of it; and as Dorothy appeared he held out one of his claws and said, "Fare, please," in quite a matter-of-fact way.

Dorothy was positively certain that she had n't any money, but she put her hand into the pocket of her apron, partly for the sake of appearances and partly because she was a little afraid of the Stork, and, to her surprise, pulled out a large cake. It was nearly as big as a saucer and was marked "ONE BISKER"; and as this seemed to show that it had some value, she handed it to the ferryman. The Stork turned it over several times rather suspiciously, and then, taking a large bite out of it, remarked, "Very good fare," and dropped the rest of it into a little hole in the wall; and having done this he stared gravely at Dorothy for a moment, and then said, "What makes your legs bend the wrong way?"

"Why, they don't!" said Dorothy, looking down at them to see if anything had happened to them.

"They 're entirely different from mine, anyhow," said the Stork.

"But, you know," said Dorothy very earnestly, "I could n't sit down if they bent the other way."

"Sitting down is all very well," said the Stork, with a solemn shake of his head, "but you could n't collect fares with 'em, to save your life," and with this he went into the house and shut the door.

"It seems to me this is a very strange adventure," said Dorothy to herself. "It appears to be mostly about people's legs," and she was gazing down again in a puzzled way at

"'THEY 'RE ENTIRELY DIFFERENT FROM MINE, ANYHOW,' SAID THE STORK."

her little black stockings when she heard a cough, and looking up she saw that the Stork had his head out of a small round window in the wall of the house.

"Look here," he said confidentially, "there 's some poetry about this old ferry. Perhaps you 'd

(continued on next page)

like to hear it." He said this in a sort of husky whisper, and as Dorothy looked up at him it seemed something like listening to an enormous cuckoo-clock with a bad cold in its works.

"Thank you," said Dorothy politely. "I 'd like it very much."

"IT SEEMED LIKE LISTENING TO AN ENORMOUS CUCKOO-CLOCK."

"All right," said the Stork. "The werses is called 'A Ferry Tale'"; and, giving another cough to clear his voice, he began:

Oh, come and cross over to nowhere,
And go where
The nobodies live on their nothing a day!
A tideful of tricks is this merry
Old Ferry,
And these are the things that it does by the way:

It pours into parks and disperses
The nurses.
It goes into gardens and scatters the cats.
It leaks into lodgings, disorders
The boarders,
And washes away with their holiday hats.

It soaks into shops, and inspires
The buyers
To crawl over counters and climb upon chairs.
It trickles on tailors, it spatters
On hatters,
And makes little milliners scamper upstairs.

It goes out of town and it rambles
Through brambles,
It wallows in hollows and dives into dells.
It flows into farm-yards and sickens
The chickens,
And washes the wheelbarrows into the wells.

It turns into taverns and drenches
The benches;
It jumps into pumps and comes out with a roar;
It pounds like a postman at lodges—
Then dodges
And runs up the lane when they open the door.

It leaks into laundries and wrangles
With mangles,
It trips over turnips and tumbles down-hill.
It rolls like a coach along highways
And by-ways;
But never gets anywhere, go as it will!

Oh, foolish old Ferry! all muddles
And puddles—
Go fribble and dribble along on your way;
We drink to your health with molasses
In glasses,
And waft you farewell with a handful of hay!

"What do you make out of it?" inquired the Stork anxiously.

"I don't make anything out of it," said Dorothy, staring at him in great perplexity.

"I did n't suppose you would," said the Stork, apparently very much relieved. "I 've

"'DEAR ME,' SAID DOROTHY TO HERSELF, 'HERE COMES ALL THE FURNITURE!'"

been at it for years and years, and I 've never made sixpence out of it yet," with which remark he quickly pulled in his head and disappeared.

"I don't know what he means, I 'm sure," said Dorothy, after waiting a moment to see if the Stork would come back, "but I would n't go over that ferry for *sixty* sixpences. It 's altogether too frolicky"; and having made this wise resolution, she was just turning to go back through the archway, when the door of the house flew open, and a stream of water poured out so suddenly that she had just time to scramble up on the window-ledge before the street was completely flooded.

"I suppose it 's something wrong with the pipes," she said to herself, in her thoughtful way; "and, dear me, here comes all the furniture!" and, sure enough, a lot of old-fashioned furniture came floating out of the house and drifted away down the street. There was a corner cupboard full of crockery, and two spinning-wheels, and a spindle-legged table set out with a blue-and-white tea-set, and some cups and saucers, and finally a carved sideboard which made two or three clumsy attempts to get through the doorway broadside on, and then took a fresh start, and came through endwise with a great flourish. By this time the water was quite up to the window-ledge, and as the sideboard was a fatherly-looking piece of furniture with plenty of room to move about in, Dorothy stepped aboard of it as it went by, and sitting down on a little shelf that ran along the back of it, sailed away in the wake of the tea-table.

The sideboard behaved in the most absurd manner, spinning around and around in the water, and banging about among the other furniture as if it had never been at sea before, and finally bringing up against the tea-table with a crash and knocking the tea-set and all the cups and saucers into the water.

(To be continued.)

THE BROWNIES IN MASSACHUSETTS.

FOURTH TOUR.

In keeping with the wishes strong
The Brownie band had cherished long,
As shades of evening closed around,
In haste they sought their meeting-ground.
No sooner had the roll been called,
And "here" or "present" each one bawled,
Than one remarked: "'T is well indeed
That all are here now to proceed,
Without delay, to carry through
The plan we long have had in view.
The old 'Bay State' is worthy ground
For us to visit in our round
Of pleasure, traveling here and there
In search of what is strange or fair."
To Boston then the Brownies made
Their way, and soon a visit paid
To Bunker Hill, where one addressed
His comrades when they reached the crest:

43

"The Brownies Through the Union," 1893, by Palmer Cox (1840–1924).

Thirteen books about the famous brownies appeared in the years 1887–1918, many of them having first enlivened the pages of *St. Nicholas.*

"This granite monument
so high
That here is pointing to
the sky,
And draws the traveler's eye
long ere
He comes within the
city fair,
Soon calls to mind the clash
and din
That bright June morning
ushered in,
When up the steep and
slippery slope

With leveled steel came Britain's hope
In even lines, with even tread,
And crimson banners overhead."
Another said: "'T is true, indeed,
As one may on the tablet read,

(continued on next page)

This is the spot where
Warren fell
Upon that day when rang
the bell
Of Freedom through the
startled land,
To call to arms each
valiant band;
Here bravely up the
grassy steep
The British came, in
columns deep,
To backward roll from
volleys hot
Of bullets, slugs, and
partridge-shot,
Or whatsoever men
could pour
Or ram into the
smoking bore."

Soon round and round the winding stair
They ran to climb the tall affair,
To reach the topmost windows small,
And gain a bird's-eye view of all.
How vain are all the arts of man,
However well he lays his plan,
To keep out creatures of the night
And have the sole, exclusive right
To shove a bolt or turn a key
That to the public is not free!

This fact is striking when we note
How easily the Brownies float
Through obstacles that are, at best,
To them but subjects for a jest.
If mortals had the power that they
Upon their nightly rounds display,
The locksmith might take down his sign,
The janitor his place resign,
The watchman sleep the hours away
And let intruders have full sway;
But only Brownies have the skill
Or gift to go thus where they will.
An hour or more their eyes were bent
On scenes around the monument.
It was, indeed, a pleasing sight:
The city in a blaze of light,
With streets and squares and pleasure-grounds
Marked out with lamps to farthest bounds.
They hurried round from place to place
With nimble feet and beaming face;
Now through the Public Gardens strayed,
Then on the Boston Common played,
Until a striking clock would prove
The time had come for them to move.
Upon the old church spire they gazed
Where long ago the signal blazed
That gave the hint to Paul Revere
To mount his steed and disappear

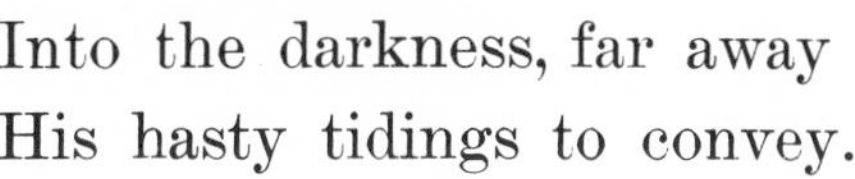

Into the darkness, far away
His hasty tidings to convey.

(continued on next page)

Not satisfied to simply stare
Upon the church from street or square,
The Brownies to the belfry went
To look around; then, well content,

They started off to make a call
On old time-honored Faneuil Hall.
It gave them great delight to range
In freedom through the building strange.
They stood around and "speechified"
From balconies on either side,
And talked about the times when there
The angry people did repair,

THE BROWNIES IN MASSACHUSETTS.

Till every nook and foot of space
Was crowded with the populace.
To Cambridge, with inquiring mind,
The Brownies traveled next, to find
The ancient elm beneath whose shade
Stood Washington to draw his blade,

48

(continued on next page)

With solemn vows to take command
Of his bold, patriotic band.
They tarried there to climb about
And study old inscriptions out,
And then away to Plymouth Rock
The Brownies ran, a lively flock;
For lightly does the Brownie go,
And skims the meadow like a crow,
When there is need of extra haste,
Or few the minutes he can waste.
When that historic spot was found,
In groups the Brownies stood around
To talk about the daring few
Whose spirit nothing could subdue.

However dark the night
may be,
Without a lantern
Brownies see.

They entered boats,
and, pulling out
Some space from shore,
they turned about

And made a rush, to show the way
The Pilgrims acted on that day

When it was counted much to be
The first to place a foot or knee
Upon the rough, though welcome beach,
So far from persecution's reach.
Some jumped while water still was deep,
And down they went to take a peep
At submarine attractions spread
Where clams and lobsters make a bed;
But, rising, found a friendly hand
Prepared to drag them to the land;
For Brownies note each other's woe,
And quickly to the rescue go—
Through flood or fire they 'll dash amain,
Nor let companions call in vain.
They don't look round to see who 'll fling
His coat aside, the first to spring
Without a thought but one—to save
A fellow-creature from the grave:
They go themselves. Thus oft you 'll find
A dozen with a single mind—
Each striving to be first to lend
Assistance to a suffering friend.

A cloud can hide the brightest stars, So trouble oft ones pleasure bars.

Said one, when he had gained the ear
Of dripping comrades standing near:
"No wonder that the Pilgrims drew
A lengthy breath when they got through
The jumping in and crawling out
That marked their landing hereabout;
And much the Indians must have been
Surprised to see those stalwart men

(continued on next page)

So eager to find footing here
Upon the Western Hemisphere."

The Brownies now to Lowell sped,
And then away to Marblehead;
On Salem next their eyes were thrown—
That has a history of its own.
And then to old Nantucket strand
With eager glances moved the band,
Where they could gain no stinted view
Of ocean rolling deep and blue.

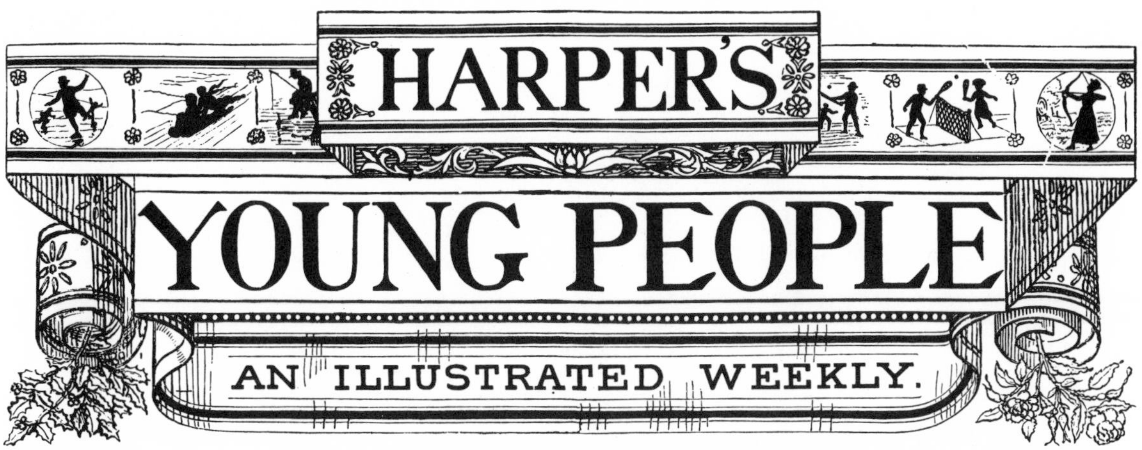
HARPER'S
YOUNG PEOPLE
AN ILLUSTRATED WEEKLY.

VOL. II.—No. 58. PUBLISHED BY HARPER & BROTHERS, NEW YORK. PRICE FOUR CENTS.

Tuesday, December 7, 1880. Copyright, 1880, by HARPER & BROTHERS. $1.50 per Year, in Advance.

HARPER'S YOUNG PEOPLE. Vols. 1–15, Vol. 16, Nos. 1–26, November 4, 1879–April 23, 1895. New York: Harper & Brothers. 29½ cm. The title varies: April 30, 1895–October 1899, Harper's Round Table.

Harper and Brothers began the publication of an "illustrated journal of amusement and instruction," under the editorial guidance of Kirk Munroe, a writer for young people. In competition with the older *St. Nicholas* for twenty years, it presented adventure stories, poetry, articles on art, nature, travel, and miscellaneous features for fun. It attracted the work of Howard Pyle—his *The Merry Adventures of Robin Hood, Men of Iron,* and fairy tales which were later to appear in *The Wonder Clock. Toby Tyler; or, Ten Weeks with a Circus by James Otis* (pseudonym of James Otis Kaler) was serialized, followed by its sequel, *Mr. Stubbs and His Brother.* W. O. Stoddard and Thomas W. Knox contributed boys' stories; and Louisa May Alcott, such tales as "A Christmas Dream, and How It Came About."

Ample illustration gave an attractive look to the magazine: Palmer Cox's "Animal Fables," occasional drawings by Thomas Nast, and Randolph Caldecott's "Hey Diddle Diddle," "The Milk Maid," and other rhymes.

TOBY TYLER; OR, TEN WEEKS WITH A CIRCUS.

BY JAMES OTIS.

TOBY STRIKES A BARGAIN.—Drawn by W. A. Rogers.

CHAPTER I.

TOBY'S INTRODUCTION TO THE CIRCUS.

"COULDN'T you give more'n six pea-nuts for a cent?" was a question asked by a very small boy with big, staring eyes, of a candy vender at a circus booth. And as he spoke he looked wistfully at the quantity of nuts piled high up on the basket, and then at the six, each of which now looked so small as he held them in his hand.

"Couldn't do it," was the reply of the proprietor of the booth, as he put the boy's penny carefully away in the drawer.

The little fellow looked for another moment at his purchase, and then carefully cracked the largest one.

A shade, and a very deep shade it was, of disappointment that passed over his face, and then looking up anxiously, he asked, "Don't you swap 'em when they're bad?"

The man's face looked as if a smile had been a stranger to it

"Toby Tyler; or, Ten Weeks with a Circus," 1880, by James Otis, pseudonym of James Otis Kaler (1848–1912).

This famous circus story appeared in book form in 1881 and was followed by *Mr. Stubbs and His Brother* in 1883. The former is still in print and regarded as a supremely successful picture of circus life.

for a long time; but one did pay it a visit just then, and he tossed the boy two nuts, and asked him a question at the same time. "What is your name?"

The big brown eyes looked up for an instant, as if to learn whether the question was asked in good faith, and then their owner said, as he carefully picked apart another nut, "Toby Tyler."

"Well, that's a queer name."

"Yes, I s'pose so, myself; but, you see, I don't expect that's the name that belongs to me. But the fellers call me so, an' so does Uncle Dan'l."

"Who is Uncle Daniel?" was the next question. In the absence of any more profitable customer the man seemed disposed to get as much amusement out of the boy as possible.

"He hain't my uncle at all; I only call him so because all the boys do, an' I live with him."

"Where's your father and mother?"

"I don't know," said Toby, rather carelessly. "I don't know much about 'em, an' Uncle Dan'l says they don't know much about me. Here's another bad nut; goin' to give me two more?"

The two nuts were given him, and he said, as he put them in his pocket, and turned over and over again those which he held in his hand, "I shouldn't wonder if all of these was bad. Sposen you give me two for each one of 'em before I crack 'em, an' then they won't be spoiled so you can't sell 'em again."

As this offer of barter was made, the man looked amused, and he asked, as he counted out the number which Toby desired, "If I give you these, I suppose you'll want me to give you two more for each one, and you'll keep that kind of a trade going until you get my whole stock?"

"I won't open my head if every one of 'em's bad."

"All right; you can keep what you've got, and I'll give you these besides; but I don't want you to buy any more, for I don't want to do that kind of business."

Toby took the nuts offered, not in the least abashed, and seated himself on a convenient stone to eat them, and at the same time to see all that was going on around him. The coming of a circus to the little town of Guilford was an event, and Toby had hardly thought of anything else since the highly colored posters had first been put up. It was yet quite early in the morning, and the tents were just being erected by the men. Toby had followed, with eager eyes, everything that looked as if it belonged to the circus, from the time the first wagon had entered the town, until the street parade had been made, and everything was being prepared for the afternoon's performance.

The man who had made the losing trade in pea-nuts seemed disposed to question the boy still further, probably owing to the fact that trade was dull, and he had nothing better to do.

"Who is this Uncle Daniel you say you live with--is he a farmer?"

"No; he's a Deacon, an' he raps me over the head with the hymn-book whenever I go to sleep in meetin', an' he says I eat four times as much as I earn. I blame him for hittin' so hard when I go to sleep, but I s'pose he's right about my eatin'. You see," and here his tone grew both confidential and mournful, "I am an awful eater, an' I can't seem to help it. Somehow I'm hungry all the time. I don't seem ever to get enough till carrot-time comes, an' then I can get all I want without troubling anybody."

"Didn't you ever have enough to eat?"

"I s'pose I did, but you see Uncle Dan'l he found me one mornin' on his hay, an' he says I was cryin' for something to eat then, an' I've kept it up ever since. I tried to get him to give me money enough to go into the circus with; but he said a cent was all he could spare these hard times, an' I'd better take that an' buy something to eat with it, for the show wasn't very good anyway. I wish pea-nuts wasn't but a cent a bushel."

"Then you would make yourself sick eating them."

"Yes, I s'pose I should; Uncle Dan'l says I'd eat till I was sick, if I got the chance; but I'd like to try it once."

He was a very small boy, with a round head covered with short red hair, a face as speckled as any turkey's egg, but thoroughly good-natured-looking, and as he sat there on the rather sharp point of the rock, swaying his body to and fro as he hugged his knees with his hands, and kept his eyes fastened on the tempting display of good things before him, it would have been a very hard-hearted man who would not have given him something. But Mr. Job Lord, the proprietor of the booth, was a hard-hearted man, and he did not make the slightest advance toward offering the little fellow anything.

Toby rocked himself silently for a moment, and then he said, hesitatingly, "I don't suppose you'd like to sell me some things, an' let me pay you when I get older, would you?"

Mr. Lord shook his head decidedly at this proposition.

"I didn't s'pose you would," said Toby, quickly; "but you didn't seem to be selling anything, an' I thought I'd just see what you'd say about it." And then he appeared suddenly to see something wonderfully interesting behind him, which served as an excuse to turn his reddening face away.

"I suppose your uncle Daniel makes you work for your living, don't he?" asked Mr. Lord, after he had re-arranged his stock of candy, and had added a couple of slices of lemon peel to what was popularly supposed to be lemonade.

"That's what I think; but he says that all the work I do wouldn't pay for the meal that one chicken would eat, an' I s'pose it's so, for I don't like to work as well as a feller without any father and mother ought to. I don't know why it is, but I guess it's because I take up so much time eatin' that it kinder tires me out. I s'pose you go into the circus whenever you want to, don't you?"

"Oh yes; I'm there at every performance, for I keep the stand under the big canvas as well as this one out here."

There was a great big sigh from out Toby's little round stomach, as he thought what bliss it must be to own all those good things, and to see the circus wherever it went. "It must be nice," he said, as he faced the booth and its hard-visaged proprietor once more.

"How would you like it?" asked Mr. Lord, patronizingly, as he looked Toby over in a business way, very much as if he contemplated purchasing him.

"Like it!" echoed Toby; "why, I'd grow fat on it."

"I don't know as that would be any advantage," continued Mr. Lord, reflectively, "for it strikes me that you're about as fat now as a boy of your age ought to be. But I've a great mind to give you a chance."

"What!" cried Toby, in amazement, and his eyes opened to their widest extent, as this possible opportunity of leading a delightful life presented itself.

"Yes, I've a great mind to give you the chance. You see," and now it was Mr. Lord's turn to grow confidential, "I've had a boy with me this season, but he cleared out at the last town, and I'm running the business alone now."

Toby's face expressed all the contempt he felt for the boy who would run away from such a glorious life as Mr. Lord's assistant must lead; but he said not a word, waiting in breathless expectation for the offer which he now felt certain would be made him.

"Now I ain't hard on a boy," continued Mr. Lord, still confidentially, "and yet that one seemed to think that he was treated worse and made to work harder than any boy in the world."

"He ought to live with Uncle Dan'l a week," said Toby, eagerly.

"Here I was just like a father to him," said Mr. Lord, paying no attention to the interruption, "and I gave him his board and lodging, and a dollar a week besides."

"Could he do what he wanted to with the dollar?"

(continued on next page)

"Of course he could. I never checked him, no matter how extravagant he was, an' yet I've seen him spend his whole week's wages at this very stand in one afternoon. And even after his money had all gone that way, I've paid for peppermint and ginger out of my own pocket just to cure his stomach-ache."

Toby shook his head mournfully, as if deploring that depravity which could cause a boy to run away from such a tender-hearted employer, and from such a desirable position. But even as he shook his head so sadly, he looked wistfully at the pea-nuts, and Mr. Lord observed the look.

It may have been that Mr. Job Lord was the tender-hearted man he prided himself upon being, or it may have been that he wished to purchase Toby's sympathy; but, at all events, he gave him a large handful of nuts, and Toby never bothered his little round head as to what motive prompted the gift. Now he could listen to the story of the boy's treachery and eat at the same time, therefore he was an attentive listener.

"All in the world that boy had to do," continued Mr. Lord, in the same injured tone he had previously used, "was to help me set things to rights when we struck a town in the morning, and then tend to the counter till we left the town at night, and all the rest of the time he had to himself. Yet that boy was ungrateful enough to run away."

Mr. Lord paused as if expecting some expression of sympathy from his listener; but Toby was so busily engaged with his unexpected feast, and his mouth was so full, that it did not seem even possible for him to shake his head.

"Now what should you say if I told you that you looked to me like a boy that was made especially to help run a candy counter at a circus, and if I offered the place to you?"

Toby made one frantic effort to swallow the very large mouthful, and in a choking voice he answered, quickly, "I should say I'd go with you, an' be mighty glad of the chance."

"Then it's a bargain, my boy, and you shall leave town with me to-night."

[TO BE CONTINUED.]

When Toby got into the circus, he found his master to be anything but a kind man. And he had further misery when he had to learn to ride a horse bareback. There was, however, his friend Mr. Stubbs the monkey with whom he was to have real adventures, escaping from the cruelties of the circus.

The book is still in print, published by Harper and Row and by Grosset and Dunlap.

ON OPPOSITE PAGE:
"Sing a Song o' Sixpence," 1880, by Randolph Caldecott (1846–1886).

The rhyme with pictures shown here appeared in *Picture Book No. 2* (1879)—one of the artist's four books with four rhymes each—and also separately as a picture book (1880).

SING A SONG O' SIXPENCE.

DRAWN BY R. CALDECOTT.

SING a Song o' Sixpence,

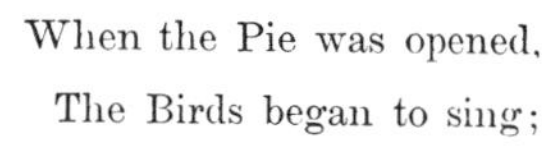

When the Pie was opened,
The Birds began to sing;

A Pocketful of Rye;

Four-and-Twenty Blackbirds
Baked in a Pie.

Was not that a dainty Dish
To set before the King?

(continued on next page)

The King was in his Counting-house
Counting out his Money.

The Maid was in the Garden,
Hanging out the Clothes;

The Queen was in the Parlor,
Eating Bread and Honey.

There came a little Blackbird,

And nipped off her Nose,
But there came a Jenny Wren
And popped it on again.

SING A SONG O' SIXPENCE *(continued from page 441)*

"The Merry Adventures of Robin Hood," 1883, by Howard Pyle (1855–1911).

As a writer of imaginative tales, a reteller of legends, and as an artist, Pyle contributed generously to the magazines. Soon after appearance there, his work found recognition in book form as well. Among these writings were *The Merry Adventures of Robin Hood* (1883); two famous collections of short fairy tales based on folklore motifs—*Pepper and Salt, or, Seasoning for Young Folks* (1886) and *The Wonder Clock; or, Four and Twenty Marvelous Tales* (1888); *Otto of the Silver Hand* (1888); and *Men of Iron* (1892). His famous retellings of the King Arthur legends came later (1903–1910).

(continued on next page)

THE MERRY ADVENTURES OF ROBIN HOOD.

BY HOWARD PYLE.

I.

IN merry England in the time of old, when King Henry II. ruled the land, there lived in Sherwood Forest, in Nottinghamshire, a famous outlaw whose name was Robin Hood. No archers ever lived who could excel him and the sevenscore merrymen that gathered about him, all outlaws like himself.

When Robin Hood was a youth of about eighteen years of age the sheriff of Nottinghamshire proclaimed a shooting match, offering as a prize to the best bowman a cask of stout old ale. Then Robin Hood said to himself, "I will go too"; so up he took his stout bow and a score or more of broadcloth-yard arrows, and started off all in the dawn of a sweet May day, from Locksley Town to Nottingham. Onward he walked briskly until in Sherwood Forest he came upon a party of the King's Foresters, all clad in Lincoln green, and seated beneath the shade of a great oak-tree, making themselves merry over a huge pasty and a barrel of ale.

When they saw Robin one of them called out, "Halloa! where goest thou, little boy, with thy penny bow and thy farthing shafts?"

"Now," quoth Robin, "my bow and eke my arrows are as good as thine, and, moreover, I go to the shooting match at Nottingham Town to try my skill with other yeomen there."

Then all shouted with laughter, and one said, "Why, boy, thou hast scarce lost thy milk-teeth, and yet thou pratest of standing up with the best archers in all Nottinghamshire."

Then Robin grew angry, and, quoth he, "I'll hold the best of ye twenty marks that I cleave the clout at threescore rods."

At this all laughed louder than before, and one cried, "Well boasted, boy, when no target is nigh to make good thy wager."

"Harkee!" cried Robin, his cheeks red with anger; "yonder at the glade's end is a herd of deer. Twenty marks upon it I cause the best hart among them to die."

"Now done!" cried he who had spoken first. "Twenty marks that thou causest no beast to die."

Then Robin took his stout bow and strung it, and drawing a gray-goose shaft to his ear, loosed the string. Straight flew the shaft, and the noblest hart of all the herd leaped aloft and fell dead in the forest path.

"Ha!" cried Robin, "I wot the wager were mine were it a hundred pounds."

Then all the Foresters were filled with rage, and he who had lost the wager was madder than all the rest. "Nay," cried he, "the wager is none of thine, and get thee gone, for by the law of the land thine ears should be clipped close to thy head."

"Catch him!" cried another.

"Nay," said another still, "let him e'en go, because of his tender years."

Never a word said Robin, but he turned on his heel with a grim look and strode away, but his heart was full of anger. Then he who had lost the wager, and whose head was dizzy with ale, seized his bow, and crying, "I'll hurry thee anon," sent an arrow whistling after Robin. But for the ale, Robin had never taken another step, for the arrow whistled within a palm's-breadth of his head. Then he turned quickly, and bending his own bow, sent a shaft back in return. "Ye said I was no archer," cried he, "but say so now again." But the Forester never spake more, for he fell upon the grass, his shafts rattling about him, and Robin's arrow in his heart. But all before the others could gather their wits, the youth was gone.

ROBIN ON HIS WAY TO NOTTINGHAM.

Then the other Foresters lifted the dead man up and bare him away to Nottingham Town.

Meantime Robin ran through the greenwood, and all the joy and brightness was gone from everything, for he had slain a man. "Alas!" cried he, "thou hast found me an archer that will make thy wife wring her hands in sorrow."

So a hundred pounds reward was set upon his head, and he became an outlaw, and lay hidden for two years within Sherwood depths. But in those two years many others joined him, and formed a famous band, and chose him to be their leader and their chief, and many merry adventures they had, as you shall read hereafter.

"Two Opinions," 1883, by Howard Pyle.
This is by Pyle in another mood.

FRANK LESLIE'S CHATTERBOX. Vols. 1–7, 1879–1886. New York: Frank Leslie's Publishing House, 25½ cm. Monthly, January 1879–1886.

Publisher of many magazines, Mr. Leslie was successful in turning this one with its stories, articles, and pictures into the *Chatterbox* annual, in which form its content was more widely read than in the monthly. The annual published in 1886 has the title: *Frank Leslie's Chatter Book*. A British magazine and annual of the same name had been initiated in 1866 and continued publication until 1948.

Vol. I.—No. 5.] MAY, 1879. [Price 10 Cents.—$1 per Year.

FRANK LESLIE'S CHATTERBOX

Entered according to the Act of Congress, in the year 1879, by Frank Leslie, in the Office of the Librarian of Congress at Washington

Frank Leslie's Publishing House, 53, 55 & 57 Park Place, New York.

400 Frank Leslie's Chatterbox.

LITTLE JOHNNY GREEN'S FIRST EXPERIMENT ON STILTS.

1. THINKS ANY ONE CAN DO IT.

2. FINDS IT NOT SO EASY, AFTER ALL.

3. "OH! OH!! OH!!!"

4. "DIDN'T EXPECT THAT."

5. "WELL, NEVER MIND!"

6. "THAT'S THE WAY TO ASTONISH THEM."

7. THINKS HE CAN TAKE A SHORT CUT HOME.

8. THINKS HE CAN'T!

9. "HELLO! HELP!! HELP!!!"

"Little Johnny Green's First Experiment on Stilts," 1879.

Humor was a feature of *Chatterbox,* in addition to stories, poems, and articles.

Immense Success of the New Juvenile Monthly!

FRANK LESLIE'S

CHATTERBOX

The peculiar adaptability of this periodical to the objects intended in its publication has been fully recognized by the heads of families, who find in the **"CHATTERBOX"** *a work which they can confidently place in the hands of the little folks, and consequently the demand is constantly increasing, and it has already attained*

AN IMMENSE CIRCULATION!

In presenting the above monthly publication to our readers, we have three objects in view:

I. The Improvement of the Mind. II. The Diffusion of Knowledge.

III. To provide Good, Healthy and Interesting Literature for the Young.

The **"CHATTERBOX"** *is composed of a choice variety of Sketches, written in a clear and forcible manner, and its numerous Illustrations are of a superior and interesting character.*

Each sketch will convey either a moral or useful information for the young.

The purest tone and language will prevail throughout its pages, and we shall be able to present our readers with a periodical that has long been wanting, which it is hoped will interest and at the same time instruct the young.

Its small cost, **ONE DOLLAR A YEAR,** *places it at the command of every household.*

FRANK LESLIE'S PUBLISHING HOUSE,

53, 55 & 57 Park Place, New York.

Selected Bibliography

Selected Bibliography

GENERAL

Andrews, Siri, ed. *The Hewins Lectures, 1947–1962.* Boston: Horn Book, 1963.
Annual papers on the writing and publishing of children's books in New England: *The Youth's Companion,* Mrs. A. D. T. Whitney, Jacob Abbott, Eliza Orne White, Laura E. Richards, Lucretia P. Hale, Susan Coolidge, Kate Douglas Wiggin. Later lectures, printed in the *Horn Book Magazine,* dealt with Samuel Goodrich, Thomas Bailey Aldrich, and "The Lachrymose Ladies" (Susan Warner, Maria Susanna Cummins, and Martha Finley).

Barry, Florence V. *A Century of Children's Books.* New York: George H. Doran Co., 1923.
An evaluation of the eighteenth century, with a chronological list of books, 1700–1825.

Blanck, Jacob N. *Peter Parley to Penrod; A Bibliographical Description of the Best-loved American Juvenile Books.* Cambridge, Mass.: Research Classics, 1961.

Chicago University Library. *Science in Nineteenth-century Children's Books; An exhibition based on the Encyclopaedia Britannica Historical Collection of Books for Children.* Chicago: 1966.

Crandall, John C. "Patriotism and Humanitarian Reform in Children's Literature, 1825–1860." *American Quarterly,* Vol. 21, Spring 1969.

Cruse, Amy. *The Victorians and Their Reading.* Boston: Houghton Mifflin, 1935.

Darling, Richard L. *The Rise of Children's Book Reviewing in America, 1865–1881.* New York. Bowker, 1968.

Darton, Frederick J. H. *Children's Books in England; Five Centuries of Social Life.* 2nd ed. Cambridge: Cambridge University Press, 1958.

Davidson, Gustav. *First Editions in American Juvenilia and Problems in Their Identification.* Chicago: Normandie House, 1939.

Halsey, Rosalie V. *Forgotten Books of the American Nursery; A History of the Development of the American Story-book.* Boston: Charles E. Goodspeed, 1911.
From Newbery to nineteenth-century American writers.

Haviland, Virginia, ed. *Children's Literature: A Guide to Reference Sources.* Washington: Library of Congress, 1966. First Supplement, 1972.

Haviland, Virginia. *The Travelogue Storybook of the Nineteenth Century.* Boston: Horn Book, 1950.
Thomas W. Knox, Hezekiah Butterworth, Charles A. Stephens, Elizabeth Champney, Edward Everett Hale and Susan Hale, and others, with a bibliography.

Hewins, Caroline M. "The History of Children's Books." *Atlantic Monthly,* Vol. 61, January 1888.

Hewins, Caroline M. *A Mid-Century Child and Her Books.* Introduction by Anne Carroll Moore. New York: Macmillan, 1926.
A librarian's reminiscences, with nineteenth-century books cited and illustrated.

Jordan, Alice M. *From Rollo to Tom Sawyer, and Other Papers.* Decorations by Nora S. Unwin. Boston: Horn Book, 1948.
Samuel Goodrich, Jacob Abbott, Susan Warner, Elijah Kellogg, Horace E. Scudder, Mary Mapes Dodge, and others are represented.

Kiefer, Monica M. *American Children Through Their Books, 1700–1835.* Philadelphia: University of Pennsylvania Press, 1948.
An appraisal in terms of social history.

Lucas, Edward V., comp. *Forgotten Tales of Long Ago.* With illustrations by F. D. Bedford. London: Wells-Gardner-Darton; New York: F. A. Stokes, 1906. Also, *Old Fashioned Tales,* 1906?
Collections of tales, with critical commentary.

Meigs, Cornelia L., ed. *A Critical History of Children's Literature; A Survey of Children's Books in English.* Decorations by Vera Bock. Rev. ed. New York: Macmillan, 1969.
The first three parts, up to 1920, are written by the editor, Anne T. Eaton, and Elizabeth Nesbitt.

Mother Goose. *Mother Goose's Melodies.* Facsimile edition of the Monroe and Francis "Copyright 1833" Version. With an introduction and bibliographic note by E. F. Bleiler. New York: Dover Publications, 1870.

Muir, Percival H. *English Children's Books, 1600–1900.* London, Batsford, 1953; New York: Praeger, 1954.
Refers to various genres of books which emigrated to America.

Neuburg, Victor E. *Chapbooks; A Bibliography of References to English and American Chapbook Literature of the Eighteenth and Nineteenth Centuries.* London: Vine Press, 1964. 2nd ed. London: Woburn Press, 1972.

Neuburg, Victor E. *The Penny Histories; A Study of Chapbooks for Young Read-*

ers over Two Centuries. Illustrated with facsimiles of seven chapbooks. London: Oxford University Press, 1969.

NYE, RUSSELL B. *The Unembarrassed Muse: The Popular Arts in America.* New York: Dial Press, 1970.
Chapter 3 discusses "Subliterature."

QUAYLE, ERIC. *The Collector's Book of Children's Books.* New York: Clarkson N. Potter, 1971.

ROSENBACH, ABRAHAM S. W. *Books and Bidders; the Adventures of a Bibliographile.* Limited ed. Boston: Little, Brown, 1927.

ROSENBACH, ABRAHAM S. W. *Early American Children's Books. With Bibliographical Descriptions of the Books in His Private Collection.* Portland, Maine: Southworth Press, 1933. Facsimile edition: New York, 1971, with all the reproductions in black and white.
Annotated, illustrated entries for books published 1682–1836.

SLOANE, WILLIAM. *Children's Books in England & America in the Seventeenth Century: A History and Checklist, Together with* The Young Christian's Library, *the First Printed Catalogue of Books for Children.* New York: King's Crown Press, Columbia University, 1955.

TARG, WILLIAM, ed. *Bibliophile in the Nursery; a Bookman's Treasury of Collectors' Lore on Old and Rare Children's Books.* Cleveland: World Publishing Co., 1957.
An anthology of writings by collectors.

THOMPSON, LAWRENCE. "The Printing and Publishing Activities of the American Tract Society from 1825 to 1850." *The Papers of the Bibliographical Society of America.* Vol. 35, second quarter, 1941.

THWAITE, MARY F. *From Primer to Pleasure in Reading: an Introduction to the History of Children's Books in England from the Invention of Printing to 1914, with an outline of some developments in other countries.* 2nd ed. London: Library Association, 1972; Boston: Horn Book, 1973.
Contains a chapter on North American books. Chronological list, 1479–1798.

TUER, ANDREW W. *Stories from Old-Fashioned Children's Books, Brought Together and Introduced to the Reader.* Adorned with 250 Amusing Cuts. London: Leadenhall Press; New York: Scribner, 1899–1900.

WEISS, HARRY B. *A Book about Chapbooks, the People's Literature of Bygone Times.* Trenton [Ann Arbor, Mich., Edwards Bros.], 1942.

WELCH, D'ALTÉ ALDREDGE. *A Bibliography of American Children's Books Printed Prior to 1821.* Worcester, Mass.: American Antiquarian Society, 1972.
An ample introduction gives a chronological history of eighteenth-century American children's books and notes important institutional and private collections.

WELSH, CHARLES. "The Early History of Children's Books in New England." *New England Magazine,* Vol. 26, April 1899.

RELIGIOUS AND INSTRUCTIVE WORKS

BOBBITT, MARY R. *A Bibliography of Etiquette Books Published in America Before 1900.* New York: New York Public Library, 1947.

Reprinted from the *Bulletin* of the New York Public Library, December 1947.

CARPENTER, CHARLES. *History of American Schoolbooks.* Philadelphia: University of Pennsylvania Press, 1963.

EAMES, WILBERFORCE. *Early New England Catechisms. A Bibliographical Account of Some Catechisms Published Before the Year 1800, for use in New England.* Worcester, Mass.: C. Hamilton, 1898.

FOLMSBEE, BEULAH. *A Little History of the Horn-Book.* Boston: Horn Book, 1942,

FORD, PAUL L., ed. *The New-England Primer: a History of its Origin and Development.* New York, Printed for Dodd, Mead, 1897. Reissued, New York: Published for the Book Lovers' Library of Early American Literature, by Dodd, Mead, 1962.

HEARTMAN, CHARLES F. *American Primers, Indian Primers, Royal Primers, and Thirty-seven Other Types of Non-New England Primers issued Prior to 1830.* Highland Park, N.J.: Printed for Harry B. Weiss, 1935.

HEARTMAN, CHARLES F. *The New-England Primer Issued Prior to 1830: a Bibliographical Check-list for the More Easy Attaining the True Knowledge of This Book.* 3d. ed. New York: Bowker, 1934.

LIVERMORE, GEORGE. *The Origin, History and Character of the New England Primer. Being a Series of Articles Contributed to "The Cambridge Chronicle."* New York: C. F. Heartman, 1915.

MCGUFFEY, WILLIAM H. *Old Favorites from the McGuffey Readers.* Edited by Harvey C. Minnich. New York: American Book Co., 1936; Detroit: Singing Tree Press, 1969.

NIETZ, JOHN A. *Old Textbooks: Spelling, Grammar, Reading, Arithmetic, Geography, American History, Civil Government, Physiology, Penmanship, Art, Music, as Taught in the Common Schools from Colonial Days to 1900.* Pittsburgh: University of Pittsburgh Press, 1961.

STONE, WILBUR MACY. *The Thumb Bible of John Taylor.* Brookline, Mass.: The LXIVMOS, 1928.

TUER, ANDREW W. *History of the Horn-Book.* London: Leadenhall Press; New York: Scribner, 1897.

AUTHORS

ABBOTT, JACOB (1803–79)

WEBER, CARL J., comp. *A Bibliography of Jacob Abbott.* Waterville, Maine: College Press, 1948.

ALCOTT, LOUISA MAY (1832–88)

GULLIVER, LUCILE. *Louisa May Alcott; a Bibliography.* With an Appreciation by Cornelia Meigs. New York; B. Franklin, 1973.

A reprint of the 1932 edition.

MEIGS, CORNELIA L. *Louisa M. Alcott and the American Family Story.* London: The Bodley Head; New York, Henry Z. Walck, 1971.

Jacob Abbott, Susan Coolidge, and Margaret Sidney, as well as Louisa May Alcott.

ULLOM, JUDITH C., comp. *Louisa May Alcott: a Centennial for Little Women; an Annotated, Selected Bibliography.* Washington, D.C.: Library of Congress, 1969.

Contemporary reviews are quoted.

ALGER, HORATIO, JR. (1832–99)

GARDNER, RALPH D. *Horatio Alger; or, The American Hero Era.* Mendota, Ill.: Wayside Press, 1964.

BURNETT, FRANCES HODGSON (1849–1924)

LASKI, MARGHANITA. *Mrs. Ewing, Mrs. Molesworth, and Mrs. Hodgson Burnett.* London: A. Marker, 1950.

CASTLEMAN, HARRY (1824–1915)

BLANCK, JACOB. *Harry Castleman, Boys' Own Author.* New York: Bowker, 1941.

GOODRICH, SAMUEL GRISWOLD (1793–1860)

DARTON, FREDERICK J. HARVEY. "Peter Parley and the Battle of the Children's Books." *Cornhill Magazine,* Vol. 73, November 1932.

An account of the conflict between Goodrich and his London publishers.

GOODRICH, SAMUEL. *Recollections of a Lifetime.* 2 vols. New York: Miller, Orton, 1857.

ROSELLE, DANIEL. *Samuel Griswold Goodrich, Creator of Peter Parley; a Study of His Life and Work.* Albany: State University of New York Press, 1968.

HALE, SARAH JOSEPHA (1788–1879)

FINLEY, RUTH E. *The Lady of Godey's, Sarah Josepha Hale.* Philadelphia: Lippincott, 1931.

HARRIS, JOEL CHANDLER (1848–1908)

BROOKES, STELLA (BREWER). *Joel Chandler Harris, Folklorist.* Athens, Georgia: University of Georgia Press, 1950.

COUSINS, PAUL M. *Joel Chandler Harris; a Biography.* Baton Rouge: Louisiana State University Press, 1968.

JOHNSTON, ANNIE F. (1863–1931)

JOHNSTON, ANNIE (FELLOWS). *The Land of the Little Colonel; Reminiscence and Autobiography.* Boston: L. C. Page, 1929.

MOORE, CLEMENT CLARKE (1779–1863)

PITTSBURGH BIBLIOPHILES. *"The Night Before Christmas"; an Exhibition Catalogue.* Compiled by George H. M. Lawrence. Foreword by Anne Lyon Haight. Pittsburgh, 1964.

PYLE, HOWARD (1853–1911)

ABBOTT, CHARLES D. *Howard Pyle, a Chronicle.* New York and London: Harper, 1925.

Biography, with illustrations and with an appreciation by Pyle's pupil, N. C. Wyeth.

MORSE, WILLARD S., and BRINCKLÉ, GERTRUDE, comps. *Howard Pyle; a Record of His Illustrations and Writings.* Wilmington, Del.: Wilmington Society of the Fine Arts, 1921.

NESBITT, ELIZABETH. *Howard Pyle.* London: The Bodley Head; New York: Henry Z. Walck, 1966.

RICHARDS, LAURA E. (1850–1943)

RICHARDS, LAURA E. *Stepping Westward.* New York and London: D. Appleton, 1931.

Reminiscences of a poet and writer, with a chapter on authorship.

STEPHENS, CHARLES ASBURY (1844–1931)

HARRIS, LOUISE. *The Star of the Youth's Companion: C. A. Stephens.* Providence, R.I.: C. A. Stephens Collection, Brown University, 1969.

STOCKTON, FRANK R. (1834–1902)

GRIFFIN, MARTIN I. J. *Frank R. Stockton; A Critical Biography.* Philadelphia: University of Pennsylvania Press; London: H. Milford, Oxford University Press, 1939.

STRATEMEYER, EDWARD (1862–1930)

"For It Was Indeed He." *Fortune,* Vol. 9, April 1934.

Discusses Stratemeyer and other writers of his syndicate.

PRAEGER, ARTHUR. "Edward Stratemeyer and His Book Machine." *Saturday Review,* Vol. 54, July 10, 1971.

WIGGIN, KATE DOUGLAS (1856–1923)

BRENNER, HELEN F. *Kate Douglas Wiggin's Country of Childhood.* Orono, Maine: Maine University Press, 1956.

ILLUSTRATORS

BIRCH, REGINALD (1856–1943)

HAMILTON, ELISABETH, B., ed. *Reginald Birch—His Book.* New York: Harcourt, Brace, 1939.

Literary selections featuring Birch's illustrations.

FROST, A. B. (1851–1928)

REED, HENRY M. *The A. B. Frost Book.* With a foreword by Eugene V. Connett. Rutland, Vt., C. E. Tuttle Co., 1967.

Reproductions and a bibliography.

PYLE, HOWARD, see under Authors

Bland, David. *A History of Book Illustration.* 2nd. rev. ed. Berkeley: University of California Press, 1969.

Hamilton, Sinclair. *Early American Book Illustrators and Wood Engravers, 1670–1870; A Catalogue of a Collection of American Books, Illustrated for the Most Part with Woodcuts and Wood Engravings, in the Princeton Library.* With a Foreword by Frank Weitenkampf. Princeton, N.J.: Princeton University Press, 1969.

Latimer, Louise P., comp. *Illustrators: A Finding List.* Boston, F. W. Faxon, 1929.
Includes American and foreign illustrators. The District of Columbia Public Library has assembled the listed books in an Illustrator Collection.

Miller, Bertha (Mahony), Louise P. Latimer, and Beulah Folmsbee, comps. *Illustrators of Children's Books, 1774–1945.* Boston, Horn Book, 1947.
Essays, brief biographies, and bibliographies.

Muir, Percival H. *Victorian Illustrated Books.* New York: Praeger, 1971.
Includes "American landmarks."

Pitz, Henry C., ed. *A Treasury of American Book Illustration.* New York: American Studio Books and Watson-Guptill Publications, 1947.

Pitz, Henry. *The Brandywine Tradition.* Boston: Houghton Mifflin, 1969.
Howard Pyle and his "school."

Tuer, Andrew W. *1,000 Quaint Cuts from Books of Other Days Including Amusing Illustrations from Children's Story Books, Fables, Chapbooks.* London: Field & Tuer; New York: Scribner & Welford, 1886.

MAGAZINES

Egoff, Sheila A. *Children's Periodicals of the Nineteenth Century;* A Survey and Bibliography. London, Library Association, 1951.
Essay and bibliography.

Frye, Burton C. *A* St. Nicholas *Anthology; the Early Years.* Foreword by Richard L. Darling. New York: Meredith Press, 1969.

Harris, Louise. *None but the Best; or, The Story of Three Pioneers:* The Youth's Companion, *Daniel Sharp Ford [and] C. A. Stephens.* Providence: C. A. Stephens Collection, Brown University, 1966.

Our Young Folks. Yesterday's Children; an Anthology, Compiled from the Pages of *Our Young Folks,* 1865–1873. Selected and edited by John Morton Blum. Boston, Houghton Mifflin, 1959.

St. Nicholas. The St. Nicholas *Anthology,* Edited by Henry Steele Commager, with an Introduction by May Lamberton Becker. 2 vols. New York: Random House, 1948, 1950.

See also Alice M. Jordan's *From Rollo to Tom Sawyer* for discussion of the *Juvenile Miscellany, Riverside Magazine, St. Nicholas,* and *Our Young Folks.*

PUBLISHERS

BRAGIN, CHARLES. *Dime Novels, 1860–1964;* A Bibliography. Brooklyn, N.Y.: 1964. Publishing history, in brief.

JOHANNSEN, ALBERT. *The House of Beadle and Adams and Its Dime and Nickel Novels, the Story of a Vanished Literature.* With a foreword by John T. McIntyre. 2 vols. Norman, Okla.: University of Oklahoma Press, 1970.

JONES, HELEN L. "The Part Played by Boston Publishers of 1860–1900 in the Field of Children's Books." *Horn Book* magazine, Vol. 45, February–June 1969.

ROSCOE, SYDNEY. *Newbery-Carnan-Power; A Checklist of Books for the Entertainment, Instruction and Education of Children and Young People.* Issued Under the Imprints of John Newbery and His Family in the Period 1742–1802. Wormley, Herts.: Five Owls Press, 1973.

SHIPTON, CLIFFORD K. *Isaiah Thomas, Printer, Patriot and Philanthropist, 1794–1831.* Rochester, N.Y.: Printing House of Leo Hart, 1948.
Illustrated biography.

WEISS, HARRY B. *The Printers and Publishers of Children's Books in New York City, 1698–1830.* New York: New York Public Library, 1948. Reprinted from the *Bulletin* of the New York Public Library, Vol. 52, August 1948.

WELCH, CHARLES. *A Bookseller of the Last Century. Being Some Account of the Life of John Newbery, and of the Books He Published with a Notice of the Later Newberys.* London: Griffith, Farran, Okeden & Welsh, 1885; Clifton, N.J.: Augustus M. Kelley, 1932.

THE LIBRARY OF CONGRESS RARE BOOK COLLECTIONS

"Collections of Rare Children's Books." A Symposium; Parts 1–6. *Library Journal,* Vol. 63, January 1–July 1, 1938.
Part I describes American children's books in the Rare Book Collection, Library of Congress.

NOLEN, ELEANOR W. "The National Library Builds a Children's Book Collection." *Horn Book* magazine, Vol. 14, July 1939.
Mentions authors and trends.

U. S. Library of Congress. Rare Book Division. The Rare Book Division: A Guide to Its Collections and Services. Washington: Library of Congress, 1965.

Index

Index

About Virginia Haviland

Virginia Haviland is known the world over as one of America's leading authorities in the field of children's literature. She has been Head of the Children's Book Section of the Library of Congress in Washington, D.C., since the inception of that division in 1963. Prior to this, she was for many years a children's librarian and book-selection specialist in the Boston Public Library and a lecturer in Library Service at Simmons College. She is a distinguished critic, whose writings appear regularly in American and international journals, and is the author of over sixteen books of retellings of famous fairy tales for children, as well as many scholarly publications in the field of children's literature.

and Margaret N. Coughlan

Margaret N. Coughlan, now Reference Librarian and Bibliographer of the Children's Book Section of the Library of Congress, was formerly Children's Librarian at the Baltimore County Public Library, and before that held the same title at the Enoch Pratt Free Library in Baltimore, Md. Ms. Coughlan received her master's degree in Library Science from the Carnegie Institute of Technology, where she came under the influence of Elizabeth Nesbitt, who encouraged and stimulated her interest in the history of children's literature—an interest first sparked by her father.